Lead the Way

Lead the Way

PRINCIPLES AND PRACTICES IN COMMUNITY AND CIVIC ENGAGEMENT

Revised Second Edition

Edited by Forrest D. Toms and Sylvia Willie Burgess

cognella®

SAN DIEGO

Bassim Hamadeh, CEO and Publisher
Carrie Montoya, Manager, Revisions and Author Care
Kaela Martin, Project Editor
Celeste Paed, Associate Production Editor
Jess Estrella, Senior Graphic Designer
Alexa Lucido, Licensing Manager
Natalie Piccotti, Director of Marketing
Kassie Graves, Vice President of Editorial
Jamie Giganti, Director of Academic Publishing

Cover image copyright © 2019 iStockphoto LP/Nadezda_Grapes.

Printed in the United States of America.

cognella® | ACADEMIC PUBLISHING
3970 Sorrento Valley Blvd., Ste. 500, San Diego, CA 92121

Contents

Acknowledgments

ANY BOOK REFLECTS the product of multiple energies, support, and sharing of one's experiences and gifts with others. This is surely the case with this book. I am deeply humbled and indebted to the contributing authors for their willingness to share their experiences and gifts to produce this book. It would not be possible without the commitment of spiritual capital that we all shared with each other, entrusted in each other, and committed to each other to produce a product we believed was needed and timely. I extend my personal gratitude to each contributing author for their collective contributions to bringing this second edition to fruition. We owe a special debt of gratitude to Dr. Abul Pitre for his leadership and guidance; without it, this book would not have been possible the first time. We also thank Dr. Alexander Erwin, a pioneer for the Leadership Studies Program at North Carolina A&T State University.

To my coeditor, Dr. Sylvia Willie Burgess, I am both blessed and thankful for your undying support, energy, trustworthiness, and collective spirit. Sylvia, you have truly been a blessing for me, for this project, and all the other projects we are involved with. We have spent countless hours conceptualizing, discussing, and formulating strategies that we believe can make a difference in the lives of people and communities; this one has indeed challenged us the most. I continue to be amazed at the depth and breadth of your knowledge of leadership, community engagement, and management capabilities.

As I reflect on the essence of this book, I cannot help but think of my mentors, from childhood through graduate studies. My early memories of community engagement start in Shelby, North Carolina, with four men: Mr. Willie "Flip" Caster, Mr. Clarence Palmer, Mr. Mitchell Terrell, and Mr. Eli Black. I watched these men—who had limited education and resources—organize youth for football, basketball, and baseball teams in the segregated South, using their own money and money raised to buy uniforms and transport other youth and me. Mr. "Flip," as we called him, used his own resources to purchase a building that he developed into a teen club for us, an interracial teen club, when it was not popular to do so. Mr. Palmer was the first African American school board member in the county. He and his wife, Pat, spent many hours talking with me, explaining and answering questions about race and racism. There are three other men I wish to acknowledge who were instrumental in me getting involved in community development work during my middle and high school years: Ben Watson,

John Watson, and J. C. Coles. They administered urban renewal programs at the time. All were heroes because they had attended and/or completed college and came back to give to the community. These gentlemen made me attend staff meetings on Fridays to learn about planning, community development, and implementation of community programs. It was years before I realized the gift they had given me. To them, I am forever blessed by their gift.

I am equally indebted to Dr. William "Beryl" West and Dr. A. Wade Boykin, my mentors and friends. These two men I credit with shaping my intellectual, professional, and personal development. Their masterful "shepherding" of my development is reflected throughout this book and the work of the students I have mentored.

I am also grateful for the friendship and partnership of Dr. Calvin Ellison, former CEO of the Community Empowerment Network (CEN) of North Carolina. Our partnership resulted in the development of community engagement training programs and processes covering 15 counties and more than 50 churches in eastern North Carolina. It was through CEN that the genesis for this book originated as we toiled in the "vineyards" of like-minded, committed citizens determined to harvest the fruit promised for tomorrow. To Mr. Richard Hooker of the North Carolina Alliance of Black Elected Officials and North Carolina Caucus of Black School Board Members, I am deeply appreciative of your friendship and the organizational and operational support you gave to me, my students, and the Department of Leadership Studies at North Carolina A&T State University. To Drs. Cheryl Lemay and Pamela Palmer, I offer a heartfelt thanks for your assistance and guidance and for being central members of our community engagement efforts.

I would especially like to thank the coauthors of our new chapter in the second edition: Richard Hooker, Forrest Toms II, Marcus Bass, and Masonya Ruff for their commitment to learning and engagement in practice and writing. Your efforts have resulted in a timely contribution to the documented legacy of CORE's footprint and effect on African American leadership and engagement in Cleveland County.

To all the members and participants in CORE over the years and to community members attending events and programs, I am truly thankful for your support. Several CORE members must be recognized for their extraordinary efforts over the years and their long-standing commitment to leadership, change, and growth in our communities. They are Richard Hooker, Larry Corry, Ron Harrill, Mary Accor, Rev. James Smith, and Rev. Billy Houze. Many others came, went away, and came back to serve over a 20-year period. These men and women, and many more, I have known since preschool and have maintained contact and relationships with in varying capacities for more than 2 decades. I have always told them how much I respect their gifts, commitment to our community, persistence to keep battling, and their will. More importantly, I am honored and grateful for how they have always accepted, supported, and championed my presence back home—for their trust in me as a "native son" to bring back to our community the fruits from seeds planted by our elders before us (see the complete list of CORE members at the end of Chapter 12).

Finally, I would like to thank my friend, soul mate, and wife, Phyllis J. Toms, for her unyielding support, encouragement, and love. We have been connected as soul mates since high school, and I am blessed to have her in my life. I would also like to thank my children, Forrest II and Zakiya, a coauthor and doctoral student, respectively, for their assistance and support.

—Forrest D. Toms, PhD

Apart from my personal efforts, the success of any project of this magnitude depends largely on the encouragement and contributions of many others. This book would not be possible without all the contributing authors and their knowledge about the various aspects of community engagement and how it connects with their areas of expertise. I take this opportunity to express my gratitude to each contributor because, collectively, we were successful in completing this second project.

A special heartfelt thank you goes to Dr. Forrest D. Toms, who is the inspiration behind the first book project. Dr. Toms, I personally thank you for the opportunity to coauthor this project with you, as well as work alongside you. Thank you for the many conversations and knowledge when we engage in a project. You have one of the most powerful minds that I have had the pleasure of working and interacting with. On behalf of all the contributing authors, thanks again for another opportunity to play in the "sandbox" of community engagement.

I would like to especially thank my coauthor on Chapter 8, "Spiritual Capital and Community Engagement," Dr. Calvin Ellison. Dr. Ellison, thank you for your knowledge and contributions based on all the work you have previously done with CEN and how this is such a true example of community engagement. I have enjoyed supporting your book projects and look forward to working with you again.

My gratitude extends to my mother, Geraldine, who as she rests in peace continues to have an impact on my life. I often think about her encouraging words and often-heard whispered prayers with my name included. Thanks, Mom. I am a better woman because of your influence. To my sisters, Yvonne and Terry, thank you for being there for me and supporting each endeavor that I undertake with sisterly love. To my spiritual sister, Lora, thank you for continuing to listen to me when I get tired and for encouraging me to keep going.

Finally, I would like to thank my daughter, Avigayil, for her support and love as I complete each endeavor on this journey. Avigayil, all that I do is in support of your future and the legacy I want to leave for your life.

—Dr. Sylvia Willie Burgess

Introduction

THE IDEAL OF community and civic engagement is something most laypersons, practitioners, and researchers generally agree on as worthy and necessary. The reality of community and civic engagement in terms of what it is, how it should be practiced, who the stakeholders are, the amount of influence some stakeholders have versus others in a given context, and the extent to which all parties have equitable and mutually beneficial outcomes is another matter. It is at this juncture where, so to speak, "the rubber meets the road." It is at this point where the ideals and the reality of community and civic engagement clash, where potentially successful plans between collaborating groups stall, and, in many cases, stop in their tracks. You see these philosophical and ideological clashes in multiple settings and partnerships, such as between government agencies and communities, between universities and neighborhoods, and between traditional and nontraditional stakeholders within ethnic/racial group communities.

Our work in communities at the grassroots level, within local governing bodies, with state and national government agencies, and advocacy groups has provided invaluable observations, experiences, and levels of analyses regarding the multidimensional aspects of community and civic engagement. The "big" lesson learned is that community and civic engagement are not easy; that's why not everyone can do it, and not everyone can do it effectively. It is developmental in nature; it can and is driven by context, and, more importantly, it takes a lot of time and patience.

It is important for those interested in addressing community engagement to gain a fundamental understanding of the why, what, and how of engagement. The terminology has been loosely used to describe everything from organizing games to voting for political candidates. What one group describes as community engagement, another group would disagree. For the purpose of this book, community engagement is defined as the process by which individuals and communities work collaboratively to build ongoing permanent relationships toward the goal of using a collective vision for the benefit of the community (CDC, 1997). The ultimate goal for community engagement is to move communities toward change from past positions of inertia to more intentional and interactive practices of engagement, both within their culturally specific groups and communities and between their communities and government agencies, businesses, and elected officials and other diverse citizens.

On the other hand, we know that leadership requires a greater understanding of self and the core values that determine individual actions. Leadership for community engagement requires a focus on how leaders of the communities identify their roles in building the foundations for capacity and change to address health, educational, justice, social, and economic challenges, to name a few. There has never been a greater need than now for leaders to create the vehicles, tools, and processes for capacity building and sustainable engagement. Those leaders who take on the responsibility of representing others must be prepared to work proactively to build the necessary relationships, partnerships, and collaborations that provide the "place" and "space" to hear and receive the "voices" of those they represent so as not to leave people disengaged or disenfranchised.

Historically, community, leadership, and engagement have been viewed and approached as separate entities, at times with an individual's and/or particular group's agendas and outcomes taking precedence over the collective will and needs of communities. Or, as is the case at the local level in many communities, how leadership, community, and engagement are defined and approached depends on who are the perceived and/or preferred stakeholders (e.g., private businesses, elected officials, agency/institutional leaders) and to what extent they exercise their power and influence.

For instance, in the view of leadership, community, and engagement from what can be described as the "mainstream of American civic and community engagement"—that is, where all economic, policy, and resource distribution decision making takes place in any city/town—there are common structural practices that define the what, how, and why of leadership and engagement practices. Toms (1997) captured this through his observations and descriptions of what he labeled the "civic service game." He stated:

> These frequent meetings formulate a pool of networks and partnerships involving many of the same individuals and organizations. The majority of the individuals participating in these networks are involved at the board level or volunteer level; moreover, they also share interactions on multiple levels in terms of personal relationships, business partnerships and through general social encounters involving their children in recreational and other community activities. Thus, there is a familiarity, a similarity in terms of core values, beliefs and worldviews about how things are and how things should be. In addition, they generally serve on two or more boards and committees in businesses and other organizations simultaneously. The overlapping of these individuals in business and semi-social contexts creates an unstated, yet predictable, sense of comfortableness with each other regardless of the setting. Knowingly or unknowingly, this formulates a silent bond and networks that produces an amenable group of people, with similar perceptions, values, beliefs, and action strategies, who know and work well with each other while striving to create a better community life. This consistent and persistent interaction across different business, civic, and social contexts, provides mainstream Americans with credibility by default. Their influence is valued highly when other community and civic ventures arise in the future producing an implicit selection criterion for participants in existing and future organization

and planning endeavors. Within the mainstream of American society is a *"silent language"* understood by all those labeled or perceived to be a *"player"* by others in the community. A player is looked upon as one who serves in and has influence on the community. In addition, the community evaluates a player by: (1) the methods used to achieve their influence, and (2) the extent of one's *"power"* and *"respect."* This, in turn, provides the player with more leverage in influencing major issues, projects, events, and future directions of community resources. This process can be defined as the "civic service game." (p. 45)

In the case of African American, Latino, American Indian, and other ethnic/racial/cultural groups, the structure and process of identifying key stakeholders and the process of being a key stakeholder vary, depending on the history and culture of the groups. For instance, a view of leadership, community, and engagement from an African American perspective suggests that, historically, churches have been known to be at the center of how leaders, leadership, and engagement are viewed and practiced. That is, history and literature document the role of ministers and churches prior to, during, and even post–civil rights movements as being selected or elected representatives of African American interests in the mainstream of American life. Even though churches and ministers were known to provide leadership in communities, this leadership was not necessarily with a focus on intentional civic engagement around policy and resource distribution issues facing their communities. Engagement in those areas was generally believed to be the domain of those individuals who were elected by the community to represent their interests on governing boards. Notwithstanding the fact that African American elected officials in the United States have grown from 1,469 in 1970 to 9,000 in 2016, there remains concern about whether and to what extent these elected official are representing the interests of the communities, particularly when nationally and locally, African American communities and their citizens remain in the top categories of disparities in the areas of health, poverty, unemployment, and education.

More and more, the expectation for leaders to be effectively connected to the communities they represent is diminishing. Often, leaders are not necessarily culturally or physically connected to their representative communities. In fact, in some cases, leaders have been known to consciously distance themselves from their own ethnic/racial groups in terms of their perspectives, policy orientation, and actual support of issues and concerns that disproportionately affect citizens. These are all indicators of the fact that the "rules of engagement" have changed, and the face of community and civic engagement is changing. With that in mind, we prepared *Lead the Way: Principles and Practices in Community and Civic Engagement* as a resource for laypersons, practitioners, and researchers in the hope that the information, insights, and practices included can help inform current and future engagement activities and processes.

This book approaches leadership and engagement from three different perspectives: Part I conceptual/historical, Part II challenges and opportunities, and Part III community/civic engagement in action. Part I of the book offers a conceptual and historical perspective of leadership and engagement. The authors explore and set forth a multidimensional and multifaceted framework for understanding and thinking about community engagement by suggesting that it must be viewed from an "insider/outsider" perspective. Next, the authors offer a comprehensive historical analysis of the challenges and necessity of fusion reconstruction and social/political activism in the 21st-century South. The analysis provides the most in-depth description of the current "Moral Monday" movement in North Carolina. Lastly, the authors explore leading and leadership in African American communities by offering a brief history of African American leadership typologies and suggesting that to understand leadership in African American communities fully, we must better understand the psychology of the African American experience in America.

Part II of the book examines the challenges and opportunities for leadership and community engagement. The chapters present the challenges of health equity and disaster/risks in communities. The opportunities explored in Part II are related to capacity building, leadership, and community-based research and spiritual capital. The final section of the book, Part III, explores community and civic engagement in action. The chapters offer a review of readiness and preparedness, the effect of students and universities in the engagement process, a faith-based capacity building model, Latino and American Indian perspectives on leadership and engagement, the role of Black elected officials and their civic responsibility, and an examination of community reinvestment and community/civic engagement.

Considering current events in the world, community engagement has shifted in the United States. The COVID-19 pandemic has reduced personal interactions in communities with the "stay at home" order. This pandemic is devastating and overwhelming communities across the country but particularly marginalized communities that are already struggling with poverty, health-care issues, food deserts, and problems with the justice system. COVID-19 has magnified the historical social ills of the United States and the impact on the quality of life for Black, Brown, and poor people. As such, all systems are pushed beyond the capacity to serve, raising more questions about the equity and fairness of our systems in serving its citizens.

In the midst of COVID-19, the digital capture of the murder of George Floyd by the Minneapolis police added another level of complexity to an already devastated nation. This murder among others in a short time frame literally "blew the top off," creating the largest protest movement, along with cases of civil unrest, in the history of cities across the country. The outrage across races, communities, and the country to urge change because "black lives matter" has unfolded the broadest continuum of diversity and transformation ever documented in the history of the United States. These two incidents will profoundly affect community engagement. As such, there is an increased need for community and national leaders to willingly lead with and through this time to intersect a divided country plagued with racial, socioeconomic, health, fairness in the justice system, and educational issues. These incidents are a clarion call for leaders to *lead the way* for change and equity for the future of our country.

After reading this book, it is our hope that readers will have an enhanced understanding of the depth and breadth of approaches, activities, and processes related to leadership and community/civic engagement. More importantly, it is our hope that the information, framework, and action examples will reinforce the need for and importance of intentionality in the development of shared visions to create permanent change in communities where citizens have been—and continue to be—marginalized and underserved. While the process of change from low engagement to higher levels of motivation and action for engagement is a slow one, it is beneficial when mutuality and reciprocity are "lifted up" as core principles and practices.

—Forrest D. Toms, PhD
—Sylvia W. Burgess, PhD

REFERENCES

Centers for Disease Control and Prevention. The social-ecological model: A framework for prevention. Atlanta (GA): Centers for Disease Control and Prevention; 1997.

Toms, F. D., (1997). Challenges and opportunities of communities in transition. In F.D. Toms & A. D. Hobbs (Eds.), *Who are we?: Building a knowledge base of ethnic, racial, and cultural groups in America*. Diverse Books.

PART I

Conceptual and Historical Perspectives on Leadership and Community Engagement

CHAPTER ONE

Community Engagement
A MULTIFACETED FRAMEWORK AND PROCESS

Forrest D. Toms, PhD, and Zakiya L. Toms, LCSW-C

If the agencies are not reaching out to you, you have to be prepared to reach into them.

— Dr. Barbara Pullen-Smith
Former Director, NC Office of Minority
Health and Health Disparities

INTRODUCTION

The opening quote by Dr. Barbara Pullen-Smith (2008) captures the focus and essence of this chapter. That is, community engagement is a multifaceted process that includes an in-depth understanding of the nature and processes of an "inside-out" and "outside-in" framework. The "inside-out" (organizational frame) suggests that a process, plan, and strategies are needed to continuously assess, examine, and revise organizational structures, policies, practices, and processes to ensure the readiness and preparedness of personnel and the organization to provide culturally competent service delivery and effectively engage increasingly diverse consumers and communities. Likewise, the "outside-in" (community frame) suggests that target communities and leaders have to be prepared to participate and engage organizations through planning/development on committees and engaging organizations in decision making, policy development, and community program implementation to address disparities in such areas as education, health, and economic development, to name a few.

Nationally, regionally, and locally, the "rules of engagement" with communities have shifted from an organization-first perspective to recognize the need to invest the time, energy, and resources to engage communities and build relationships through peer-related exchanges, more mutually beneficial partnerships, and mutual trust with citizens reflective of legitimate partnerships. This shift has emerged from efforts to decentralize government authority to regional and local decision-making bodies. The result has been an increased focus on community engagement activities and processes among government agencies, human service agencies, and service providers. It has resulted in changes in policy, organizational practices, and procedures and assessment of how effective organizations work with and through communities to achieve program and organizational goals. Relatedly, federal, state, and private funding agencies have changed their funding policies, criteria, and requirements for partnering with community members to solve problems. The hope is that by elevating the importance and significance of community engagement policies and practices among government leaders, private- and public-sector providers, and community organizations, critical problems and issues can be responded to in a more culturally responsive and efficient way.

This chapter will offer a philosophical framework for defining and understanding community engagement by making a connection between an individual's and/or organization's beliefs (philosophy), ideals, and theories and their engagement practices (methods). It will explore various concepts, definitions, and frameworks describing community engagement and will discuss the relationship between culture and engagement. The context for community engagement will then be examined by looking at the demographic shifts and changing social climate. Next, we will offer a conceptual framework for viewing community engagement as a multifaceted approach that includes an organizational and a community frame of reference. Finally, we will discuss how our communities are in transition and the importance of expanding the spheres of participation, involvement, and engagement across various stakeholder groups, as well as how this can create more equitable representation and transformative change in meeting the needs of a changing citizenry.

FRAMEWORK FOR DEFINING AND UNDERSTANDING COMMUNITY ENGAGEMENT: MAKING THE CONNECTION BETWEEN PHILOSOPHY, IDEOLOGY, AND ENGAGEMENT

Figure 1.1 presents a framework for understanding the connection between individual and organizational beliefs, ideals, theories, and actions. In more general terms, *philosophy* can refer to "the most basic beliefs, concepts, and attitudes of an individual or group." Our beliefs inform and, in many ways, guide our ideals. Michael Appleton (1983) described *ideals* as a set of ideas that explains or legitimates social arrangements, structures of power, or ways of life in terms of the goals, interests, and social positions of individuals or groups. That is, ideals or ideologies attempt to "prescribe" what ought to be and contain a distinguishable evaluative or judgmental element. Prager (1982) argued that as a norm, ideology serves to set parameters for individual expression.

While there are many in society who may wholeheartedly and unreflectively embrace the ideology, there are also those who, while not fully sharing in its expression, are constrained in both thought and action by its presence (Prager, 1982).

Appleton (1983) went further to suggest that using these stated and unstated ideals as an evaluative and judgmental yardstick has served an important function in U.S. society, particularly as it relates to race, ethnicity, and culture, by relating belief to action to justify and guide social action. These

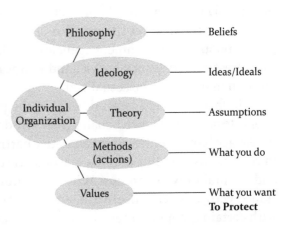

FIGURE 1.1 Framework for Defining and Understanding Community Engagement

ideals have thus served as a guidepost for formulating and evaluating social policy in the areas of education, health care, banking, and government-supported human services and the distribution of resources (Toms, 1997). Pratte (1972) pointed out that the more ingrained an ideology is into the fabric of one's thoughts, feelings, and day-to-day experiences, the stronger the intellectual hold and the more difficult it will be to change the practices and policies arising out of it. He further suggested that the test of strength of any ideology is the extent to which basic assumptions remain not merely unquestioned but literally unrecognized (Pratte, 1972).

Theory can be defined as a set of interrelated assumptions, propositions, or beliefs about "what ought to be" or "is thought to be." Theories can also be described from a scientific perspective as a well-confirmed type of explanation made in a way that is consistent with the scientific method and fulfilling of the criteria for modern science. Here we refer to the more generalized use of theory used daily by nonscientists. In this case, we ask how you would describe your theory of community engagement.

Methods, in the general sense, refer to "actions," what you do (individually/organizationally). In the case of community engagement, the actions you take or do not take can, in fact, say a great deal about what your philosophy (beliefs), ideals, and theories are of community engagement. On the other hand, if we were to examine an organization's mission, values, and beliefs and then compare them to their methods, we could, in fact, determine if there is a connection between stated beliefs and ideals and actual methods (action). *Values* are protected by methods. That is, if you look closely at the "actions" or "methods" of an individual, organization, or group, you can clearly see what is valued.

There appears to be a general agreement that citizens should be able to act on their own behalf and have the power and right to participate in decisions that affect their quality of life and well-being (White, 2009). These ideals and discussions can be heard daily in workplaces, homes, classrooms, and even on various media platforms throughout the day. Yet the practice of this philosophy and set of ideals by private, public, nonprofit, government agencies, and human service agencies in their attempt to address everyday social, civic, and political challenges in our communities more often than not fail to be actualized.

If, in fact, there is a general belief in the participatory democracy (the will of the people to act on their own behalf), then why do institutions and organizations struggle to "engage" communities in collaborative partnerships or work effectively with citizens in community-building efforts—particularly citizens from low-income and ethnically and culturally diverse groups? Why do institutions and organizations appear to be less skilled with, or not as effective in, establishing ongoing connections and relationships with certain groups and certain areas of the community? And why do certain groups of citizens or certain areas of a community tend to feel disrespected, not valued, and even hindered in their efforts to build partnerships and secure the support and resources needed to address and advance their issues and concerns? Collectively, the changing demographics in the United States, combined with the history of exclusion of certain groups, or at the least the inability and/or unwillingness to be inclusive, have created serious questions about the readiness and preparedness of U.S. citizens and institutions to live up to the ideals of "equality and justice for all." Understanding the connection between beliefs, ideals, theories, and methods is a critical first step in understanding the principles and practices of community engagement. This framework provides building blocks for gaining a clearer understanding of the concepts and definitions related to community engagement.

Concepts and Definitions of Community Engagement

Over the past 2 decades, the emerging and expanding importance of collaborative processes with communities has resulted in federal, state-level, and private agencies, including in their funding criteria and requirements goals and objectives for community engagement. The growing commitment to community engagement is reflected in a number of major federal initiatives, including the Clinical and Translational Science Awards program and the Research Centers in Minority Institutions program of the National Institutes of Health, Center for Disease Control and Prevention's (CDC) Prevention Research Centers, and the practice-based research networks of the Agency for Healthcare Research and Quality (AHRQ). In addition, new work by AHRQ highlights the potential benefits of engaging patients and families in the redesign of medical care (Scholle et al., 2010). The CDC (2010) lays out our national health objectives and emphasizes collaboration among diverse groups as a strategy to improve health. Relatedly, national standards and accreditation agencies have infused collaboration and community engagement as core areas of assessment and evaluation for mental health providers, health departments, and for-profit and nonprofit human service providers.

The concept of community engagement can be viewed and described differently, contingent upon the individual, the community, and/or the organization potentially looking to help implement change. Community engagement consists of more than one element; it is inclusive of fairness, justice, empowerment, participation, and self-determination (Alinsky, 1962; Chávez et al., 2007; Freire, 1970; Wallerstein et al., 2006). The CDC Agency for Toxic Substances and Disease Registry Committee for Community Engagement developed a working definition of community engagement that has been widely used and quoted over the years: "Community engagement is the process of working collaboratively with and through groups of people affiliated by geographic proximity, special interest, or similar situations to address issues affecting the well-being of those people" (p. 1). Fawcett et al. (1995) stated that community engagement often involves partnerships and coalitions that help mobilize resources and influence systems, change relationships among partners, and serve as catalysts for changing policies, programs, and practices.

McCloskey et al. (2011) reported four different perspectives in which communities can be understood; they include (1) systems, (2) social, (3) virtual, and (4) individual perspective(s). The social perspective consists of everyone who makes up a community, along with the individuals who may be considered "outsiders," who are trying to help find common ground. The virtual perspective takes into account the powerful nature and use of technology as a resource and tool in today's society. Lastly, the individual perspective attests to one's sense of interconnectedness as an entity within and throughout communities.

Many people consider themselves to be a part of multiple communities, ranging from families to political ties. This suggests that a person's sense of and identification with a community can go beyond the definitions applied by researchers and engagement leaders (McCloskey et al., 2011).

Adler and Coggins (2005) posited the need to think of engagement as a continuum that ranges from the private sphere to the public. The former includes individual actions, such as helping one's neighbor; the latter focuses more on collaborative action with groups or organizations. Eliasoph (1998) proposed the notion of "zones of engagement" as a way of examining and challenging the assumption that nonpolitical engagement and social capital formation easily transfers into political engagement. She offered the following frames as zones of engagement: family relationships, peer and work relationships, civic engagement (e.g., social, communality, community), and political engagement (e.g., policy, electoral). She indicates that each zone has invisible boundaries that individuals must negotiate and cross psychologically and behaviorally, which suggests shifting their commitment, time, and energy across different activities and relationships (Eliasoph, 1998, p. 404).

The Carnegie Elective Classification Report stated, "Community Engagement describes the collaboration between institutions of higher education and their larger communities for the mutually beneficial exchange of knowledge and resources in a context of partnership and reciprocity" (Carnegie Foundation for the Advancement of Teaching, 2006, p. 34).

This focus on mutuality, reciprocity, and knowledge exchange has the potential to be a "game changer" in the world of engagement. In short, if applied as described and intended, the outcome for both parties can—and will—achieve a certain level of desired success.

Why Practice Community Engagement?

Stanley's (2009) literature review on community engagement revealed nine areas wherein it's been identified as having a positive impact, along with several perceived risks, both outlined to follow, respectively. Impact areas referenced included an increase in preparedness to explore concerns through the use of an agenda and improved design and delivery, which aided in informing implementation and change, as well as increased stakeholder participation. Risks were characterized in terms of issues of time, money, and other resources needed to develop new skill sets and increased expectations.

To counterbalance benefits and risks, there should be an understanding of what the community has to offer (outside-in) and vice versa, what the organization has to offer to the community (inside-out). Relationship building and garnering of support can be accomplished through immersion efforts, such as spending time and participating with community members in the community. These interactions can aide in rapport development, as well as increased cultural awareness from both perspectives, thus improving the exploration of needs and desired outcomes, in addition to creating opportunities for communities and constituencies that allow for shared power through active participation that can serve to empower and mobilize efforts for decision making and social action (Hatcher et al., 2008). Other elements essential to community engagement include capacity building, community empowerment, and coalition building. Capacity building includes fostering shared knowledge, leadership skills, and an ability to represent the interests of one's constituents (McCloskey et al., 2011). Empowerment takes place at three levels: (1) individual, (2) organization or group, and (3) community (McCloskey et al., 2011). Finally, coalition building occurs when different organizations in the process cannot reach the goal alone. It is at this point that all parties recognize that it will take a collective effort to achieve the stated goals; this is the starting point of coalition building.

Culture and Community Engagement

Dr. A. Wade Boykin (1985), Howard University, suggested that "culture is to be defined as that which is cultivated" (p. 102); it is the very essence of culture. It is all-encompassing; it varies depending on the individual, the community, and the circumstance (Boykin, 1985). Christie Kiefer (2007) defined culture as a complex integrated system of thought and behavior shared by members of a group—a system whose whole pattern allows us to understand the meanings that people attach to specific facts and observations. An individual's culture influences his or her attitude toward various health issues, including perceptions of what is and is not a health problem, methods of disease prevention, treatments for illness, and use of health providers. As Spector (2004) noted, "We learn from our own cultural and ethnic backgrounds *how* to be healthy, *how* to recognize illness, and *how* to be ill ... meanings attached to the notions of health and illness are related to basic, culture-bound values by which we define a given experience and perceptions" (p. 59).

Another way to understand this concept is to think of culture as the "luggage" we always carry with us—"the sum of beliefs, practices, habits, likes, dislikes, norms, customs, rituals ... that we have learned from our families" (Spector, 2004, p. 60). Cultural identity influences "the group's design for living, the shared set of socially transmitted perceptions about the nature of the physical, social, and spiritual world, particularly as it relates to achieving life's goals" (Airhihenbuwa, 1995, p. 5). Cultural experiences also can influence how individuals and groups relate to each other (within group) and to people and institutions of other cultures (between group).

Initiating community engagement activities (individually and organizationally) requires an understanding of the beliefs and value systems held by different ethnic/racial/cultural groups in target communities, especially if they are different from their own. Understanding the connection between culture and community engagement is a prerequisite to any and all engagement plans and processes. Failure to fully grasp the complexities of culture and cultural differences in planning for engagement activities and processes will surely result in "faulty assumptions," which generally result in "faulty outcomes."

Demographic Shifts and Changing Social Climate

The United States, today and in the future, represents one of the most diverse countries in the world. America's diverse blend—racially, ethnically, socially, culturally, and politically—has made her more colorful than ever imagined. Over the past 2 or more decades, this increasing blend of different people, cultures, values, beliefs, and actions has changed the cultural dynamics of how individuals and organizations view and deal with racial/ethnic differences, particularly in terms of government agencies, human service providers, and educational institutions (Toms, 1997). These demographic changes have sparked emerging sensibilities in the public, civic, and private sectors to acknowledge and, in varying ways, respond to the market presence and market value of the current and projected racial, ethnic, cultural, economic, and political differences in communities across the nation.

Indeed, the United States is involved in a struggle to confront the new challenges and opportunities created by an array of mixed and diverse peoples of many kinds and origins. This struggle to define and redefine who we are has forced everyone (individuals, communities, organizations, and institutions), as Isaacs (1975) has pointed out, "to stumble around amid the rubble and ruins looking for new ways of existing and coexisting on new and largely unfixed terms" (p. 108). It has meant "trying to cope with all the social, economic, psychological carry-overs and consequences of how it was while trying to shape how it is to be hereafter" (Isaacs, 1975, p. 108).

The current and projected demographic changes in the U.S. ethnic/racial composition have begun to challenge the very core values and capabilities of how leadership and organizations define and develop policies, procedures, and practices for workplace interactions. It has also begun to challenge how leaders and organizations must respond to the changing dynamics of community involvement, participation, and engagement of citizens as consumers and collaborative partners.

According to a 2010 release by the U.S. Census Bureau, the U.S. population will be considerably older and more racially and ethnically diverse by 2060. Acting Director Thomas L. Mesenbourg stated, "The next half century marks key points in continuing trends—the U.S. will become a plurality nation, where the non-Hispanic white population remains the largest single group, but no group is in the majority" (U.S. Census Bureau, 2012, para. 2). The non-Hispanic White population is projected to peak in 2024 at 199.6 million, up from 197.8 million in 2012. Unlike other racial or ethnic groups, however, its population is projected to slowly decrease, falling by nearly 20.6 million from 2024 to 2060 (U.S. Census Bureau, 2012).

In 2012, the Hispanic population was 53.3 million. It is projected to more than double to 128.8 million by 2060. Consequently, by the end of the period, nearly one in three U.S. residents will be Hispanic, up from about one in six today. The black population in 2012 was estimated at 41.2 million and projected to increase to 61.8 million by 2060. The Asian population is projected to more than double, from 15.9 million in 2012 to 34.4 million in 2060, with its share of the nation's total population climbing from 5.1% to 8.2% in the same period (U.S. Census Bureau, 2012).

American Indians and Alaska Natives would increase from 3.9 million in 2012 to 6.3 million by 2060, a percentage population jump from 1.2% to 1.5%. The Native Hawaiian and Other Pacific Islander population is expected to nearly double from 706,000 to 1.4 million. The number of people who identify themselves as being of two or more races is projected to more than triple from 7.5 million to 26.7 million over the same period. It is projected that the United States will become a majority-minority nation for the first time in 2043. While the non-Hispanic White population will remain the largest single group, no group will make up a majority. At present, 37% of the U.S. population is represented by minority groups; the number is expected to grow to 57% by 2060 (U.S. Census Bureau, 2012).

These types of projections have been made for many years. However, the realities of these demographic changes are being felt, personally and socially, by individual Americans and institutions with whom they participate with regularity. That is, whether in our schools, businesses, civic government, and political organizations or in social and recreational settings, American citizens are experiencing contact with people from different ethnic/racial origins as parents, professionals, service providers, customer representatives, and consumers. As a result, individuals and organizations are directly or indirectly and/or consciously or unconsciously affected by the increase in the demographic changes occurring in society (Toms, 1997).

The Changing Social Climate: Participatory Democracy

It is not only the demographic shifts but also the effect of the shifts on the social, cultural, and civic climate in the country. One clear effect of these population shifts has been a need to build collaborative relations among and between increasingly diverse consumers and institutions, such as human services agencies, higher educational institutions, and local governments. Another noticeable effect has been the need to reexamine and change the policies and practices of how leadership and organizations view and approach building the capacity of individuals and institutions to intentionally engage populations that historically have been excluded, or not included, in civic decision making and community-building programs and processes (Toms, 1997).

At issue here is the ideal of participatory democracy, which implies the right and expectation that different ethnic/racial/cultural groups have representative representation of their groups' interests in decision-making bodies that develop and implement policies. Philosophically, participatory democracy is believed to be fundamental to citizenship. McBride et al. (2006) argued that the engagement of citizens in participatory democracy is the defining construct of this Americanized form of governance. Saltmarsh et al. (2009) in their research on engaged higher education institutions suggested a need to shift focus from civic engagement to what they described as "democratic engagement" (p. 6). The authors indicated that "the norms of democratic culture are determined by the values of inclusiveness, participation, task sharing, lay participation, reciprocity in public problem solving, and an equality of respect for the knowledge and experience that everyone contributes to education and community building" (Saltmarsh et al., 2009, p. 6). They argued that the key components to democratic engagement include mutually beneficial relationships, reciprocity, and "processes and purpose." Mutually beneficial relationships are critical to the development of trust, equity, and fairness in partnership development. Reciprocity (processes) operates to facilitate the involvement of individuals, and purpose (its democratic dimensions) maintains focus on the norms of a democratic culture. Such a democratic framework is shaped by attention to processes and purpose and is based on "both sides bringing their own experience and expertise to the project ... this kind of collaboration, they suggest, requires substantial change in the institutional culture" (Saltmarsh et al., 2009, p. 9).

Few, if any, would argue that the concept and ideal of participatory democracy and local decision making are not noteworthy. However, the reality for groups that have not been represented at the decision-making table is that they are grossly underrepresented in terms of inclusion in leadership positions and policy and resource distribution decisions that affect their quality of life and community well-being (Toms, 1997). Because of the increased demographics, social and political activity, and marketplace presence and value of a growing diverse customer and consumer base, no longer can diverse populations be blatantly ignored. In more and more cases, their voices are being sought out.

Readiness and Preparedness for Engagement

Readiness is a construct most examined in the public health literature as a prevention strategy. It most often has a professional service outcome. Community readiness is the extent to which communities are prepared to engage in or improve the level of networking, which is theorized to lead to more effective community engagement (Grasby et al., 2005).

Foster-Fisherman et al. (2007) found that different components of capacity and readiness mattered for different levels of community engagement. Their research suggested that what helps individuals move from inaction to action may be different from what inspires them to become more highly engaged residents in their communities. Readiness is thus defined by the outcome expected (Lloyd, 2010). Foster-Fisherman et al. (2007) viewed readiness as separate from skill and infrastructure capacity to imply attitudes and beliefs that impel members to work toward change. They found nurturing strong community leadership infrastructure to be critical to collective efficacy and hope for change. Although social ties and leadership were important, these are the critical indicators of readiness. Fisherman-Foster et al. (2009) suggested that readiness is thus defined as hope for change and collective efficacy mediated by social networks. All other constructs are seen as contributing factors to civic participation.

Toms et al. (2008) identified a number of factors as indicators of readiness for community action. These include (1) a powerful vision and mission; (2) a strong presence; (3) organizational expertise and access to potential consumers or markets; (4) extensive communication, programs, and projects; (5) well-known respected leaders; (6) access to community leaders and influential people, facilities, and equipment, fundraising and financial capacity, family and community engagement; and (7) a willingness to learn and build capacity as factors that predict community readiness for partnerships. This literature suggests that readiness is influenced by varying degrees of social capital, leadership community capacity and character, and an orientation to the outcome/product or the process (Lloyd, 2010).

COMMUNITY ENGAGEMENT: A MULTIFACETED APPROACH— ORGANIZATIONAL FRAME

In order for an organization to be effective and culturally competent, community stakeholders (traditional and nontraditional) need to be integrally involved in the design, implementation, and evaluation of all programs, services, and supports. Their participation on governance boards, advisory committees, task forces, and work groups is instrumental in facilitating their authentic involvement and voice in all areas of the organization. It is essential that organizations create an environment that is conducive to trust building, respect, and shared power. The following quote from Chappell (2008) captures the risk involved when organizations build (knowingly and/or unknowingly) unrealistic expectations about community engagement, particularly in relation to consultation:

> Consultation has been used as a general term to describe how local councils approach communities about decisions that affect them. This general use has the potential to create unrealistic expectations and confusion. Most commonly, communities become disengaged when they are asked to provide input on a decision that has already been determined. If a decision has been made, the community needs to be informed about how and why it was made and not have raised expectations that they are being consulted for their input on a final decision. There will always be times when councils must make decisions without input from communities as part of their governance role. There will be other times when it will be relevant to increase the public impact on a decision by working at the more participatory levels of involve, collaborate or empower. (p. 8)

Figure 1.2 offers a framework for understanding and building the internal capacity of organizations to develop, implement, and sustain an effective community engagement process. Organizational capacity building can and does take on many forms. This should go beyond the general yearly goals and plans to include or, should we say,

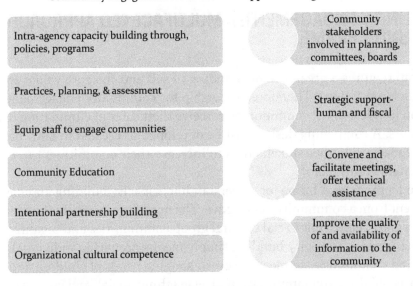

Community Engagement A Multifaceted Approach - Organizations

Intra-agency capacity building through, policies, programs	Community stakeholders involved in planning, committees, boards
Practices, planning, & assessment	Strategic support–human and fiscal
Equip staff to engage communities	
Community Education	Convene and facilitate meetings, offer technical assistance
Intentional partnership building	Improve the quality of and availability of information to the community
Organizational cultural competence	

FIGURE 1.2   A Multifaceted Approach—Organizations

intentionally build into the fabric of the plan intraorganizational capacity building around policies, procedures, practices, and planning and assessment directly focused on community engagement—that is, not a separate organizational plan but a plan that is inclusive of principles, goals, objectives, strategies, and processes focused on community engagement. These goals and processes should include how community stakeholders will be involved in planning committees and advisory boards, how human and fiscal resources will be targeted to help achieve engagement goals, and how resources will be targeted to communities to address their identified needs (e.g., program support and technical assistance).

A critical and often overlooked or underestimated aspect of organizational capacity building in the 21st century is organizational cultural competency. Davis (1997) defined cultural competence as "the integration and transformation of knowledge, information, and data about individuals and groups of people into specific clinical standards, skills, service approaches, techniques, and marketing programs that match the individual's culture and increase the quality and appropriateness of mental health care and outcomes" (p. 3). Organizational cultural competency is important to community engagement because it provides a "baseline" for the assessment of how well and to what extent individuals and the organization are prepared to deliver culturally relative and competent services and programs to diverse consumers and communities. We suggest that cultural competency, in many ways, serves as an "indicator of" and "prerequisite to" organizational readiness for developing and implementing a community engagement process.

COMMUNITY ENGAGEMENT: A MULTIFACETED APPROACH—COMMUNITY FRAME

Leadership requires a greater understanding of self and the core values that determine individual actions. Therefore, leadership for community engagement requires a focus on how leaders of communities perceive their roles in eliminating disparities for followers. A compelling desire must be developed or created in faith-based community leaders and other stakeholders to increase their commitment to effectively lead followers (Toms, 2010).

Figure 1.3 provides a frame for understanding capacity building and community engagement from a community perspective. The need for capacity building in African American and other ethnic/racial cultural group communities and organizations has never been greater. Capacity building simply means preparing individuals, organizations, and communities to meet the ever-changing needs of children and families, particularly children and families from diverse ethnic, racial, and cultural heritages. This means concerned citizens and leaders must organize, plan, develop, and implement programs and processes to improve the quality of life in their communities

Community Engagement A Multifaceted Approach - Communities

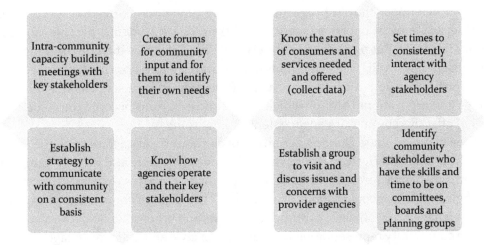

FIGURE 1.3 A Multifaceted Approach—Communities

through intentional and consistent participation in community engagement activities. This suggests that plans and processes must be implemented to convene meetings regularly with key stakeholders in the community, create forums for community input, identify needs, and strategies to communicate with community leaders and residents on a consistent basis.

Identified stakeholders (community leaders) must seek avenues to provide intentional representation of the issues, needs, and concerns of their groups within the fabric of mainstream institutions, programs, and service delivery vehicles. In addition, it also means that those persons identified as leaders—whether selected by their communities or self-selected—must, at the same time, create avenues, vehicles, and processes to transfer the knowledge and necessary information back to the people they represent. It means that those who accept the responsibility of representing others are ethically and morally accountable to create avenues to hear the voices of those they represent and build those voices into the center of all discussions regarding programs, service needs, and resource distribution.

These leaders, who represent the voices of the people, must take an active organizing role within the community to get more individuals and organizations directly involved and participating in the process of civic engagement. The areas of engagement include access to services, more community education on the status of health, mental health, and education disparity data, provider accountability, and culturally relevant and competent service delivery. These areas and others must be systematically and strategically addressed and monitored.

The process requires that participants make clear distinctions between events, programs, and processes (Toms, 2010). Events bring people together, many times celebrating, recognizing, and supporting people and groups. Or they can include informational meetings, church programs, etc. Programs provide needed services (e.g., tutoring, academic support), education, and training for students, parents, and community residents. But processes are the critical link. Processes include thinking about the "what," "how," and "when" methods of identifying and recruiting key stakeholders and coordinating activities, to name a few. Processes, in fact, serve as the engine for change and innovations through which events and programs become the vehicles and tools of effective community engagement (Toms, 2010).

To be clear, we share Goode's definition of community engagement as the process of working collaboratively with and through groups of people affiliated by geographic proximity, special interest, or similar situations to address issues affecting the well-being of those people (Goode et al., 2006). The "with" of community engagement suggests that elected officials, community leaders, and other stakeholders must seek to include community representation in all aspects of civic and political engagement. The "through" of community engagement implies working relationships and partnerships with communities to ensure participation in and engagement of issues and policies affecting their well-being (Toms, 2010; Toms et al., 2011).

COMMUNITIES IN TRANSITION: EXPANDING THE SPHERES OF ENGAGEMENT

Without a doubt, our communities have undergone, and continue to undergo, a transition involving the action and interaction between parents and children, educational institutions, and communities, and human service agencies, local governments, and diverse citizenry. The external environment is rapidly changing, as reflected through the reported demographic shifts and future demographic projections, along with the changing social climate in areas of participatory democracy, cultural conflict, and cultural transition. These examples are clear indicators of how our society and communities are in transition.

Furthermore, community leaders and stakeholders in the mainstream of civic affairs are affected by this transition, as are the underrepresented ethnic, racial, and cultural groups that seek and expect their voices to be included in the community-building process through participation and involvement in policy development and decision-making processes (Toms, 1997).

Figure 1.4 attempts to provide a visual representation and conceptual frame for understanding the multifaceted and multidimensional nature of the transitions occurring in our communities. We suggest that as these transitions continue to evolve in our communities, we must expand the spheres of community participation and engagement in civic affairs by increasing and involving more stakeholders in the center of community, economic, and civic activity. The graphic includes three separate—yet

Communities in Transition
Expand The Sphere
Community Participation and Civic Affairs

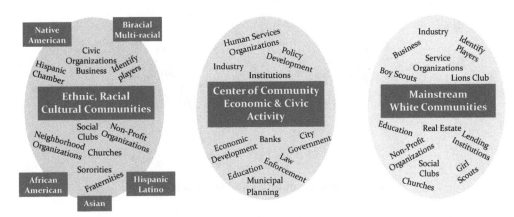

FIGURE 1.4 Communities in Transition: Expand the Sphere

interconnected—circles, each identifying selected stakeholders central to participation in civic affairs. The circle on the left of the graph represents various ethnic, racial, cultural groups potentially involved in community/civic engagement in their communities. Keeping in mind that there are five groups—(1) African American, (2) Asian, (3) Hispanic/Latino, (4) Native American, and (5) multiracial—highlighted around the circle representing a separate community participation and engagement process operating in each group's community. Not all of these groups will have the same target organizations or groups participating; not all will have equal or representative representation of organizations identified around the circle; not all will have formal or informal engagement processes operating consistently inside their communities nor within the mainstream of the overall community. The circle to the far right represents the mainstream of White communities and selected identifiable groups or agencies known to participate and engage in civic affairs within their community. The center circle represents the center of community, economic, and civic activity in any community. This center of community activity is where policy development, economic development, and decision making occurs through governing boards, such as city councils, county commissioners, economic development boards, school boards, and chambers of commerce. While we recognize that members of various ethnic, racial, and cultural groups are represented on these governing boards, we suggest that as our communities transition, there will be a greater need to expand the participation and involvement of more citizens in the participatory democracy process (i.e., it is not enough just to have someone who looks like you at the table. They must be ready to represent the group's interests by being responsive to citizens' needs. Thus they must

Communities in Transition

Build Bridges Through Engagement

Ethnic, Racial Cultural Communities

Center of Community Economic & Civic Activity

Mainstream White Communities

Between Communities and Stakeholders

FIGURE 1.5 Communities in Transition: Build Bridges Through Engagement

be prepared to provide opportunities to build capacity for citizens to participate in civic/community affairs on a consistent basis).

Figure 1.5 suggests that with intentional community engagement processes and efforts in various diverse communities and in the mainstream of White communities, we can produce a "bridge builder" for engagement to expand the voices in the center civic governing processes. In terms of diverse communities, this means efforts must be enhanced to create vehicles and tools designed to increase the awareness, knowledge, and skills of citizens regarding participation in the mainstream of civic affairs. This includes community education forums around issues of disparities in the areas of education, health care, mental health, and economic development, to name a few. It means developing vehicles and tools to identify, recruit, and prepare citizens to serve on planning committees and advisory groups associated with and appointed by local governing boards. On the other hand, it means that agencies and individuals in the mainstream can be bridge builders for more inclusive engagement and representation of diverse groups, both within their communities and between their communities and diverse communities. To be clear, this same proposition applies to diverse stakeholders and their communities.

Figure 1.6 indicates that we can expand the sphere of engagement and increase equitable representation in the center of civic affairs if we intentionally expand the bridge builders from diverse communities and mainstream communities and agencies. In order for this vision to be achieved, more efforts must be directed toward enhancing the relational context and interpersonal interactions among and between diverse communities and mainstream stakeholders and organizations.

What we are suggesting has been described as transformative change by Eckel and Green (1998). These authors argued that transformation requires a shift in an

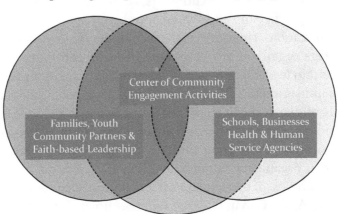

Expanding the Spheres of Community Engagement

Center of Community Engagement Activities

Families, Youth Community Partners & Faith-based Leadership

Schools, Businesses Health & Human Service Agencies

Equitable Representation
& Participation in Identifying Needs & Services

FIGURE 1.6   Expanding the Spheres of Community Engagement

institution's (community's) culture—an altering of the common beliefs, values, and behaviors. Transformational change involves altering the underlying assumptions so that they are congruent with the desired changes (Eckel & Green, 1998).

SUMMARY

There is a great deal of "chatter" surrounding community engagement and partnering in and around government agencies, nonprofits, human service agencies, service providers, and the community. These terms extend beyond the need for benchmarks to maintain the status quo. When the discussion of these terms move beyond status quo fulfillment and benchmark data, it can become clearer that traditional beliefs, ideals, and assumptions used to implement and execute community engagement efforts lacked intentionality for the development and sustainment of a mutually beneficial partnership. Brukardt et al. (2004) argued, "True partnerships are spaces within which the questions are created, there is genuine reciprocal deliberation, and the work to find answers begun" (p. 9). White (2009) extended this thinking. He stated, "Such visions of parity are laudable but not necessarily realistic"; he went further by stating, "Notions of reciprocal deliberation" and "equal partnerships" are far-fetched concepts to community leaders, who are fully aware of their own under-resourced capacity in comparison to institutions' abundance (p. 14).

In their study of civic and public organizations, Creighton and Harwood (2007) interviewed institutional leaders that expressed deep and passionate concern for the communities in which they worked, while their institutions' operational forces were not aligned with their expressed sentiments, as their engagements with the communities lacked true partnership and shared power.

In most organizations, there are certain people or offices assigned with the responsibility to engage organizations or groups within a community. Likewise, in the community, certain leaders, groups, and organizations are generally viewed to represent the community's interest. Within this particular formula, many communities and their voices are often not included at the table, particularly citizens from low-income and diverse groups. And even when they are included in the engagement process, White (2009) suggested two groups usually emerge as the primary partners. It is at this juncture that organizations must intentionally build in a process committed to "expanding the spheres" of participation and inclusion of voices to represent a broader community base. As Dr. Calvin Ellison, executive director of the Community Empowerment Network in North Carolina has stated, "If you are not at the table, then you are probably on the menu" (Ellison, 2008). Clearly, citizen leaders, community residents, and community organizations are not simply satisfied with a seat at the table. They want to be included in the discussion about who will be at the table, the menu, and other issues that can help define their community's problems and identify solutions to help solve them.

There are many examples of institutions and communities that are effectively navigating the multifaceted dimensions of community engagement. Yet there is a greater need to continue to expand the spheres of engagement to prepare increasingly diverse citizens and communities to participate in the civic affairs of local communities. It will require organizations to look inward to assess the readiness and preparedness of the institution and its personnel to be purposeful, reciprocal, and culturally competent in how they engage and work with communities. It will require those community citizens and leaders to be consistent and persistent in the efforts to represent the "will" and "voice" of the people they were intended to represent and to be willing and committed to finding and creating the vehicles and processes to transform communities of place by consistently reaching out, educating, and informing citizens.

DISCUSSION QUESTIONS

The following questions can be used to facilitate further discussions and understanding of the multifaceted nature of community engagement through guided small and/or large group discussions. Participants should be assigned to small groups of four to five, depending on the size of the groups, and given 10–15 minutes to discuss assigned questions. Each small group should have a facilitator and recorder. The facilitator will make sure that every participant has a chance to respond to the questions, and the recorder will write down responses.

1. What is community engagement?
2. What role, if any, do philosophy, ideology, theory, and methods play in decision making, policy development/implementation, and resource distribution as they relate to inclusion and community engagement? Please list and discuss current-day examples of how philosophy and ideology are manifested in today's educational, social, political, and economic practices.
3. How, and in what ways, do demographic shifts in the U.S. population relate to the need for a more multifaceted approach to inclusion and community engagement?
4. Discuss the "inside-out–outside-in" framework for community engagement and what makes it different from more traditional methods of community engagement.
5. What are the elements of a multifaceted community engagement framework and process?
6. Why do certain groups of citizens or certain areas of a community tend to feel disrespected, not valued, and even hindered in their efforts to build and secure the support and resources needed to address and advance their issues and concerns?
7. Why do institutions and organizations struggle to "engage" communities in collaborative partnerships and work effectively with citizens in community-building efforts, particularly citizens from low-income and ethnically and culturally diverse groups?

REFERENCES

Adler, R. P., & Coggin, J. (2005). What do we mean by "civic engagement"? *Journal of Transformative Education, 3*(3), 236–253.

Airhihenbuwa, C. O. (1995). *Health and culture beyond the western paradigm.* SAGE Publications.

Alinsky, S. D. (1962). *Citizen participation and community organization in planning and urban renewal.* Industrial Areas Foundation.

Appleton, M. (1983). *Cultural pluralism in education: Theoretical foundations, Arizona State University.* Longman, Inc.

Boykin, A. W., & Toms, F. D. (1985). Black child socialization: A conceptual framework. In H. P. McAdoo & J. L. McAdoo (Eds.), Sage focus editions, Vol. 72. Black children: Social, educational, and parental environments (p. 33–51). Sage Publications.

Brukardt, M. J., Holland B., Percy S., & Zimpher, N. (2004). *Calling the question: Is higher education ready to commit to community engagement?* University of Wisconsin.

Carnegie Foundation for the Advancement of Teaching. (2006). *Carnegie elective classification report.* http:classifications.carnegiefoundation.org/descriptions/communityengagement.php

Center for Disease Control and Prevention. (2010). *Healthy People 2020.* (2010). National Center for Health Statistics Hyattsville, MD.

Chappell, B. (2008). To engage or consult? That is the question! *Incite, 29*(3), 8.

Chávez, V., Minkler, M., Wallerstein, N., & Spencer, M. S. (2007). Community organizing for health and social justice. In L. Cohen, V. Chávez, & S. Chehimi (Eds.), *Prevention is primary: Strategies for community well-being* (1st ed., pp. 95–120). John Wiley and Sons.

Creighton, J. A., & R. C. Harwood. (2007). The organization-first approach: How intermediary organizations approach civic engagement and communities. Bethesda, MD: The Harwood Institute for Public Innovation.

Davis, K. (1997). Race, health status, and managed care. In L. Epstein & F. Brisbane (Eds.), *Cultural competence series* (pp. 1–33). Center for Substance Abuse Prevention.

Eckel, P., Hill, B., & Green, M. (1998). *En route to transformation.* On change: Occasional Paper, No. 1. Washington, DC: American Council on Education.

Eliasoph, N. (1998). Avoiding politics: How Americans produce apathy in everyday life. Cambridge University Press.

Ellison, C. (2008). *Expanding the Spheres of Community Engagement.* [Paper presentation]. Community Empowerment Network Annual Meeting. Farmville, NC, United States.

Fawcett, S. B., Paine-Andrews, A., Francisco, V. T., Schultz, J. A., Richter, K. P., & Berkley-Patton, J. (1995). Evaluating community initiatives for health and development. In I. Rootman & D. McQueen (Eds.), *Evaluating health promotion approaches* (pp. 241–277). World Health Organization.

Foster-Fisherman, P., Cantillon, D., Pierce S., & Van Egeren, L. (2007). Building an active citizenry: The role of neighborhood problems, readiness and capacity for change. *American Journal of Community Psychology, 39,* 91–106.

Foster-Fisherman, P., Pierce, S., & Van Egeren, L. (2009). Who participates and why: Building a process model of citizen participation. *Health Education and Behavior, 39,* 550–69.

Freire, P. (1970). *Pedagogy of the oppressed.* Herder and Herder.

Goode, T. (2002). Promoting cultural diversity and cultural competency: Self-assessment checklist for personnel providing services and supports to children with disabilities and special health care needs. Georgetown University National Center for Cultural Competence. https://nccc.georgetown.edu/documents/ChecklistCSHN.pdf

Goode, T., Dunne, C., & Bronheim, S. (2006). The Evidence Base for Cultural and Linguistic Competence in Health Care. The Commonwealth Fund.

Grasby, D., Zammit, C., Pretty, G., & Bramston, P. (2005, August 14–17). Ready, set, go: Using the community readiness method to engage social networks for sustainable natural resource management in the Queensland and Murray-Darling basin [Conference session]. International Conference on Engaging Communities, Queensland, Australia.

Hatcher, H., Planalp, R., Cho, J., Torti, F. M., & Torti, S. (2008). Curcumin: From ancient medicine to current clinical trials. Cellular and molecular life sciences: CMLS. 65. 1631–52. 10.1007/s00018-008-7452-4.

Holland, B., & Ramaley, J. A. (2008, July 1–4). *Creating a supportive environment for community university engagement: Conceptual frameworks* [Paper presentation]. HERDSA, 2008: Engaging Communities, Rotorua, NZ.

Isaacs, H. R. (1975). *The idols of the tribe: Identity and political change.* Harvard University Press.

Kiefer, C. W. (2007). *Doing health anthropology: Research methods for community assessment and change* (1st ed.). Springer.

Lloyd, C. M. (2010). *University relations* [Unpublished doctoral dissertation]. North Carolina Agricultural and Technical State University.

McBride, A., Sherraden, M., & Pritzker, S. (2006). Civic engagement among low-income and low-wealth families: In their words. *Family Relations, 55,* 152–162.

McCloskey, D. J., Aguilar-Gaxiola, S., & Mitchner, J. L. (Eds.). (2011). *Principles of community engagement* (2nd ed., Publication No. 11–728). Clinical and Translational Science Awards (CTSA) Program and the Research Centers in Minority Institutions Program of the National Institutes of Health (NIH), CDC's Prevention Research Centers NIH.

Prager, J. (1982). American racial ideology as collective representation. *Ethnic and Racial Studies, 5,* 99–119.

Pratte, R. (1972). *The concept of cultural pluralism* [Paper presentation]. Philosophy of Education, 1972: Proceedings of the Twenty-Eighth Annual Meeting of the Philosophy of Education Society. Salt Lake City, Utah, United States.

Saltmarsh, J., Hartley, M., & Clayton, P. H. (2009). *Democratic engagement white paper.* New England Resource Center for Higher Education.

Scholle, S. H., Torda, P., Peikes, D., Han, E., & Genevro, J. (2010). Engaging patients and families in the medical home (Publication No. 10-0083-EF). Agency for Healthcare Research and Quality.

Smith, B. P. (2008). *Leadership Role of Community Health Ambassadors.* [Paper presentation]. Community Empowerment Network Annual Meeting. Farmville, NC, United States.

Spector, R. E. (2004). *Cultural diversity in health and illness* (5th ed.). Pearson.

Stanley, K. (2009). *Exploring impact: Public involvement in NHS, public health and social care research.* INVOLVE.

Toms, F. D. (1997). Challenges and opportunities of communities in transition. In F.D. Toms & A. D. Hobbs (Eds.), *Who are we?: Building a knowledge base of ethnic, racial, and cultural groups in America.* Diverse Books.

Toms, F. D. (2010). Black elected officials and community/civic engagement [Paper presentation]. Annual Meeting of the American Education Research Association. Denver, CO, United States.

Toms, F. D., Lloyd, C. L., Edwards-Carter, L., & Ellison, C. (2011). The Faith-Based Community View of Improving Health and Health Care Advocacy through Engagement. *Practical Matters Journal, 4,* 1–13.

Toms, F. D., Glover, S., Erwin, A., & Ellison, C. (2008). Leadership and community engagement: A faith-based capacity building model. *Leadership Studies Magazine, 1,* 13–15.

U.S. Census Bureau. (2012, December 12). *U.S. Census Bureau projections show a slower growing, older, more diverse nation a half century from now* [Press release]. http://www.census.gov/newsroom/releases/archives/population/cb12-243.html

Wallerstein, N. B., & Duran, B. (2006). Using community-based participatory research to address health disparities. *Health Promotion Practice, 7*(3), 312–23.

White, B. P. (2009). *Navigating the dynamics between institutions and their communities. A study for the Kettering Foundation.* The Kettering Foundation.

Figure Credits

Fig. 1.4: Communities in Transition: Challenges and Opportunities of Community Building, Training and Research Development, Inc.

Fig. 1.5: Communities in Transition: Challenges and Opportunities of Community Building, Training and Research Development, Inc.

Fig. 1.6: Communities in Transition: Challenges and Opportunities of Community Building, Training and Research Development, Inc.

CHAPTER TWO

The History, Challenges, and Continuing Necessity for Fusion Reconstruction Social/Political Activism in the 21st-Century South

William Barber, DMin, and T. Anthony Spearman, DMin

> Gentlemen of the Convention, There has never been before and there would probably never be again so important an assemblage of the colored people of North Carolina as the present in its influence upon the destinies of the people for all time to come .... Let us have faith, and patience, and moderation, yet assert always that we want three things, first, the right to give evidence in the courts; second, the right to be represented in the jury-box; and third, the right to put votes in the ballot box. These rights we want, these rights we contend for, and these rights, under God, we must ultimately have.

Rev. James Walker Hood spoke the previous words on the floor of the Constitutional Convention of 1868 in North Carolina. He spoke as an African American Lincoln Republican and a Reconstruction politician who believed in fusion politics. In his words, we hear three pillars of public policy that would be used to unite Whites and Blacks, fresh out of the ravages of the Civil War, into a common bond to move forward and begin the arduous task of reconstruction in North Carolina and the nation. When the convention was over, the fusionists had framed these words as a new vision for a new North Carolina:

NORTH CAROLINA STATE CONSTITUTION

Preamble

We, the people of the State of North Carolina, grateful to Almighty God, the Sovereign Ruler of Nations, for the preservation of the American Union and the existence of our civil, political and religious liberties, and acknowledging our dependence upon Him for the continuance of those blessings to us and our posterity, do, for the more certain security thereof and for the better government of this State, ordain and establish this Constitution.

Article I

Declaration of Rights

That the great, general, and essential principles of liberty and free government may be recognized and established, and that the relations of this State to the Union and government of the United States and those of the people of this State to the rest of the American people may be defined and affirmed, we do declare that:

Section 1. The equality and rights of persons.

We hold it to be self-evident that all persons are created equal; that they are endowed by their Creator with certain inalienable rights; that among these are life, liberty, the enjoyment of the fruits of their own labor, and the pursuit of happiness.

Sec. 2. Sovereignty of the people.

All political power is vested in and derived from the people; all government of right originates from the people, is founded upon their will only, and is instituted solely for the good of the whole.

Sec. 3. Internal government of the State.

The people of this State have the inherent, sole, and exclusive right of regulating the internal government and police thereof, and of altering or abolishing their Constitution and form of government whenever it may be necessary to their safety and happiness; but every such right shall be exercised in pursuance of law and consistently with the Constitution of the United States.

Sec. 4. Secession prohibited.

This State shall ever remain a member of the American Union; the people thereof are part of the American nation; there is no right on the part of this State to secede; and all attempts, from whatever source or upon whatever pretext, to dissolve this Union or to sever this Nation, shall be resisted with the whole power of the State.

Sec. 5. Allegiance to the United States.

Every citizen of this State owes paramount allegiance to the Constitution and government of the United States, and no law or ordinance of the State in contravention or subversion thereof can have any binding force.

Source: https://www.ncleg.gov/EnactedLegislation/Constitution/NCConstitution.html.

Sec. 6. Separation of powers.

The legislative, executive, and supreme judicial powers of the State government shall be forever separate and distinct from each other.

Sec. 7. Suspending laws.

All power of suspending laws or the execution of laws by any authority, without the consent of the representatives of the people, is injurious to their rights and shall not be exercised.

Sec. 8. Representation and taxation.

The people of this State shall not be taxed or made subject to the payment of any impost or duty without the consent of themselves or their representatives in the General Assembly, freely given.

Sec. 9. Frequent elections.

For redress of grievances and for amending and strengthening the laws, elections shall be often held.

Sec. 10. Free elections.

All elections shall be free.

Sec. 11. Property qualifications.

As political rights and privileges are not dependent upon or modified by property, no property qualification shall affect the right to vote or hold office.

Sec. 12. Right of assembly and petition.

The people have a right to assemble together to consult for their common good, to instruct their representatives, and to apply to the General Assembly for redress of grievances; but secret political societies are dangerous to the liberties of a free people and shall not be tolerated.

Sec. 13. Religious liberty.

All persons have a natural and inalienable right to worship Almighty God according to the dictates of their own consciences, and no human authority shall, in any case whatever, control or interfere with the rights of conscience.

Sec. 14. Freedom of speech and press.

Freedom of speech and of the press are two of the great bulwarks of liberty and therefore shall never be restrained, but every person shall be held responsible for their abuse.

Sec. 15. Education.

The people have a right to the privilege of education, and it is the duty of the State to guard and maintain that right.

Sec. 16. Ex post facto laws.

Retrospective laws, punishing acts committed before the existence of such laws and by them only declared criminal, are oppressive, unjust, and incompatible with liberty, and therefore no ex post facto law shall be enacted. No law taxing retrospectively sales, purchases, or other acts previously done shall be enacted.

Sec. 17. Slavery and involuntary servitude.

Slavery is forever prohibited. Involuntary servitude, except as a punishment for crime whereof the parties have been adjudged guilty, is forever prohibited.

Sec. 18. Court shall be open.

All courts shall be open; every person for an injury done him in his lands, goods, person, or reputation shall have remedy by due course of law; and right and justice shall be administered without favor, denial, or delay.

Sec. 19. Law of the land; equal protection of the laws.

No person shall be taken, imprisoned, or disseized of his freehold, liberties, or privileges, or outlawed, or exiled, or in any manner deprived of his life, liberty, or property, but by the law of the land. No person shall be denied the equal protection of the laws; nor shall any person be subjected to discrimination by the State because of race, color, religion, or national origin.

This new vision of liberty and citizenship outlined in the 1868 North Carolina Constitution predated the passage of the Fifteenth Amendment to the U.S. Constitution. Readily available research reveals the Fifteenth Amendment, ratified on February 3, 1870, provided that

> the right of U.S. citizens to vote shall not be denied or abridged by the United States or by any state on account of race, color, or previous condition of servitude.

In addition, under this amendment, the Congress was given the authority to enforce those rights and regulate the voting process. With new constitutions at the state and local levels, fusion political alliances began to be born.

On a per capita and absolute basis, more Blacks were elected to public office during the period from 1865 to 1880 than at any other time in American history, including a number of state legislative bodies, which were effectively under the control of strong African American caucuses. During this period of "fusion politics," Blacks and Whites joined together to reconstruct the nation toward the noble goals of justice and equality and passed some of the most progressive economic, educational, and labor laws in our nation's history.

Almost a century before the Voting Rights Act (VRA), 16 African Americans won seats in the U.S. Congress, and more than 600 black men took the oath of office in southern state legislatures in the years between 1865 and 1880 (Foner & Garrity, 1991, pp. 917–923). While they never held office in proportion to their numbers, African Americans wielded significant power in every statehouse. In North Carolina, more

African Americans served in the legislature than there are today. Although southern White terrorism and northern White indifference destroyed Reconstruction, the redefinition of American citizenship is unimaginable without the framework of rights won by these Black and White pioneers (Foner, 1990, pp. 254–255).

Between 1865 and 1900, Black-majority interracial alliances in every southern state rose to push public education, protect the right to vote, and curb corporate power by reaching across the color line. They outraged White conservatives by raising taxes for public education. They attacked the divisive rhetoric of White solidarity and pointed to the common interests of most Black and White southerners (Dailey, 2000, pp. 1–14). These "fusion" coalitions took power: during that decade, more than a quarter of White voters in the region cast their ballots for Black-majority coalitions. In the 1890s, a "fusion" of Republicans and Populists in North Carolina swept the state legislature and won both U.S. Senate seats and the governorship (Edmonds, 1951). These "fusion" coalitions of Blacks and Whites in the South passed some of the most progressive educational and labor laws in our nation's history (Kousser, 1974, pp. 171–175).

The radical and racist Dixiecrats of this period could not stand for this. Near and around 1870, they started a campaign to "redeem" America from the influence of Black political power and progress. They launched a frontal attack. These radical Dixiecrats found the means to deny the vote to Blacks through violence, intimidation, and Jim Crow laws. From 1890 to 1908, 10 southern states wrote new constitutions with provisions that included literacy tests, poll taxes, and grandfather clauses. State provisions applied to all voters and were upheld by an ultraconservative, radical Supreme Court beginning in 1875. Later, in the 20th century, when the Supreme Court began to find a few of the provisions unconstitutional, states reacted rapidly in devising new legislation to continue the disenfranchisement of most Blacks.

Declaring their intention to "redeem" America, the White conservatives of the South organized the Ku Klux Klan and the Red Shirts to create what one editor termed "permanent good government by the party of the White Man" (Tyson, 2006, p. 1A). Everywhere and always, conservatives howled about the use of tax money to support public education—especially for Black children—and sought to suppress the African American vote. "Race riots" in New Orleans, Wilmington, Atlanta, Springfield, and other cities destroyed interracial democracy and created a Jim Crow political economy rooted in low taxes, low wages, and fewer and fewer voters (Cecelski & Tyson, 1998; Godshalk, 2005; Mixon, 2005; Prather, 1984; Senechal, 1990). These backlash brigades were the political ancestors of the "Dixiecrats" of the Strom Thurmond and Jesse Helms genre, the paranoid right wing of the John Birch Society. In many ways, they were precursors of the Tea Party today.

Between 1901 and 1902, George White, the last African American congressperson of the Reconstruction era, who was from North Carolina, was effectively driven out of office because he saw the tactics being implemented to prevent his reelection. The strategy to stop any effort at reconstruction and fusion politics has always consisted of five direct actions: (1) attacking voting rights, (2) attacking tax revenue and government programs and agencies designed to promote social uplift, (3) attacking public educational policy, (4) attacking labor rights, and (5) attacking or assassinating White and Black progressive leaders.

At the end of the first Reconstruction, the North Carolina General Assembly passed, in 1900, a constitutional amendment restricting the Black vote. Literacy tests, grandfather clauses, and poll taxes were used to limit the number of Black votes. The U.S. Supreme Court declared the grandfather clause unconstitutional in 1915 but the North Carolina General Assembly in North Carolina continued with literacy testing that was prohibitive towards Blacks being able to vote. The promises of the Fifteenth Amendment were all but nullified. Black voting decreased in some places to nearly zero, and it wasn't until the fight was waged to pass the VRA of 1965 that hope of power and participation began to be renewed. Speaking about the genesis and ending of the first Reconstruction, renowned sociologist W. E. B. Du Bois said,

> What is the object of writing the history of Reconstruction? Is it to wipe out the disgrace of a people which fought to make slaves of Negroes? Is it to show that the North had higher motives than freeing black men? Is it to prove that Negroes were black angels? No, it is simply to establish the Truth, on which Right, in the future, may be built. We shall never have a science of history until we have in our colleges men who regard the truth as more important than the defense of the white race, and who will not deliberately encourage students to gather thesis material in order to support a prejudice or buttress a lie.

– W. E. B. Du Bois in *Black Reconstruction in America*

THE SECOND RECONSTRUCTION

Some would note that the second Reconstruction occurred from 1955 to 1968. Framing the second Reconstruction between the years 1954 and 1965 is certainly not to negate the fact that some significant events subsequent to the first Reconstruction and predating this period more than likely began to bring form to this era. Such events that ushered in and catapulted the second Reconstruction period would have to include the election of President Franklin Delano Roosevelt, who served this country during one of the worst periods in history. The allegiance of Black voters had shifted from Republican to Democrat by the year 1940. Through Roosevelt's New Deal policies of relief, recovery, and bank reform, a valiant effort to drive this nation closer to her constitutional ideology and further away from her national practice was launched. A new era was on the horizon. Dewey W. Grantham stated,

> The white man had imposed a way of life on the Negro which was at variance with the "American Creed" which the white man himself espoused, and it was the responsibility of white men to formulate and effect a more adequate and morally correct treatment of Negroes. (Bunche, 1973, p. xxv)

President Roosevelt may have been wrestling with this idea in mind when he set up a meeting with Black leaders to discuss discrimination in the military on September 27, 1940.

The term "separate but equal," made famous by the U.S. Supreme Court case *Plessy v. Ferguson*, remained a staple as the law of the land with regard to racial policy. The euphemistic phrase was really a "policy of separate and unequal treatment of blacks" (Mershon & Schlossman, 1998, p. 8). Whites saw segregation as a way to prevent racial conflict and tension. Yet this way of life may have actually generated more tension. In June 1941, President Roosevelt issued Executive Order 8802, which created the Fair Employment Practices Committee (FEPC), which enforced the banning of discrimi-natory hiring. The FEPC was one of the most important federal moves in support of the rights of African Americans between Reconstruction and the Civil Rights Act of 1964. Yet by February 1946, following the death of President Roosevelt in 1942, a Senate filibuster killed it.

Another significant event occurred in 1935 when the National Association for the Advancement of Colored People (NAACP) began challenging segregation in graduate and secondary schools. Charles Hamilton Houston, the African American attorney credited with dismantling Jim Crow, developed a strategy positing, first of all, that the cost of establishing separate but equal facilities would become too burdensome for states and, secondly, that those who received education in the nation's finest schools could not possibly suggest that attorneys of color received equal legal training. The NAACP won its first major federal victory in a case on behalf of Lloyd Gaines, an honors graduate from Lincoln University who was denied admission to the University of Missouri Law School (Ogletree, 2004, p. 121). This began setting precedents for other states to attempt equalization of school movements. After World War II, there was an increase in the number of black applicants to college and graduate programs. This provided the NAACP with a wealth of plaintiffs with which to launch direct attacks on educational segregation. Victories in two such cases cleared the way: *Sweatt v. Painter* and *McLaurin v. Oklahoma State Regents* paved the way to the *Brown* decision. By 1948, the NAACP endorsed the ideology of Thurgood Marshall, one of Houston's students, of attacking segregation in education head-on. This endorsement led to the naming of Marshall as the lead counsel on the *Brown v. Board of Education* case.

There were actually five individual cases bundled together under the heading of *Brown v. Board*. The Supreme Court combined them because each sought the same legal remedy. The combined cases emanated from Delaware, Kansas, South Carolina, Virginia, and Washington, D.C. The following is a brief description of those cases:

Delaware—*Belton v. Gebhart (Bulah v. Gebhart)*

First petitioned in 1951, these local cases challenged the inferior conditions of two schools designated for African American children. In the suburb of Claymont, African American children were prohibited from attending the area's local high school. Instead, they had to ride a school bus for nearly an hour to attend Howard High School in Wilmington. Located in an industrial area of the state's capital city, Howard High School also suffered from a deficient curriculum, pupil-teacher ratio, teacher training, extracurricular activities, and physical plant. In the rural community of Hockessin, African American students were forced to attend a dilapidated one-room schoolhouse and not provided transportation to the school, while White children in the area were provided with transportation and a better school facility. In both cases, Louis Redding, a local NAACP attorney, represented the plaintiffs: the African American parents. Although the state supreme court ruled in favor of the plaintiffs, the decision did not apply to all schools in Delaware. These class action cases were named for Ethel Belton and Shirley Bulah.

Kansas—*Brown v. Board of Education*

In 1950, the Topeka NAACP, led by McKinley Burnett, set out to organize a legal challenge to an 1879 state law that permitted racially segregated elementary schools in certain cities based on population. For Kansas, this would become the 12th case filed in the state focused on ending segregation in public schools. The local NAACP assembled a group of 13 parents who agreed to be plaintiffs on behalf of their 20 children. Following directions from legal counsel, they attempted to enroll their children in segregated White schools, and all were denied. Topeka operated 18 neighborhood schools for White children, while African American children had access to only four schools. In February of 1951, the Topeka NAACP filed a case on behalf of the African American children. Although this was a class action, it was named for one of the plaintiffs, Oliver Brown.

South Carolina—*Briggs v. Elliott*

In Clarendon County, South Carolina, the state NAACP first attempted, unsuccessfully and with a single plaintiff, to take legal action in 1947 against the inferior conditions African American students experienced under South Carolina's racially segregated school system. By 1951, community activist Rev. J. A. DeLaine convinced African American parents to join the NAACP's efforts to file a class action suit in the U.S. district court. The court found that the schools designated for African Americans were grossly inadequate in terms of buildings, transportation, and teachers' salaries when compared to the schools provided for Whites. An order to equalize the facilities was virtually ignored by school officials, and the schools were never made equal. This class action case was named for Harry Briggs Sr.

Virginia—*Davis v. County School Board of Prince Edward County*
One of the few public high schools available to African Americans in the state was Robert Moton High School in Prince Edward County. Built in 1943, it was never large enough to accommodate its student population. Eventually, hastily constructed tar paper–covered buildings were added as classrooms. The gross inadequacies of these classrooms sparked a student strike in 1951. Organized by 16-year-old Barbara Johns, the students initially sought to acquire a new building with indoor plumbing. The NAACP soon joined their struggle and challenged the inferior quality of their school facilities in court. Although the U.S. district court ordered that the plaintiffs be provided with equal school facilities, they were denied access to the White schools in their area. This class action case was named for Dorothy Davis.

Washington, D.C.—*Bolling v. Melvin Sharpe*
Eleven African American junior high school students were taken on a field trip to the city's new modern John Philip Sousa School (for Whites only). Accompanied by local activist Gardner Bishop, who requested admittance for the students and was denied, the African American students were ordered to return to their grossly inadequate school. A suit was filed on their behalf in 1951. After review of the *Brown* case in 1954, the Supreme Court ruled "segregation in the District of Columbia public schools ... is a denial of the due process of law guaranteed by the Fifth Amendment." This class action case was named for Spottswood Bolling (*Bolling v. Sharpe*, 1954).

Brown v. Board of Education triggered tremendous backlash; violent reactions began once again to surface. A recapitulation of the five areas that ultra-right-wing conservatives attack: (1) educational laws, (2) labor laws, (3) fair justice, (4) taxes, and (5) voting rights.

The case also had a profound and indelible effect on the United States. Declared the "case of the century," it established that intentional segregation was unconstitutional. This ruling served to fuel the civil rights movement and to challenge the legitimacy of all public institutions that embraced segregation. However, there was significant political and legal resistance to *Brown*'s mandate, and some commentators assert that, because the mandate was not bolstered by vigorous enforcement, political leaders opposed to *Brown* could easily thwart its promise. Given the *Brown* court's lack of firm resolve, as evidenced in its express refusal to order an immediate injunction against segregation and in its "all deliberate speed" modification, public resistance was inevitable (Ogletree, 2004, p. 124).

One such violent reaction occurred in the state of Mississippi: the murder of a 14-year-old African American youth from Chicago, Emmett Till, who was butchered beyond recognition and lynched on August 28, 1955, while on vacation in Money,

Mississippi. His murder called into question relations between North and South, segregation, and law enforcement. Rather than agree to a closed-casket funeral, Emmett's mother courageously decided to keep the casket open for the whole world to see. Thousands of people lined up to view the remains, arousing furor among Whites and people of color. Violence against Blacks increased all over Mississippi; in May, the Rev. George Lee, an African American voter registration activist, was murdered in Belzoni, Mississippi. On August 13, Lamar Smith, another African American activist, was shot to death in Brookhaven, Mississippi.

A few months after the slaying of Till and the release of his murderers, another violent reaction was sparked by the arrest of Rosa Parks on December 1, 1955. The Montgomery, Alabama, bus boycott was a 13-month mass protest that ended with the U.S. Supreme Court ruling that segregation on public buses is unconstitutional. The Montgomery Improvement Association coordinated the boycott, and its president, Dr. Martin Luther King Jr., became a prominent civil rights leader as international attention focused on Montgomery. The bus boycott demonstrated the potential for nonviolent mass protests to successfully challenge racial segregation and served as an example for other southern campaigns that followed.

Once, during an interview with the noted Black child psychologist and educator, Kenneth B. Clark, Dr. King was asked, "What is the relationship between your movement and such organizations as the NAACP, CORE, and the Student Nonviolent Coordinating Committee? They're separate organizations, but do they work together?"

King responded,

> Yes, we do. As you say, each of these organizations is autonomous, but we work together in many, many ways. Last year we started a voter-registration drive, an intensified voter-registration drive. And all of the organizations are working together, sometimes two or three are working together in the same community. The same thing is true with our direct-action programs. In Birmingham we had the support of Snick [SNCC, Student Nonviolent Coordinating Committee] and CORE and the NAACP. CORE sent some of its staff members in to assist us and Snick sent some of its staff members. Roy Wilkins came down to speak in one of the mass meetings and to make it clear that even though the NAACP cannot operate in Alabama, we had the support of the NAACP. So we are all working together in a very significant way, and we are doing even more in the days ahead to coordinate our efforts. (Washington, 1986, pp. 337–338)

Therein, one gets the sense that "fusion coalition" building was among the priorities that stimulated this movement; experienced and inexperienced alike, professionals and novices, students and career folk, young and old, Black and White, women and men were all passionately involved. In *Stride Toward Freedom*, King's 1958 memoir of the boycott, King declared the real meaning of the Montgomery bus boycott to be the power of a growing self-respect to animate the struggle for civil rights.

The roots of the bus boycott began years before the arrest of Rosa Parks. The Women's Political Council (WPC), a group of Black professionals founded in 1946, had already turned their attention to Jim Crow practices on the Montgomery city buses. In a meeting with Mayor W. A. Gayle in March 1954, the council's members outlined the changes they sought for Montgomery's bus system: no one standing over empty seats, a decree that Black individuals not be made to pay at the front of the bus and enter from the rear, and a policy that would require buses to stop at every corner in Black residential areas, as they did in White communities. When the meeting failed to produce any meaningful change, WPC president Jo Ann Robinson reiterated the council's requests in a May 21 letter to Mayor Gayle, telling him, "There has been talk from twenty-five or more local organizations of planning a city-wide boycott of busses" ("A Letter from the Women's Political Council"; Robinson, 1954).

The second Reconstruction of fusion politics from 1954 to 1968 resulted in the creation of some tremendous, substantive social policy. In addition to the aforementioned, the implementation of the following policies is noteworthy:

On March 6, 1961, President John F. Kennedy issued Executive Order 10925, which made the first reference to "affirmative action" and created the Committee on Equal Employment Opportunity. This executive order mandated that projects financed with federal funds "take affirmative action" to ensure that hiring and employment practices are free of racial bias, but it never defined the term. I am convinced, however, that Tim Wise hits the nail on the head by stating,

> Affirmative action is, as it has always been, about moving this nation toward racial equity and justice. That is what is at stake, and to ignore that basic truth is to imperil the victories of the past, and to diminish the opportunities for future victories. (Wise, 2005, p. 10)

I like the manner in which Wise sums up the issue when he argued that privileged White America has always benefited from affirmative action. Consider the Naturalization Act of 1790, the first U.S. statute to codify naturalization law, hence writing discrimination into the Constitution by offering to "any alien, being a free white person" who had been in the United States for 2 years affirmative action. Or what about the Homestead Act of 1862, which encouraged Western migration with the offer of 160 acres of land. There has always been affirmative action for those who are "always three laps ahead in a five lap contest" (Wise, 2007). It only becomes problematic and contested when attempts to level the playing field occur.

The Social Security Amendments of 1965 resulted in the creation of Medicare and Medicaid. When President Roosevelt signed the Social Security Act in 1935, it did not include medical benefits. While President Truman did embrace the idea, he had no success integrating medical care into a national program. During the administration of President Eisenhower, when the House Ways and Means Committee was created, the members were mainly Republicans and southern Dixiecrats who spent their time complicating the issue. By 1962, President Kennedy did succeed in obtaining a minimum wage increase and increases in Social Security benefits, but it would be after the election of Lyndon B. Johnson in 1964, when Democrats controlled Congress in both the House and the Senate, that a national medical program would be enacted under Social Security. However, it was Wilbur Mills, a Democrat from Arkansas's second district and the chair of the Ways and Means Committee, often referred to as the most powerful man in Washington during his time, who played a very important role in the creation of the Medicare program. Mills was also acknowledged as the primary tax expert in Congress and leading architect of the Tax Reform Act of 1969.

All of this culminated in the Civil Rights Act of 1964 and, subsequently, the VRA of 1965 being signed into law on August 6. President Johnson referred to August 6, 1965, as "a triumph for freedom as huge as any victory that has ever been won on any battlefield" (Johnson, 1965, p. 840). The law came 7 months after Martin Luther King launched a Southern Christian Leadership Conference campaign based in Selma, Alabama, with the aim of pressuring Congress to pass such legislation.

Fusion politics had gained tremendous ground during this 11-year reconstruction period. Two years after the March on Washington, the nation, in the middle of a second Reconstruction, faced the blood sacrifice (literally) of Whites and Blacks, Jews and Christians, and so many others fighting to undo the legalized systems of Jim Crow that had been put in place in the late 1800s to stop the first Reconstruction, and the power of a broad Black and White fusion coalition in this nation. This forced White supremacists and strong regressive forces to pass the VRA of 1965. The language of the VRA is clear. It is an act to enforce the provisions of the 15th Amendment and to ensure that no federal, state, or local government may in any way impede people from registering to vote or voting because of their race or ethnicity.

This VRA was introduced in the Senate as S1564 by Mike Mansfield (D) and Everett Dirksen (R) on March 18, 1965—11 days after the brutal beatings the whole world saw on March 7, Bloody Sunday, in Selma, Alabama, at the Edmund Pettus Bridge. Although discrimination existed in all 100 counties, only 40 North Carolina counties came under the provisions of VRA 65.

But the passage of the bill increased African American voting participation and made it possible for African Americans to be elected once again to political office. In 1948, only 15% of the Black population was registered, and by 1962, it had risen slowly to 36%. The percentage increased to 50% 1 year after the passage of VRA 65.

In the 1966 election, for the first time since the 19th century, a substantial number of Blacks voted in North Carolina. Approximately 281,000 Blacks voted.

With this revived political power and ability to create a fresh fusion alliance, North Carolina Blacks helped elect Henry E. Frye (Guilford County) to the state House in 1968, Frederick Douglass Alexander (Mecklenburg County) to the state Senate in 1974, and John W. Winters Sr. (Wake County) to the state Senate in 1974. Ironically, Henry Frye later became a state supreme court justice but had been denied suffrage in 1956 because during the literacy test, he forgot the names of the signers of the Declaration of Independence.

SOUTHERN STRATEGY: A 20TH-CENTURY RESPONSE TO THE SECOND FUSION RECONSTRUCTION MOVEMENT

The transformative power of fusion politics once again came under attack. The attacks defined and developed by Kevin Phillips, a Nixon and Republican strategist, came to be known as the White southern strategy. It was a strategy deliberately designed to play the race card in a way to drive southern Whites to vote for conservative White politicians and leave the ranks of the Democratic Party, which had elected persons like John F. Kennedy and Lyndon B. Johnson, who had helped to usher in the public policy goals and demands of the civil rights movement.

The Republican Party liked it, and this strategic effort ended the second Reconstruction. Tim Wise noted that this strategy was not new, per se. In a starkly revealing interview, former GOP strategist Lee Atwater boldly described how the southern strategy worked to undermine fusion-type political movements:

> You start out in 1954 by saying, "Nigger, nigger, nigger." By 1968, you can't say "nigger"—that hurts you. Backfires. So you say stuff like forced busing. State's rights and all that stuff. You're getting so abstract now [that] you're talking about cutting taxes, and all these things you're talking about are totally economic things and a by-product of them is [that] blacks get hurt worse than whites. (Lamis, 1999)

Atwater, who would manage George H. W. Bush's successful run for the presidency in 1988 (the Willie Horton campaign) and then serve as national party chairman, was talking with Alexander P. Lamis, a political science professor at Case Western Reserve University. Mr. Lamis quoted Atwater in his book, *Southern Politics in the 1990s*.

The target of the southern strategy was all of the southern states of the "old confederacy" with the goal of developing a "solid South" that ensured that the majority of southern Whites would resist and repel any fusion political alliances with African Americans.

On June 11, 1963, Governor George Wallace stood stiffly in the door of Foster Auditorium at the University of Alabama and pretended to defy a desegregation order delivered by Assistant Attorney General Nicholas Katzenbach. Within a week of Governor Wallace's performance, carefully choreographed for a national television audience, more than 100,000 congratulatory telegrams and letters rained onto his desk. More than 95% of his mail was positive, and half came from admirers north of the Mason-Dixon line. The fan mail persuaded the slick-haired demagogue from Alabama to run for the 1964 Democratic presidential nomination. It was arguably a pointless candidacy against a popular incumbent and ordinarily would not have been taken seriously.

In Wisconsin's Democratic primary, however, more than a third of the state's Democrats cast their ballots for George Wallace, although his campaign had not spent a dime. Three weeks later, Wallace landed 30% of the votes cast in the Indiana primary; two Ku Klux Klansmen ran a shoestring campaign out of a service station phone booth. In Maryland's Democratic primary, Wallace won 16 of the state's 23 counties and 43% of the final tally, although Black opposition and a suspicious tally by President Johnson loyalists probably defeated the notorious segregationist. "Without the nigger block vote," Wallace himself argued, "we would have won the whole thing" (Rawls, 1982).

Wallace's surprising performance suggested to Republican George H. W. Bush that volcanic White opposition to the Democratic Party's embrace of civil rights opened the door for Republicans in the "solid South." A hopeful Bush decided to run for the U.S. Senate, although he had never before held elective office. Bush declared himself "emphatically opposed" to the Civil Rights Act of 1964, saying that it "trampled upon the Constitution" (Holmes, 1991, p. 1). by mandating equal access to restaurants, hotels, restrooms, and other public accommodations. Bush explained to a crowd, "The new civil rights act was passed to protect 14 per cent of the people. I'm also worried about the other 86 per cent" (Holmes, 1991, p. 1).

After President Johnson signed the Civil Rights Act of 1964 into law, he told his staff, "I think we just gave the South to the Republicans for your lifetime and mine" (Farber, 2010, p. 125). As Richard Nixon, who campaigned for the Arizona Republican candidate, put it, "Barry Goldwater ran as a racist candidate" (*New York Times*, 1964, p. 20). If Nixon's assessment smacks of the pot's critique of the kettle, Goldwater certainly made opposition to the Civil Rights Act the centerpiece of his campaign. Goldwater ranted during the Senate debate that the bill's passage would impose a "police state" in America. He failed to mention Mississippi, America's undeniable police state, where FBI agents at that very moment were dragging the rivers and swamps for the bodies of three murdered civil rights workers. Goldwater won Mississippi, Alabama, Louisiana, Georgia, and South Carolina. For decades to come, the Republican Party's new base would be in the South. But the conservative realignment in the South, which eventually would inspire Nixon's own "southern strategy" that entrenched the new base, did not begin with the Supreme Court's ruling in *Brown v. Board of Education* or the mid-1960s civil rights legislation. Instead, the battle lines became clear in the early days of the New Deal.

The enduring political conservatism of many White southerners should hardly have been news to the nation. But when racial tensions flared in the 1950s and the Citizens' Councils mobilized the White South, many observers at the time (and historians ever since) found it convenient to pin the troubles on the NAACP, the U.S. Supreme Court, and "massive resistance" to the *Brown* decision. But the segregationist movement went back to the mid-1930s when White southern conservatives began to sour on Franklin Delano Roosevelt.

The Goldwater campaign, Black and Black (2003) argued, "attracted many racist Southern whites but permanently alienated African American voters" (p. 4). The 1964 presidential race marked the moment when "more Southern whites voted Republican than Democratic, a pattern that has recurred in every subsequent presidential election." Although Goldwater lost the election to President Johnson in a landslide, his candidacy unified many elements of the American right and electrified a generation of conservative activists. Rooted in racial backlash, the Goldwater campaign launched a new conservatism that redrew the political map of America (Black & Black, 2003, p. 4).

Although he campaigned hard for Goldwater, Strom Thurmond became the indispensable linchpin of Richard Nixon's southern strategy, the critical turn that made the phrase famous. Nixon's other tutors on the subject included Goldwater himself and especially George Wallace, whose American Independent Party candidacy that year was the only real threat to Nixon's presidential candidacy. George Wallace followed up on Goldwater's successes with his phenomenal 1968 third-party campaign, which historian Dan Carter said made him "the most influential loser in twentieth-century American politics" (Carter, 2000, p. 468). Certainly, Wallace taught the new—and far more conservative—Republican Party how to use the language of anti-elitism, anti-communism, and various euphemisms of race to inflame White voters. Nixon also used his friendship with the Rev. Billy Graham to appeal to White southerners, inviting the evangelist to counsel him on whether to run for the presidency, although he clearly had already decided. In public, Nixon began to claim that Graham had been the person most responsible for his decision to enter the 1968 campaign (Perlstein, 2009, p. 343).

Nixon's southern strategy had a number of authors, among them Patrick Buchanan, a young, right-wing editorial writer from the St. Louis *Globe-Democrat*, and Harry Dent, an aide to Strom Thurmond. Spiro Agnew, Nixon's running mate, and John Mitchell, who would become his attorney general, were also strong advocates. Nixon had chosen Agnew, governor of the border state of Maryland, primarily because of Agnew's diatribes against mainstream Black leaders in Baltimore after the riots in the 1968 wake of the King assassination. Agnew became "Nixon's Wallace," using acerbic attacks to say things Nixon could not quite say and to make visceral racial appeals to create what the Nixon strategists called "positive polarization."

The real architect, however, was Kevin Phillips, whose book, *The Emerging Republican Majority*, was published after the election but in manuscript form had become virtually the bible of Nixon's 1968 campaign. Phillips (1969) called America, "the melting pot that never melted" and explained that "all you've got to do with American politics is work out who hates whom and you've got it" (p. 326). Phillips advised Nixon that the Republican Party could win without Negro votes, in fact, by painting the Democrats as a "black party." Phillips (1969) predicted "a new American revolution coming out of the South and West" (p. 477) because of fears and objections raised by the civil rights movement's victories. He also noted that "white ethnics" in the North were also ripe for the picking, correctly predicting, for example, that the Irish Democrats in New York would turn Republican "because they don't like the Jews and Negroes who run the New York Democratic Party" (Phillips, 1969, p. 108). The South, Phillips said, would become the base for a new Republican Party (O'Reilly, 1995, pp. 285–286). Harry Dent urged Nixon to use racially coded language strong enough to persuade white southerners that Wallace was "not a viable alternative and [they will] turn to Republicanism in droves" (Carter, 1999, p. 44). The GOP should "follow Phillips' plan," said Dent, but "disavow it publicly" (Carter, 1999, p. 44).

Nixon intended for his southern strategy to go beyond Election Day and establish a new Sunbelt power base for the Republican Party in the South and West. By 1968, many southern white conservatives—Jesse Helms, Strom Thurmond, and most of those who would become the New Right in the South—left the Democratic Party. Thurmond organized conservative Democrats across the South to abandon their party and become Republicans. Sure, he said, they preferred Wallace or even Reagan. Hell, he did, too, Thurmond said. Nixon can win, however, and—here comes Thurmond's wink—Nixon is our friend on the issues that matter. Throughout the campaign, Nixon derided school integration as arbitrary federal interference with state and local prerogatives and endorsed the so-called freedom of choice plans that Wallace touted. He promised Thurmond that he would lift federal guidelines that called for cutting funding to school districts that refused to desegregate. The television commercials and newspaper ads that Thurmond cut for Nixon in 1968 did not even argue that Wallace was wrong but instead that Wallace couldn't win. The white South, Thurmond insisted, would never go back to the party of civil rights and urban riots (Perlstein, 2009, pp. 344–345).

Nixon took the entire South except for the four states that Wallace carried; his narrow victory in 1968 would have been a landslide, except that Wallace siphoned off 13.5% of the vote. The greatest threat to Nixon's southern strategy was not from the Democrats on his left but from Wallace to his right. Nixon barely eked out his victory with 43.4%, compared to Vice President Hubert Humphrey's 42.7%. Less than three out of five eligible voters bothered to cast a ballot (Chafe, 1999, p. 384). Following the inauguration, Nixon set out to win all the Wallace voters in 1972 via a still deeper southern strategy.

Kevin Phillips was optimistic. White southerners would "ease their way into the Republican Party by way of the American Independents," (Phillips, 1969, p. 259) Phillips assured Nixon. "We'll get two-thirds to three-fourths of the Wallace vote in nineteen seventy-two" (Phillips, 1969, p. 259). With an astute level of strategic complexity, he advised his new boss to promote African American voting rights in the South, not because Black southerners were citizens but because Black political participation would quicken the pace at which White Democrats became Republicans. Nixon read *The Emerging Republican Majority* carefully over his 1969 Christmas vacation and issued orders to his chief of staff, H. R. Haldeman: "Use Phillips as an analyst—study his strategy—don't think in terms of old time ethnics, go for Poles, Italians, Irish, must learn to understand Silent Majority ... don't go for Jews & blacks" (Carter, 1999, p. 42–44).

Because of the White House tapes, we now know that, in private, Nixon frequently referred to African Americans as "jigaboos" and "niggers" (Chafe, 1999, p. 428). One of his top aides, John Erlichman, later wrote that Nixon genuinely believed that Blacks could only "marginally benefit from federal programs because blacks were genetically inferior to whites" (Erlichman, 1982, p. 213). The president, Erlichman insisted, "did use the words 'genetically inferior.' He thought they could not achieve on a level with whites" (Erlichman, 1982, p. 213; Lemann, 1991, pp. 203–204). Nixon's private attitudes, however, were less important than the divisive politics that passed for public policy in his administration. Nixon's new chief political adviser, Attorney General John Mitchell, believed intensely that the president's reelection depended on that "positive polarization" of the electorate, along the lines drawn in Phillips's southern strategy. President Nixon saw votes for the taking in widespread White objections to busing and no votes whatsoever in pushing compliance with the courts. He used terms like "compulsory racial balancing" and "forced integration" as a matter of course. "The Federal Courts were ordering the busing of white kids and black kids," (O'Reilly, 1995, pp. 304) Erlichman explained. "And Richard Nixon wanted every one of their parents to know he opposed it" (Perlstein, 2009, pp. 464–465).

Almost immediately after the administration moved into the White House, the Justice Department began to grant stays for Mississippi's compliance with federal court orders to desegregate their public schools. Senator John Stennis of Mississippi, chair of the Senate Armed Services Committee, had implied that he might interfere with Nixon's defense outlays if he did not help Mississippi avoid school desegregation; this was probably unnecessary since it also served Nixon's ends with respect to the South's role in his reelection. When the stay by the Fifth Circuit Court of Appeals went to the U.S. Supreme Court, the Nixon administration argued against school desegregation, the first time that had happened since *Brown v. Board of Education* (Perlstein, 2009, pp. 464–465).

Nixon's appointments to the court also reflected the southern strategy. First, the president nominated Clement F. Haynsworth of South Carolina, his heavy segregationist baggage notwithstanding. J. Edgar Hoover's Federal Bureau of Investigation dispatched a glowing report, calling Haynsworth "the foremost jurist in this area" and "very conservative," as well as "well disposed toward law enforcement" (O'Reilly, 1995, pp. 306–307). Harry Dent and Kevin Phillips ran interference in Congress, leaning on "contributors who are important to uncommitted Senators," (O'Reilly, 1995, pp. 306–307) in addition to releasing negative information on the uncooperative. Haynsworth was a mediocre nominee at best and had all manner of objectionable civil rights decisions on his record. The Senate killed the appointment on November 21, 1969. Nixon instructed Harry Dent: "Find a good federal judge further South and further to the right!" (Perlstein, 2009, p. 465).

When the Nixon administration put forward the name of G. Harrold Carswell of Florida for the Supreme Court instead, Senator Birch Bayh remarked that Carswell "made Hayneworth look like Learned Hand." The dean of Yale Law School testified that Carswell had "more slender credentials than any nominee for the Supreme Court put forth in this century" (Carter, 2000, p. 397). Carswell's record on civil rights—or even common decency—was abysmal. One NAACP lawyer explained that Carswell was such a vicious racist that he would prepare his Black subordinates for what they could expect by having them practice their arguments while he screamed epithets at them. While both of the nominees were segregationists, Carswell had referred to Blacks as "monkeys" from the federal bench (O'Reilly, 1995, p. 307). One of Nixon's own aides later admitted, "They think he's a boob, a dummy. And what counter is there to that? He is" (Perlstein, 2009, p. 465).

When Democratic senators, joined by a few moderate Republicans, managed to block the nominations of both Haynsworth and Carswell, President Nixon blamed their southern origins and conservative politics in ways that advanced his political goals more than their confirmations could ever have done. "When you strip away all the hypocrisy," Nixon said, the "real reason for their rejection was their legal philosophy ... [and] the accident of their birth" (Perlstein, 2009, p. 397). He announced that he could certainly understand the "bitter feeling of millions of Americans who live in the South about the act of regional discrimination that took place in the Senate" (Perlstein, 2009, p. 397). Never again, said the president, would he ever "nominate another Southerner and let him be subjected to the kind of malicious character assassination accorded both Judges Haynsworth and Carswell" (Perlstein, 2009, p. 398). Nixon's polls in the South quickly headed due north (Perlstein, 2009, pp. 397–398). "You know," one aide to Nixon said, "the President really believes in that Southern strategy—more than he believes in anything else" (Chafe, 1999, p. 386).

Hodding Carter called Ronald Reagan part Wallace and part Nixon and a more effective southern strategist than both put together. In the end, it was Reagan who capitalized on, and perhaps made permanent, the Republican realignment brought about by Nixon's southern strategy. In 1980, American conservatives finally nominated their darling, Reagan, the man who had won their hearts back in 1964 with his nomination speech for Barry Goldwater and with his opposition to the Civil Rights Act. In 1966, Reagan became governor of California by becoming the champion of a movement to repeal the 1964 Rumford Act, which prohibited property owners from refusing to rent or sell property on the basis of the race or religion of the prospective occupants. Reagan consolidated and expanded his power by attacking the University of California at Berkeley, Martin Luther King Jr., the Black Panthers, and the counterculture. In the 1968 contest for the Republican nomination, Reagan made a last-minute run at Nixon, which Nixon had squelched by meeting with southern political leaders and promising to stop enforcement of the Supreme Court's rulings on school desegregation.

In 1980, having secured the nomination, Reagan's campaign staff chose to kick off his presidential campaign in Philadelphia, Mississippi, which had been made famous because of the 1964 murders of three civil rights workers there. At the Neshoba County Fair, right down the road from the earthen dam where the bodies of James Chaney, Andrew Goodman, and Michael Schwerner had been found, Reagan delivered a speech trumpeting "states' rights." Reagan called the Civil Rights Act of 1964 "bad legislation that infringed upon the individual rights of citizens" and the VRA of 1965 "a humiliation to the South" (O'Reilly, 1995, pp. 350–351). His stump speeches that year featured apocryphal tales of "welfare queens," whom he could not identify, and undeserving criminals who drove fleets of Cadillac® cars that they somehow purchased with food stamps. Another favorite yarn was his assertion that he'd been in the grocery store line beside "a strapping young buck" with "a fistful of food stamps and a stack of porterhouse steaks" (O'Reilly, 1995, pp. 350–351).

Reagan won in a landslide. The South went Republican in percentages so high that it became clear that the southern strategy had worked overwhelmingly, the wedge driven far more deeply than any one victory could drive it. The hammer behind it carried a weight far beyond the backlash to the *Brown* decision or resistance to the gains of the freedom movement in the South. The deep thrust came from "the long segregationist movement" that emerged from the southern conservative revolt against Franklin Roosevelt. Its landmarks were the Dixiecrat challenge in 1948 in which four Deep South states went to Strom Thurmond's third-party candidacy and the Goldwater campaign of 1964, which won five southern states and launched a new conservative movement.

Reagan's victory was the triumph of southern strategies over much of the 20th century. It revealed a conservative realignment driven by the politics of race and by lesser revolts against banning mandatory prayer in public schools, feminism, abortion, and homosexuality. Richard Viguerie, Phyllis Schlafly, Paul Weyrich, and most of the other key activists in the early New Right were all veterans of the Goldwater campaign (Diamond, 1995, p. 172). Viguerie, one of the most important architects of the New Right and the "guru" of direct mail fundraising, used the Goldwater list to raise $6 million for George Wallace in 1968. The list produced three quarters of all the money Wallace raised; it then became the starting point for the direct mail campaigns of the New Right in the 1970s and 1980s (Carter, 2000, pp. 455–456). Virtually all of the New Right organizations employed Viguerie as their fundraiser: the Moral Majority, New Conservative Political Action Committee, Congressional Caucus, and Jesse Helms's Congressional Club (Diamond, 1995, pp. 128–174). William Rusher, one of America's leading conservative activists, noted that the mailing lists from the Goldwater and Wallace campaigns were the foundation of all subsequent organized political activity on the part of American conservatives (Thimmesch, 1975, pp. 58–63). Lee Atwater, one of the political architects of the New Right who managed George Bush's campaigns, referred to Nixon's southern strategy as "a brilliant campaign ... a blueprint for everything I have done in the South since then" (O'Reilly, 1995, p. 381).

A SYNOPSIS OF THE HISTORY OF RECONSTRUCTION FUSION MOVEMENTS

Summing up the aforementioned history, it could be said that after the Civil War, something phenomenal happened called fusion politics, which was unique to the South. Lincoln Republicans joined with former slaves or freedmen to rewrite constitutions all over the South. Right here in North Carolina, in 1868, they rewrote the constitution. The promises of Reconstruction were that we were going to reconstruct the nation to be closer to its noble ideals—what it said on paper, not what it did in practice.

By 1870 in North Carolina, there were more African Americans serving in the general assembly than there are today. Those legislators, joined with progressive Whites, wrote some of the most progressive education laws, labor laws, voting laws, and criminal justice laws. And I'm talking 144 years ago.

By 1872, however, there was a violent reaction from the former planters, and they called it the redemption movement. They needed to redeem America, and particularly the South, from the influence of Black political power; they needed to stop fusion politics. The Klan was formed in 1872 as a political organization, and on November 10, 1898, there were vicious, violent riots called the Wilmington Riots. Duly elected Blacks and Whites were run out of office. White supremacists took over the state legislature. There were always five things they attacked: (1) educational laws, (2) labor laws, (3) fair criminal justice laws, (4) taxes, and (5) voting rights. These supremacists wanted to cut taxes so that the government wouldn't have any money to fulfill the promises that had been made to the former slaves. Lastly, they attacked voting rights. If your grandfather was a slave, then you couldn't vote or you had to pay a poll tax—you had to pay something to be able to exercise your right to vote.

White supremacy was rewritten into the laws of the state, and by 1910, Black voting power was virtually nothing. Zero. So the Reconstruction movement was ended by the late 1800s.

Then we come to the 1960s, the second Reconstruction: Dr. King and the March on Washington, D.C.; five score years ago, a man in whose shadow we stand talked about emancipation, but he also said that things were not yet where they should be.

From 1954, *Brown v. Board of Education*, all the way to the death of Dr. King, there was a massive movement—Blacks and Whites, Jews and gentiles, all coming together and reconstructing the nation. How was that stopped? They attacked voting rights; they attacked education; they attacked progressive tax policy, but they also attacked leaders. They killed King, Medgar Evers, Malcolm X, John and Robert Kennedy, and hundreds of others. And that shut down the second Reconstruction.

EMERGENCE OF THE POSSIBILITY OF A THIRD RECONSTRUCTION

Then something strange happened. A guy named Barack Obama ran for the presidency in 2008. And guess what he did? He ran a campaign rooted in the idea of fusion politics—like in the 1800s and the 1960s. And guess what? Obama won—in places like North Carolina and in the South. And how did he win? The electorate was broad and deep, and it was young, and it was old; it was lesbian, gay, bisexual, or transgender (LGBT); it was Black; it was Hispanic, and it was Asian; it was people who wanted to push America beyond the visages of racism. And so Obama's election represented the possibility of a third Reconstruction.

And it just might work this time. It just might work. The demographics are changing; there are more Black and Brown people, and younger folks are not as bound as they once were. But that new electorate scares the daylights out of those who have a homogeneous view of life. It does not fit their worldview. So what do you see? An all-out assault once again. The attack on voting rights started immediately after President Obama was elected.

VIEWING THE THIRD RECONSTRUCTION IN NORTH CAROLINA FROM THE BOTTOM UP

What is important to note is that the seeds for success in a fusion coalition in North Carolina were planted in 2005 and 2006—before Senator Obama considered running.

In the fall of 2006, the NAACP leadership considered a bold proposal to invite other progressive organizations that were predominantly White to join the NAACP in a massive People's Assembly in Raleigh on the Saturday nearest the NAACP's 98th birthday, February 12, 2007. The aim of the assembly and agenda was based on the radical prophets of the Old Testament and a need for a fresh 21st-century fusion movement. To set a *people's agenda* that would challenge the lawmakers' habit of doing business for business, the new coalition would demand that they do the people's business for the people.

After much debate, the NAACP leadership voted unanimously to sponsor the "Historic Thousands on Jones Street" People's Assembly. This was quickly shortened to *HKonJ*. They did not want to set a number—some proposed 50,000 and some proposed 2,000—so they agreed on "historic." But they wanted to convey that this was a *grassroots movement* of the people, by the people, and for the people. This wasn't just a couple of lobbyists going over to Jones Street with policy papers begging for some crumbs for poor people. This was a people's lobby assembling at the people's house on Jones Street.

The best thinkers were gathered to help write the 14-point agenda. They were guided by several principles. First, the central organizing principle was its antiracism.

Past efforts to build broad Black-White fusion movements had always collapsed when racist appeals to the White sections of the alliance were made as the struggle heated up. We wanted our White friends to know from the get-go that the people's agenda was centered on dismantling the system of racism—the institutional legacies of slavery and Jim Crow that insidiously replicate themselves in our daily lives.

Second, the agenda had to be against poverty. The NAACP and its progressive partners, by definition, fight for the poor, the least of these, the disenfranchised, the miseducated, the imprisoned, the hungry, and the homeless. The shortest war in U.S. history was the war on poverty! Declared in late 1964, mortally wounded in 1966 when governors got the veto power over any antipoverty program in their states, and put to death in 1969 by Nixon's hatchet man, Donald Rumsfeld. This righteous war must be declared again—with long-term commitments, lots more money, and millions of people fighting for good jobs, living wages, decent health care, decent housing, and new hope for the increasing number of sisters and brothers of all colors who are broke. Today, the politically expedient language is to talk about the problems of the "middle class." It's not popular to advocate for the poor. Prophets don't care about what is popular. Prophets care about what is right. Prophets teach how to reduce fear and poverty.

And third, the people's agenda had to be against the unjust war in Iraq, specifically, and extreme militarism or the military-industrial complex that President Eisenhower warned against. We learned from the trap that was laid for Dr. King and other civil rights leaders. They had remained silent for years while the United States invaded and used napalm against the sovereign nation of Vietnam. When Dr. King, in April 1967, strongly criticized President Johnson and the government's racist occupation of Vietnam, the movement's enemies used this criticism to create divisions *within* the movement and within the Democratic Party.

On the Saturday of Thanksgiving weekend in 2006, leaders of 16 organizations drove to Goldsboro for the first People's Assembly meeting. The text that morning was from the prophet Ezekiel's experience in the valley full of dry bones:

> And the Lord told Ezekiel to say to the bones: "O ye dry bones, hear the word of the Lord ... I will cause breath to enter into you. I will lay sinews upon you. I will bring up flesh upon you and cover you with skin. And ye shall live." Ezekiel did as the Lord told him to do. Behold, there was a noise, and a shaking, and the bones came together. But, Ezekiel saw, *there was no breath in them*. And the Lord told Ezekiel to say to the wind, "Come from the four winds, O Breath, and breathe upon these slain, so they may live."
>
> And behold, the breath came into them, and they lived, and they stood upon their feet, and they were an exceeding great army. (Ezekiel 37 King James Version)

After the meeting, a call to fusion coalition and actions were written that would serve as the trumpet announcement for the first HKonJ People's Assembly, entitled

"Why HKonJ? Our Values, the Rationale for Our Work and the Action Steps to Be Taken" by Reverend Dr. William J. Barber II on behalf of the North Carolina NAACP and its coalition partners.

More than 7,000 people of all races responded. They met in February 2007 for a 2-hour teach-in and voted unanimously on a 14-point agenda with 81 actions steps. They then marched and delivered it to the North Carolina General Assembly. The agenda is presented next.

HKonJ 14-Point People's Agenda

    a. All children need high-quality, well-funded, diverse public schools
    b. Livable wages and support for low-income people
    c. Health care for all
    d. Redress ugly chapters in North Carolina's racist history: The overthrow of the biracial, 1898 Wilmington government and the sterilization of poor, mainly Black, women from 1947 to 1977
    e. Expand and improve same-day registration and public financing of elections
    f. Lift every historically Black college and university
    g. Document and redress 200 years of state discrimination in hiring and contracting
    h. Provide affordable housing and stop consumer abuse
    i. Abolish the racially biased death penalty and mandatory sentencing laws. Reform our prisons
    j. Promote environmental justice
    k. Collective bargaining for public and private employees and worker safety
    l. Protect the rights of immigrants from Latin American and other nations. North Carolina must provide immigrants with health care, education, workers' rights, and protection from discrimination
    m. Organize, strengthen and provide funding for our civil rights enforcement agencies and statutes now
    n. Bring our troops home from Iraq now

The NAACP knew it had to embark upon a journey to build a 21st-century fusion movement called the HKonJ People's Assembly Coalition—a name provided by renowned civil rights attorney Al McSurely. The organization came together around a 14-point agenda, including the goal of fighting all forms of discrimination 2 years before the election of President Obama. The members said it was time to inject a new politics into the veins of North Carolina's body. The HKonJ movement has captured the four winds of the state. It has breathed the sacred spirit of a Black-Brown-White community of action into the dry bones of many single-issue, often single-race, organizations. The Sweet 16 is now the Sweet 145. The 4,000-member army gathered on

February 9, 2007, doubled to 8,000 on February 10, 2008. And every year, it has reached historic proportions, both the number who came to Raleigh on an unusually cold Saturday morning in February to show their support for the people's agenda and the quality and diversity of our movement. In February 2012, more than 13,000 people, representing 125 different organizations and churches, participated; a year later, in 2013, the largest turnout of a civil rights demonstration in North Carolina was reached—more than 17,000 people. Like Ezekiel's dry bones, we are becoming an exceeding great army.

We have seen the fruit of this fusion: winning same-day registration/early vote and Sunday voting. It should be noted that President Obama actually lost the election on Election Day but won during early voting, which had been secured by the fusion movement a full 2 years before he was even considered a candidate. The fusion movement, represented by HKonJ, was able to take on the general assembly in 2012 when it passed a budget that was unconstitutional and that hurt 64,000 poor children eligible for the More at Four and win in court. The NAACP, Democracy North Carolina, the League of Women Voters, and the A. Philip Randolph Institute—allies in the HKonJ movement—have taken on the race-based redistricting plan passed by the general assembly.

The Truth and Hope Poverty Tour visited 27 North Carolina communities, putting a face on poverty with state and national attention. We raised the demand that North Carolina address the fact that in our state, 1.6 million people—including 600,000 children—live in deep poverty.

Being able to mount a campaign in North Carolina against Amendment One and on the side of the LGBT community is the fruit of fusion. Although we temporarily lost at the ballot, we changed the national dialogue; we moved the NAACP National Board to refine its position, and we inspired the coalition work in Maryland that helped that state support marriage equality.

Seeing more than 17,000 people gather in front of the general assembly in February, the most diverse coalition of its type in the South, consisting of more than 140 organizations—Black, White, Latino, labor, gay, and straight—holding hands together, that is the fruit of this fusion.

That's why the extremists have opened their checkbooks, pouring money into North Carolina to take us backward. That's why they have exerted so much energy to divide us. The tree is known by the fruit it bears. The forces of regression know the signs.

More than one million African Americans and Latinos have participated in early voting. African Americans make up more than 23% of the electorate this year. Just think about that for a minute. African Americans make up 23%—elementary mathematics shows that 51% is the majority of 100%. So if we work together, stay in coalition together, don't become despondent while building this fusion movement, then progressive Whites, labor, Latino, and the LGBT community can make up the other 28%.

All the signs say we are in the middle of a third Reconstruction that once again is being caused by the force of fusion politics.

Many believe that HKonJ is growing so fast because of the politics of hate and hypocrisy that have become the hallmark of the right-wing extremists who have seized Mr. Lincoln's Grand Old Party. These extremists have used racism and homophobia and sexism to try to divide us. They use their old tricks, refined and sharpened over the last 40 years. But their fundamental tactic remains the same: aggravate, scratch, and claw away at the old racial fault lines in our society. They believe our White sisters and brothers are still vulnerable to direct and indirect appeals to the racist stereotypes that have been carefully planted in all of our minds, unconsciously associated with most men's (and some women's) sexist and homophobic anxieties.

The right wing's main weapon—tried and true since it created the Ku Klux Klan after the Civil War—is to flash daily images of Black men in orange jumpsuits who are out to kill and rape their mothers, take their jobs, and take college slots away from their darling children and who are only interested in White women, with the aim of making everyone a biracial person, like our president. Obama's two victories put these splitters and their lies in perspective. They are losers. Their lies are increasingly transparent.

We in the NAACP, the oldest civil rights organization in the world, with 103 years' experience in dealing with these splitters and their lies, believe the HKonJ assembly is strategically positioned to tackle the job of healing these false divisions and suspicions. We have learned that doing things together, eating together, praying together, and getting to know each other in joint struggles for the common good of all people represent the best balm for aching, dry bones. We know that challenging the old way of doing business in Raleigh and in Washington, D.C., will bring new, sometimes unlikely, partners into our growing circle of trust and hope.

The Rev. Dr. William J. Barber II, coauthor of this chapter, from time to time eloquently states that "'we' is the most important word in the social justice vocabulary." The essential sentiment of his statement has actually echoed through the genuine social justice corridors of America since antebellum times. It rings out the ethos of progressive Americans and strongly suggests that they are ever striving toward a common destiny: the rich, the poor, Blacks and Whites, creditors and debtors, gay and straight all moving in the same productive direction. Over the course of 8 short years, I (Spearman) have been deeply empowered by the "we" that Barber articulates. This "we" loves the souls of people and practices doing no wrong to their neighbors. This "we" wills them to open their hearts of compassion toward the least, the last, and the lost. Yet in this nation, the "we" Barber speaks of is too often juxtaposed with another "we" that reverberates cacophonously throughout this land. That "we" has yet to spread its wings in an effort to brood over and cover the entire brotherhood of man in the great nation that is called the United States of America. Over the course of her 237-year history, striving toward a common destiny in America has yet to be realized, despite two of her founding documents that contain, in this case, the incongruous term *we*. Consider the preamble of the United States Constitution:

> **We** the People of the United States, in Order to form a more perfect Union, establish Justice, insure domestic Tranquility, provide for the common defence, promote the general Welfare, and secure the Blessings of Liberty to ourselves and our Posterity, do ordain and establish this Constitution for the United States of America.

Then consider again the preamble of the Constitution of the State of North Carolina:

> **We**, the people of the State of North Carolina, grateful to Almighty God, the Sovereign Ruler of Nations, for the preservation of the American Union and the existence of our civil, political and religious liberties, and acknowledging our dependence upon Him for the continuance of those blessings to us and our posterity, do, for the more certain security thereof and for the better government of this State, ordain and establish this Constitution.

Why does it appear as though some subversive forces have infringed on our constitutional covenant and resulted in an America plagued by national double-mindedness? It is all too self-evident that embedded within these founding documents is the stronghold of hypocrisy that will take a mightier "we" to disintegrate—a "we" who would dare not pass legislation that kills anything faintly resembling neighborliness or expressing ingratitude to God.

This time around, we will not be split. This time around, our dry bones are going to keep walking around, an exceeding great army of people whose ancestors honored this land for centuries before European immigrants arrived, before the slave traders seized Africans who knew how to take care of the land and brought them in chains to this land of no opportunity for them, and before people of color from Latin America and Asia were brought to pick vegetables and build railroads. Yes, an exceedingly great army is forming in the first 2 decades of the 21st century, taking risks to build new friendships while working together to dismantle the systems of militarism, racism, and poverty and create a new society based on respect, love, and productive work.

REFERENCES

Black, E., & Black, M. (2003). *The rise of southern Republicans*. Belknap Press.

Boiling v. Sharpe. 347 U.S. 497 (1954).

Bunche, R. J. (1973). *The political status of the Negro in the age of FDR*. University of Chicago Press.

Carter, D. T. (1999). *From George Wallace to Newt Gingrich: Race in the conservative counter-revolution, 1963–64*. LSU Press.

Carter, D. T. (2000). *The politics of rage.* LSU Press.

Cecelski, D. S., & Tyson, T. B. (1998). *Democracy betrayed: The Wilmington race riot and its legacy.* University of North Carolina Press.

Chafe, W. H. (1999). *The unfinished journey: America since World War II.* Oxford University Press.

Dailey, J. (2000). *Before Jim Crow: A history of race in postemancipation Virginia.* University of North Carolina Press.

Diamond, S. (1995). *Roads to dominion: Right-wing movements and political power in the United States.* Guildford Press.

Du Bois, W. E. B. (1962). *Black Reconstruction in America: 1860–1880.* The Free Press.

Edmonds, H. G. (1951). *The Negro and fusion politics in North Carolina, 1894–1901.* University of North Carolina Press.

Erlichman, J. (1982). *Witness to power: The Nixon years.* Simon & Schuster.

Farber, D. (2010). *The rise and fall of modern American conservatism: A short history.* Princeton University Press.

Foner, E. (1990). *A short history of Reconstruction, 1863–1877.* Harper and Row.

Foner, E., & Garrity, J. A. (Eds.) (1991). *The reader's companion to American history.* Houghton Mifflin.

Godshalk, D. F. (2005). *Veiled visions: The 1906 Atlanta race riot and the remaking of American race relations.* University of North Carolina Press.

Goldwater Rift with Nixon Deep: Senator 'Disinherits' Rival Over Romney Boom. June 12, 1964 p. 20.

Holmes, S. A. (1991). The Nation: When the Subject is Civil Rights, There are Two George Bushes. *The New York Times. Section 4* p. 1.

Johnson, L. B. (1965). Public Papers of the Presidents of the United States: Volume II, entry 394, pp. 840–843. Washington, D. C.: Government Printing Office, 1966.

Kousser, J. M. (1974). *The shaping of southern politics: Suffrage restriction and the establishment of the one-party South, 1880–1910.* Yale University Press.

Lemann, N. (1991). *The promised land: The great migration and how it changed America.* Knopf.

Lamis, A. P. (1999). *Southern politics in the 1990s.* Louisiana State University Press.

Mershon, S., & Schlossman, S. (1998). *Foxholes & color lines: Desegregating the U.S. Armed Forces.* John Hopkins University Press.

Mixon, G. (2005). *The Atlanta riot: Race, class and violence in a New South city.* University of Florida Press.

Ogletree Jr., C. J. (2004). *All deliberate speed: Reflections on the first half century of Brown v. Board of Education.* W. W. Norton & Company.

O'Reilly, K. (1995). *Nixon's piano: Presidents and racial politics from Washington to Clinton.* Free Press.

Perlstein, R. (2009). *Nixonland: The rise of a president and the fracturing of America.* Scribner.

Phillips, K. (1969). *The emerging Republican majority.* Arlington House.

Prather, H. L. (1984). *"We have taken a city"; the Wilmington racial massacre and coup of 1898.* Associated University Presses.

Robinson, J. (1954). *Everyday Americans, Exceptional Americans: A Teaching American History Project Primary Source Activity "Rosa Parks and the Montgomery Bus Boycott"* http://chnm.gmu.edu/tah-loudoun/blog/psas/rosa-parks-and-the-montgomery-bus-boycott/

Senechal, R. (1990). *The sociogenesis of a race riot: Springfield, Illinois in 1908.* University of Illinois Press.

Thimmesch, N. (1975, June 9). The grass-roots dollar chase—ready on the right. New York Magazine, 58–63.

Tyson, T. B. (2006, November 17). Ghosts of 1898: Wilmington's race riot and the rise of white supremacy. *Raleigh News & Observer.* https://media2.newsobserver.com/content/media/2010/5/3/ghostsof1898.pdf

Washington, J. M. (Ed.) (1986). *The essential writings and speeches of Martin Luther King, Jr.* Harper Collins Publishers.

Wise, T. (2005). *Affirmative action: Racial preference in black and white.* Routledge Taylor & Francis Group.

Wise, T. (2007). Flashback: Affirmative action debate: Destroying conservative nonsense. TimWise.org. http://www.timwise.org/2013/03/flashback-affirmative-action-debate-2007-destroying-conservative-nonsense/.

CHAPTER THREE

Leadership and Engagement in African American Communities

A PSYCHOSOCIAL FRAMEWORK

Forrest D. Toms, PhD, Cheryl LeMay Lloyd, PhD, and Sylvia Willie Burgess, PhD

INTRODUCTION

Even before emancipation, there were discussions about the need for more sustainable, effective leadership and civic/community engagement in African American communities. Now in the 21st century, the enigma persists. There are long-standing themes in many of these dialogues focused on (1) the lack of visibility and participation of African American leaders and organizations in the public discourse at school board, city council, county commissioners, and public health board meetings; (2) why participation and involvement in these decision-making arenas remain limited to nonexistent; and (3) what could and should be done to prepare citizens for more substantive, consistent, and persistent engagement and involvement in civic/community decision making. Such activity explicitly affects policies and resource distribution. At the community level, many citizens believe that this lack of representation and participation in the civic process directly affects the consistent and mounting disparities in African American communities. These disparities are most evident in data reflecting early educational achievement and performance, health-care outcomes, employment compensation and access, gaps in employment with livable compensation, and, ultimately, in the desperately declining individual economic net worth and collective access to capital. A central concern is that even though, numerically, there are more African Americans serving as elected officials than at any other time in history (Bositis, 2001), there is less community participation and involvement in local and state civic activity. The lack of participation in civic/community activities at the local level translates into the development of policy and distribution of needed resources that ultimately can, and do, negatively affect children, families, and communities. At the very least, the lack of policy development and resource distribution compounds the already historic disparities affecting African American communities.

These concerns suggest the need for more intentional, focused efforts to develop and implement comprehensive community capacity-building models, programs, and processes for community-based and faith-based leaders and organizations designed to enhance participation and involvement in local decision making, both inside their own communities and within the mainstream of the broader community. The framework for such requires a firm grasp of leadership in the African American community from historic and current perspectives, a concrete conceptual view of readiness to accept leadership in such a precocious community, and, finally, a comprehensive model for developing community capacity to lead. The development of more tactical strategies to increase engagement at the local, state, and national levels around policies and resource distribution requires analysis of the psychosocial challenges facing individuals, leaders, and the institutions in African American communities. There is a need to develop and implement strategies that address these needs and challenges.

Without doubt, the changing demographic makeup; dynamic knowledge-based economy; changing social, political, and economic challenges; and increasing demand for intentional civic/community participation at the national, state, and local levels in the mainstream of American society present the need for a new framework for examining the current nature and processes of leading and leadership in African American communities.

For the individual African American, civic and political socialization are filtered through their families' orally transmitted histories, political attitudes, and sense of engagement (Rosenzweig & Thelen, 1998). Boykin and Toms (1985) captured this notion in their article "Black Child Socialization: A Conceptual Framework." They suggested that the "tacit socialization" by African American parents is the most powerful transmitter of cultural values, beliefs, and worldviews because it is primarily "unspoken." That is, it occurs through observation, modeling, and life experiences obtained within the fabric of one's cultural experience. Thus history and identity combine to create a powerful narrative of membership and obligation that "both echoes and reinforces the African American civic counter-narrative of struggle, duty, and opportunity" (Rosenzweig & Thelen, 1998, p. 90).

This chapter explores the historical and psychosocial perspectives of the African American leadership experience, which, we believe, is critical in understanding and reframing leadership for a new generation. These perspectives are focused on examining the leadership typologies, styles, and challenges that initiate the development of a framework from which African American leaders and institutions might create a new reality in their engagement civically with the mainstream. It serves as the framework for understanding the African American experience—a contextual schema for civic engagement readiness, trust, leadership, and learning in public (LIP). It briefly reviews the methodology and findings of previous research and provides discussion and analysis for the development of a framework for individual and communal capacity building.

Leadership

Bass (1990) stated, "There are almost as many different definitions of leadership as there are persons who have attempted to define the concept" (p. 11). Leadership can be framed as the capacity to effectively guide self and others in providing awareness, knowledge, and skills in creating a shared vision and information and knowledge in a direction that ethically benefits the whole. However, as noted, how leadership is defined depends on who is doing the defining, whether it is from a business perspective, an educational context, a sports team's viewpoint, a grassroots citizen's point of view, or from the perspective of a minority disenfranchised community of color.

From a sociological frame, leadership is viewed from three levels: (1) macro, (2) meso, and (3) micro. The macrolevel group is often a large social unit, usually bureaucratic, which operates at a national or a global level. Most members are unlikely to know the leaders personally or ever have communicated with them. These include national leaders, government officials, megachurches, and corporations. Mesolevel groups are intermediate in size, usually large enough that members may never have heard the names of many of the other members, yet they are not so large as to seem distant or the leader unapproachable. In this group, if you do not know the leader yourself, you probably know someone who knows or who is friends with the leader. The microlevel is a small unit, such as a local community social network, in which everyone within that group knows everyone or is within one acquaintance of knowing every person in the group. This includes your nuclear family or a local chapter or club, such as civic clubs, sororities, fraternities, churches, sports teams, or even a family reunion. Each level is critical to community progress, requiring individuals to find their place in the order or risk disassociation and disenfranchisement.

Burns (1978) posited that leadership "changes both leader and followers" (p. 14). Northouse (2004) provided the following definition of leadership:

> Despite the multitude of ways that leadership has been conceptualized, the following components can be identified as central to the phenomenon of leadership: (a) Leadership is a process, (b) leadership involves influence, (c) leadership occurs within a group context, and (d) leadership involves goal attainment. Based on these components, the following definition of leadership will be used in the text. Leadership is a process whereby an individual influences a group of individuals to achieve a common goal. (p. 3)

This definition of leadership corresponds with the way African American leadership has historically been defined by writers such as Smythe (1950) and Cothran and Phillips (1960). The next section builds the foundation for the historical backdrop of African American leadership.

Historical Backdrop to African American Leadership

In his 1950 article entitled "Changing Patterns in Negro Leadership," Smythe defined leadership as involving a group of individuals in which one assumes dominance over the other; the dominant person may change the attitudes and values of the group. He suggested that leadership customarily works toward some specific goal, which when achieved may call for another form of leadership (Smythe, 1950).

Smythe (1950) provided an insightful definition of Negro leaders for the time period: "A Negro leader is defined here as a person who exerts special influence over a number of people for a period of a decade or more and who has helped to change significantly the position of the Negro in America. Further, he stands as a distinctive symbol in the struggle, growth and development of the Negro" (p. 191).

Cothran and Phillips (1960) argued that there were two major conceptual dimensions of the notion of Negro leadership in their study, awareness, and prominence notoriety. They suggested that these two elements were essential to the legitimation of leadership of Negro leaders: (1) the degree to which an individual is known and (2) the degree to which the relevant role and status (power) of the individual are known (p. 108). Hines and Pierce (1965) described a concept of "leader" in their study as "that individual identified as sufficiently influential to direct or control collective behavior and having a number of followers who, implicitly or explicitly, legitimize his leadership function" (p. 163).

Smythe contended that until the 1950s, there were only three notable Negro leaders: Frederick Douglass, Booker T. Washington, and W. E. B. Du Bois. Standing, in his 1934 article "Nationalism in Negro Leadership," made a similar argument about Negro leaders and leadership; however, he reluctantly included Marcus Garvey in the list. Standing made the point that Washington was the most significant because he was the only one who actually had an ongoing national audience.

Guy Johnson (1937), in his article "Negro Racial Movements and Leadership in the United States," wrote,

> Leadership and racial movements among Negroes have reflected the changing intraracial and interracial situations. So far only two significant Negro philosophies have crystallized. One was personified in Booker T. Washington, who preached patience and good will and was as much a leader of white as Negro opinion; the other W. E. B Dubois who believed in the full emancipation of Negroes through education and mobilization. (p. 57)

African American Leadership Typologies and Styles

Donn Davis (2007) proposed that there were three stages of African American leadership development prominent during the 19th century to the 20th century. The first stage represented the accommodationist leadership style readily identified with Booker T. Washington. Washington's leadership style was contrasted by the intellectually progressive leadership style of Dr. Du Bois. The second stage is characterized as the protest stage, which was more aggressive, nonviolent direct action, at times militant and often confrontational to long-standing discriminatory segregationist policies and practices. The third stage Davis suggested includes African American elected officials who were members of the civil rights movement but evolved into an increasing number of elected offices in the 1970s (Davis, 2007). Watson and Rosser (2006) posited that there were three types of leadership: (1) accommodation, (2) social organizing, and (3) guidance/mobilization.

Samuel A. Stouffer (1955) offered his observations and analysis of leadership types. He stated,

> The existence of different types of leadership must be recognized and the reactions of each given situation demands further analysis. One fundamental distinction in regard to the leaders can be advanced, and that is the distinction between the "zealots" or "innovators" and the "influential." The former are more mobile, less rooted or established in their communities. They will initiate changes, and will often be sacrificed to the resistance of the community. The 'influential', on the other hand, seldom initiate change. They tend to remain on the sidelines until an issue has developed and its ultimate outcome seems fairly assured. (p. 27)

Cothran and Phillips (1960) suggested that Stouffer's "innovator" compares with Myrdal's protest leader in that they attempt to alter the power and prestigious arrangements in the community through the manipulation of economic and political influence. Likewise, they see Stouffer's "influential" as comparable to Myrdal's accommodation leader. That is, the "influential" will seldom seek change; the accommodation leader seeks change as long as it can be done quietly and without the kind of publicity that will single them out for attack (Cothran & Phillips, 1960, p. 109).

Two studies form a foundation for examining African American leadership. First, in 1903, Du Bois theorized that members of the African American "Talented Tenth" during the postslavery era had an obligation to provide leadership to the majority of their race (Battle & Wright, 2002). Du Bois advocated that "from the very first it has been the educated and intelligent of the Negro people [the Talented Tenth] that have led and elevated the mass" (Battle & Wright, 2002, p. 656). To determine if the Du Bois philosophy of the "Talented Tenth" was still evident in African American leaders today, Battle and Wright (2002) conducted a study of current members of the "Talented Tenth." They concluded that current members of the "Talented Tenth" represent evidence of higher levels of community and political activism. The debate regarding Du Bois's original "Talented Tenth" philosophy remains a prominent component of the public discourse of African American leadership.

A second study establishing a foundation for examining African American leadership involves research conducted by Gunnar Myrdal and Ralph Bunche (2005). In 1944, funding provided by the Carnegie Corporation supported Myrdal and Bunche in their examination of African American leadership in the South. The researchers traveled the South, interviewing African American leaders as a part of a massive study to research the "Negro problem." Their findings would become part of a larger monograph entitled *An American Dilemma: The Negro Problem and Modern Democracy* (Myrdal, 1944). Myrdal and Bunche identified six Negro leadership typologies and related behavior patterns. The six typologies are as follows: (1) aggressive, (2) cautious, (3) liaison, (4) symbolic, (5) prestige, and (6) designated (Bunche, 2005). The leadership typologies identified by Myrdal and Bunche serve as a foundation for future typologies associated with African American leadership.

TOWARD AN UNDERSTANDING OF THE AFRICAN AMERICAN PSYCHOSOCIAL EXPERIENCE IN AMERICA: IMPLICATIONS FOR LEADERSHIP AND COMMUNITY ENGAGEMENT

There is an inherent complexity in negotiating the African American experience in America. W. E. B. Du Bois captured the essence of the African American experience and its complexity in his research dating back to the early 19th century (Du Bois, 1903). He stated, "One ever feels his two-ness—an American, a Negro; two souls, two thoughts, two unreconciled strivings; two warring ideals in one dark body, whose dogged strength alone keeps it from being torn asunder" (Du Bois, 1903, p. 20). He described this twoness as "double consciousness," the reality of having to negotiate no less than two different and competing psychosocial realities at the same time. We suggest this inherent complexity must be posed, queried, and understood before we can develop and offer adequate prescriptions to address the challenges associated with the need for more sustainable leadership and consistent civic/community engagement.

A. Wade Boykin (1983), professor of psychology at Howard University, built on the early work of Du Bois by suggesting that African Americans, in fact, must negotiate no less than three realms of experiences. Boykin offered a framework that posits that African Americans face a "triple quandary" in terms of their ethnic/group status in the United States. Boykin described his framework as an Afrographic analysis of the African American experience in the United States. This means he offered a descriptive appraisal of the scope and range of psychological realities and experiences of African Americans in the United States (Boykin, 1983/1986; Boykin & Toms, 1985).

Boykin asserted that African Americans must negotiate different—and not necessarily interchangeable—realms of psychological experiences as an ethnic/racial group in the United States. These experiences are believed to be products of the interplay among three realms of experiences: (1) the mainstream, (2) the minority, and (3) the Afrocultural (Boykin, 1983/1986; Boykin & Toms, 1985; Boykin & Ellison, 1993 Cole, 1970; Jones, 1979). African Americans grow within the reaches of these three realms

and are provided varying opportunities and situations in which they observe, participate, and acquire various roles, values, competencies, and allegiances from childhood
through adulthood (Boykin & Ellison, 1995).

The mainstream experience in the United States is the most persuasive, and all
members of the society have contact with the mainstream realm. This experience
includes participation in work systems, educational systems, the judicial system, consumption systems, bureaucratic systems (both as clients and employees), and mass
media (Boykin, 1983/1986, 1986; Young, 1974). The minority experience is based on
exposure to social, economic, and political oppression resulting from one's minority
status in the United States. Boykin pointed out that, although other groups maintain a minority status in America, this status is not necessarily linked to race. The
Afrocultural experience is rooted in the traditional African ethos and has a culturally indigenous basis from which African Americans interpret and negotiate social
reality. The triple quandary is likely to exist for African Americans because (1) they
are likely to be incompletely socialized to the Euro-American cultural ethos (White
Anglo-Saxon Protestant ethic); (2) they typically develop negotiating styles that arise
out of their African heritage but are at odds with mainstream ideology; and (3) they
are victimized by racial and economic oppression (Boykin, 1983/1986; Boykin & Toms,
1985; Toms & Hobbs, 1997).

Toms (1997) continued this line of thinking in a study of the psychological orientations and the psychosocial adjustment of African American college students. He
defined psychological orientations as the multiple ways that individual African Americans orient themselves to cope with the demands of participating in and balancing
no less than multiple societal and cultural experiences simultaneously. Like most
Americans, Toms (1997) suggested that African Americans feel a need to participate
in, endorse, and sometimes value mainstream American values, expectations, and
standards for success. For African Americans, though, that need for success in the
mainstream must be reconciled with an equally pressing need to develop adaptive
coping strategies to address racism and discrimination associated with participation
in American institutions (Boykin, 1983/1986; Toms, 1997). The following section will
explore how and in what ways the triple quandary framework can be used to examine
African American leaders' psychosocial experiences to better inform our understanding of their leadership and community engagement practices.

Triple Quandary, Leadership, and Engagement

Applying the "triple quandary" framework to leadership and engagement in African
American communities has multiple implications. Wilson (1960) describes the difference between militant and moderate political styles as a way to understand the
ways leaders approach the world. He noted that militant and moderate styles can be
described by observing the way Negro leaders approach the world. It is important how
they see the world, feel it, describe it, and act toward it.

In terms of connecting the triple quandary framework to leadership and engagement, clearly, not all African Americans, such as those in leadership positions as elected officials and those leading at the community-based level, have acquired or maintain the necessary competencies, values, behavioral repertoires, and orientations for successful participation within the fabric of mainstream American institutions. As Boykin and Ellison (1995) noted, "The level, frequency of participation, and the level and areas of competency will vary among African Americans. The orientation toward the mainstream institutions will vary as well. The utilization and embracement of behavior patterns, values, and roles of the mainstream will also differ among African Americans" (p. 99). The implication here is that adaptive reactions, coping styles, and adjustment techniques have surely become part and parcel of the negotiational reality for African Americans (Boykin & Toms, 1985, p. 44). Thus you can expect to see varying levels of styles, participation, and orientations as to how different African American leaders negotiate in the mainstream of American institutions personally and through how they lead and provide leadership. That is, is their leadership style more of a "to and for" or a "with and through the community"? Do they provide opportunities for community education and participation? Are there opportunities for communities to provide feedback and participate in the decision-making process?

This suggests that even those who seek to lead and engage in leadership in African American communities may, in fact, not have the readiness and preparedness to be successful, depending on their own psychosocial orientation (e.g., the amount of involvement, participation, time, types, and levels of experiences with the mainstream or, for that matter, within their own African American cultural experiences). As Wilson (1960) proposed, citizens will have to assess for themselves how prospective leaders approach the world, how they feel about it, describe it, and act toward it in their leadership roles. That is, how comfortable are they in participating in mainstream civic arenas as leaders and representative voices for their communities? This also means citizens must actively engage leaders through observations, conversations, and evaluation of their actions to ensure that they are, in fact, aligned with the community's expectations and needs.

Second, Boykin and Toms (1985) offered further insight into the minority experience that has implications for leaders and those seeking to get more involved in civic/community engagement. They extend their thinking on the nature of the minority experience for African Americans in terms of three critical axes: (1) whether one takes an active or passive role in reacting to racism and oppression, (2) whether one takes a mainstream system engagement or system disengagement posture, and (3) whether one is oriented toward system change or system maintenance. Another factor in understanding the minority experience and its significance to African American leaders is a concern with impression management.

Boykin and Ellison (1985) suggested, "Given the persistence of negative images of black people in U.S. society at large, there is often the persistent suspicion that white people are constantly judging black people and often are primed to judge pejoratively. Then, it would be reasonable that many African Americans would have a preoccupation with how they are perceived by others and how they want to be perceived. In some instances, the concern is with making a good impression on white people. Yet in some instances the concern is to attempt to consciously present the opposite from mainstream normative expectations" (Boykin & Ellison, 1985, p. 102).

For African American leaders, this is a daily reality; for some, it is a daily and situational concern with how they are perceived and how they seek to be perceived. Depending on how much they value maintaining a positive image and position in the eyes of their mainstream counterparts, personal and collective conflict can readily affect their decision making, thus impacting their "will" and "ability" to effectively represent the interest and voice of the community. On the other hand, this idea of image management can also be a factor in whether African American leaders get a seat at the decision-making table, simply based on the perceptions of key stakeholders. For example, while attending a community engagement meeting, the question came up about the lack of African American and/or minority participation in the process, to which one of the mainstream stakeholders in the room responded, "Well, I just have a problem with how some of them act ... and if they are going to participate, they will have to be professional" (Fordham & Ogbu, 1986, 1988). This example reinforces the quote above by Boykin and Ellison (1985) regarding "image management" and African Americans. African Americans at local levels continue to be challenged by overt and covert forms of individual and institutional racism—many times operating in a way that it essentially goes unnoticed and unquestioned.

There are many questions that must also be posed and answered regarding leaders and leadership in African American communities, such as have the leaders developed the necessary coping strategies to deal with forms of overt and covert personal and institutional racism? Are their personal coping strategies, leadership styles, behaviors, and methods more oriented toward mainstream cultural values and beliefs, more toward those of their own ethnic/racial group, or have they acquired the competencies to successfully negotiate between both? These questions and others are necessary and critical because the answers can determine to what extent they are able to connect with and engage members of their own community, as well as influence their ability to provide effective representation in deliberations with mainstream stakeholders and agencies around policy development and resource distribution. These questions relate to aspects of both the mainstream and minority experience, as described in the triple quandary.

These questions and others will help citizens gain a better understanding of the complexities of participation and engagement. These particular questions provide insight into the extent that individuals who seek to lead and engage understand the "insider versus outsider status" of the African American experience and leadership and engagement in American society.

Figure 3.1 offers further thoughts and inquiries that will provide additional assessment questions for discussion about the characteristics and psychosocial orientation of prospective and current leaders and their leadership in African American communities.

We cannot leave this section without addressing the important implications for a more inclusive and expanded capacity-building process, particularly for young African Americans and grassroots populations. Further exploration of the triple quandary framework leads us to a discussion about the multifaceted, intergenerational nature and context of leading and leadership in African American communities. We would be remiss in this discussion if we did not address emerging issues regarding the widening gap between African American baby boomers, Generation Xers, and millennials. In the arena of leading and leadership, this gap within and between groups is a constant in the workplace, at conferences, community events, and even family reunions. The generational divide seems to dictate that millennials need to take on leadership roles and learn the necessary skills while operating in those roles. This is in direct opposition to conventional or more mainstream leadership, which promotes more experience as the caveat to better leadership (Bottomley & Burgess, 2018). The lack of connection or disconnect between generations of African Americans is evident in multiple contexts of leadership and within our communities.

Charles Payne's work would suggest that the response to this quandary has resulted in a generation of African Americans who have chosen to distance themselves from their history. Payne further asserted that confusion and fear about their history raise important questions about their civic engagement and their capacity to engage in the collective struggling that helped liberate their ancestors (Payne, 2003, p. 23).

In a perusal of attendees at meetings in community settings, such as churches, town halls, or community-sponsored events addressing important issues or training, one will quickly note limited representation of Generation X and the almost nonexistent representation of millennials and Generation Z. Why is this? Do we assume that they do not care to be involved? Are intentional plans developed to be inclusive of members of each generational group? What are the barriers or roadblocks to engaging these groups in the leadership process that historically have been grounded in the energy and synergy of youthful leaders?

There is the perception among many African Americans, particularly those representing Generation X and millennials (and to some degree Generation Z), that there are limited opportunities to participate in leadership activities at the community level. They believe that those who currently hold positions of leadership, whether elected, appointed, or self-selected, are apt to hold on to those positions if possible. The underlying assumption is that of "power" and maintaining it. Stated bluntly, for many persons, it took them a long time to get their positions ("power and recognition"), and they will hold on until death. Bunche (2005) responded to this observation in his research on Black leaders when he stated, "Most black leaders would never relinquish power once they had their first taste of it" (p. 4).

Leadership Challenges: Readiness and Preparedness to Lead and Provide Leadership

- **Why Were They Selected? Or Why Did They Choose to Serve?** *Are they the best representative? For what purpose were they selected/chosen to serve? Whom do they appear to represent? Themselves or the community's voice?*

- **To What Extent Are They Skilled or Unskilled?** *Do they have the necessary expertise? How aligned are their personal beliefs, values, and goals with those of the community? Are they open to critical discussion with constituents on issues with differing perspectives? Or is their leadership style one that suggests they alone are the decision maker because they have the title and power and are in the leadership role?*

- **To What Extent Are They Known for Their Integrity or Lack Thereof?** *Are they known for their integrity within their own community as a leader, and do they have the respect of mainstream leaders? Do they have a track record of being a "person of their word"? Do they walk the talk? Are they the type that follows up after meetings and planning, or are they the type who must be contacted consistently and rarely return communications?*

- **What Is Their Capacity to Lead and Provide Leadership?** *Do they have a perspective of "shared leadership and community-capacity building," or is their vision of leading one that centers on their own beliefs? Do they have the capacity to connect with and mobilize diverse groups of constituents to create a "critical mass" to champion efforts with civic and elected officials around critical issues and policies impacting the community? Do they understand and readily support the vision of developing and reproducing leaders for the future through intentional mentoring and development of leadership sustainability plans and processes?*

- **To What Extent Do Their Personal Coping Strategies Support Their Ability to Negotiate for Critical Issues and Needs? How Are They Oriented Psychologically?** *Do their beliefs and actions align more with maintaining things as they are, or are they more aligned with system change? Are they more concerned about being understood and accepted by mainstream stakeholders rather than representing the community's interests? Are they more concerned with their personal status and access to power than important issues and policies that affect the community they represent?*

- **To What Extent Can They Be Counted on to Substantially Contribute Regarding Their Group's Issues, Needs, and Recommendations?** *Are they secure enough with themselves, with their ethnic/racial group heritage, to maintain a tough position at the bargaining table? Do they have the necessary confidence and knowledge to contribute to discussions and think through structural and procedural hurdles to make a contribution on behalf of the community? Or do they have a tendency to be quiet, to have "lockjaw" when tough political issues and policies are being debated? In short, how prepared are they to represent the interests of the group?*

FIGURE 3.1   Leadership Challenges: Readiness and Preparedness to Lead and Provide Leadership

For young African Americans, there seems to be a great deal of discontent, a sense that they have had to wait too long to participate or take on leadership roles that they are clearly qualified for, but the opportunity remains limited or nonexistent. Their inability to penetrate existing leadership roles and structure (e.g., churches, community organizations, and elected positions) may be one explanation for the limited participation and engagement in civic/community affairs in African American communities. This point returns us to our earlier discussion of the psychology of the African American experience—in particular, the minority experience, which asks, "Is one (who seeks to lead and engage) about system change or system maintenance?"—not just as it relates to participation in mainstream American institutional public discourse and policies but also within one's own community/cultural context. Stated another way, one who seeks to lead cannot be about "change" within mainstream American institutions and processes and about "maintenance" (keeping it the same) when it comes to themselves and their leadership context.

We suggest that gaining a better understanding of the psychosocial experiences of African American leaders and communities provides the necessary insight into developing social capital, trust, and relational context for increased leadership and engagement. To be sure, efforts to gain a more in-depth understanding of African American psychosocial experiences will enhance the decision-making processes of local leaders and organizations. Gaining this understanding will assist in the development of more effective strategies and tactics to educate, organize, and mobilize citizens to be more involved with civic- and community-based issues.

COMMUNITY ENGAGEMENT IN AFRICAN AMERICAN COMMUNITIES—WHAT DIFFERENCE DOES IT MAKE?

Historian Charles Payne (2003) noted, "This generation of African Americans" (p. 24) is the generation that has been least exposed to some important forms of social education and least supported by the accumulated understandings of previous generations. This changes the individual paradigm of not only leadership but also community.

African American institutions face questions of their relevance and capacity to serve diverse audiences while using their cultural expertise and experience to address the needs of monolithic—yet not so monolithic—constituents. Regarding churches and historically Black colleges and universities (HBCUs), the most prominent of these institutions are uniquely equipped to address the challenges that face the African American community: the economic, health, and educational disparities exacerbated by limited and ineffective civic engagement (Lloyd, 2010). Yet the institutions are challenged by the fact that, although African Americans have traditionally had very distinctive norms with regard to civic participation, since the 1980s, their rates of group membership have fallen to approximate those of White Americans (Putnam, 2000). The sharpest decline has been within communities of the less well-educated and suggests serious questions about the transmission of participatory norms that have characterized past African American civic life (Payne, 2003; Putnam, 2000).

Andrea Harris, executive director of the North Carolina Institute for Minority Economic Development (NCIMED), discussed community development and the difference it makes in minority communities through HBCUs:

> Community engagement is not new to Historically Black Colleges and Universities, and HBCUs should not entertain this notion as some new phenomenon. HBCUs are products of community engagement. They are not silos that sit separate and apart from the rest of those living on the same dirt in and around the institutions. Nor are they separate and apart from the very network of people who share or uphold their mission, interests, or with whom they collaborate on ideas, resources, and who identify with the institutions as a part of who they are as a community or a people or a neighborhood. These institutions were started through community engagement. (Harris, 2013, p. 2)

Harris described how HBCUs in North Carolina were founded and supported largely through individuals and groups of community leaders who bought and denoted slots of land, organized to establish schools, and collaborated with Black businesses and religious organizations to develop and sustain the schools, as well as how those institutions were vehicles of pride and growth for surrounding communities. She pointed out, for example, that the founders of North Carolina Central University were also founders of what is known as Black Wall Street. These founders also established North Carolina Mutual Life Insurance Company, Mechanics & Farmers Bank, and Mutual Community Savings and Loan. The founders saw themselves, the future of the institutions they created, and the future of their people as tied to one another (Harris, 2013, p. 4). So, there is little doubt that community engagement in African American communities has made a difference and continues to do so through HBCUs, minority businesses, and grassroots citizens.

However, it must be pointed out that Harris (2013) has concerns about the current relationships between HBCUs and the communities they are surrounded by. She stated,

> Today, HBCUs continue to see themselves as the institutions of higher education that they are. However, too many lack the relationship with the low-to-moderate income working class black community they once enjoyed. Economic stratification of neighborhoods, gentrification, classism, and to some extent elitism, have had unhealthy consequences on the relationship between many HBCUs and the neighborhoods within which they are located, as well as their relationship to historically

Black civil rights and political organizations to which they once turned for support and voice. (p. 4)

The North Carolina Institute of Minority Economic Development (NCIMED) commissioned Dr. Jeffrey Humphreys of the Selig Institute, Terry College of Business, and the University of Georgia to conduct an analysis of the economic impact of North Carolina's 10 accredited HBCUs on their host communities. The combined economic effect in 2007 for the 10 HBCUs was $1.6 billion (sales), currently updated to $1.8 billion. These HBCUs add $939 million in value (gross regional product), $683 million in labor income, and 18,369 full- and part-time jobs (Harris, 2013, p. 5). Harris (2013) argued that in the future, it will take community engagement to reshape thinking, perception, and how the larger community values the HBCU community.

This is just one example of the difference community engagement makes in African American communities. Other examples include the relentless work of faith-based leaders and organizations that provide and sustain food and clothes drives, shelter and assistance to battered women and children, and housing development and job training programs for the unemployed, underemployed, and youth. There are several community-based organizations, community development corporations, and individuals who engage communities on a daily basis, providing support and services to those who cannot get assistance anywhere else. Even though these examples capture aspects of community engagement in African American communities, there remains a need to focus attention on more community capacity building among leaders, community organizations, and community members to intentionally engage elected officials, human service providers, and educational institutions to shape and direct policies and fiscal resources.

Building Capacity for Civic/Community Engagement in African American Communities

African Americans are viewed and described as occupying an "insider-outsider" existence within American society (Boykin & Ellison, 1993). This existence has varied throughout history, from having no legal rights as a citizen, with no access to representation in civic and community decision making, to representation with limited possibilities to express the concerns of the African American citizenry, to full access and representation in governing bodies, with limited participation and engagement of its citizens in the participatory democracy process. Each status was persistently colored by ancestry, unique immigration to this country in bondage, and socialization to a new culture as a "subculture."

Leaders in the African American community are cognizant of the need for new knowledge, skills, and abilities. In an exploratory sample of African American clergy from rural eastern North Carolina churches, Carter-Edwards et al. (2006) indicated a perceived need to increase the capacity of the churches to promote health, improve financial and infrastructural capacity, and create internal and external collaborative partnerships. Governmental agencies denote the need for community/social context that includes knowledge and understanding of (1) African American cultural values, (2) community capacity (e.g., identification of individual stakeholders, as well as organizations), (3) participation patterns of individuals and organizations in civic and community affairs, and (4) effectiveness of outreach strategies to the African American population within the community (Pullen-Smith et al., 2008).

Toms (1997), Boykin (1985), and Payne (2003) would suggest an emphasis on strengthening communities through collaborative leadership and citizen participation. Understanding how to nurture citizen participation is important to the survival of the African American community in an increasingly diverse and complex world. Critical constructs for developing such leadership for civic engagement are trust, spiritual capital, social capital, and the ability to learn in public (LIP). The literature denotes correlations between leadership capacity, trust, and individual social capital (Foster-Fishman et al., 2007; Toms et al., 2011). The following four focus areas are believed to be critical to capacity-building efforts related to civic/community engagement. They may be described as the precursors to engagement. Each focus area plays a critical role in the planning, organizing, development, and implementation of capacity-building strategies. While addressed separately, they are intimately interconnected in the capacity-building process within African American communities—overtly, covertly, consciously, and unconsciously. Readiness for engagement requires the ability to trust others, build spiritual capital individually and social capital collectively, and a willingness to LIP.

Trust

Trust has been defined as a social phenomenon that is based on anticipated behavioral integrity. Yet trust is the factor least abundant in African Americans' social capital constructs. Multiple aspects of trust are described in the literature. Trust involves risk taking, positive expectations, or an intention to accept vulnerability (McEvily et al., 2003). As a social practice, it is defined by choices and is always relational (Flores & Solomon, 1998). The partnerships that emerge from such an orientation are dependent on relational context rather than disciplinary content. Trust is affected by one's social, physical, and fiscal environment and implies a willingness to be vulnerable. This description reiterates the difficulty in acquiring this first construct of readiness.

Spiritual Capital

There is a need to first explore more extensively the importance of the tacit power of individual relationships to organizational partnerships. This is described as spiritual capital. The initial creation of a shared vision, reciprocity, and trust as contributors to engaged partnerships can have catalytic effects on organizational effectiveness. This exchange cannot be built organization to organization but lies in the interpersonal relationships between leaders. Spiritual capital is not a religious construct but a relational connection that transcends the logical and contractual and is dependent on faith in the individuals (Lloyd, 2010). It lies in the relational engagement among and between partners that permits individuals to develop a degree of faith in each other that goes beyond just dependability to perform a task. Leaders in such partnerships mutually allow for the acceptance of risk that accompanies the establishment of new relationships and innovations. Spiritual capital shared by individuals is critical to building sustainable leadership prepared for civic engagement (see Chapter 8 for more on spiritual capital).

Social Capital

Social trust influences interpersonal relationships at multiple levels, including individual and group performance in organizational settings, between organizations, and in social groups. Building and maintaining trusting relationships are critical for effective, sustained leadership. This unique form of social trust acts like building blocks for spiritual capital, and spiritual capital is the foundation for productive and intentional relationships, which are critical components of leadership and civic/community engagement, particularly in African American communities (Lloyd, 2010; Toms et al., 2011). For African American communities to be "players" in the civic engagement process at local levels, intentional efforts must be exercised to build social capital among and between individuals, community, and faith-based organizations, as well as like-minded broader community stakeholders, for the purpose of addressing pervasive disparities and inequities affecting the community. Building social capital is critical to policy change. The community's social capital is necessary for the successful engagement in city council, county commissioner, and school and health department board meetings and wherever policies are developed and decisions made on resource distribution that will impact quality of life.

Learning in Public

The acquisition of skills and knowledge is important to organizational and community capacity building. Like all other readiness characteristics, "trust" rears its head. When positive interpersonal relationships are established across organizations, trust can influence interorganizational performance (Zaheer et al., 1998).

Models of leadership must not only take into consideration the individual leader but also organizational leadership capacity. Zaheer and associates (1998) shifted the focus of trust from an individual level to review its effect on interorganizational leadership. These relationships between people facilitate successful business operations and actions with other organizations. The qualitative research in rural and urban African American North Carolina communities suggests that an ability to innovate and learn collectively must accompany these trusting relationships if we anticipate the development of new skills, knowledge, and capacity.

Toms et al. (2011) described this as "LIP." This paradigm for knowledge flow requires that institutions, communities, and individuals become far more adept at a process that has evolved toward social learning. It is specialized, complex, and dynamic, requiring the reciprocal contributions of expertise and experience from all of its stakeholders. Toms suggested that LIP includes the history of engagement; the nature of protocol, both overt and tacit; the psychocultural context; types of intentional collaborations; communication skills; understanding of the metrics of engagement; and capacity to plan, develop, and innovate (Toms et al., 2011). LIP can only occur if all participants are predisposed to recognize and value the equitable sources of historical and emerging expertise in realms of knowledge, skill, and ability. This diverges from the historical expert model that anoints formal leaders as conveyers of knowledge. This is of particular importance in the African American community where, historically, leadership and decision making have been seen as the echelon of the educated and those with formal religious appointment (Bunche, 2005).

LIP presupposes a different paradigm. Successful communities have strong informal and formal leadership. The engagement of citizens in participatory democracy is the defining construct of the Americanized form of governance (Toms & Hobbs, 1997). For many communities, the reality is that, in terms of numeric representation, they remain underrepresented. The connection between successful communities and leadership practices is documented in the literature. Such communities are intentional about diversity, engaging new leaders, using the assets of their members, and transitioning leadership over time (Flora, 1998; Green et al., 1990; Wall & Luther, 2005). These are functions of individuals who have the confidence and willingness to learn from others and to do so in collaborative environments.

SUMMARY

The African American community and its partners are challenged in the 21st century to respond to rapidly changing environments. Community potential for contextual leadership will be affected by African American history, intergenerational changes, self-efficacy and attitude, access to and participation in decision-making bodies, and the community's propensity to think and act as a global and local dynamism. What will such vitality require of leaders and followers? The African American community will need leaders capable of leading and following, boundary-spanning competencies, and team-building ability. Current and prospective leaders who seek to lead and guide a change process within African American communities today and in the future will need to be grounded in leadership skills that encompass and span the following five levels of leadership: (1) inner (oneself), (2) interpersonal, (3) organizational, (4) community, and (5) systems (see Figure 3.2).

FIVE LEVELS OF LEADERSHIP (TOMS, 2010)

- **Inner (Oneself).** This level relates to the inner world and concerns effective ways for a person to lead themselves and develop fully as a human being. These lessons are developmental in nature, involving a transformation of the manager's self-beliefs, attitudes, identities, and habits of self-improvement and self-development (Van Velsor & McCauley, 2004, p. 14).*

- **Interpersonal (Others With Whom Leadership Is Shared).** This level relates to the world of people and involves interpersonal and social skills that equip leaders to lead and work with people effectively. These lessons are social in nature, involving insights into other people's perspectives and group dynamics and a greater appreciation of the social process of influence and leadership (Van Velsor & McCauley, 2004, p.14).*

- **Organizational (the Base From Which Leaders Act).** This level relates to working in organizations to address strategic, systemic, and cultural issues. These lessons are technical in nature, concerning strategic, operational, and functional knowledge for getting work done and managing and transforming an organization (Van Velsor & McCauley, 2004, p. 14).*

- **Community (the Place Leaders Are Concerned With Changing).** This level relates to how connected or disconnected leaders are with the community of place they are concerned about or seek to change. Have they worked to build the necessary relationships/partnerships with individual stakeholders, churches, and organizations to formulate a constituent group that can be organized to "act collectively" around critical policy issues in the areas of education, health care, and economic development?

- **Systems—Policies/Procedures/Practices (Local, State, National).** This level relates to the readiness and preparedness of leaders to provide leadership as internal representatives on boards, commissions, and committees through their knowledge and skills. Have they invested time educating and informing the community on critical issues and prepared them to intentionally participate in formal civic settings through letter writing, meetings, and engagement with other elected officials who need to hear their voices and concerns as a representative of all citizens?

*Van Velsor, E., and McCauley, C. (Eds.). (2004). *Handbook of leadership development,.*. San Franciso: Jossey-Bass.

FIGURE 3.2   Five Levels of Leadership

Although leadership and its constructs are diverse across the literature, there is a common need to engage communities in the creation of a vision and then focus on goal achievement on multiple levels. This focus must occur inside the leaders' own communities and between their communities and mainstream stakeholders. This requires leadership to be less focused on personal preeminence and more intent on skill development on multiple levels, as described earlier.

This chapter denotes the need to create capacity-competent leadership with demonstrated skills in planning, developing, and the implementation of shared visions. Competent leadership is also accepting of the shared responsibility for the workload and shared recognition of achievement. The 21st-century leader will refine the art of communication, embracing the rules of effective decision making and the ability to engage in robust discussions without internalizing responses as personal affronts—that is, leaders who have developed the psychosocial maturity and skill sets to lead themselves and their communities of "place" into a new era of intentional participatory engagement.

REFERENCES

Bass, B. M. (1990). From transactional leadership: Learning to share the vision. *Organizational Dynamics, 18*, 19–31.

Battle, J., & Wright, E. (2002). W. E. B. Du Bois's talented tenth: A quantitative assessment. *Journal of Black Studies, 32*(6), 654–72.

Bositis, D. (2001). *Changing of the guard: Generational differences among black elected officials.* Joint Center for Political and Economic Studies.

Bottomley, K., & Burgess, S. W. (2018). Millennials in leadership: An examination of the practice immediacy model. In J. Marques & S. Dhiman (Eds.), *Engaged leadership: Transforming through future-oriented design thinking* (pp. 223–234). Springer.

Boykin, A. W. (1983, 1986). The academic performance of Afro-American children. In J. Spence (Ed.), *Achievement and achievement motives* (pp. 5–27). Freeman.

Boykin, A. W. (1986). The triple quandary and the schooling of Afro-American children. In U. Neisser (Ed.), *The school achievement of minority children* (pp. 57–92). Erlbaum.

Boykin, A. W., & Ellison, C. (1993). The multiple ecologies of black youth socialization: An afrographic analysis. In R. Taylor (Ed.), *Black youth* (pp. 93–127). SAGE Publications.

Boykin, A. W., & Toms, F. D. (1985). Black child socialization: A conceptual framework. In A. McAdoo & J. M. McAdoo (Eds.), *Black children* (pp. 33–51). SAGE Publications.

Bunche, R. (2005). *A brief and tentative analysis of negro leadership* (J. S. Holloway, Ed.). New York University Press.

Burns, J. M. (1978). *Leadership.* Harper and Row.

Carter-Edwards, L., Jallah, Y. B., Goldmon, M. V., Roberson Jr., J. T., & Hoyo, C. (2006). Key attributes of health ministries in African American churches: An exploratory survey. *North Carolina Medical Journal, 67*(5), 345–350.

Cole, J. (1970). Black culture: Negro, black and nigger. *Black Scholar, 1*, 40–43.

Cothran, T. C., & Phillips Jr., W. (1960). Negro leadership in crisis situations. *Phylon, 22*(2), 107–118.

Davis, D. G. (2007). Learning for leaders: Notes on a pedagogy for the praxis of Black political leadership. In J. Davis (Ed.). *Perspectives in black politics and black leadership* (pp. 47–39). University Press of America.

Du Bois, W. E. B. (1903). *The souls of black folks.* McClurg.

Flora, C. (1998). Social capital and communities of place. *Rural Sociology, 63*(4), 481–506.

Flores, F., & Solomon, R. C. (1998). Creating trust. *Business Ethics Quarterly, 8*(2), 205–232.

Fordham, S., & Ogbu, J. U. (1986). Black students' school success: Coping with the "burden of 'acting white.'" *Urban Review, 18*(3), 176–206.

Fordham, S., & Ogbu, J. (1988). Racelessness as a factor of black student success: Pragmatic strategy or Pyrrhic victory? *Harvard Educational Review, 58,* 54–84.

Foster-Fishman, P., Cantillon, D., Pierce, S., & Van Egeren, L. (2007). Building an active citizenry: The role of neighborhood problems, readiness and capacity for change. *American Journal of Community Psychology, 39,* 91–106.

Green, G., Flora, J., Flora, C., & Schmidt, F. (1990). Local self-development strategies: National survey results. *Journal of Community Development Society, 21 (55–73).*

Harris, A. (2013, April 17). *Community engagement* [Paper presentation]. NCCU Health Disparities Conference. Durham North Carolina, United States. http://web.nccu.edu/hbcu-conferencespeaker/Harrispaper.pdf

Hines, R. H., & Pierce, J. E. (1965). Negro leadership after the social crisis: An analysis of leadership changes in Montgomery, Alabama. *Phylon, 26*(2), 162–172.

Johnson, G. B. (July 1937). Negro racial movements and leadership in the U.S. *American Journal of Sociology, 43*(1), 57–71.

Jones, J. (1979). Conceptual and strategic issues in the relationship of black psychology to American social science. In A. W. Boykin, A. J. Franklin, & J. F. Yates (Eds.), *Research directions of black psychologists* (pp. 391–432). Russell SAGE Publications.

Lloyd, C. L. (2010). *Indicators of community-land grant university readiness for engagement from the community perspective.* North Carolina A&T State University.

McEvily, B., Perrone, V., & Zaheer, A. (2003). Trust as an organizing principle. *Organization Science, 14*(1), 91–103.

Myrdal, G. (1944). *An American dilemma: The Negro problem and modern democracy.* The Carnegie Foundation.

Northouse, P. (2004). *Leadership: Theories and practice.* SAGE Publications.

Payne, C. M. (2003). More than a symbol of freedom: Education for liberation and democracy. *Phi Delta Kappan, 85*(1), 22–28.

Pullen-Smith, B., Carter-Edwards, L., & Leathers, K. (2008). Community health ambassadors: A model for engaging community leaders to promote better health in North Carolina. *Journal of Public Health Management and Practice, 14*(Suppl:S), 73–81.

Putnam, R. D. (2000). *Bowling alone: The collapse and revival of American community.* Simon & Schuster.

Rosenzweig, R., & Thelen, D. (1998). *The presence of the past.* Columbia University Press.

Smythe, H. A. (1950). Changing patterns in Negro leadership. *Social Forces, 29*(2), 191–197. UNC Press.

Standing, T. G. (1934). Nationalism in Negro leadership. *American Journal of Sociology, 40*(2), 180–192.

Stouffer, S. A. (1955). *Communism and conformity and civil liberties.* Transaction Publishers.

Toms, F. D. (1997). Challenges and opportunities of communities in transition. In F.D. Toms & A. D. Hobbs (Eds.), *Who are we?: Building a knowledge base of ethnic, racial, and cultural groups in America.* Diverse Books.

Toms, F. D. (2010). Black elected officials and community/civic engagement [Paper presentation]. Annual Meeting of the American Education Research Association. Denver, CO, United States.

Toms, F. D., & Hobbs, A. D. (1997). *Who are we?: Building a knowledge base of ethnic, racial, and cultural groups in America.* Diverse Books.

Toms, F., Lloyd, C. L., Carter-Edwards, L., & Ellison, C. (2011). A faith-based community view of improving health and health care advocacy through engagement. *Practical Matters, 4,* 1–13.

Van Velsor, E., & McCauley, C. (Eds.). (2004). *Handbook of leadership development.* Jossey-Bass.

Wall, M., & Luther, V. (2005). *20 clues to rural community survival: An annotated list.* Heartland Center for Leadership Development.

Watson, A. C., & Rosser, M. (2006). *The emergence of African-American leaders in American society.* Praeger Publishers.

Wilson, J. Q. (1960). *Negro politics: The search for leadership.* The Free Press.

Young, V. (1974). A black American socialization pattern. *American Ethnologist, 1,* 405–413.

Zaheer, A., McEvily, B., & Perrone, V. (1998). Does trust matter? Exploring the effects of inter-organizational and interpersonal trust on performance. *Organization Science, 9*(2), 141–59.

PART II

Challenges and Opportunities for Leadership and Community Engagement

CHAPTER FOUR

Adaptive Leadership

*APPLYING COMMUNITY ENGAGEMENT PRINCIPLES IN
DESIGNING AND DELIVERING PUBLIC HEALTH INTERVENTIONS*

Lori Carter-Edwards, Elizabeth A. Moyer, and Barbara Pullen-Smith

This chapter will

- Define adaptive leadership and community engagement,
- Provide a critique of the current literature intersecting adaptive leadership with principles of community engagement,
- Describe a set of engagement strategies for leaders to use for their organizations and the communities they serve when designing and implementing public health interventions, and
- Discuss recommendations for community-engaged adaptive leadership.

There is a growing, collective consciousness emerging among multiple sectors that authentic, meaningful community partnerships are critical for successfully designing and implementing health and health-care programs and services that reduce health disparities and improve health outcomes (CDC, 2020; PCORI, 2020). While the importance of such relationships is not new for some sectors, the current national thrust reveals clear signs of the shift taking place to value health equity and the need and responsibility of organizations and systems to address the social determinants of health. Public Health 3.0 (DeSalvo et al., 2017), the 3.0 Transformation Framework for Health System Reform (Halfon et al., 2014), and the framework for the upcoming Healthy People 2030 (Healthypeople.gov, 2020) all refer to prevention and shared understanding and responsibility for achieving optimal health. Through cross-sector partnerships (DeSalvo et al., 2017), communities must be a part of the equation in the design and execution of viable solutions (Halfon et al., 2014). Thus, leadership must be shared (Halfon et al., 2014).

Effective leadership among all sectors is essential for health transformation, particularly in an ever-changing public health and health-care environment (Snebold, 2015). Leaders must prepare to adapt to different environments and stakeholders in dynamic settings rapidly. To do so requires practicing iterative self-reflection, diagnosing and mobilizing organizations and systems (Heifetz et al., 2009), and taking and managing courageous steps toward innovation. In terms of working with communities to address health, principles of engagement must be integrated to establish trustworthy relationships for sustainable change. Since change authentically and meaningfully involves differing views and levels of influence and power, leadership must also involve creating a culture that manages conflict, bringing value to often-marginalized voices, and establishing shared goals for collective buy-in.

This chapter will connect adaptive leadership in health with the principles of community engagement. Through a public health lens, characteristics of effective public health leaders will be described, and, through examples, a series of engagement strategies will be provided as tools for building the types of relationships needed to codesign interventions. We conclude the chapter with a summary and set of recommendations for future efforts for engaged leadership that supports community interventions for systems change that promote health equity.

ADAPTIVE LEADERSHIP AND COMMUNITY ENGAGEMENT DEFINED

The practice of *adaptive leadership*, a theory dating back to 1994 (Heifetz et al., 2009), is built on the belief that leadership is a process of "mobilizing stakeholders to address challenging problems and to perform adaptive work in support of stated goals" (Heifetz et al., 2004, p. 92; Moore, 2018). As Heifetz and colleagues stated (2009), the process is built on the capacity to thrive, where successful adaptation is iterative, forging into the future using the best from prior history. Through a trial-and-error approach, adaptive leadership embraces the exploration of innovation, recognizing the importance of "failing forward" or the concept that leveraging mistakes fosters learning, innovation, and resilience (Maxwell, 2007). Adaptive leaders diagnose the system (including the landscape, adaptive challenges, and capacities and qualities of the organization) and mobilize the system (including framing the diverse interpretations, designing effective interventions, managing relationships and conflict, and creating an adaptive culture). Adaptive leaders see themselves as systems (by understanding their roles, bandwidth, loyalties, and "tuning," where how they react is rooted in historical personal and/or professional life experiences) and deploy themselves (by purposefully and courageously engaging and inspiring others, receiving support from others, and taking risks to do things differently without the fear of failing forward) (Heifetz et al., 2009).

Adaptive leadership is different from transformational leadership, which centers on a single leader's ability to inspire, possess a vision, and model one's values (Mason et al., 2014). Within an organization, transformational leaders operate by motivating their supporters to action, to buy into the mission and vision set forth, and to provide the support and encouragement for the supporters to maximize their own goals and aspirations (Frey et al., 2009). Transformational leadership skills are essential but not sufficient in flat, matrixed, or decentralized organizational structures that do not operate using a traditional hierarchical leadership model. Transformational leadership focuses on leading related to supporters, whereas adaptive leadership focuses on leading in relation to the contextual environment (Cojocar, 2008; Moore, 2018). Often in these environments, decision making involves a shared approach (Weger et al., 2018).

Community engagement is the "process of working collaboratively with and through groups of people affiliated by geographic proximity, special interest, or similar situations to address issues affecting the well-being of those people" (CDC, 1997, p. 9; U.S. DHHS, 2011). A blend of science and art (U.S. DHHS, 2011), community engagement's influence from science comes from numerous disciplines (e.g., sociology, political science, anthropology, organizational development, social work, psychology) and organizing from such concepts as community participation, mobilizations, and psychology and cultural influences. Its influence from art comes from the ability to adapt the science to fit the community's interests and purposes for engagement through understanding, skill, and sensitivity (U.S. DHHS, 2011). It is rooted in achieving health equity, where every person has the opportunity to "attain his or her full health potential" and no one is "disadvantaged from achieving this potential because of social position or other socially determined circumstances" (CDC, 2020, para. 1). There are nine principles of community engagement (Box 4.1). All are important and may apply in different ways and combinations in varying settings among diverse populations. However, one of the most prominent principles is trust, which is fundamental to collaboration and partnership building (Alio et al., 2014; Frerichs et al., 2017; McCloskey et al., 2011).

Community engagement evolved from *community benefit* in the late 1800s (legally defined by four charitable organizations, including trusts for charity, education, religion, and other purposes), *community organizing* from the late 1800s to the 1950s (which, based in the principles of social action and social justice [Alinsky, 1972], involved conflict strategies to address socioenvironmental health disparities), and *community participation* from the 1960s to the 1970s (a period of prominence for public participation as reflected in the World Health Organization [WHO] 1948 Constitution, which declared the importance of public involvement [WHO, 1948] and efforts and implementation of community-based participatory research) (Wallerstein et al., 2015). The period of *community engagement* from the late 1970s to the present focuses on empowerment and participation rather than conflict strategies and social action. However, in a climate of a global health crisis and civil unrest because of systemic burdens and insults (Galea & Abdalla, 2020), a shift back to community organizing is emerging.

BOX 4.1: PRINCIPLES OF COMMUNITY ENGAGEMENT

- *Be clear about the purposes or goals* of the engagement effort and the populations and/or communities you want to engage
- Become *knowledgeable* about the community (cultural and social structures and norms)
- Go to the community, establish relationships, *build trust*
- Remember and accept that *collective self-determination* is the responsibility and right of all people in a community
- *Partnering with the community* is necessary to create change and improve health
- All aspects of community engagement must *recognize and respect the diversity of the community*
- Community engagement can only be sustained by *identifying and mobilizing community assets*
- Community collaboration requires long-term *commitment*
- Organizations that wish to engage a community, as well as individuals seeking to effect change, *must be prepared to release control* of actions or interventions to the community

(U.S. DHHS, 2011)

Central to the process of community engagement is establishing a common goal or goals among a team of stakeholders (Box 4.2). Adaptive leadership also seeks to take collective action toward a common goal or goals; however, its focus is on readily acclimating to changing environments through approaches tailored to a specific situation. Both promote the exploration of ideas related to a common goal, involve clear communication, seek to achieve agreement on the goal, require time for building relationships, and values others' contributions to the process. In the example "Tale of Three Towns" (Box 4.2), there are eight different types of stakeholders but one common goal: to build the highway. Leaders react differently to the environment across the towns where cross-sector partnerships, or lack thereof, affect the outcome. Each stakeholder has a unique role and purpose but should be viewed as equal partners at the table. Critical in this example is that context and leadership style matter.

BOX 4.2: TALE OF THREE TOWNS: VALUING A COMMON GOAL IN COMMUNITY ENGAGEMENT

In the tale of three towns (Figures 4.1, 4.2, and 4.3), each town set out to build a highway within 1 year. Each town had adequate land; neighboring towns but limited road access to them; a standard blueprint for a 5-mile highway; a mayor, town manager, accountant, engineers, construction company, pavers, and ditch diggers; limited material resources; and access to large equipment and a gravel yard. Were they successful?

FIGURE 4.1 Town A

Town A Did Not Finish the Highway. The town manager and mayor were in close contact throughout the planning but did not include the construction company in the initial discussions. The construction company had to wait to get materials from the gravel yard, but there was a back order. Since the construction company did know what the full planning schedule was, it could not get the materials on time. The accountant had the budget set for the cost of the highway based on what the mayor and town manager planned, but it did not account for the need for additional pavers when there was a crunch period late summer after a long rain when no one could work. Consequently, the pavers went and did other jobs. When sought for the highway in Town A, there were not enough pavers to fulfill the job. The result? A half-finished highway, with traffic backed up such that people had to leave home earlier than usual to get to work.

Town B Finished Building the Highway, but It Was of Poor Quality. Town B had a town manager who often failed to listen to the engineer. The engineer was well respected by the construction company and the pavers for the work that he'd done for many years in another town. The town manager considered him an outsider who did not belong, despite the positive sentiment of and respect from the construction company and pavers who grew up in Town B like the town manager. The engineer pleaded with the town manager to wait to build the road until he could negotiate for additional funding for appropriate soil testing and additional materials to make the ground firmer and thus safer for the travelers. The town manager wanted to rush to meet the

FIGURE 4.2 Town B

1-year deadline to show the mayor his leadership abilities and accomplishments—all at the cost of a quality road.

Town C Successfully Completed a Quality Highway. A reporter in the town and her television crew came to the opening of the highway. She and her crew marveled at the town's ability to complete the beautiful highway in a year with limited material and human resources. The reporter had heard about what happened with the highways in Towns A and B and as a result was very interested in sharing the story about Town C's success so that maybe others could benefit. She interviewed the mayor of Town C, asking him why he was successful in building the highway in his town. The mayor said, "Thanks so much for the compliment, but I did not build the highway. Our town built this highway. When I found out two years ago that we needed to build a highway in a year so that we could reach our neighboring towns, which needed access to our hospital and our high school, the town manager and I convened a large meeting with the accountant, the engineer, the construction company, the pavers, and the ditch diggers. Collectively, we discussed the plan to make sure all of us understood the primary purpose of the highway. Then, with the help of the engineer, we identified the best land area to make the highway. We knew we didn't have all of the resources to build a four-lane highway, so we asked for help from the governor. Our construction company has a great relationship with another construction company a few towns over, and we were able to borrow some of their large equipment for a fraction of the cost of buying equipment. The accountant was very happy with that. We knew after hearing from our pavers that this job would require them to work triple time, or we would need to hire additional pavers. Since we had a few people who were out of work but had some skills and a good work ethic, some of our

FIGURE 4.3   Town C

pavers and ditch diggers tag-teamed in getting safety clearance for these individuals. They got them qualified for temporary employment (with which the accountant assisted) and taught some of these men and women some basics in protecting the pavers on the road and daily cleanup. This freed the pavers to do paving and the ditch diggers to share the use of the heavy equipment. So, you see, our town built this wonderful highway ... and I'm glad to be a resident!"

(Carter-Edwards L. East Carolina University Mills Symposium, Keynote Presentation, 2014; photos accessed through www.pixabay.com)

ATTRIBUTES OF EFFECTIVE COMMUNITY-ENGAGED LEADERS IN HEALTH: STAKEHOLDER PERCEPTIONS

While there is ample literature on adaptive leadership and leadership in general, there is very little on leadership attributes in community engagement. Burns even stated in 1978 that "leadership is one of the most observed and least understood phenomena on earth". To gain a better understanding of the type and mode of delivery of content for the design of a course on community engagement and leadership in health, a survey was sent in 2016 to 65 academic and community stakeholders where a total of 35 individuals (53.8%) responded within 2 weeks. Two reviewers (EAM and BPS) independently coded and generated key themes from the stakeholders' responses to the open-ended survey question, "In your own words, what are the qualities of an effective community-engaged leader in health?" After independently generating themes, the reviewers convened, discussed their results, and reached consensus. They found that the stakeholders expressed feedback that can be categorized as character traits (Table 4.1) and leadership skills (Table 4.2).

TABLE 4.1 *Stakeholder Feedback: Qualities of an Effective Community-Engaged Leader in Health—Character Traits*

TRUSTWORTHY	INTERPERSONAL	INNOVATIVE	TEAM BUILDER
• authenticity	• appreciate issues impacting community	• adaptability*	• collaboration*
• commitment	• build relationships	• create sustainable programs	• engage diverse individuals, groups, organizations*
• dependable	• build trust*	• creativity	
• do the right thing	• collaboration	• curiosity*	
• ethical	• comfortable with community	• flexible*	• galvanize
• fairness	• compassion	• forward-looking	• group facilitation
• follows up on commitments	• empathize	• malleability	• inspire others
• genuine connection with engaged community	• enjoy working with diverse populations	• modifies one's perspective with new information	• inspire others to do the right thing
• good reputation	• equitable and open partnerships	• nimble	• mobilize others
• honest	• humility	• open-minded	• motivate others to actively seek out ways to improve their own health
• in "for the long haul"	• inspire others	• receptive to new ideas	
• integrity	• invest adequate time and resources to gain trust	• willing to learn	
• keeps promises	• liaison		• partnerships
• reduces need to be judgmental	• passionate*		• relationship builder
• retains respectfulness	• patient*		
• transparency	• personable		
• true to their word	• relationship oriented		
• values contributions of all community members	• respectful		
	• sensitivity		
	• supportive		
	• understanding		
	• value community input		
	• willingness to be close to target community		
	• work with diverse populations		

Feedback from 35 stakeholders completing a survey on engagement skills and content for a course on community engagement and leadership in health. Actual responses from participants are listed alphabetically.
*Response mentioned by more than one respondent.

TABLE 4.2 *Stakeholder Feedback: Qualities of an Effective Community-Engaged Leader in Health—Skills*

LEADERSHIP SKILLS	COMMUNICATION SKILLS	ORGANIZATIONAL SKILLS	CONTENT EXPERTISE
• advocate* • allows stakeholders to own the solutions • altruistic • amplify energy of community • bridge needs and desires and health-care system • builds up others • change agents* • creates a collective vision • determined • foster leadership • future thinking • keep community focused and moving • lead by example • motivate others • needs of community first • provides guidance • resilience • seek ways to improve own health • self-aware • shared leadership • shared power and resources • sharing vision • team building* • transformative change • visionary • well connected to resources	• active listening • convey complex data, research/ outcome/stats in simplified format • excellent communication skills • good listener* • keep community informed • meeting facilitation • negotiation skills • process input from people • provide feedback/ solicits input • seeks to improve quality of engagement process • spend time together • strong communication	• assessments • attention to details • builds capacity • connect resources (time, people, and money) • data collection • implement activities* • inclusiveness • integrate health systems and policies • leveraging resources • more work, less talk • partnerships • planning • willing to travel and work outside of normal hours and locations	• ability to understand data from people's perspective • aware of resources • chronic health issues • cultural norms/diversity* • culture and historical perspective • direct experiences • diverse populations* • health inequities issues • health issues* • health priorities • health trends and strategies • identifies assets in community • identify gaps and missing data • knows community strengths and ailments • political, social, health-related landscape • population's health needs* • social and environmental factors • understands strengths and weaknesses • understands system-level influences • use data to learn how to improve community • well-informed

Feedback from 35 stakeholders completing a survey on engagement skills and content for a course on community engagement and leadership in health. Actual responses from participants are listed alphabetically.
*Response mentioned by more than one respondent.

The key themes that emerged for character traits were the ability to be trustworthy, interpersonal, innovative, and a team builder (Table 4.1). Authenticity and commitment were vital traits for being trustworthy; however, a large, broad number of interpersonal traits were identified, including such factors as demonstrating a willingness or enjoyment in working with diverse populations, building trust, and being passionate, sensitive, and patient. Common innovative traits included adaptability or flexibility and curiosity. In team building, the ability to collaborate and engage diverse individuals, groups, and organizations were common traits.

Key themes that emerged for skills were in the areas of leadership, communication, organization, and content expertise (Table 4.2). Numerous skills were classified as leadership skills or expertise in content. Team building, advocacy, and serving as change agents were commonly listed leadership skills, and in terms of content, having expertise in health and population health issues, particularly skills in cultural diversity, were common.

These findings serve as a useful guide regarding the traits and skills leaders engaging communities to address health issues should possess.

LITERATURE LINKING ADAPTIVE LEADERSHIP WITH ENGAGEMENT IN HEALTH

While engagement is inherent in the volume of literature on adaptive leadership, health literature directly linking adaptive leadership with engagement is limited. In a targeted search of title/abstract key words "adaptive leadership" and "engagement" or "community engagement" (using PubMed as the search engine), only five articles were identified that included "adaptive leadership" and "engagement." None included "community engagement."

Cohen and Tedesco (2009) called for adaptive leadership and staff engagement to fundamentally address resistance to change in necessary dental education reform. The authors refer to the concept of thriving as defined by Heifetz et al. (2009) and the need to shift the culture to an adaptive rather than technical framework for innovation and sustainable change. In an integrative review, de Zulueta (2015) discussed the practice of compassionate health care; the need to shift from punitive, rigid leadership; and adopting a culture that fosters shared learning, open communication, interpersonal connections, skills building, and cross-cutting workloads across silos. To thrive, de Zulueta acknowledged the importance of providing space for authentic dialogue between patients, clinicians, and managers. The Cohen and Tedesco (2009) and de Zulueta (2015) articles involve adaptive leadership and staff engagement, with de Zulueta including the patient community.

Three recent studies reveal lessons from assessing or taking action to adapt to changes in the health-care environment. In a study using the Public Health Workforce

Interests and Needs Survey, Raskind and colleagues (2019) evaluated the existing capacity of the maternal and child health (MCH) workforce to maximize opportunities during ongoing change. The results revealed a low awareness of MCH public health trends but high reported proficiency in skills related to these trends. Not surprisingly, the lowest proficiency was reported for systems integration. However, for capacity in change management or adaptive leadership, workplace support was the strongest correlate. The findings from this study provide a springboard for engaging staff in the development of meaningful training to adapt to trends and implies a need for gaining a greater understanding of systems so that staff can articulate leverage points for developing systems strategies for transformation in the workplace. In a study conducted in Australia, Petriwskyi and Power (2020) explored the effect of staff leading change in a consumer-engaged practice in elder care. Staff members were empowered to identify issues, generate solutions, and transform their organizations. While they were able to engage in adaptive leadership by creating solutions, barriers to progress were technical, practical, systemic, and philosophical in nature. These findings, as with the study by Raskind and colleagues (2019), indicate a clear need to understand and address systems change at a higher level. Finally, Noble and colleagues (2020) described their rapid, multipronged process and lessons learned from the accelerated preparation of their San Francisco emergency department to be responsive to coronavirus disease 2019 (COVID-19). In their approach, they engaged their workforce; created a set of logistics for new care areas; deployed two accelerated care units, each composed of military-grade, negative-pressure medical tents; and managed personal protective equipment. Their approach is already serving as a model for other states in response to this public health crisis.

A brief review of this literature reveals the perceived importance and/or willingness of organizations to use adaptive leadership approaches to respond to rapid changes in the health-care environment. Staff engagement and workplace buy-in may be essential for sustainable change in organizational infrastructures. However, larger systems issues remain ill defined and unaddressed, indicating an area for continued exploration. Furthermore, since these studies demonstrated limited to no involvement of communities in the process of engagement, additional work is needed in applying adaptive leadership principles in settings where community engagement occurs.

COMMUNITY ENGAGEMENT TOOLS, STRATEGIES, AND PUBLIC HEALTH LEADERSHIP

Public health leaders understand that authentically engaging individual, organizational, and community stakeholders can generate effective health-care solutions to persistent health disparate issues. Despite this awareness, the strategies used are often insufficient and/or not sustainable. Principles of community engagement are mentioned but not fully realized. Furthermore, the leaders frequently design strategies and solutions without the input of the communities served.

Community engagement tools and strategies exist that leaders can use to, for example, initiate relationships, identify power structures, understand systems, manage conflict, clarify responsibilities, break down silos, align goals, and, most importantly, establish trust. In adaptive leadership, having a series of accessible tools and strategies is essential for rapid decision making and planning.

There exists a wide range of engagement tools and strategies, many of which originated or was derived from organizational psychology or leadership theory. While most strategies or tools are delivered by trained professionals, the following is a brief description of a sample of engagement resources and examples of their utility.

Appreciative Inquiry

Appreciative inquiry (AI) is a concept that builds on what works and then replicates it through constructive communication. It is a strengths-based approach and method for promoting transformative change. Cooperrider and Srivastva (1987) elucidated the concept of AI through the following question:

> How can we better inquire into organization existence in ways that are economically, humanly, and ecologically significant, that is, in ways that increasingly help people discover, dream, design, and transform toward the greatest good? (p. 154)

Within its four-dimensional cycle is a positive core that places the organization at the center of its assets. *Discover* (the best of what is), *dream* (envisioning or articulating what might be), *design* (co-constructing what should be the ideal), and *destiny* (experimenting collectively what it can be) are the cycle components. AI uses a strength rather than a deficit approach. In health care, AI has promoted positive change through workforce engagement and organizational learning (Trajkovski et al., 2013). AI is a useful strategy when an organization or community relationship is stagnant or a focus on the deficits keep the partnership from creating change.

> Example: A community-academic team is unable to move forward in a partnership because of a lack of clarity of the roles and communication barriers. Instead of unpacking the barriers, an AI approach tries to discover the true desire so that the conversation continues, and trust can be built. AI: "What do you really want from this partnership? What are your greatest hopes and dreams?" Deficit: "What barriers did you experience in the partnership?"

Charrettes

A charrette is an intensive workshop or session where key stakeholders are convened, build on each other's thoughts and ideas, and develop a solution to a specific problem (Lennertz & Lutzenhiser, 2006). This structured, in-depth de-intensification model has five stages: (1) *empathize* (work to understand the people for whom you are trying to find a solution), (2) *define* (clearly articulate the problem), (3) *ideate* (brainstorm as many creative ideas as possible), (4) *prototype* (create representations of the types of identified solutions), and (5) *test* (illicit feedback on the prototypes) (Klamerus et al., 2019; Lennertz & Lutzenhiser, 2006). Charrettes are useful not only when the partnerships are stagnant but also when tension exists and an approach toward consensus is necessary for making collective progress in a program or initiative.

> Example: Reducing the burden of receiving food vouchers to make purchases at a farmers' market. The location and time for getting the vouchers conflict with recipients' work schedules. A charrette is implemented to identify the inefficiencies in the process, the gaps in communication, and a series of ideas for solutions.

Community Engagement Studio

A community engagement studio is a consultative method designed for researchers to garner input from multiple stakeholders, including patients, caregivers, health-care providers, community members, and nonresearcher stakeholders (Joosten et al., 2015). The community-engagement studio faculty and staff team use their expertise to recruit the stakeholders for the research who are seeking to use the service, thus minimizing the researchers' burden of time to convene the group. While relationship building is important to the process, it occurs at the studio session through the facilitation team. The stakeholders have a lived experience pertinent to the specific topic raised by the researcher. A 2-hour face-to-face facilitated meeting is held. A co-learning experience is fostered through the process, and a summary is compiled and used to guide the next phases of the research effort. This approach is useful when a researcher is seeking guidance on where to start with a population and/or topic for which they are unfamiliar.

> Example: A researcher seeks to understand the systemic barriers to home care for elders after a stay in the hospital. A community engagement studio may include transportation service representation, providers from the hospital, caregivers, supermarket managers, pharmacists, etc., as participants. The facilitation team guides the discussion so that the key issues emerge and are documented, and a plan can be put in place that includes the community's input.

Give-Get Grid

The Give-Get Grid is a partnership tool used to guide facilitated discussion that can be used for program planning (Southerland et al., 2013). It is designed to have two parties describe or list their expectations ("gets") and their contributions ("gives"). The 2 × 2 matrix is used to record the comments from the guided discussion. The use of the tool helps to build sustainable partnerships because both parties are aware up front of what each party will do and want. A list is populated in each cell of the matrix, followed by collective discussion. Negotiations for specific activities and resources become more feasible, and conflict is minimized. The tool is especially useful in clarifying roles and responsibilities, as well as the other partner's expectations.

> Example: A researcher team and a community organization seek to design a youth nutrition program for teen girls and boys who live in a food desert. The Give-Get Grid is used to spell out one of the community's expectations ("get"), which is to receive from the researcher training and compensation for assistance with recruitment and data collection. The community's "give" is access to members of the community for the project. The researcher's expectation ("get") is for the community to submit the recruitment data in a timely fashion. The researcher's contribution ("give") is training on the recruitment methods.

Stakeholder Power Analysis and Mapping

Stakeholder power analysis and mapping are methods for identifying stakeholders *who* will negatively or positively influence your program, study, or initiative; the *type* of influence they may have; and the *strategies* for receiving the most effective support possible (Carter-Edwards et al., 2015; WHO, n.d.). Through a systematic process, stakeholders are listed, reviewed, and rated based on the perceived level of support they will contribute and their level of impact during the development and execution of the program or initiative. Once the rating is complete, the stakeholders are placed on a 2 × 2 matrix that describes their power (low/high) and their interest (low/high). Stakeholders placed in the high-power/high-interest group are the most influential stakeholders to advance the work. Stakeholders with high power/low interest must be engaged so that the work can continue. Stakeholders with high interest/low power are kept informed, and those with low interest/low power should be monitored. This approach is useful for strategic planning, developing communication approaches, and developing dissemination strategies.

> Example: Use of stakeholder power analysis for developing a mobile testing unit and community health worker training program through a community of faith-based organizations to address COVID-19. Stakeholders may include pastors, health ministers, staff from the state health department, health professionals, clergy, community health workers, and hospital administrators/business staff. The facilitator notes the interest and the power of each stakeholder. Stakeholders with great interest and power include the hospital administrators who support instituting the program. Stakeholders with great power but the least interest are staff members from the health department who think the task should not include the community. Convening of the stakeholders and discussion for strategic planning and negotiation subsequently occur.

These tools and strategies represent a small number of resources available to assist leaders with engaged, inclusive strategies for promoting programs and initiatives.

SUMMARY AND RECOMMENDATIONS

This chapter provided an overview of adaptive leadership, community engagement, stakeholder-generated attributes necessary for community-engaged leads in health, a review of the current literature that combines adaptive leadership with engagement, and tools and strategies for engaged leadership for programs and initiatives. The integration of adaptive leadership and community engagement in health is a relatively new approach that requires much greater attention. For example, to the authors' knowledge, this is the first community-academic stakeholder documentation of attributes for an effective community-engaged leader in health. While the traits and skills identified are not new to leadership, they do point to a set of competencies that those with lived experiences see as essential for building the types of partnerships needed in changing health and health-care landscapes. In addition to the need for increased understanding of adaptive leadership actions in organizational settings for health professionals, the literature review also revealed a gap in the study of adaptive leadership *with* community engagement. Leaders in communities where patients reside, where trust exists, and where daily living drives behaviors must be a part of the discussion, design, and decision making within the systems that are seeking, now more than ever, methods for authentic partnership. Furthermore, the tools and strategies for engagement, while powerful and often effective, are used primarily to advance the efforts of individual studies, programs, and initiatives without a deeper understanding of how to link such leadership and engagement to systems-level change where national dialogue currently exists.

In the transformation of health and health care, there will be an increasing need for leaders with the appropriate traits and skills to adapt rapidly to impending change. Indeed, as indicated in the literature review, organizational change and engagement of staff members as essential partners for designing solutions to current pressing issues are necessary. However, there is also a critical need for transformative approaches to involve citizen leaders, respected, knowledgeable individuals who represent the best, with the communities in which they reside. Public Health 3.0, Health Care System Transformation 3.0, and the framework for Healthy People 2030 recognize the importance of achieving health equity with the participation of communities. Nevertheless, until community leadership is integral to the discussion of adaptive leadership, change will remain incremental and not sustainable.

To advance the dialogue and the work in this field, recommendations for next steps include the following:

- Engaged discussions with community leaders from multiple regions across the country on adaptive leadership, natural experiences, and lessons learned from the field
- Engaged discussions with a diverse set of stakeholders from the academic, community, faith, business, and local and state government sectors on the leverage

  points within systems that can address the drivers and social determinants of
  health
- Implementation of studies of adaptive leadership and community engagement
- Development of specific leadership training opportunities around adaptive leadership and community engagement

By making the effort to engage in necessary dialogue about such complex topics as systems change, adaptive leadership, and community engagement, social consciousness may lead to more prescriptive action for large policy-level changes. Self-reflection and bidirectional learning may help generate discussion about new structures of communication and operation in rapidly changing health environments. The dynamic nature of adaptive leadership will require us to support a new workforce to address the enormity of systems change. Community leaders must not only be a part but also integral to this movement and offered the same opportunities as others to help lead necessary change.

ACKNOWLEDGMENTS

The authors acknowledge Dana Rice, DrPH, assistant professor of public health leadership in the University of North Carolina at Chapel Hill Gillings School of Global Public Health, and Diana Derige, DrPH, director of health equity strategy and development for the American Medical Association for their tireless efforts and work with Dr. Carter-Edwards in graduate instruction for the course on Community Engagement and Leadership in Health.

REFERENCES

Alinsky, S. D. (1972). *Rules for radicals. A pragmatic primer for realistic radicals.* Vintage.

Alio, A. P., Lewis, C. A., Bunce, C. A., & Wakefield, S. (2014). Capacity building among African American faith leaders to promote HIV prevention and vaccine research. *Program Community Health Partnerships, 8*(3), 305–316.

Burns, J. M. G. (1978). *Leadership.* New York: Harper & Row.

Carter-Edwards, L. (2014). Health Care: Looking Forward. [Keynote Presentation]. East Carolina University Mills Symposium. Greenville, NC, United States.

Carter-Edwards, L., Lowe-Wilson, A., Mouw, M. S., Jeon, J. Y., Baber, C. R., Vu, M. B., & Bethell, M. (2015). Community member and stakeholder perspectives on a healthy environment initiative in North Carolina. *Prevention of Chronic Disease, 12,* E127.

Cohen, P. A., Tedesco, L. A. (2009). Willing, ready, and able? How we must exercise leadership for needed change in dental education. *Journal of Dental Education, 73*(1), 3–11.

Centers for Disease Control (CDC). (1997). *Principles of community engagement* (1st ed.). Centers for Disease Control and Prevention: CDC/ATSDR Committee on Community Engagement.

Centers for Disease Control (CDC). (2020). Health equity. www.cdc.gov/chronicdisease/health equity/index.htm

Cooperrider, D. L., & Srivastva, S. (1987). Appreciative inquiry in organizational life. In W. Pasmore & R. Woodman (Eds.), *Research in organization change and development* (Vol. 1, pp. 129–169). JAI Press.

DeSalvo, K. B., Wang, Y. C., Harris, A., Auerbach, J., Koo, D., & O'Carroll P. (2017). Public health 3.0: A call to action for public health to meet the challenges of the 21st century. *Preventing Chronic Disease, 14.* https://www.cdc.gov/pcd/issues/2017/17_0017.htm

de Zulueta, P. C. (2015). Developing compassionate leadership in health care: An integrative review. *Journal of Healthcare Leadership, 8,* 1–10.

Frerichs, L., Kim, M., Dave, G., Cheney, A., Lich, K. H., Jones, J., Cene, C. W., Varma, D. S., Schaael, J., Black, A., Striley, C. W., Vassar, S., Sullivan, G., Cottler, L. B., Brown, A., Burke, J. G., & Corbie-Smith, G. (2017). Stakeholder perspectives on creating and maintaining trust in community-academic research partnerships. *Health Education Behavior, 44*(1), 182–191.

Frey, M., Kern, R. M., Snow, J., & Curlette, W. L. (2009). Lifestyle and transformational leadership style. *Journal of Individual Psychology, 65*(3), 212–240.

Galea, S., & Abdalla, S. M. (2020, June 12). COVID-19 pandemic, unemployment, and civil unrest: Underlying deep racial and socioeconomic divides. *JAMA, 324*(3), 227–228.

Halfon, N., Long, P., Chang, D. I., Hester, J., Inkelas, M., & Rodgers, A. (2014). Applying a 3.0 transformation framework to guide large-scale health system reform. *Health Affairs (Millwood), 33*(11), 2003–2011.

Healthypeople.gov. (2020). Development of the national health promotion and disease prevention objectives for 2030. https://www.healthypeople.gov/2020/About-Healthy-People/ Development-Healthy-People-2030.

Heifetz, R. A., Grashow, A., & Linsky, M. (2009). *The practice of adaptive leadership: Tools and tactics for changing your organization and the world.* Harvard Business Press.

Heifetz, R. A., Kania, J. V., & Kramer, M. R. (2004). Leading boldly. *Stanford Social Innovation Review, 2*(3), 20–31.

Joosten, Y. A., Israel, T. L., Williams, N. A., Boone, L. R., Schlundt, D. G., Mouton, C. P., Dittus, R. S., Bernard, G. R., & Wilkins, C. H. (2015). Community engagement studios: A structured approach to obtaining meaningful input from stakeholders to inform research. *Academic Medicine, 90*(12), 1646–1650.

Klamerus, M. L., Damschroder, L. J., Sparks, J. B., Skurla, S. E., Kerr, E. A., Hofer, T. P., & Caverly, T. J. (2019). Developing strategies to reduce unnecessary services in primary care: Protocol for user-centered design charrettes. *JMIR Research Protocols, 8*(11), e15618.

Lennertz, B., & Lutzenhiser, A. (2006). *The charrette handbook: The essential guide for accelerated, collaborative community planning.* APA/Planners Press.

Mason, C., Griffin, M., & Parker, S. (2014). Transformational leadership development. *Leadership & Organization Development Journal, 35*(3), 174–194.

Maxwell, J. C. (2007). *Failing forward*. Harper Collins.

McCloskey, D. J., McDonald, M. A., Cook, J., Heurtin-Roberts, S., Updegrove, S., Sampson, D., Gutter, S., & Eder, M. (2011). Community engagement: Definitions and organizing concepts from the literature. In *Principles of community engagement* (2nd ed.). (pp. 1–42). (NIH Publication No. 11–7782). U.S. Government Printing Office. (Note there is no editor ... this is a NIH publication).

Moore, S. (2018, February 3). Transformational and adaptive leadership. *Moore Innovation and Quality Management*. https://moore-management.com/blog/f/leadership-2fdfa5be5067

Noble, J., Degesys, N. F., Kwan, E., Grom, E., Brown, C., Fahim, J., & Raven, M. (2020). Emergency department preparation for COVID-19: Accelerated care units. *Emergency Medicine Journal*, *37*(7), 402–406.

PCORI Virtual Annual Meeting: Accelerating Impact on Care and Patient-Centered Outcomes. (2020, September 16). PCORI Annual Meeting.

Petriwskyi, A., & Power, S. (2020). Supporting staff as change leaders in consumer engagement in aged care: Learnings from action research. *Journal of Nursing Management*, *28*(3), 643–652.

Raskind, I. G., Chapple-McGruder, T., Mendez, D. D., Kramer, M. R., Liller, K. D., Cilent, D., Wingate, M. S., Castrucci, B. C., Gould, E., & Stampfel, C. (2019). MCH workforce capacity: Maximizing opportunities afforded by a changing public health system. *Maternal Child Health Journal*, *23*(7), 979–988.

Snebold, L. (2015). Public health transformation: Helping local health departments navigate change through adaptive leadership. *Journal of Public Health Management Practices*, *21*(3), 310–312.

Southerland, J., Behringer, B., & Slawson, D. L. (2013). Using the give-get grid to understand potential expectations of engagement in a community-academic partnership. *Health Promotion Practice*, *14*(6), 909–917.

Trajkovski, S., Schmied, V., Vickers, M., & Jackson, D. (2013). Using appreciative inquiry to transform health care. *Contemporary Nurse*, *45*(1), 95–100.

U.S. DHHS. (2011). *Principles of community engagement* (2nd ed., Publication No. 11–7782). NIH.

Wallerstein, N., Minkler, M., Carter-Edwards, L., Avila, M., & Sanchez, V. (2015). Using community engagement, community building, and social action to improve health. In K. Glanz, B. K. Rimer, & K. Viswanath (Eds.), *Health behavior: Theory, research & practice* (5th ed., pp. 277–300). Jossey-Bass Wiley.

Weger, E. D., Vooren, N. V., Luijkx, K. G., Baan, C. A., & Drewes, H. W. (2018). Achieving successful community engagement: A rapid realist review. *BMC Health Services Research*, *18*(1). https://doi.org/10.1186/s12913-018-3090-1

WHO. (1948). 1948 constitution. https://www.who.int/governance/eb/who_constitution_en.pdf

WHO. (n.d.). *Stakeholder power analysis*. https://www.who.int/hac/techguidance/training/stakeholder%20analysis%20ppt.pdf?ua=1

Figure Credits

CHAPTER FIVE

Health Equity and Community Engagement

Monique Bethell, PhD

ADVANCING HEALTH EQUITY by reducing and eliminating health disparities and promoting social justice is one of the most complex and elusive public health challenges of the 21st century (Williams & Purdie-Vaughn, 2016). Over the last 20 years, initiatives to promote health equity have focused on upstream social policies, community economic investments, and health promotion programs that sought to increase access to social and economic opportunities and foster support for the fair distribution of health resources for the most vulnerable populations and marginalized communities. While some improvements have been made, most of the progress has been slow and fragmented. Despite the accumulation of robust literature on the social, economic, and environmental disadvantage as primary root causes of health disparities and health inequities, these could only partially account for the persistent racial ethnic differences in health risk and outcomes. The reality is that factors that contribute to patterns of poor health outcomes among racial ethnic populations are deeply entrenched, complex, interdependent, and constantly evolving. As such, future directions for advancing health equity must take into account the extent to which historical factors (e.g., racism, discrimination, and oppression) contributed to social disadvantage and how mechanisms of power and privilege were central drivers of social inequities. Furthermore, the lens of health equity must carefully examine the salient intersection of racial identity and lived experiences across populations and how they shape the intergenerational transmission of health outcomes for marginalized populations.

The nature of intersecting factors that created social disadvantage and increased vulnerability to poor health outcomes, particularly for

The year 2020 will forever be marked, not by the vision we chose to have, but by the clear sight we needed in the present moment, to reflect on the hindsight of past injustices, in order to give us the foresight to plan for a better future.

African-Americans and marginalized communities of color, became the central focus of recent events that completely transformed our vision about what how we experience health.

This is not a year that Americans and people worldwide are likely to forget. As Americans we grappled with the social and economic crisis that resulted from the widespread outbreak of the COVID-19 global pandemic that nearly crippled the world. Within months of the first U.S. case, we were once again thrown into the spotlight as Americans grappled with the deep emotions of witnessing the death of an unarmed Black man that resulted from the immense force of racialized police brutality.

As a nation and society, we struggled to come to terms with how a deeply entrenched history of racism, oppression, and discrimination collided with present social and economic disadvantage, and for many created very uncertain health futures. During a time characterized by the global impact of the COVID-19 pandemic, nationwide and global protests against racial injustice and racialized policing, and social and economic crisis, we are in the midst of a perfect storm.

The COVID-19 global pandemic clearly exposed the persistent systemic and structural inequities across historically racial ethnic and socially disadvantaged populations. The greatest impact was felt in marginalized communities that struggled to recover from the drastic and sweeping policy changes that resulted from COVID-19 recommendations and restrictions. Recent data collected from the COVID-19 pandemic revealed that racial ethnic minority groups were at increased risk for and disproportionately affected by COVID-19, which negatively impacts their health and lived experiences. Across the U.S., reports indicated that African-Americans and Latinos were three times more likely to contract COVID-19 that their White counterparts and are more than twice as likely to die from it (Wen & Sadeghi, 2020).

"It's time to refocus, reinforce, and repeat the message that health disparities exist and that health equity benefits everyone."

Disentangling the nature of advancing health equity starts by laying the foundation of core concepts that are central to understanding the dimensions of health equity, including the moral obligation to focus on social justice. Concepts such as health disparities and social determinants of health are central to ensuring that health equity is understood within the proper context of social justice. A second aspect of health equity is understanding the historical perspectives of social inequities that is centered on the impact of racism, oppression, and privilege and how they created an environment that allowed the growth and persistence of health disparities and the present reality of health inequities. Making progress towards health equity also requires a rigorous analytical approach that takes into account the intersection of multiple identities and social location that punctuate the lived experiences of population subgroups through mutually reinforcing patterns of power dynamics, discrimination, and bias. Another core feature of health equity is the need to engage in authentic dialogue and partner with communities of color and minority led organizations and apply the health equity lens process. The application of the health equity lens process can be used to empower community members to advocate for community-based solutions. And finally, in order for health equity to truly have meaningful and sustained progress, there must be adaptive leadership in public health agencies that embraces diversity and inclusivity and builds an infrastructure that supports multi-disciplinary perspectives. Adaptive leadership is the cornerstone of building the bridge between the history of injustice, the current realities of inequities, and the future of health equity.

ADVANCING HEALTH EQUITY: CORE CONCEPTS

Health equity was explicitly stated as an overarching goal of public health and health promotion in Healthy People 2020 and included as a foundational principle of Healthy People 2030. While there is no standard definition of health equity, in general, the primary theme is that it supports the right for everyone—including the most disadvantaged members of the population—to have an equal opportunity to achieve the highest attainable standard of health. Attaining health equity results when no one is disadvantaged from achieving their full potential because of their social position or other socially determined circumstances (Braveman, 2006; Whitehead, 1992; Whitehead & Dahlgren, 2006). It also reflects the absence of systematic differences in one or more aspects of health status across populations defined by social status, race/ethnicity, or geography (Sparks, 2010).

Health equity is grounded in our moral obligation to support human rights, address issues of social justice, and is centered on the belief that differences in age, gender, race, ethnicity, social class, or other socially determined circumstance should not affect the opportunities for achieving optimal health (Daniels et al., 2009; National Collaborating Centre for Determinants of Health, 2013; WHO, 2016). Despite ample evidence about the nature, distribution, and effect of social inequities, previous efforts to advance health equity have met with limited policy success. We must acknowledge that advancements in health equity cannot be driven by one-size-fits-all policy solutions that fail to account for the convergence of multiple intersecting factors that shape both the short- and long-term social, contextual, and collective experiences of marginalized populations. Effective progress toward health equity requires a shift in the dialogue, policies, and actions that align with interventions that can redistribute power and resources at the local, national, and global levels (Plamondon et al., 2019).

Social Justice: A Moral Obligation
Applying a health equity lens means that we are addressing issues of justice and fairness. From an ecological perspective, health equity is a product of the relationships that are inclusive of agents from multiple sectors of society. Social justice issues that

are reflected in health inequities stem from using social stratification as a determinant for the distribution of resources. Also known as the social gradient view of health inequalities, it means that those who are more socially and economically advantaged can attain higher levels of health than those who are poor and socially disadvantaged. As a key indicator of social inequities, the slope (or steepness) of the gradient suggests the need to examine the macrolevel factors that have a direct or indirect effect on health (Li et al., 2008).

As early as the 1970s, researchers identified the need to address social justice issues as moral and ethical issues to improve the health of minority and low-income populations. Beauchamp (1976) discussed the need to break existing ethical and political barriers that continue to unfairly protect the wealthy, powerful, and more socially advantaged members of society. The focus of social justice was on "fairness" and the benefits to society when resources are "equally distributed" to support the development of health for all citizens. However, key questions aimed at the heart of social justice advocates are what criteria should be used to make decisions about resource allocation, and how should we make decisions about priorities when resources are scarce (Powers & Faden, 2006)? Such questions appear to resonate politically controversial tones of ethics, values, and shared responsibilities.

To adequately address social justice issues from a health equity perspective, some researchers argue that contemporary public health models should seek to realign priorities and explicitly focus on those populations that have poor life prospects across multiple dimensions of public health (Powers & Faden, 2006). From this perspective, public health is charged with a moral and ethical responsibility to prioritize the distribution of resources in areas and within populations where there is a disproportionately high burden of adverse conditions and persistent health disparities. Yet, the strength of current evidence shows that policy solutions that focus on downstream solutions for addressing social disadvantage are inadequate to fully address the racialized history of injustice and trauma suffered by racial ethnic populations.

Health Disparities: Social and Structural Determinants of Health

According to Healthy People 2020, health disparities are the measurable outcomes of health differences that are linked to social, economic, or environmental disadvantage (USDHHS, 2008). They adversely affect groups of people who have systematically experienced social or economic challenges based on socially identified characteristics, such as age, gender, race/ethnicity, and socioeconomic status. The characteristics of health disparities are important to define and explicitly clarify because they influence how disadvantage becomes manifested through the social determinants of health and serve as an indicator to measure our progress toward health equity. By definition, health disparities are unfair and unjust because they put economically and socially disadvantaged groups at a further disadvantage with respect to their health (Braveman, 2014).

Social determinants of health reflect the places where people live, work, pray, and play. They are the result of social policies, discriminatory processes, and structural segmentations of social groups that reflect differences in power, privilege, and status (Braveman et al., 2011). Concentrated poverty, differences in educational quality and attainment, racialized discriminatory housing policies, and limited access to healthy food, clean air, and water are some examples of the social, environmental, and economic determinants of health that reflect how the landscape of social inequities produce health inequities. These and other structural barriers give rise to large, preventable differences in life experiences as they shape the composition of communities, social networks, and institutions and influence the nature of social relationships across social environments and impact the social conditions which are key drivers of poor health outcomes (e.g., life expectancy).

Uprooting the Foundation of Health Inequities: Historical Perspectives and Current Realities

Evidence of the persistent and widening gap of health disparities has increased the urgency to firmly understand the historical patterns of underlying root causes of health inequities and disrupt the ongoing cumulative effect of social and racial injustices that have adversely affected the health status and quality of life for socially disadvantaged populations. Plamodon (2020) acknowledges that despite having consensus about the cause, health inequities persist, which reflects an uncomfortable paradox—good intentions and good evidence do not necessarily lead to meaningful action.

Health inequities, which are measured by the persistent and widening gaps in health outcomes across socially defined population categories or groups (i.e., health disparities) that are avoidable or unfair, are the result of social, economic, and environmental disadvantage and are reflected in the social conditions in which people are born, grow, live, work, and age (Braveman, 2014; WHO, 2016). Essentially, health inequities, therefore, are the result of social conditions and economic circumstances that negatively affect health outcomes, are avoidable, and not caused by behavior or genes. The circumstances are shaped by unfair, unjust policies that govern the distribution of power and resources (Graham, 2004). They reflect structural and systemic inequalities in systemic, social, and economic inequality that result in social divisions that become manifested through social determinants of health (Bryant, 2010; Graham, 2004; Hofrichter, 2011; WHO, 2016; Singh et al., 2017).

Understandably, there are questions about the persistence of health disparities among racial-ethnic minorities and disadvantaged communities and how social disadvantages that result from systemic and structural injustices increase the risk of poor health outcomes over time. Earlier definitions of health equity and inequities were critiqued for their inability to explain persistent differences in racial ethnic health outcomes, even after accounting for differences in socioeconomic status. The core issue with the prior definition was that it proposed that systematic differences in health outcomes between groups can be reduced or eliminated by removing social and economic inequalities to advance our efforts to reduce health disparities.

However, emerging evidence has shed light on how racism, oppression, and power are interwoven with multiple social factors that are linked to disadvantage and lead to contextualized differences across population segments and groups. It is these contextualized differences rooted in social justice, racism, discrimination, and privilege that have become the starting point for researchers regarding transforming our approach to advancing health equity. Meaningful progress toward health equity means that we need to address the "entrenched racism" that contributes to sustained disparities, with an explicit focus on the complex web of social inequities (e.g., power, oppression, structured and systemic racism) as the root causes of health disparities.

Realistically, long-term success in the elimination of health disparities will require an emphasis on intervention strategies that move beyond discussions about fairness, equality, and moral responsibility. Successful strategies will have to delve into deeper territory and engage members of the community at various levels to address the power imbalances and resistance to structural changes that contribute to sustained disparities. According to Eliassen (2013), this "entrenched resistance" includes a segment of the population that benefits from maintaining a vested interest in systems and societal arrangements that see the functional advantages of the ongoing presence of health disparities. For these powerful stakeholders, there is a hidden cost for health disparities that would present greater consequences than the benefit of reducing and eliminating the conditions that support and perpetuate health disparities. Public health professionals and community partners will be required to collaborate with these stakeholders to develop alternative strategies that can minimize the potential perceived risks of socioeconomic drift (downward mobility) and social stunting (inhibiting the initial capital needed for upward mobility) (Haas et al., 2011).

Political or societal transformation encompasses the broad context of interpreting social justice issues at the macrolevel of society. It reflects the extent to which societal policies and systems are changed to support a commitment to fairness and justice in policies that affect all members of society. It also means looking at the big picture and creates a fundamental understanding of how systems, policies, and environments need to shift to synergistically create transformational impact at all levels of society.

Transforming Our Vision of Health Equity: Creating a Lasting Legacy

Although there is no universal consensus about the single best approach to reducing/eliminating health disparities, there are some key factors that must be considered when transforming our approach to advancing health equity. First, we must acknowledge that health equity is a dynamic process that requires an ongoing commitment to interdisciplinary research, encourages critical reflection about the impact of racism and discrimination on African American and marginalized communities, and integrates emerging knowledge about societal inequities using the application of a health equity lens. It also requires engaging various stakeholders in meaningful dialogue about overcoming the generational effect of historical traumas and past injustices and empowering communities to advocate for sustainable progress toward health equity. And, finally, it requires a sustained commitment of leadership to build a racially diverse workforce and public health infrastructure that is adequately prepared to adapt to environmental hazards and unforeseen public health challenges that threaten the health and well-being of vulnerable, marginalized populations.

Transforming public health and taking action to advance health equity in the 21st century requires a second paradigm shift. The initial shift from measuring differences in health outcomes across population groups, to investing in community-based solutions that address the historical inequalities and past injustices in social and economic conditions that served as precursors to understanding large gaps in health outcomes between socially stratified groups. However, emerging models suggest the need to re-examine what it means to transform health. A radical shift in making progress towards achieving health equity means undoing the harms and traumas of centuries of racism, discrimination, and oppressive power dynamics that created a legacy of disadvantage for racial ethnic populations that create systematic differences in health experiences (Plamondon, 2020). The National Science Foundation defined transformative research as "research driven by ideas that have the potential to radically change our understanding of an important scientific ... concept or leading to the creation of a new paradigm or field of science or engineering. Such research is also characterized by its challenge to current understanding or its pathway to new frontiers" (NSF, 2007, para. 1).

Over the past decade, these transformation models have received broad multi-agency support at the federal and global levels (Dankwa-Mullan et al., 2010). In a call to action, John Ruffin, director of the National Institute on Minority Health and Health Disparities, addressed the complex nature of health disparities. He said that we have a "moral obligation in our society to do what is necessary to improve health" (Ruffin, 2010, p. S9). He considered this a time for transformation and emphasized the importance of community and individual empowerment, both nationally and globally. This statement is further reinforced by global efforts to transform public health by ensuring that the intended beneficiaries of public health programs are able to negotiate their level of inclusion in the decisions about policies and resources that are intended to affect the health of their communities. More specifically, McFarlane et al. (2000) posited that the essence of transforming public health with a focus on community engagement requires that the framework be re-crafted. This requires locating organized and active communities at the center. The communities become initiators and managers of their own health. This creates a paradigm where non-governmental, governmental, private sector and stakeholders operate on the periphery. They listen and learn from the communities and collectively discuss and make decisions.

The Next Generation of Health Equity Research: Interdisciplinary Approaches

Concerns about the widening gap in health disparities across racial ethnic populations and marginalized communities have increased the need to rethink the approach to addressing health inequity, in an effort to advance social justice and advance health equity. Communities and public health practitioners across the nation continue to face ongoing challenges in removing the structural and systemic barriers that limit opportunities to promote health in disadvantaged communities. While policy and programmatic solutions have shown modest improvements in some health outcomes, researchers continue to search for solutions that extend beyond marginal progress. Previous research on the social determinants of health as root causes of health disparities has failed to capture the effect of mutually reciprocating social factors that intersect to maintain the status quo.

The use application of intersectionality approaches allows researchers to broaden their perspectives on health disparities by examining the context of oppressive systems of power that undermine progress toward health equity. It provides an opportunity to understand how social and political conditions are governed by the organization of power and influence in society and how they work together to shape human experiences (Collins & Blige, 2016).

Rather than simply examining the effect of upstream factors on downstream outcomes, intersectionality approaches enourage researchers to consider the interlocking systems of oppression (e.g., racism, sexism, power dynamics) that shape the experiences and lives of population subgroups and limit the life chances of individuals based on multiple social identities (Green et al., 2017). Critiques of social determinants frameworks have focused on the idea that contextual forces, such as racism, discrimination, and social class, do not operate in isolation but interact with each other in a reciprocal manner that is mutually reinforced over time by underlying power dynamics. Opponents of the linear approach to social determinants frameworks as the cornerstone of understanding health inequities have acknowledged that disparities are generated through multiple intervening factors and social risk mechanisms that will vary over time.

Lopez and Gadsden (2016) eloquently summarized the literature about the potential power of using intersectionality as a transformational paradigm for addressing the relationship between social determinants of health and health equity. They argued that the power of intersectionality lies in two primary domains: (1) it provides critical knowledge that raises questions about the meaning and relationship between social categories and intersecting systems of social categories and oppression (Bowleg, 2008; Collins, 2008, 2015; Collins & Bilge, 2016), and (2) it focuses on power relations at the individual, institutional, and global levels, along with the convergence of experiences in a given sociohistorical context and situational landscape. These domains adequately lay the groundwork for understanding how intersecting factors of oppression (e.g., racism, sexism, ethnocentrism) interact to produce major differences in the lived experiences of individuals with multiple overlapping identities that become embodied and shape the social determinants of health. By reframing the discussion of examining social disadvantage as an outcome of individual behaviors and shifting the focus to the system of power dynamics and oppression that is unique to the lived experience of people with intersecting identities, questions about patterns and factors that shape social determinants become firmly anchored in a social justice and racial justice framework.

The intersection of the various forms of racism that are manifested through discriminatory practices and behaviors (e.g., implicit bias, microaggressions) are concepts that become embodied in the experience of minority populations, which interact with social status and social position to form the basis of social identity. These social identities are fortified by power and dominance structures that operate through established social systems and reinforce the inequalities that limit life opportunities.

Moreover, as racism becomes internalized and embedded in the body through social and environmental stressors, those stressors can shift the trajectory of health over the life span. For this reason, it is important to give equal consideration to the effect of life-course theory on health equity.

DISCUSSION QUESTIONS

- What are some of the intersecting power dynamics that contributed to the increased risk of exposure and infection of COVID-19 in African Americans?
- How do existing power structures and dynamics contribute to differences in exposure to COVID-19 or other diseases, infection, and mortality rates for African American men and women?
- How should researchers examine the intersecting role of racism, discrimination, and social exclusion (e.g., race, gender, age, disability), economic, and behavioral factors to determine the effect of COVID-19 on minority communities?

Intergenerational Transmission of Health Disparities

Intersectionality concepts are useful for broadening our understanding of the complex network of interacting social factors that contribute to ongoing health disparities. However, the explanation is incomplete without understanding how these disparities are transmitted over time and across generations. Contemporary health researchers have started to examine how life-course perspectives are central to understanding differences in risk exposure at different stages of human development and how these perspectives alter health trajectories within and across generations (Jones et al., 2019).

Developmental life-course perspectives help to explain how socially patterned exposures during childhood, adolescence, and early adult life influence disease risks in middle-aged and older adults (Kuh et al., 2003). Life-course epidemiologists argue that social factors at different life stages create differential health outcomes depending on the timing and duration of exposure. The integration of life-course theory for advancing health equity is particularly relevant for examining the ecological and historical causes of disease and illness during sensitive growth. For example, environmental exposure to undernutrition or maternal psychological stress during the critical periods of fetal development may have long-term effects on chronic disease outcomes in adulthood by altering genetic programming or the structure and function of organs or body systems (Ben-Shlomo & Kuh, 2002).

Combined with intersectionality approaches, we have an integrated multidimensional framework that demonstrates how health trajectories are shaped by early life experiences that influence developmental processes and outcomes. Scientists studying social epigenetics have come to understand how our history becomes embedded in our genes and how genetic expression influences our bodies' ability to adapt to environmental threats.

Across the life span, health outcomes are further affected by overlapping and mutually reinforcing social factors that have the potential to intersect with multiple social identities at various stages throughout the life span. These intersections may alter the experiences of social and environmental conditions that in turn can alter health trajectories. For example, African American women have multiple social identities and experience various levels of disadvantages across multiple indicators that place them at higher risk for poor health outcomes. Studies have shown that African American women are more likely to experience chronic and perpetual social stressors, such as higher poverty rates, lower wealth, and increased exposure to chronic psychological stressors, such as racism, sexism, and oppression. As a result, African American women experience higher rates of chronic stress-related morbidities than other racial-ethnic gender groups (e.g., Black men). Despite higher mortality rates in African American men and lower life expectancy, African American women are more likely to have a lower quality of life and higher health burdens. Insights from the emergent fields of social epigenetics help provide a better understanding of how adverse childhood experiences can genetically modify the interaction of cells that influence growth and development, as well as increase vulnerability to various diseases and health conditions. Contributions from social neuroscience also demonstrate how chronic social, psychological, or environmental stressors can affect the development of neuronal pathways that influence individual responses to environmental stimuli.

DISCUSSION QUESTIONS

- What are some current trends in public health that can have a lasting effect across multiple generations?
- What are some of the intersecting social, structural, and systemic factors that pose barriers and obstacles to developmental processes?
- How can power dynamics and social policies that promote inequality negatively affect health across the life span and long-term community health?

With growing interest in expanding the understanding of social inequalities to include intersectionality and intergenerational approaches that help to explain differences in health disparities among population groups, the application of a health equity lens to guide the development of health research, policy, and programs has greatly improved.

Setting the Stage for Advancing Health Equity Through Multilevel Community Engagement

Now that we have a deeper and broader understanding of the dimensions of health equity and the factors that contribute to health inequities, we need to explore the strategies needed to engage and mobilize communities to address issues of unjust social conditions that have adversely affected the health of community residents. Seen as a foundational principle for public health planning, promotion, and research, health equity researchers emphasize the importance of developing sustainable relationships with communities to inform public health decision making. Research also indicates that community engagement is most effective when there is an intentional and explicit focus on an "active process of change and transformation rather than merely static outcomes for health improvements" (Rifkin, 2003, p. 169). Community engagement involves the dynamic relationships and mutually beneficial exchange of resources that occur between community members and local health departments (Morgan & Lifshay, 2006).

Community engagement, defined as "the process of working collaboratively with and through groups of people affiliated by geographic proximity, special interest or similar situations to address issues affecting the well-being of people" (CDC, 1997, p. 9), has become a powerful vehicle for addressing health inequities. From a broader sociological perspective, communities have been instrumental in progressive social change movements and are likely to be an active force in bringing about the policy, systems, and environmental changes that are needed to tackle the complex issues related to health disparities.

To effectively tackle these complex issues, local health departments must be willing to expand their ability to effectively engage communities to determine public health priorities and create plans that incorporate local community concerns. Guided by a broad vision of improving health and well-being for all individuals, combined with the mobilization of the community through the process of mutually beneficial engagement, long-term solutions can emerge that are an evolving response to the changing population's health issues. Essentially, public health must shift to adopt transformational strategies to address major challenges in the 21st century and work through and with the communities to stimulate change that addresses the elimination of health inequities.

As public health leaders, we need to deconstruct the concept of community engagement to construct a conceptual framework for how it is applied to efforts to achieve health equity. Within the public health context, modern community engagement focuses on working with various segments of the community, particularly populations within underserved, disadvantaged communities. Consequently, public health leaders are increasing their efforts to expand strategic partnerships and collaborate with communities to explore innovative and sustainable strategies for eradicating health disparities. Despite the disproportional burden of disparities suffered by low-income minority communities, traditional policy structures have often excluded communities from participating in the dialogue about public health solutions. With fewer resources available, more restrictive statutory mandates, and increased political pressure, public health leaders must be willing to engage the community as a partner in program planning and service delivery rather than simply being a recipient of services.

While this is a standard desirable outcome for public health interventions, there are four levels of community engagement that must be taken into account when developing a transformative approach to addressing issues of health inequity: (1) *multisector partnership development*, (2) *community collaboration*, (3) civic leadership, and (4) *community outreach and mobilization*. While community collaboration and community outreach/mobilization are commonly defined notions that are described in various public health literature, the focus here is on understanding multisector partnerships and civic leadership.

Multisector Partnerships

Notions of inclusion, partnership, and intention serve as cornerstones for how the meaning of community engagement is transformed as a model to address health equity in the 21st century. Effective solutions require interorganizational coordination and collaboration by pooling resources, talents, and strategies from a broad range of sectors (Woulfe et al., 2010).

Multisector partnership is considered a subset of community engagement that focuses on the collaboration between agencies to address a particular societal issue or achieve social improvements (Sparks, 2010). Collaboration refers to the process of system change, shifting the focus from responsibilities and effectiveness of individual institutions to collective efforts of multiple institutions to affect population health (Woulfe et al., 2010). The WHO Commission on Social Determinants of Health (WHO,

2008) recommended that public health leaders collaborate with other sectors of government and society to more effectively influence factors that affect health and well-being.

Civic Leadership

The process of civic leadership has been demonstrated to effectively develop a more informed and engaged public, with views and opinions that have been transformed by a deeper understanding of the complex issues that need to be addressed (Abelson et al., 2003; Dolan et al., 1999; Luskin et al., 2002; Pesce et al., 2011). Recent research on community-based participation in democratic processes has further legitimized the policy decisions and political actions that represent community interests. These actions have been shown to lead to increased public trust and a growing appreciation of the critical importance of seeking collaborative approaches to addressing the social determinants of health. Rifkin (2003) argued that people who engage in civil and political actions can forge new futures and gain greater confidence when they are fully committed and their efforts to contribute to changing situations are successful. However, she noted that the converse was also true. When communities do not act or allow inequities to continue in existence, this leads to poor health outcomes, as well as other adverse consequences.

Beyond the increased awareness of the need for community input as an essential component for developing equitable public health solutions, it is also critical to understand the different strategic and tactical approaches to community engagement (Table 5.1). The premise for a multilayered approach was to develop a way to further improve the efficiency and effectiveness of communication across community partners. As an extension of public health efforts to create meaningful relationships in the community, it became essential to understand how the different levels of community can offer different values. By creating an awareness of the depth and breadth of the community, public health leaders have the foundation for creating integrative experiences and developing a comprehensive approach to health equity.

TABLE 5.1 *Strategic and Tactical Approaches to Community Engagement*

LEVEL OF ENGAGEMENT	PURPOSE	STRATEGIC APPROACH	TACTICAL APPROACH
Multisector Partnerships	Extend the reach of government agencies	Systems change	Community investment Contribute to vision
Coalition/Collaboration	Focus on neighborhood-based and community initiatives	Community connections and relationships Community capacity	Trust building Shared power Consensus building
Civic Leadership	Engage in the democratic (policy) process	Stakeholder inclusion in equitable governance	Empowerment Access to decision making
Community Outreach	Social networking approaches	Social action Mobilization	Community readiness Unity

Engaging Communities to Address Health Disparities: Application of a Health Equity Lens

This section provides a road map for the implementation of a community-based engagement strategy to encourage dialogue and action on reducing and eliminating health disparities. The application of a health equity lens is an important strategy that can be used to help guide and facilitate the discussion with communities on equity solutions that are relevant to the needs, resources, and conditions of the community. Each part of the health equity lens provides the goals, strategies, and processes through which transformation occurs.

PART 1—Identify the Issues

It has become well-known among local public health practitioners that health, disease, and death are not randomly distributed in our communities. Poor health and premature death are concentrated among people with low income and people residing in certain places (Iton, 2009). Social epidemiologists acknowledge and study the etiology and distribution of social determinants and their contribution to health inequities. It is important to learn as much about the community conditions, health status of residents, and resource capacity prior to engaging them in the strategic planning process. Tracking health indicators by race or other sociodemographic characteristics provides important information about the disparate outcomes of people within different social categories (Hofrichter, 2011). The various forms of data can be grouped into three primary categories: (1) disease surveillance (disparities, population health indicators), (2) sociogeographic (place-based data, social and economic conditions), and (3) context (policy, environment, systems).

Clearly identify disparities in both health outcomes and community conditions across population groups and geographic areas in the jurisdiction through the use of existing data, community input, and environmental assessments.

- What population or geographical area has the disproportional burden of poor health outcomes or the highest health disparities?
- What are the main risk factors related to the health outcome or condition?
- What social/economic/political/environmental conditions have led to these poor health outcomes?
- What are the barriers that have existed to prevent the reduction or elimination of health disparities?
- What are the size and severity of the health outcomes? What are the priority indicators?
- How are community priorities, needs, resources, and concerns identified and documented?

PART 2—Build/Strengthen State and Local Partnerships and Promote Community Engagement

The process of engaging community members is designed to create an informed and "engaged" public that demonstrates views that have been transformed by a deeper understanding of the issues being addressed (Abelson et al., 2003; Dolan et al., 1999). Research conducted by Pesce et al. (2011) found that deliberately engaging groups about ways to address the social determinants of health can change both participant attitudes and yield informed priorities that might guide public policy aimed at affordable and effective ways to reduce health disparities. They also found that previous efforts to engage communities around public health interventions have not been as successful, usually because stakeholders believed there were more pressing issues, alternate issues could accomplish the same goal, or only a small segment of the community would benefit from the investment.

Ensure that the leadership team and coalition include voices of populations/areas identified in Step 1 and that there are meaningful opportunities for community engagement in the development of strategies.

- What existing coalitions or agencies are currently addressing issues related to the strategy?
- Do current partnerships include members of the community directly affected by this issue?
- Have population(s)/area(s) experiencing health disparities been engaged in efforts to identify possible barriers and unintended consequences of the proposed strategy?
- Does the coalition include traditional and nontraditional partners (e.g., business owners, managers, transportation, housing)?
- What are the power dynamics that must be addressed with the inclusion of nontraditional partners and community members?
- Are meetings held in the community and during times that community members are available?
- Is leadership or civic engagement training available to community members to develop their capacity to participate in the decision-making process?
- What is the plan for communication both to and from the community members and coalitions?

PART 3—Select Intervention (or Multiple Interventions) to Address Each Strategy

Using evidence-based approaches to guide the planning of public health interventions indicates the need to develop rational and transparent approaches to setting priorities. Previous efforts to approach public health interventions have depended on a single criterion to address outcomes, such as individual disease conditions, evidence-based medicine, and/or risk factors. However, the reality is that policy makers, planners, and institutions use multiple criteria for making decisions about resource distribution and policy. However, while using multiple criteria for intervention planning is critical, it does not cover all the information that is relevant to address community issues, particularly from an equity perspective.

Ensure the selection, design, and implementation of interventions are linked to the disparities identified. Consider the following when reviewing proposed strategies:

- Is the strategy <u>TARGETED</u> to a population group(s)/area(s) experiencing health disparities?
- Does the strategy rely on <u>SITE SELECTION</u> (e.g., it requires selecting X number of multiunit housing developments, or assigning X number of worksites for smoking policies, or creating X number of farmers' markets)?
- Is the strategy <u>JURISDICTION-WIDE</u> (i.e., across county/multiple counties), or does it include everyone in a specified geographical area?

Depending on the previous strategy selection criteria, consider the following when selecting specific activities to achieve the strategy:

- Is the objective measurable?
- Have members of the population experiencing disparities been involved in the planning and design of the intervention?
- Are activities/messages/materials culturally tailored to the unique needs of the population group(s)/area(s) experiencing health disparities, and are potential barriers addressed?
- Do selection criteria of sites reflect populations/areas with the highest burden? If not, are the selection criteria logical and justified (e.g., assessments, surveys)?
- What are the potential barriers, challenges, impacts, and unintended consequences that could arise because of the interventions?
- Are barriers identified regarding implementation and enforcement addressed?
- Have potential unintended consequences been considered and accounted for in proposed activities?

PART 4—*Develop and Expand Monitoring and Evaluation Systems*

Conducting an evaluation using a health equity lens focuses on shifting how empirical inquiry or research is produced, interpreted, and used, as well as understanding what constitutes "evidence." Public health surveillance systems have sharpened their measurement tools over the last few decades to capture key indicators of health, such as life expectancy, burden of disease, and injury for a population and relative subgroups. However, within the scope of understanding the cumulative effect of social-economic disadvantage, public health inquiry needs to cast a wider net to identify sources of data that can serve as a basis for understanding the complex factors that affect health in different settings for different populations.

Review evaluation and monitoring plans and questions to ensure that health equity–related efforts will be measured. In addition, ensure that appropriate data will be collected to conduct sub-analyses for assessing the differential effect of each strategy across population group(s)/area(s), as well as the overall effect of strategies on reducing health disparities.

- What data needs to be tracked or monitored? How frequently? What key variables will you use to identify and track populations experiencing health disparities?
- Are there existing sources of data available from partner agencies that can provide information about contextual factors?
- Are there other sources of data that are needed? What are some other ways and mechanisms for gathering data (e.g., surveys, photovoice, community coalition meeting notes, service mapping)?

PART 5—Develop a Plan for Sustainability

Committing to a goal of health equity means creating lasting and enduring policies, systems, and environmental changes designed to improve the social and economic conditions that impact the overall health of the population. When developing solutions that address inequities, there is a general consensus that health improvements for poor and marginalized populations are not successful when they depend on single interventions (Rifkin, 2003). Rather, researchers believe that success is more likely to depend on long-term structural improvements that ensure continuity in programs and services. Further, instead of investing in programs and services that provide temporary solutions and produce only modest gains—if any—there is a growing trend toward creating long-lasting substantive structural changes. Particularly in a climate of reduced budgets for programs and services, continued reinvestment in individualized public health programs are unlikely to succeed without support from the communities affected by the proposed intervention (Johnson et al., 2009). In fact, governments are increasingly calling for public health departments to enhance dialogue between community residents and local governments to develop concrete long-lasting policy interventions that effectively address the needs of the community (Pesce et al., 2011).

Leading the Way: Adaptive Leadership and Workforce Diversity

The future of public health will largely depend on the abilities of leaders who understand how to navigate the challenges, barriers, and obstacles presented by various health problems. From a leadership perspective, a transformational approach to addressing health disparities requires broad investment in adaptive leadership that emphasizes community engagement as a core element to inform evidence-based practices, social action, and policy changes needed to close the disparities gap. It further emphasizes an ongoing need to build trust and open communication through bridge building and power sharing that lead to viable health equity solutions (Morgan & Lifshay, 2006).

Encouraging transformative change in public health means that we begin to foster innovative thinking about how we collaborate with communities to achieve a greater collective effect on chronic disease prevention. Embedded in this philosophy is the concept of adaptive leadership (Heifetz, 1994). The adaptive leadership model is proposed as a method for creating long-term sustainable changes, where decision making is inclusive of stakeholders affected by the problem or issue and a key element of transformational change. Heifetz and Linsky (2004) stressed that leadership is the "activity of mobilizing people to tackle the toughest problems and do the adaptive work necessary to achieve progress" (p. 24). More specifically, this model provides a framework for understanding how public health practitioners can promote leadership that results in creative problem solving, fosters successful and sustainable changes, and supports positive changes in the relationship between the organization and its stakeholders (Glover et al., 2002).

Perhaps one of the most important aspects of advancing health equity is to have an institution that supports and integrates health equity principles into all aspects of the organization. The missions, policies, staffs, contracts, partnerships, and training opportunities are some examples of ways that institutions can show a commitment to preparing their workforces for achieving health equity and reducing health disparities. Two key ways that organizations can build their capacity to promote health equity is through (1) workforce diversity and (2) enhanced training opportunities.

WORKFORCE DIVERSITY

A culturally and linguistically diverse workforce is a key component in the process of planning programs that have the goals of achieving health equity and reducing health disparities. Workforce diversity ensures that the population being served is represented by the professionals who can serve as cultural brokers or liaisons to the community and can translate the unique needs or perspectives as needed.

Institutional or organizational transformation occurs because of challenging and changing previously held organizational assumptions, systems, policies, and practices. This reorientation to public health practice provides a starting point for practitioners to be adequately prepared to address racism, discrimination, and power dynamics as fundamental causes of health inequities (Hofrichter & Bhatia, 2010). Creating diversity and inclusion in the public health workforce also entails ensuring an institutional commitment to creating a diverse professional environment where staff members are exposed to culturally appropriate professional development skills that prepare them to work with less-advantaged communities where resources are low and tensions are high. Understanding the value of culturally relevant communication and developing skills to engage in courageous discussions about past social injustice perpetuated by a lack of social trust are critical for any public health professional preparing to address health equity and health disparities. Institutional policies that reflect fairness and equality are, by their nature, transformative, particularly when employees are valued and respected for their diversity of beliefs, skills, and contributions. These institutional values become translated into the treatment of consumers, community members, and anyone receiving services.

SUMMARY

Transforming public health in the 21st century requires a multifaceted approach that is defined by explicit efforts to reduce social injustices, address social determinants, and close the gap in health outcomes of those who are economically and socially disadvantaged.

Simply stated, health equity is the goal, health disparities are the measurement of progress toward that goal, social justice is the framework for action planning, and community engagement is a key ingredient for ensuring the sustainability of health improvements. At the intersection of health and policy, environmental and systems change are community-engaged interventions, which are informed by multiple disciplines, integrate social epidemiology practices, apply adaptive leadership principles, and promote effective behavior change strategies. Underlying these concepts is a focus on culturally tailored, contextually specific, evidence-based interventions, which reflect a moral and ethical commitment to investing in sustainable health improvements.

Using the socioecological framework to guide the planning, design, and implementation of health equity interventions further acknowledges the need to address overlapping structural inequalities and social barriers that are persistent and affect individuals and communities at multiple levels. Also significant are the perceptions of the community members regarding their experiences with the changes that result from the new wave of policies and practices within their community. While there has been a growing acceptance that changes are needed to achieve health equity (Beadle & Graham, 2011), do the priorities for resource allocation reflect the needs and concerns of the communities?

Summarizing the implementation framework for the National Partnership for Action to End Health Disparities, Beadle and Graham (2011) succinctly stated, "Collective action to end health disparities is possible if individuals and organizations, those with a vested interest are engaged in the work as equal partners ... and a collaborative approach to problem-solving" (para. 13).

Transforming public health leadership to address the complex challenges of the 21st century requires alignment with state and national efforts to reduce health disparities, combined with a profound sense of urgency and an intentional commitment to build structural capacity and engage communities in constructive dialogue about the range of issues and possible solutions. Building consensus and implementing sustainable change that leads to long-term health improvements is not an easy process and will not occur overnight. However, the steps we take today can lead to progress toward providing opportunities for transforming the health of communities and leading public health practice into the 21st century.

COVID-19 AND HEALTH INEQUITIES: A CASE STUDY

The public health crisis caused by the novel coronavirus disease of 2019 (COVID-19) has had an unprecedented and devastating effect on the United States and the global community. While many countries and populations have dealt with the widespread burden of the COVID-19 global pandemic, for the United States, the devastation was particularly evident among vulnerable, racial-ethnic minority populations in marginalized, underserved communities. Within the first few months of the pandemic, as illness and mortality rates started to rise rapidly across the United States, it quickly became evident that African Americans and poor, marginalized communities of color would be hit the hardest. Elevated risks of infection, spread, and fatality were disproportionately higher among minorities with underlying chronic conditions, elderly, disabled, and individuals who were susceptible to acute viral infections. Social risk factors, such as poverty, living in overcrowded housing situations, inadequate availability of resources, lack of insurance, and limited access to care meant that previously existing inequities worsened the destructive effect of this disease.

Heightened awareness about the disproportionate effect of COVID-19, particularly among poor African American populations, placed a spotlight on the effect of decades of structural inequities and social systems that were racist, unfair, and unjust, which left minority populations more vulnerable to conditions that increased their risk for becoming infected with the virus and dying from it. Long-standing health disparities among minority populations were further amplified by the acute social and economic conditions that left minority and low-income communities struggling and more vulnerable to the detrimental effects of COVID-19. By examining the effect of COVID-19 within a sociohistorical context, it becomes clear that the devastation caused by the COVID-19 pandemic extends far beyond the health dangers presented by the risk of infection. Social distancing recommendations combined with shelter in place, remote working, and stay-at-home policies enacted to control the spread of the virus left many minorities socially and economically helpless and paralyzed the health and well-being of communities. Once again, the health outcomes of poor low-income minorities were collateral damage as COVID-19 exposed the extent to which policies, systems, and structures failed to support the growing challenges faced by marginalized populations and communities of color. Income inequality, racial inequities, and social disadvantage are at the intersection of power and privilege.

Preliminary data gathered by national, state, and local agencies reveal interesting patterns that demonstrate the need to more carefully examine the convergence of intersecting factors that contribute to differences in infection and mortality rates across race/ethnicity, gender, age, and socioeconomic status categories. Initial data estimates show that while African American women are more likely to have higher rates of infection, African American men were more likely to die from the disease. The risk of infection was also higher for those aged 65 and over, individuals with underlying chronic conditions, health-care workers deemed "essential employees," and individuals in environments without access to personal protective equipment. COVID-19 has the potential to have a profound long-term effect on the social and economic viability of communities and alter the health trajectories of minority populations. Placed within a sociohistorical context, the COVID-19 pandemic has also changed health behaviors, including the way populations access health-care services and patterns of social engagement. Clearly, researchers will need to draw on emerging interdisciplinary approaches to adequately examine how these diverse and mutually influencing factors work together to affect health outcomes.

REFERENCES

Abelson, J., Forest, P. G., Eyles, J., Smith, P., Martin, E., & Gauvin, F. P. (2003). Deliberations about deliberative methods: Issues in the design and evaluation of public participation processes. *Social Science & Medicine, 57*(2), 239–251.

Assari, S. (2018). *Health disparities due to diminished return among black Americans: Public policy solutions. Society for the Psychological Study of Social Issues, 12*(1), 112–145. https://doi.org/10.1111/sipr.12042

Beadle, M. R., & Graham, G. N. (2011). Collective action to end health disparities. *American Journal of Public Health, 101*(1) 16–18.

Beauchamp, D. E. (1976). Public health as social justice. *Inquiry, 13*(1), 3–14.

Ben-Shlomo, Y., & Kuh, D. (2002). A life course approach to chronic disease epidemiology: conceptual models, empirical challenges and interdisciplinary perspectives. *International Journal of Epidemiology, 31*(2), 285–293.

Bowleg, L. (2008). When Black + Lesbian + Woman ≠ Black Lesbian Woman: The Methodological Challenges of Qualitative and Quantitative Intersectionality Research. *Sex Roles, 59*, 312–325.

Brassolotto, J., Raphael, D., & Baldeo, N. (2014). Epistemological barriers to addressing the social determinants of health among public health professionals in Ontario, Canada: A qualitative inquiry. *Critical Public Health, 24*, 321–336.

Braveman, P (2014). What are health disparities and health equity? We need to be clear. *Public Health Reports, 129*(Suppl 2), 5–8.

Braveman, P., Egerter, S., & Williams, D. R. (2011). The social determinants of health: Coming of age. *Annual Review of Public Health, 32*, 381–398.

Bryant, T. (2010). Politics, public policy and health inequalities. In D. Raphael, T. Bryant, & M. Rioux (Eds.), *Staying alive: Critical perspectives on health, illness, and health care* (pp. 239–265). Canadian Scholars' Press.

Center for Disease Control and Prevention (CDC). (1997). Principles of community engagement (1st ed.). CDC/ATSDR Committee on Community Engagement.

Collins, P. H. (2008). *Black feminist thought: Knowledge, consciousness, and the politics of empowerment.* New York: Routledge.

Collins, P. H. (2015). *Intersectionality's definitional dilemmas.* Annual Review of Sociology *41*, 1–20. https://doi.org/10.1146/annurev-soc-073014-112142

Collins, P. H., & Blige, S. (2016). *Intersectionality.* Malden, MA: Polity Press.

Collins, P. H., & Bilge, S. (2016). *Intersectionality.* Cambridge, UK: Polity Press.

Dalton, H. J., & Farley, J. H. (2017). Racial disparities in cervical cancer: Worse than we thought. Cancer, 123: 915–916. doi:10.1002/cncr.30501

Dankwa-Mullan, I., Rhee, K., Stoff, D. M., Pohlhaus, J., Francisco, S., Stinson, N., & Ruffin, J. (2010). Moving toward paradigm-shifting research in health disparities through translational, transformational, and transdisciplinary approaches. *American Journal of Public Health, 100*(1), 19–24.

Dolan, P., Cookson, R., & Ferguson, B. (1999). Effect of discussion and deliberation on the public's views of priority setting in health care: Focus group study. *BMJ, 318*(7188), 916–919.

Eliassen, A. H. (2003). The usefulness of health disparity: Stumbling blocks in the path of social equity. *Journal of Community Positive Practices, XIII*(1), 3–25.

Glover, W., Friedman, H., & Jones, G. (2002). Adaptive Leadership: When Change Is Not Enough (Part One).

Graham, H. (2004). Social determinants and their unequal distribution: Clarifying policy understandings. *Milbank Quarterly, 82*(1), 101–124.

Green, M. A., Evans, C. R., & Subramanian, S. V. (2017). Can intersectionality theory enrich population health research? *Social Science & Medicine, 178*, 214–216

Haas, S. A., Glymour, M. M., & Berkman, L. F. (2011). Childhood health and labor market inequality over the life course. *Journal of Health and Social Behavior, 52*(3), 298–313.

Heifetz, R. A. (1994). *Leadership without easy answers.* Belknap Press of Harvard University Press.

Heifetz, R. A., & Linsky, M. (2004). When leadership spells danger. *Educational Leadership, 61*(7), 33–37.

Hofrichter, R., & Bhatia, R. (Eds.) (2010). *Tackling health inequities through public health practice: Theory to action.* Oxford University Press.

Hofrichter, R. (2011). *Health equity: Exploring the social and economic dimensions.* America's Health Rankings. www.americashealthrankings.org

Iton, A. (2009). *The challenge of local public health practice in eliminating health disparities.* The Opportunity Agenda. http://www.opportunityagenda.org/mapping

Johnson, N., Oliff, P., & Williams, E. (2009). *An update on state budget cuts: At least 41 states have imposed cuts that hurt vulnerable residents; federal economic recovery funds and state tax increases are reducing the harm.* Center on Budget and Policy Priorities. https://www.cbpp.org/research/an-update-on-state-budget-cuts

Jones, N. L., Gilman, S. E., Cheng, T. L., Drury, S. S., Hill, C. V., & Geronimus, A. T. (2019). Life course approaches to the causes of health disparities. *American Journal of Public Health, 109*(S1), S48–S55. https://doi.org/10.2105/AJPH.2018.304738

Kuh, D., Ben-Shlomo, Y., Lynch, J., Hallqvist, J., & Power, C. (2003). Life course epidemiology. *Journal of epidemiology and community health, 57*(10), 778–783. https://doi.org/10.1136/jech.57.10.778

Li, J., McMurray, A., & Stanley, F. (2008). Modernity's paradox and the structural determinants of child health and well-being. *Health Sociology Review, 17*(1), 64–77.

Lopez, N., & Gadsden, V. L. (2016). Health Inequities, Social Determinants, and Intersectionality. *NAM Perspectives.* Discussion Paper, National Academy of Medicine, Washington, DC.

Luskin, R. C., Fishkin, J. S., & Jowell, R. (2002). Considered opinions: Deliberative polling in Britain. *British Journal of Political Science, 32*(3), 455–487.

Macfarlane, S., Racelis, M., & Muli-Musiime, F. (2000). Public health in developing countries. *Lancet, 356*, 841–846.

Morgan, M., & Lifshay, J. (2006). *Community engagement in public health.* Contra Health Services. http://newroutes.org/sites/default/files/live/community_engagement_in_ph_0.pdf

National Collaborating Centre for Determinants of Health. (2013). *Let's talk: Health equity.* https://nccdh.ca/images/uploads/Lets_Talk_Health_Equity_English.pdf

National Science Foundation. (2007). National Science Board Enhancing support of transformative research at the National Science Foundation. Arlington, VA: Available at: http://www.nsf.gov/nsb/documents/2007/tr_report.pdf

Pesce, J. E., Kpaduwa, C. S., & Danis, M. (2011). Deliberation to enhance awareness of and prioritize socioeconomic interventions for health. *Social Science & Medicine, 72*(5), 789–797.

Plamondon, K. M. (2020). A tool to assess alignment between knowledge and action for health equity. *BMC public health, 20*(1), 224. https://doi.org/10.1186/s12889-020-8324-6

Plamondon, K. M., Caxaj, C. S., Graham, I. D., & Bottorff, J. L. (2019). Connecting knowledge with action for health equity: A critical interpretive synthesis of promising practices. *International Journal for Equity in Health, 18*(1), 202. https://doi.org/10.1186/s12939-019-1108-x

Powers, M., & Faden, R. (2006). *Social justice: The moral foundations of public health and health policy.* Oxford University Press.

Rifkin, S. B. (2003). A framework linking community empowerment and health equity: It is a matter of CHOICE. *Journal of Health Population, Population, and Nutrition, 21*(3), 168–180.

Ruffin, J. (2010). The science of eliminating health disparities: Embracing a new paradigm. *American Journal of Public Health, 100*(S1), S8–S9.

Singh, G. K., Daus, G. P., Allender, M., Ramey, C. T., Martin, E. K., Perry, C., Reyes, A., & Vedamuthu, I. P. (2017). Social Determinants of Health in the United States: Addressing Major Health Inequality Trends for the Nation, 1935–2016. *International journal of MCH and AIDS*, 6(2), 139–164. https://doi.org/10.21106/ijma.236

Sparks, M. (2010). Strategic directions for health promotion. *Health Promotion International*, 25(4), 381–383.

U.S. Department of Health and Human Services. The Secretary's Advisory Committee on National Health Promotion and Disease Prevention Objectives for 2020. Phase I report: Recommendations for the framework and format of Healthy People 2020 [Internet]. Section IV: Advisory Committee findings and recommendations [cited 2010 January 6]. Available from: http://www.healthypeople.gov/sites/default/files/PhaseI_0.pdf.

Whitehead, M, & Dahlgren G. (2006). *Levelling up (part 1): A discussion paper on concepts and principles for tackling social inequities in health*. World Health Organization.

Wen, L. S., & Sadeghi, N. B. (2020). Addressing racial health disparities in the COVID-19 pandemic: Immediate and Long-term policy solutions. Health Affairs Blog (July 20, 2020). https://www.healthaffairs.org/do/10.1377/hblog20200716.620294/full/ (accessed August 24, 2020)

Williams, D. R., & Purdie-Vaughns, V. (2016). Needed Interventions to Reduce Racial/Ethnic Disparities in Health. *Journal of Health Politics, Policy and Law*, 41 (4), 627–651.

World Health Organization (WHO). (2016). Equity. http://www.who.int/healthsystems/topics/equity/en (accessed August 24, 2020).

World Health Organization (WHO). (2008). *Primary health care, now more than ever*. https://www.who.int/whr/2008/en/

Woulfe, J., Oliver, T. R., Siemering, K. Q., & Zahner, S. J. (2010). Peer reviewed: Multisector partnerships in population health improvement. *Preventing Chronic Disease*, 7(6), A119.

CHAPTER SIX

Capacity Building for Community Engagement

Pamela Palmer, PhD

CONSTITUENTS WHO PLAN, organize, and implement community engagement initiatives in their local communities are oftentimes faced with both challenges and opportunities that affect their ability to establish, maintain, and sustain an infrastructure for community engagement. Routinely, concerned citizens in local communities *establish and maintain nonprofit organizations* as a formal structure to navigate their community engagement efforts. This chapter introduces a capacity-building *framework* for nonprofit organizations committed to *sustaining* community engagement. The framework advances a *course of action* for building the capacity of the primary functions of what makes a nonprofit a vehicle for community engagement. Through this process, community citizens are able to *define* a collective mission and vision indicative of their communities' needs, *identify* strengths and weaknesses relative to organization capacity, and *craft and implement* a plan of action for capacity building to support the communities they represent. The *approach* of setting up a formal organizational structure for community engagement *offers an infrastructure* for meeting the challenges and opportunities that emerge within the process of community engagement. While this framework and approach remain options for building capacity with nonprofit organizations, there is an emerging concept currently used in the realm of organizational development for nonprofits, and that concept is *resilience*. More specifically, organizational resilience. Literally, resilience is written in the "Capacity Building in Action" section of this chapter; and described in the wake of the novel coronavirus disease of 2019 (COVID-19), a worldwide pandemic. As nonprofit-led task forces are engaging in micro- and macro-responses to this crisis, many are conceptualizing their response and recovery strategies in the concept of resilience.

CAPACITY BUILDING, COMMUNITY ENGAGEMENT, AND COMMUNITY RESILIENCE

Individual nonprofits and the nonprofit sector acknowledge and use capacity building as a means to enhance capacity. The definitions for capacity and capacity building adopted for this chapter were defined by Deborah Linnell (2003) in her *Evaluation of Capacity Building: Lessons Learned* report. Linnell stated that capacity building and capacity are related, but they are not the same. She refers to capacity as an organization's ability to achieve its mission effectively and to sustain itself over the long term. She described capacity building as activities that improve an organization's ability to achieve its mission. Linnell further explained that capacity building may relate to almost any aspect of its work: improved governance, leadership, mission and strategy, administration (including human resources, financial management, and legal matters), program development and implementation, fundraising and income generation, diversity, partnerships and collaboration, evaluation, advocacy and policy change, marketing, positioning, planning, etc. These same aspects of work are relative, and in some cases, they are used to support community engagement.

According to the Centers for Disease Control (CDC; National Institutes of Health, 2011), community engagement is the process of working collaboratively with and through groups of people affiliated by geographic proximity, special interest, or similar situations to address issues affecting the well-being of those people. It is a powerful vehicle for bringing about environmental and behavioral changes that will improve the health of the community and its members. It often involves partnerships and coalitions that help mobilize resources and influence systems, change relationships among partners, and serve as catalysts for changing policies, programs, and practices. Toms (1997) considered community engagement to be a systems perspective, both internally and externally, which focuses on the dynamics and interrelationships among various individual stakeholders and community organizations. Toms (1997) also supported the idea of building capacity for the development of partnerships with various stakeholders who maintain community engagement. In this context, the use of a nonprofit organization makes sense.

Historically, nonprofits have served as a vehicle for community change by providing support, resources, and services to enhance the ability of individuals and communities to engage in movements of change. This concept goes as far back as the establishment of the United Way of America (1887) and the National Association for the Advancement of Colored People (founded in 1909), to the formation of the Susan G. Komen Foundation (created in 1982) and, more recently, Organizing for Action (2013). These organizations were established and have been maintained and sustained with elements of what the CDC (National Institutes of Health, 2011) and Toms (1997) described as community engagement. Accordingly, nonprofit organizations continue to offer a formal structure for community engagement.

In eastern North Carolina, several nonprofit organizations have been established to launch and nourish community engagement. This cohort of nonprofits make up the Community Empowerment Network (CEN)—an organized following of community leaders representing grassroots organizations, who have adopted community engagement as a strategy for addressing community issues (North Carolina Office of Minority Health and Health Disparities [OMHHD], www.ncminorityhealth.org). According to OMHHD, this network embraces capacity building as a strategy for growth and development and takes part in capacity-building activities on a regular basis. For example, CEN affiliates attend the Leadership Enhancement Engagement Project (LEEP). The LEEP Project is a comprehensive and long-term community capacity-building initiative of the North Carolina OMHHD. The overall goal of LEEP is to develop capacity in three primary areas: (1) enhance CEN's organizational capacity to plan, develop, implement, and sustain ongoing community engagement efforts; (2) develop and enhance the knowledge and skills of CEN churches to intentionally engage—locally and regionally—elected officials, human service agencies, and educational institutions around policy and political issues regarding health, educational, and economic disparities; and (3) provide CEN members and communities with the training, multimedia educational tools, and community-building skills to organize and engage citizens for increased involvement and participation in the civic and political process in eastern North Carolina. Thus many leaders of nonprofit organizations who participated in the third component of LEEP used capacity building to enhance their nonprofits' ability to secure the necessary resources for continuous community engagement activities. Likewise, in the spirit of community engagement, nonprofit organizations in central North Carolina are continuously participating in capacity building to enhance their ability to engage people in community-based initiatives coordinated by various nonprofits.

As of late, nonprofit organizations throughout North Carolina are demonstrating characteristics of organizational resilience. This is according to their prompt feedback via a need survey conducted immediately after the statewide order of shelter in place (North Carolina Center for Nonprofits, 2020). These nonprofits in the wake of COVID-19, and before, have performed resiliently to maintain their missions and achieve their visions.

CAPACITY-BUILDING FRAMEWORK

In an effort to implement capacity building in central North Carolina, the Hayden-Harman Foundation (Palmer, 2006) provided funding and other resources to develop, introduce, and implement a framework for capacity building. Pamela Palmer designed the capacity-building framework for nonprofit management (Capacity Builders, www.capacitybuilderstraining.com) as a strategy to assist executive directors of nonprofit organizations with their capacity-building needs. The premise for the framework originated after more than 15 years of Dr. Palmer, as a college professor of nonprofit leadership and management, responding to questions and concerns related to "how to manage a nonprofit." As a result, this framework was developed as a guide to engage nonprofit professionals in building the capacity of the nonprofits they represent. Palmer (Guilford Nonprofit Consortium, 2013) has used this framework for nearly 5 years as the basis for facilitating the Nonprofit Management Institute held at High Point University and coordinated by the Guilford Nonprofit Consortium in partnership with the Duke University Nonprofit Certificate program (Guilford Nonprofit Consortium, 2013).

Again, the essence of what nonprofit organizations do with, for, and in communities is indicative of the fundamentals for community engagement. The framework specifies three contextual areas of work for building the capacity of nonprofit organizations. The areas of work illustrated in the framework are based on (1) phases of nonprofit growth and development, (2) primary functions of managing a nonprofit, and (3) strategies for capacity building (Figure 6.1).

Contextual Areas of Work

When nonprofit professionals and community leaders decide to "do" capacity building, it is essential that they pinpoint and understand the essence of where their organizations are in their growth and development. This is to acknowledge the degree of readiness for capacity building. Therefore, the framework distinguishes the phases of growth and development as Phase One: establish, Phase Two: maintain, and Phase Three: sustain.

ESTABLISH	MAINTAIN	SUSTAIN
Start a Nonprofit	Conduct Needs Assessments and Asset Mapping Develop a Strategic Plan	Recruit/Manage Volunteers
Research Social Issues	Human Resource Management Recruit/Manage Volunteers	Develop and Grow a Donor Base for Fundraising
Understand the Role of the Executive Director	Design, Manage, and Evaluate Community-Based Programs	Establish Business Ventures for Social Change
Create a Management Team	Write Grants to Address Community Needs Fundraise for Sustainability	Establish a Brand Use Social Media
Develop a Board of Directors Recruit/Manage Volunteers	Manage Finances Develop a Marketing Strategy	Maintain a Healthy Image
TRAINING	TECHNICAL ASSISTANCE	CONSULTATION

FIGURE 6.1   Capacity-Building Framework for Nonprofit Management © Pamela Palmer, PhD

Functions of Nonprofit Management

The primary functions of managing a nonprofit are fundamental to developing appropriate strategies for implementing capacity-building activities. As shown in Figure 6.1, there are salient functions of operating a nonprofit. Capacity building for each function is unique to the organization's phase of growth and development. In this framework, the general relativity of the management functions of each phase is Establish = Develop a Foundation, Maintain = Manage Day-to-Day Operations, and Sustain = Secure Recurrent Funds and Resources.

Strategies for Building Capacity

The tactical approach for facilitating capacity-building activities using this framework is facilitated in three forms: (1) training, (2) technical assistance, and (3) one-on-one consultation. Nonprofit organizations consider each of the three tactics based on their current level of capacity across the functions of managing a nonprofit, as well as setting up on-site technical assistance related to organizations' capacity needs and securing one-on-one consultation to ensure consistent participation in capacity building.

CAPACITY BUILDING IN ACTION

The process for building capacity employs a three-step process and advances a course of action for community engagement. The steps involve (1) defining or refining a collective mission and vision, indicative of the purpose of the nonprofit to meet its communities' needs through community engagement; (2) identifying strengths and weaknesses relative to organization capacity; and (3) crafting and implementing a plan of action for capacity building. In addition, the strategies for capacity building are employed in a customized fashion based on the organization's capacity-building needs. This three-step procedure generates a plan for capacity enhancement and the foundation for meeting the challenges and opportunities that emerge within the process of community engagement. In addition, organizational resilience has emerged as a contributing factor to a strategic mindset when nonprofits respond to a crisis like COVID-19. This worldwide pandemic has forever changed the way nonprofits will respond to crises in the context of capacity building.

Step 1

This action encompasses the development or review of the nonprofit's mission and vision statements. Collectively, stakeholders consider community engagement to be a part of the current and future plans of the organization. This is accomplished by answering the following questions about the organization: Who are we? What do we do? What do we value? What is the purpose of the nonprofit? How will the organization use community engagement to contribute to minimizing community needs related to the nonprofit's purpose? Responses to these questions will yield pertinent information to craft or revise the organization's mission and vision statements.

Step 2

The practice of identifying strengths and weaknesses relative to the organizational capacity of a nonprofit is oftentimes realized as a result of assessing capacity. For example, nonprofit professionals who participate in the Nonprofit Management Institute (Guilford Nonprofit Consortium, 2013) in central North Carolina use the McKinsey Capacity Assessment (Venture Philanthropy Partners, 2001) to determine the level of capacity across seven elements: (1) aspirations, (2) strategy, (3) organizational skills, (4) systems and infrastructure, (5) human resources, (6) organizational structure, and (7) culture. The results of the assessment give these professionals insight into their organizational strengths and weaknesses.

Step 3

As explained previously, the strategies for capacity building take shape around training, technical assistance, and one-on-one consultation. These strategies are customized based on the organization's capacity-building needs. More specifically, areas for building the capacity of nonprofit organizations are noted, based on the seven elements of the McKinsey Capacity Assessment (Venture Philanthropy Partners, 2001), and each of the three strategies is designed, planned, and implemented. The inclusivity of resilience as a helpful capacity-building resource has positively affected crisis management as nonprofits pivot to respond to COVID-19. It bears repeating: Organizational resilience has emerged as a contributing factor and strategic mindset when nonprofits engage in responding to a crisis.

SUMMARY

The use of capacity building to develop and maintain an organization's infrastructure for community engagement is essential, as demonstrated in nonprofit organizations in eastern and central North Carolina. As described, community leaders and nonprofit professionals have access to capacity-building activities in which they participate to meet the capacity enhancement needs experienced by their nonprofits. When these needs are met, nonprofit organizations are more equipped to pursue the missions and visions established by community leaders. Consequently, community engagement is better positioned to advance in communities, relevant to resilience when nonprofits respond, rebuild, and reform on their journey to bounce back from a crisis.

REFERENCES

Guilford Nonprofit Consortium. (2013). Nonprofit Management Institute. Greensboro, NC. www.guilfordnonprofits.org

Linnell, D. (2003). *Evaluation of capacity building: Lessons from the field.* Alliance for Nonprofit Management. http://seerconsulting.com.au/wp-content/uploads/2009/09/Evaluation-of-Capacity-Building-Lessons-from-Field.pdf

National Institutes of Health. (2011). *Principles of community engagement* (2nd ed., Publication #11-7782). Clinical and Translational Science Awards Consortium Community Engagement Key Function Committee Task Force on the Principles of Community Engagement. https://www.atsdr.cdc.gov/communityengagement/pdf/PCE_Report_508_FINAL.pdf

North Carolina Center for Nonprofits. (2020). *Survey of NC nonprofits measuring the impact of COVID-19.* https://www.ncnonprofits.org/

Palmer, P. (2006). Grant proposal. Pamela Palmer & Associates. https://ppalmerandassociates.com/

Palmer, P. (2013). Final report. Pamela Palmer & Associates. https://ppalmerandassociates.com/

Toms, F. (1997). Triple Quandary. [PowerPoint presentation].

Venture Philanthropy Partners. (2001). *Effective capacity building in nonprofit organizations.* McKinsey & Company.

CHAPTER SEVEN

Leadership and Community-Based Research

Seronda A. Robinson, PhD, M. LaVerne Reid, PhD, and George Cliette, PhD

LEADERSHIP IS A pivotal component of community-based participatory research (CBPR). Appropriate leadership is needed to ensure that the principles and processes of CBPR are upheld and to maximize the outcomes of the intervention. CBPR consists of a partnership between researchers, generally from academic institutions, and community members. The joining of these two diverse groups requires strong leadership to maintain relationships, promote progress, and ensure capacity building and sustainability. There are specific characteristics that an effective leader should possess, regardless of institution or community affiliation. The leader must make sure that everyone shares the vision and guide the group in attaining the overall goal. In CBPR, should the leadership represent the academic researchers, the community members, or a combination of both? The core functions of leadership, the principles of CBPR, and who should lead the research effort are discussed in this chapter.

INTRODUCTION

CBPR has become popular among health researchers and practitioners for addressing health disparities. To be most effective, interventions should be culturally tailored to the target group. The development of these interventions requires the knowledge and resources of those vulnerable to the health condition. A major strength of CBPR is that it involves collaboration with those affected by the issue being studied to develop culturally appropriate interventions. CBPR is a partnership between a local community, academic researchers, and other organizations. The partners work together to identify opportunities for conducting research interventions. To conduct CBPR successfully requires adherence to the principles of CBPR and effective leadership.

LEADERSHIP IN CBPR

The leadership for CBPR may take the form of a single individual, or multiple individuals, or a team of leaders in the form of an advisory board. The principal investigator may serve as the sole leader. Alternatively, there may be coinvestigators, one representing the research institution and one representing the primary partnering community-based organization (CBO), who provide leadership for the project. Oftentimes, CBPR projects are guided by a community advisory board (CAB) consisting of representatives of various agencies, CBOs, and residents with various levels of experience with the outcome of interest or target population.

Because the principal investigator (PI) is ultimately responsible to the funding agency for the accountability of funds and the overall success of the project, the PI naturally assumes a leadership role. As with most good leaders, the PI should be willing to receive guidance and advice from others and will ultimately make the final decision, with a willingness and preparedness to accept the consequences of the decision. If it is a true partnership, the PI should not lord authority or flaunt their position over other participants, especially the leader of the partnering CBO(s).

When there is a primary CBO, it is appropriate for a representative from that agency to serve as a coleader for the overall project. In the true sense of CBPR, the community and CBO would have been involved from the inception of the idea for the project, and their representative would have been involved as a coauthor of the grant proposal. This representative would have been listed as the coprincipal investigator from the inception of the grant. Thus, this individual would share in the responsibility of fund distribution and accountability to the funding institution.

An active CAB provides oversight and serves as a liaison between the researchers and the community. The advisory board should consist of representatives from CBOs and other institutions, such as churches, with relevance to the research topic and significance in the community of interest. There may be representation from residents related to the outcome of interest. In subsequent years, former intervention participants may be invited to share their perspectives from the other side.

The CAB provides input and oversight to the project, ensuring that the researchers conduct processes in ways that are culturally appropriate, geared for success, and in the best interests of all, particularly community members. While the entire board votes to make recommendations and final decisions, individuals may be named to serve as chair or cochairs. It is beneficial to have cochairs to assist and support each other. If the board is to exist for multiple years, it may be advantageous to have cochairs of the board, with one selected to serve as the lead chair, while the other serves in a training position in preparation for being the chair in the subsequent year. This allows the cochair to hone their skills and gain comfort in the role, and it provides a degree of consistency for the group in the following years.

The CAB may be further divided into subcommittees, each with a chairperson as the leader. The formation of subcommittees may give individuals on the board a greater sense of purpose and a more active role. This could also help to overcome potential discomfort from the feeling of intrinsic hierarchies that may interfere with full participation from all board members.

PRINCIPLES OF CBPR (ISRAEL ET AL., 2003)

1. ***CBPR Recognizes the Community as a Unit of Identity.*** CBPR partnerships seek to work with existing units of identity that may be composed of a defined geographic area (e.g., a neighborhood), a geographically dispersed group of individuals with shared beliefs or culture, or a common sense of identity (i.e., ethnicity, age, sexual orientation). The existence of a sense of community will affect the type of organizational leadership structure selected. The infrastructure of a community typically has existing leaders. These leaders may be formal, such as political leaders or directors of local organizations. There are also some informal leaders who are recognized by the community members, such as church pastors or elderly members of the community, who have their fingers on the pulse of the community and are aware of all the comings and goings in the area. These highly influential individuals are well respected in their communities and often serve as gatekeepers. To gain entry into the community and have an opportunity to be successful, it is incumbent upon the research team to build rapport with the existing leaders and work with and through them versus establishing external leadership that does not consider the importance of these preexisting roles. These leaders are very influential in garnering participation. Researchers should partner with community leaders to enhance success.

2. ***CBPR Builds on Existing Strengths and Resources Within the Community.*** Strengths may include individual skills, social support networks, and faith-based organizations or CBOs. Members of community organizations often have skills that can be enhanced through training to help with data collection and other aspects of the implementation of the project. Often, the existing relationships and ties within the community are some of the greatest assets. Social support is a key factor in health improvement, and laymen often trust the advice of their life-learned peers over that of book-educated professionals. These relationships also serve to create leadership roles within the community; thus, individuals such as cosmetologists and barbers are considered community leaders because they are sources of information and often have trusted relationships with community members. Partnerships are instrumental in uniting forces of various organizations that focus on the same issues.

An effective leader empowers others to lead and recognizes natural leaders as a resource.

3. ***CBPR Facilitates Collaborative, Equitable Partnerships in All Phases of the Research.*** As a partnership, CBPR projects are conducted according to the norms of partnerships, which consist of mutual respect, recognition of knowledge and expertise, and transparency/open communication. Community partners should be empowered through shared information and decision-making power. The PI should facilitate the research process while familiarizing community members with it and incorporating their suggestions based on personal knowledge of how things work in the community. Shared leadership through co-PIs or cochairs enhances fairness in the partnership.

4. ***CBPR Integrates and Achieves a Balance Between Research and Action for the Mutual Benefit of All Partners.*** Researchers seek to enhance the body of knowledge about health. In CBPR, this knowledge acquisition is balanced with the development of intervention strategies to address the health concern in the community. The leader must ensure that all parties are satisfied.

5. ***CBPR Promotes Co-learning and Capacity Building Among All Partners.*** Community members learn research skills (e.g., data collection, presentation preparation, manuscript development, and proposal writing), while researchers learn from the local and cultural knowledge of community members. Identifying leaders from among community members and developing their leadership skills is one way to build capacity.

6. ***CBPR Involves Systems Development Through a Cyclical and Iterative Process.*** Researchers and community members learn from each other and continue to build on the knowledge gained throughout the process. Each accomplishment builds more trust. The leader guides the research process.

7. ***CBPR Emphasizes the Local Relevance of Public Health Problems and Ecological Perspectives That Recognize and Attend to the Multiple Determinants of Health and Disease.*** An ecological approach that involves individuals, as well as interpersonal relationships and organizational networks, is used. An effective leader can effectively communicate with people at various levels.

8. ***CBPR Disseminates Findings and Knowledge Gained to All Partners and Involves All Partners in the Dissemination Process.*** Community members participate in presentations and manuscript writing, and they guide researchers in the best methods for sharing findings with the community. Leadership is fostered in a community member through the opportunity to facilitate presentations.

9. ***CBPR Involves a Long-Term Process and Commitment to Sustainability.*** Relationships and commitments are established to continue beyond the funding period. Furthermore, skills are honed through training, and resources are

provided to continue efforts. Leadership skills are essential tools that should be developed among community members to continue successful efforts in the absence of researchers.

EFFECTIVE LEADERSHIP CHARACTERISTICS

While there is no cookie-cutter recipe for leadership, in his classic leadership textbook, *Leadership in Organizations*, Gary Yukl presented what he considered to be the 10 most important leadership roles for enhancing work in teams and organizations. These characteristics are presented as they relate to CBPR (Yukl, 2010).

1. ***Help Interpret the Meaning of Events.*** Effective leaders must help others to understand why events are relevant. Because research is often unfamiliar to community partners, the researcher or research team must assume leadership in ensuring that everyone understands the various activities that occur and the consequences and opportunities resulting from each event. Particularly, the CAB must realize the importance of meeting deadlines for deliverables and conducting activities according to specified rules, such as those established by the Institutional Review Board (IRB). Chairs of CABs should be well informed of the research team's agenda prior to the CAB meeting and clearly understand items to be presented to accurately present the information to the CAB in a format that is understandable in lay terms to avoid potentially prolonging the meeting, thus seeking the best way to clarify issues for understanding versus making decisions for progress.

2. ***Create Alignment on Objectives and Strategies.*** Tasks are performed most effectively when there is agreement on the efforts toward achieving them. Effective leaders must merge the priorities of the research team and community using strategies deemed culturally appropriate by community representatives while remaining scientifically sound to provide good research.

3. ***Build Task Commitment and Optimism.*** The leader is responsible for maintaining morale to preserve enthusiasm toward the efforts and commitment to completing the tasks. Despite obstacles, team members must remain confident in the success of the project. The CAB serves as the liaison between the community and researchers. The PI and chair must ensure that CAB members and other partners—such as pastors—stay encouraged regarding the outcome of the efforts and continue to motivate community residents to participate.

4. ***Build Mutual Trust and Cooperation.*** Relationships are a major asset in CBPR. Respect for participants and recognition of the contributions of various partners are key. The leader must ensure that all partners harbor mutual respect for each other by making sure they understand each other (i.e.,

clarifying terminology and colloquialisms), are culturally sensitive, and accept diversity. An effective leader is also skilled in conflict management and can quickly resolve conflicts before they escalate.

5. ***Strengthen Collective Identity.*** While the CAB members represent members of the community who are recognized as a unit of identity, the researcher must ensure that all partners in CBPR realize that the partnership has a unique identity, with all members genuinely concerned for the improvement of the health of the community.

6. ***Organize and Coordinate Activities.*** The research process is innately replete with multiple tasks and activities. The leader must organize efforts so that the people's time and the resources are used efficiently. One useful method is to allocate a specified amount of time to each task on the agenda.

7. ***Encourage and Facilitate Collective Learning.*** All partners contribute something to the team. Leaders must encourage and facilitate active learning between all partners to enhance the benefit of shared skills and knowledge.

8. ***Obtain Necessary Resources and Support.*** The researcher must maintain access to funding and approval. Community members are key to maintaining the support of community leaders and members. They may even have access to additional resources, such as meeting facilities and refreshments. Effective leaders help to acquire the necessary resources and support.

9. ***Develop and Empower People.*** The effective leader ensures the proper training of individuals to enhance skills and empower them to assume leadership roles and accept new responsibilities.

10. ***Promote Social Justice and Morality.*** An environment of compassion and social responsibility promotes member satisfaction and commitment. An effective leader must model moral behavior and ethical practices.

SUMMARY

The identification of a potentially effective leader for community-based research requires selecting someone with motivation, organization, prioritization, and endurance.

Motivation. The leader must embrace the goal of the research and be motivated to have a successful outcome. They must see the vision of the goal and be able to influence others to share in that vision. The leader needs to be able to move followers to action. They must have the ability to persuade others to focus on the outcome of interest to the researcher while using scientifically approved methods deemed most appropriate by community members.

Organization. The leader has the responsibility of representing and serving as a liaison between the research team, practitioners, advisory board members, community members, and other partners. Therefore, the leader must remain organized to address the needs of each group appropriately. The leader must coordinate meetings and other activities to best accommodate those involved. In addition, research occurs on a timeline to meet deliverables by the deadline. Meeting this timeline will be complicated by having to accommodate the schedules of multiple community members to implement the project successfully. Therefore, excellent organizational skills are imperative.

Prioritization. The leader must prioritize the needs of the community to ensure continued participation for success. Simultaneously, the needs of the researchers to be responsive to the funders and to meet promotion and tenure requirements through papers and presentations must be considered. When working with multiple groups with similar—yet different—agendas, prioritization is critical.

Endurance. CBPR inherently poses numerous challenges by virtue of accommodating diverse groups with various levels of skills and knowledge and individual desires. Nonetheless, the process is geared to be sustainable. Although CBPR is time consuming because of the multiple opinions to be considered; to ensure success and sustainability, the leader must be able to endure to the end or at the least make sure that appropriate training is occurring to guarantee continuation.

Case Study 1: African Americans and Hypertension

The Department of Public Health Education at Robinsonville University was awarded a 3-year planning grant through the National Institute on Health Disparities. A CBPR approach was used to plan and pilot an intervention to improve the health of African Americans in Robinsonville, Georgia. The research team (RT) consisted of researchers from the university and health-care providers from a local community-based, health-care organization. A 10-member CAB was created with interested representatives from the target community—namely, members of the African American community and local health-care agencies. Participants included clinicians, ministers, local government officials and school board members, health educators from the local health department, representatives from other CBOs, and small business owners.

The planning period was used to form the CAB and to conduct an assessment to determine the major health conditions of concern in the community. The CAB met monthly to decide every step of the research project. The CAB identified local members of the community who were considered key informants. CAB members contacted these informants and introduced the researchers and the project. A member of the RT conducted the key informant interviews. Hypertension emerged as the health issue of greatest concern.

Once hypertension was identified as the leading cause of the disease of interest, researchers gave input regarding the leading causes of hypertension. CAB members informed the researchers that the churches were the best way to reach the African American community. The CAB agreed to focus on physical activity and nutrition through the church health and wellness ministries.

The group decided to work with church health ministries, an existing infrastructure, to increase the opportunity for the sustainability of the project beyond the funding period. The minister on the CAB invited representatives from the RT and CAB to his denomination's annual pastors' conference. They were allowed 10 minutes to speak to the body of pastors in attendance. Pastors who were interested in participating provided the contact information for the head of their health ministry, who would serve as the liaison between the RT and the church. Churches without an existing health ministry offered the contact information for their parish nurse.

Researchers and CAB members worked together to develop a survey and biological data collection sheet to capture participant characteristics and anticipated 6-month changes in knowledge, attitudes, behavior, and biological outcomes. At the initiation of the implementation phase, a breakfast was held with the pastors and health ministry leaders to provide more information about the project.

Physical inactivity and poor nutrition choices were addressed at each church. One of the CAB members, who was a personal trainer, agreed to meet with representatives from each church to train and certify them as fitness instructors. The church liaisons worked with the personal trainer and other members of their wellness ministries to establish fitness programs at each church. Each week, the pastors promoted the programs and encouraged congregants to participate to present their temples as healthier living sacrifices. A nutritionist from the participating health organization worked with ministry liaisons to develop healthier menus to be served after church functions. Other staff members from the community-based, healthcare organization were trained to collect data properly and completed training in the protection of human subjects to meet IRB requirements. These staff members assisted in collecting data on participants at the baseline and the 6-month follow-up.

The CAB was led by a chair and cochair, who were selected from and by CAB members. In each subsequent year, the cochair became the chair, and the CAB voted on a new cochair. Each chair and cochair received a copy of *Robert's Rules of Orders* to guide the proper conduct of the meetings. The CAB was further divided into subcommittees, such as the promotion/recruitment, finance, presentation, and celebration committees. Chairpersons were selected to facilitate committee meetings and to present a report to the CAB. Committees came up with suggestions that were presented to the CAB and voted on by a quorum of the board. Similarly, the RT met weekly to carry out activities necessary to move the project forward and to meet deliverables. Just like the subcommittees, the RT brought recommendations to the CAB, who voted to make final decisions.

After pivotal data collection points, the data were summarized and presented to the CAB. The CAB made recommendations for appropriate methods of presentation and participated in the distribution of the findings to the participating churches. Aggregated findings were presented in layman's terms with many illustrations.

The outcomes of the project were quite impressive. The project was successful in establishing new health ministries at three churches that previously did not have such a ministry. Fitness programs were formed at 15 churches, with an average of 10–15 regular participants weekly. Initially, 200 eligible participants diagnosed with hypertension or borderline hypertension were enrolled. At the 6-month follow-up, 144 of the original enrollees had been retained. A moderate reduction in weight was observed, with an average group weight loss ranging from 15 to 30 pounds. Twelve churches reported ensuring that water, fruits, and vegetables were served at every church function. Eighty-six percent of participants reported changes in physical activity or nutrition, and 78% reported reductions in blood pressure levels.

Several papers were published, and presentations were made. CAB members were invited to participate in the writing and presentation of posters and workshops to share findings and lessons learned from the study. The PI and several CAB members returned to the pastors' conference from which churches had volunteered to participate to present the aggregated findings of the project. The head of the community-based, health-care organization was invited to serve as a co-PI and to assist in writing a proposal for the next grant.

DISCUSSION QUESTIONS

1. Describe the leadership in this project.
2. Which factors made it effective or ineffective?
3. Did this project meet the principles of CBPR? Why or why not?

Case Study 2: Hispanics and Mental Health

Avanna, Texas, is a small urban city, with a population of more than 15% Hispanics. The Health Disparities Center at a university in Avanna acquired a grant to address health disparities among Latinos. Dr. Samuels, the PI, chose to focus on mental health, an area of great interest to her. She established an RT with students, staff, and other consultants from the Department of Psychology. The team expressed an interest in assessing the social determinants of health that affect the mental health of Hispanic families. In addition, Dr. Samuels established a partnership with La Plaza Hispana, a local grassroots organization dedicated to improving the quality of life of Hispanics/Latinos. The director was asked to allow the RT to conduct surveys, with adults attending some of her programs. She was also asked to have interpreters on hand for assistance in presenting the project to potential participants.

After the initial assessments were conducted to identify risk factors associated with mental health, it was determined that the inability to cope with some of the other prevalent chronic health issues, such as cancer and heart disease, must have been causing great mental distress. To assist with these mental health issues, members of the RT set up hours on campus, during which they provided free counseling services. They posted fliers at La Plaza Hispana. During the remaining time of the project funding, only a custodial worker at the university who saw the sign while cleaning offices stopped to inquire about the services. Dr. Samuels determined that a lack of interest in seeking care must have been a barrier to others taking advantage of the free services that were offered. She felt very successful in identifying the risk factors for mental health in the community and published several papers on her descriptive study.

DISCUSSION QUESTIONS

1. Describe the leadership in this project.
2. Which factors made it effective or ineffective?
3. Did this project meet the principles of CBPR? Why or why not?

Case Study 3: African American Women and Breastfeeding

A researcher at the University of Jacksontown received a small seed grant to conduct exploratory research addressing issues among African American women in the area. She partnered with local cosmetologists and the director of the cosmetology board for the area and created an advisory board consisting of several cosmetologists, the board director, and other faculty members. She wanted to address the low rates of breastfeeding among African American women.

The RT developed questions to assess barriers to breastfeeding. The team members then met with the advisory board and presented their chosen questions. The board was asked to comment on the selected questions and offer any additional remarks they felt were important. Board members made recommendations on the wording of some questions to avoid unintentional offense and to clarify meanings.

Input was also solicited from the board to determine the best method for gathering data from the target population. It was determined that focus groups to elicit an open discussion among groups of similar women would be best. The cosmetologists further offered their salons on Monday evenings, the day that most were closed for regular business, to conduct the group meetings. The shops were presented as local settings in the community that were familiar and nonthreatening to participants. In addition, some of the women volunteered to serve as childcare providers in the waiting rooms during the focus group sessions. It was suggested that the RT provide snacks for both the participants and their children as an incentive to increase participation by eliminating the need to feed the children and lack of childcare as potential barriers to participation. The head of the cosmetology school volunteered to conduct the focus groups. The PI thought this would be a good idea to avoid potentially intimidating the participants. She agreed to train the instructor in the protocol for conducting focus groups. Graduate students were hired to serve as note takers during the sessions.

After everyone had been properly trained, dates for the focus groups were set. Various dates were set to hold groups with teen moms, mothers between the ages of 21 and 40, and older women who may be influential to younger women of childbearing age. The cosmetologists advertised in their shops and encouraged customers to participate. Fliers were placed in other common local areas, such as grocery stores, the clinic, OB/GYN offices, and some day-care facilities.

After the data were analyzed, table tents were placed in the participating shops with colorful graphs of the aggregated findings. Women who did not regularly visit these shops were invited to attend a short presentation jointly presented by one of the cosmetologists and the PI on a Monday evening at one of the participating shops. In addition, one of the cosmetologists from the board was invited to attend each conference at which findings were presented. Furthermore, the head of the cosmetology school was asked to serve as a coinvestigator when a proposal was submitted for a grant to fund an intervention to address the barriers identified.

DISCUSSION QUESTIONS

1. Describe the leadership in this project.
2. Which factors made it effective or ineffective?
3. Did this project meet the principles of CBPR? Why or why not?

REFERENCES

Israel, B. A., Schulz, A. J., Parker, E. A., Becker, A. B., Allen, A. J., & Guzman, J. R. (2003). Critical issues in developing and following community-based participatory research principles. In M. Minkler & N. Wallerstein (Eds.), *Community-based participatory research for health* (pp. 56–73). Jossey-Bass.

Yukl, G. (2010). *Leadership in organizations*. Prentice Hall.

CHAPTER EIGHT

Spiritual Capital and Engagement

Sylvia Willie Burgess, PhD, and Calvin Ellison, PhD

INTRODUCTION

In many African American communities, spirituality has been a sustaining force. This notion of connecting with a higher power has been passed down from generation to generation through traditions and rituals that help those who adhere to the teachings and parables to quantify their belief in a celestial existence after death. If there are efforts from outside entities to engage African American communities, it is necessary that they have an understanding of the worth and value of spiritual experiences to both the individual and the community. By default, engaging in efforts to transform African American communities mandates a relationship between religious institutions and those external change agents. It is not merely enough to engage the purveyors of the spiritual experiences of African Americans to bring about community change; it must be accompanied by an explanation and an understanding of the value of those experiences. Thus, this chapter introduces spiritual capital as such an experience.

This chapter presents spiritual capital as a mechanism by which community engagement can be improved. It outlines the connection between spiritual capital and engagement. The chapter focuses on the role of faith-based organizations and their leadership as an example of how the effective use of spiritual capital components, in conjunction with training, added resources, and skill development, can affect community engagement. The chapter outlines a framework of practical applications and the use of training tools as a means for maximizing individual spiritual capital within the context of participatory engagement in an effort to create permanent change in disparate communities.

SPIRITUAL CAPITAL AND COMMUNITY ENGAGEMENT

For the purposes of this chapter, spiritual capital is defined as an individual's intrinsic values that are associated with trust, culture, and deep commitment to building relationships, to better serve society, and to satisfy the internal human need to serve. Lloyd (2010) noted that these intrinsic factors associated with spiritual capital are value-based characteristics.

Lloyd (2010) described spiritual capital not as a religious construct but a relational connection that extends beyond the logical and contractual and is dependent on faith in one another. In addition, Burgess (2011) later noted that spiritual capital has nothing to do with an individual's personal religious preference. However, the church has played an important part in helping to formulate these intrinsic values—especially for African American communities where the church has often been the springboard for much community change. From this perspective, the effective use of spiritual capital helps foster an environment that compels individuals to go beyond just working together to complete tasks. It perpetuates a repeatable and sustainable foundation for engagement.

Conceptually, when used effectively, spiritual capital can affect community engagement in significant ways. According to Burgess (2011), there is a positive relationship between spiritual capital and engagement. Her research revealed that as an individual's spiritual capital rises, so does their ability to participate and be more engaged. Spiritual capital is a resource that can be used to build participation and establish engagement in a deliberate fashion. In her research, Burgess (2011) noted that leaders tend to resonate with the idea of spiritual capital. Thus, this provides an opportunity to alter engagement practices. By helping leaders understand that they already possess the intrinsic nature to behave in this manner, based on their values and ability to trust others, they can build better relationships for working together for change within their communities. To this end, it is relevant to emphasize the relationship between spiritual capital and engagement as a means of raising the individual's level of participation, connecting them to appropriate resources, and building skills to change their current levels of engagement. The connection begins with defining community engagement within the context of spiritual capital.

Community engagement is defined as people working collaboratively with and through groups of people who are associated by geographical proximity, have some common interest, are attempting to address issues that affect the well-being of the groups, and are working to include a wider range of people in processes and outcomes to achieve the desired goal of greater engagement (Goode et al., 2006). Putnam (1995) defined engagement as people's connection with the life of their communities, which includes political activities. These connections involve local entities, such as school boards, city councils, and county commissions, as well as interacting with public agencies, such as health departments. Engagement is an important component to the success of communities (Toms, 2010). According to Centra and McDonald's (1997) study, engagement requires that all individuals communicate with leaders and others from different backgrounds, values, concerns, and priorities. Further, community engagement involves using the appropriate tools to mobilize communities and their citizens for engaging in public decision making that focuses on community issues. It is essential to find the right tools to support the emerging importance of engagement. These tools should focus on building knowledge development and providing skills training to change how people engage and participate (Burgess, 2011).

Spiritual capital is one such tool to be used toward better community engagement. While many readers will automatically connect spiritual capital to religion, it is important to note that spiritual capital is not focused on the religious perspective. However, faith-based organizations and their leadership play a significant role in assisting communities where citizens are living in oppressed or marginalized conditions. Thus, this creates a platform by which the use of spiritual capital can influence participation and improve engagement (Burgess, 2011). According to Sewell (2003), it takes such leaders who are not afraid to challenge the status quo to work to change the ills of society and to create action plans for change. The intrinsic nature of spiritual capital provides such a foundation for these "organic leaders" (Sewell, 2003, p. 14) to work from to change the way engagement occurs within the community.

Burgess (2011) suggested that it is critically important to those seeking to be better engaged to emphasize the necessity to connect to their communities in a genuine way. This requires not only the community leaders and representatives but also the community members to gain the required skills to effectively tap into the necessary resources to support and create better opportunities for engagement. The leaders, representatives, and community members must all join together to bring about change in their communities. This requires building the right relationships within and across communities to create these opportunities for more engagement. Further, the engagement practices must be intentional and focused on building meaningful, mutually beneficial, and reciprocal relationships with all community citizens.

Key Components of Spiritual Capital

When society begins to view spiritual capital as an intrinsic value and intentional resource that all individuals possess to create change through building relationships and enhancing trust and faith among one another, better engagement practices will follow. When examining the components of spiritual capital, it becomes clear that there are also tactical applications for understanding their effect on engagement (Table 8.1). The more leaders and community members can resonate with building spiritual capital as an asset, the more likely they will think of it as a tool to be used to enhance engagement.

When coupled, spiritual capital and community engagement have the potential—through well-defined and planned tactics and strategy-building processes—to help

TABLE 8.1 *Key Components of Spiritual Capital*

COMPONENT	ASPECTS OF THE COMPONENTS	TACTICS FOR USE	IMPACT ON ENGAGEMENT
Relationship building	Builds leadership among individuals in the community	Engage and empower others. Does not build programs that leave people alienated and disengaged	Creates sustainable changes in engagement practices
Spiritual capital investment	Views spiritual capital as an investment with a high return	Helps individuals use their personal sacrifice, giving, and volunteering in communities as a must	Builds reliable engagement practices that can be repeated in future community endeavors
Trust and faith building	Creates a foundation for spiritual capital to affect community relationships on a long-term basis	Establish planned ways to help leaders connect through trust building	Establishes a long-term platform of positive engagement
Intentionality of spiritual capital as a resource	Enhances and positions spiritual capital as a resource that can be used to improve or better communities	Plan, develop, and implement ongoing community engagement opportunities that are directly related to the local community	Uses spiritual capital in conjunction with other resources to help communities deliberately engage locally

Adapted from Burgess, S. (2011). Spiritual capital: Relationship with civic engagement among faith-based leaders [Unpublished doctoral dissertation]. North Carolina Agricultural and Technical State University.

community leaders and community members understand the value of engagement and participation. This leads to better decision making about challenges faced by the community and improvement in communication with civic leaders to bring about sustainable change. The most important of all these components, from a community perspective, is trust and faith building among individuals and leaders within the community (Lloyd, 2010).

The idea of incorporating trust as a primary component to ensure that the effect of spiritual capital on engagement lasts plays a major role in unfolding the process for creating more participatory environments. This makes trust even more important at the grassroots level for engaging citizens. According to Toms (1997), citizens at this level are already more mistrustful because of past dealings by leaders that did not yield positive results for those involved. Trust appears to be a major component for opening doors to engagement. The level of trust and honesty among individuals will affect their behavior and enhance the potential for more sustainable engagement in their communities (Lloyd, 2010). The ultimate goal and simultaneous challenge are to create more opportunities for community leaders and community members working together to use their spiritual capital as an asset to promote community growth and change in engagement practices (Burgess, 2011).

SPIRITUAL CAPITAL AND THE CHURCH

The enormity of the power and influence of the church in African American communities is hard to describe to anyone not familiar with the experience of hearing the deliverance of an ecclesiastical message that rings within the ears of those parishioners who hold on to it until the Wednesday night service. Such influence is exceeded only by the power of the head of the church themselves. It is only with their blessings that programs can begin and become successful. If there is any hint that the pastor, bishop, or evangelist is opposed to the effort, or if they merely do not support it, nothing will take place. Church leaders are the most powerful "politicians" in African American communities—without the title of *politician*.

It is important to work with the established leadership of church organizations to accomplish the change needed in communities. For example, if a particular program or service is seen as beneficial to the community, then the pastorate and the church must be brought to the table as legitimate contributors. If not, many pastors have the power to silence the initiative before it starts (see the story excerpt in Table 8.2).

TABLE 8.2 *Importance of Involving the Church*

A gentleman recently approached me to obtain my input on a project that he wanted to see begun in the community. As we met and discussed his plan, it was difficult for me to contain myself regarding what I knew would be the not-so-positive response he did not want. However, I recognized that he had been very active in our local community, and he had taken a sabbatical of sorts. Once he finished, I told him that I thought the concept was different from any program that had been introduced in this community, as far as I was aware. I could not deny that the timing for the program was quite appropriate given the state of African American males in our community. Yet I explained to him that I knew his participation in the community was superior to anyone's, and with that being the case, he was aware of the effort that would be required for this initiative to succeed: the full and complete cooperation of the local clergy from the African American churches. There could not be merely a representative from the church, but there would need to be a seat at the table, exclusively, for the pastors themselves. If they were being asked to have their churches make monetary contributions to the effort, the pastors would have to personally be involved. This can be a positive or negative based on the overall perception of the pastor or the church.

As seen in the story, the importance of involving the church and its leadership is often the critical component to getting certain community initiatives started. Often, there are hurdles that must be overcome to create community change. Sewell (2001) noted that even though there are significant challenges to overcome, the Black church still plays a pivotal role in building and enhancing communities. It is important for future researchers and scholars to assess the role of church leadership and how to partner with them and ensure that they have a legitimate seat at the table in an effort to influence change in the community.

Sewell (2003) further added that the role of the Black church in the community has changed from one of direct concern for the personal well-being of its citizens to one where the greater concern is based on social capital and personal gain by Black pastors. He noted that public service organizations have replaced the role of the Black church in communities, particularly in the South and in the Baptist denomination. However, despite the shifts in the way Black churches support communities and the disparities within, there is still a strong role played by select leaders who care about and are compassionate toward those who are oppressed by circumstances.

Historically, churches are the one place that African Americans have felt completely safe. It is there that family secrets can come out, financial problems can be revealed, and all manner of ailments and illnesses can be made known. The church is the one place in the African American community that people can feel as if they are a part of a community. Two people can live next door to each other and not see one another in the course of a week, but they will greet each other lovingly at church. So, it is in the church that there is a greater degree of consensus than there is anywhere else in the community. Thus, positioning spiritual capital in conjunction with engagement can provide the opportunity for enhanced engagement, especially since there is an established connection between community engagement and spiritual capital (Burgess, 2011).

Even though the study of spiritual capital and civic engagement is a relatively new area of research sociologically, it has been in existence from the beginnings of the African American church. Historians and writers have written about how African Americans sought from the church the sense of purpose that the White establishment tried to deny them (Sewell, 2001). It was in the church, in their "Sunday-go-to-meetin' clothes," that they felt dignified and walked with their heads held high and chests out. It was there that they were as good as anybody else. That sense of importance led members to be diligent workers in, outside, and on behalf of the church. In no other community is the church as vital a part of a group's existence as in African American communities. The church continues to meet the needs of the communities, not only as a place to receive a spiritual balm but also as an information source for education and awareness. As an institution, it has historically operated as a conduit between communities and agencies that seek to deliver any number of services to the local residents. As a result, it is important for church leaders to understand how to connect spiritual capital to community engagement for better outcomes when engaging (see Table 8.3).

TABLE 8.3 *Steps for the Church to Connect Spiritual Capital and Community Engagement*

1. Build leadership capacity among individuals and organizations and their ability to participate in a process that involves multiple institutions and structures designed to engage and empower individuals and communities.

2. Develop and enhance the knowledge and skills of organizational leaders and community members to intentionally engage, locally and in the regions with elected officials and agencies, around policy and political issues regarding health, education, social, and economic disparities.

3. Enhance opportunities to build trust between community and church leadership.

4. Foster a culture that allows relationships to be enhanced for purposes of engagement.

5. Enhance the faith-based organization's capacity to plan, develop, implement, and sustain ongoing community engagement activities.

6. Provide training, access to multimedia tools, and community-building skills to organize, engage, and train citizens for increased engagement.

MAKING IT WORK—PRACTICAL APPLICATIONS

Civil rights activist and Baptist preacher Martin Luther King Jr. made a profound statement that has stirred the passions of communities and churches for decades: "Any religion that professes to be concerned about the souls of men and not the slums that damn them, the economic conditions that strangle them or the social conditions that cripple them is as a dry as dust religion" (King, 2008, p. 64). This statement should challenge every religious leader to think outside the box and to dare to do more than preach to people about the eternal destiny of their souls. In addition to spiritual well-being, the components of human existence and welfare must be addressed. It is imperative that faith-based leaders work with communities to address issues that plague disparate and underserved populations.

Leaders and community members must do more than just organize awareness, education, and prevention programs to serve disparate communities. They must become more deliberate about identifying and addressing the challenges and barriers to engagement around health, education, economic, and social disparities, particularly with human service providers and civic and government leadership. Partnerships need to be forged with other faith-based leaders to help everyone understand that the disparities must not only be addressed at a local level but also approached on all levels: community, county, regional, and national.

Using effective tools in a purposeful manner will certainly support this effort. Incorporating the power of spiritual capital as a tool for effective engagement, along with the intrinsic spirituality of the church, provides an option for faith-based leaders to build the foundation for having a sustainable effect on the community. The African American church leadership is a key player in connecting spiritual capital and engagement. According to Burgess (2011), spiritual capital is an important component of leadership, which leads to higher levels of engagement and participation. Many community-changing events have found their beginnings within the walls of the church, especially in African American communities, so what better connector than using the church as a springboard for spiritual capital and engagement? Bruning et al. (2006) agreed that, primarily, the church was the only place where more than a few Blacks could gather without immediate repercussions. Thus engagement for many communities began in the church because of the need for individuals to rally together and act. Still, today, in the 21st century, the church is often used as the launching pad for many community endeavors. If the faith community and its leadership get behind a cause, there will be more traction toward that cause.

THE INFLUENCE OF FAITH-BASED LEADERS

Crawford and Olson (2001) described spiritual leaders as those called by God within the framework of their faith communities to guide God's people. This puts faith-based leaders in a unique position to influence the communities in which they are located. Often, you find faith-based leaders engaging in subtle political activities, such as forming partnerships with police and other nonprofits to bring about reform in communities. While these activities and partnerships are needed and necessary, faith-based leaders will have to be more purposeful, intentional, and focused on building relationships and capacity internal to their own communities as well.

Faith-based leaders have a responsibility to help others live out their callings in all areas of life. According to Jackman (2005), people called as spiritual leaders have a unique connection to the big picture of God's agenda. Ideally, faith-based leaders lead with faith—for both themselves and their followers—while creating community. The faith community's primary purpose is to transform lives. They transform individuals, who in turn can positively affect the community as a whole (Winseman, 2002). The key to expanding engagement practices as a tool for empowerment and change is to help faith-based leaders understand the power of spiritual capital and relationship building as a unifying force that can, and will, transform lives and build sustainable communities. Frequently, faith-based leaders feel they have a certain obligation to preach and teach about issues that affect their church communities. As a result, the difficulty with this lies in keeping people motivated who have become passive with regard to community engagement. Throop (2008) noted that this works both ways. It is also challenging for church members to stay motivated if their leadership has become passive. This is often because of a lack of skill development and relationship building, as well as a lack of trust.

Faith-based leaders play an important role in promoting skill development for themselves and their congregations. The importance of enhancing skill development and supporting congregants is conveyed when faith-based leaders see more opportunities for all involved parties. What appears to be happening today is a decline in the value and execution of skill development and engagement. According to Ellison (2010), it is imperative that faith-based leaders pass on to their congregations not only the concepts of engagement but also the associated actions required to make engagement happen. In a study conducted by Carter-Edwards et al. (2012), findings suggest that the clergy plays a significant role in the area of garnering participation among its membership. They note that it is important to build collaborative individual and church models to implement programs and activities that will mobilize members to improve engagement behaviors (i.e., health behaviors to diminish disparities) with the church and community.

The authors of this chapter note that one such avenue for improving engagement practices is the use of spiritual capital to promote change in participatory behaviors. Spiritual capital sways people to act through a level of higher motivation and service for the well-being of those involved. Its critical component is to build better relationships, thus providing a natural platform for the willingness to engage. Further, spiritual capital, according to Zohar and Marshall (2004), improves society and provides for more than material needs. In addition, it builds a correlation between the physical and spiritual well-being of individuals working for a common purpose. This leads to the conceptualization that when faith-based leaders understand the power of spiritual capital and learn ways to use it effectively, engagement is a natural outcome. It allows for a greater connection between people and the organizations they work with.

THE CHALLENGES AND OPPORTUNITIES OF WORKING WITH FAITH-BASED LEADERS

The primary challenge involves influencing faith-based leaders to step outside their theological, denominational, local, and personal boxes to consider the reality of disparities that stagnate and threaten the well-being of communities. Another challenge is convincing leaders to stay true to the process that will bring about changes in disparities and to encourage key leaders from their churches to engage as well. An example of providing leaders with the tools to improve participatory engagement includes helping them build skills in using tools such as community forums and established monthly meetings to ensure that they stay with the process. It is also important to help faith-based leaders understand that the disparities that do exist in their communities did not come overnight and that the problems from the disparities will not leave immediately. Lastly, a further challenge is getting faith-based leaders to reecho what they were taught about engagement to their congregations. Table 8.4 depicts the Community Empowerment Network (CEN) story, describing an example of how this engagement works when done well.

TABLE 8.4 *The CEN Story*

The Community Empowerment Network (CEN) of North Carolina was a collaboration of multicounty faith-based organizations whose mission was to advance their communities through partnerships that thrive on economic development, superior education, and elimination of health disparities. The CEN of North Carolina was an outgrowth of program development activities initiated by Success Dynamics Community Development Corporation in Farmville, North Carolina. Dr. Calvin Ellison served as the executive director of Success Dynamics and the chair of CEN. CEN was established in 2005 through support for Success Dynamics from the Office of Minority Health and Health Disparities. The CEN leadership and community engagement model (developed from work with Dr. Forrest Toms and North Carolina Agricultural and Technical State University's doctoral program in leadership studies) is an outgrowth of an identified need on the part of faith-based leaders to be intentional about developing the knowledge, skills, and planning necessary to address policy issues and disparities among poor and underrepresented people and a commitment to find ways to collectively use the power of the church to leverage resources to improve the quality of life of communities in the eastern regions of North Carolina. The CEN of North Carolina began with 12 churches in one regional chapter and has grown to eight regional chapters with more than 100 churches. This growth was a result of leaders understanding the need for community empowerment and engagement.

Note: Because of losing its primary funding source, CEN was dissolved in 2012. However, the churches involved in the initiative were equipped with the capacity to continue engagement practices.

The CEN of North Carolina was one example of the way communities can come together to begin engaging and working to change communities on a more permanent basis. The CEN model began by engaging more faith-based organizations in an educational process to empower, impact, and advance their community. The churches involved were instructed and trained on how to design, develop, and implement nontraditional outreach programs, establish resource centers, and lead and manage an effective organization. They were given training in organizational, programmatic, and leadership development, as well as community engagement practices.

Another opportunity given to the participating organizations was exposure to community and state agencies (i.e., Department of Commerce, community colleges and universities, local health departments, and others) with which many had never interacted. Further, the CEN of North Carolina participated in two signature programs that were developed by Toms et al. (2008). The first program, the Leadership Enhancement and Engagement Project, is a capacity-building program that focuses on leadership development and community engagement. The second program, Participation, Engagement, and Practice, is focused on civic and community advocacy. Both of these programs were implemented within the CEN.

Further, more generic opportunities can involve faith-based leaders taking a closer look at the levels of spiritual capital among their leaders and themselves. They must seek ways to help leaders understand the connections involved in community engagement and the importance of such connections. For example, pastors can use spiritual capital as a teaching topic to help leaders recognize that it is positively related to personal willingness to participate and that it has an effect on engagement within communities. In an effort to take the ideology of spiritual capital to the next level, it is important to go beyond the immediate leadership and include as many community members as possible in the learning and implementation process. This allows for using spiritual capital as a bridge and motivator for more engagement. Lastly, faith-based leaders can seek methods by which to increase spiritual capital among individuals in an effort to counteract the notion that people are not willing to engage. Using existing structures within faith-based organizations, such as missions, is another way to create value around engagement. This is an opportunity to garner existing resources for a common cause while working toward sustainable practices for continuous engagement.

FORGING RELATIONSHIPS FOR ENGAGEMENT

The realization regarding effective engagement is that to see systems change and create greater community impact, leaders and community members must involve and empower their communities. This can be done by engaging more faith-based leaders, community leaders, and community members in a synergistic effort of using spiritual capital as a tool for engagement. The relationship-building component of spiritual capital is one of the greatest aspects of empowering the community; emphasis must be placed on the importance of unity in the group and the equity of relationships. For example, pastors can take the opportunity to put this process to work by getting mission leaders to discuss spiritual capital and how they might collectively develop/support existing community programs by each one taking on separate responsibilities for the benefit of the whole group. This provides an opportunity for intentional engagement with each other. Other examples would include inviting expert speakers on specific subject matters, ensuring that both leadership and community members are in attendance, and hosting monthly roundtable meetings to discuss specific community issues.

Further, forging relationships with community and state organizations is critically important to the growth and overall success of a community and to faith-based organizations. Building collaborations with other organizations opens doors for increased resources, funding, training, and program development. Addressing the challenges and opportunities that exist when building and sustaining relationships with faith-based leaders is beneficial to the advancement of the elimination of health, social, educational, and economic disparities. Problems do not go away because they are ignored; it is imperative that communities address these issues and engage in the process of change (Ellison, 2010).

MAXIMIZING SPIRITUAL CAPITAL

Another important viewpoint to consider is the use of spiritual capital outside the arena of faith-based organizations. Since spiritual capital is not determined by religious denominations, leadership outside the religious purview may opt to give attention to the notion of spiritual capital. Viewing spiritual capital from the perspective of intrinsic values, power, relationships, and influence will allow other leaders to use it to facilitate avenues for engagement that are not faith-based related. As a result, the stigma often associated with people as spiritual beings or the focus on religion can be capitulated through spiritual capital, as it is viewed as an intrinsic value that any person can use, no matter their religious preferences.

Spiritual capital is universal in that it requires an intentional plan focused on engagement activities. Intentional training and development among all people about how to engage and what to engage in will create processes for building more focused relationships that connect engagement that is lasting. The ultimate goal is to help leaders and communities understand the necessity of their influence in engagement practices and the importance of exercising personal spiritual capital as a resource for participation. The use of spiritual capital is an avenue by which faith-based leaders may connect to other leaders through building trust and exercising their faith among themselves to facilitate more engagement in communities. Burgess (2011) noted that spiritual capital is one way to highlight the opportunity for transforming behavior among community leaders and members, thus creating participatory mindsets. It is important to help leaders first understand the benefits of using spiritual capital and then how to expand it to provide greater opportunities for engagement and participation. As noted in Table 8.5, the expansion of spiritual capital includes viewing it as (a) values based, (b) a resource, (c) a type of wealth, (d) a leadership tool, and (e) a component for policy changes.

SUMMARY

While spiritual capital is a relatively new phenomenon, helping communities consider the value of it and how to use it with specific learning tasks is a necessity. Also, creating learning environments for spiritual capital will be important for continuing engagement through this avenue. This involves gaining an understanding of the key components of spiritual capital, understanding the role of the church and its leadership and how they connect it to engagement, and expanding engagement outside the arena of faith-based institutions. Further, helping communities build leadership capacity among community members and individuals through the use of spiritual capital is a key element in continuing to improve engagement practices (Burgess, 2011). This involves helping communities understand the power of intentionally engaging and

TABLE 8.5 *Spiritual Capital Expanded*

COMPONENT	EXPLANATION
1. Values Based	Gives an advantage in situations where material wealth cannot
	Raises the common good among people
	More sustainable than social capital
2. Expanded Resource	Valuable resource
	Physical and mental resource
	Positive cultural impact
	Relational asset (family, groups, community activities, and social connections)
3. Type of Wealth	Viewed as nonphysical wealth
	Builds leadership capacity
4. Leadership	Connects spiritual capital to engagement through leadership
	Serves as a bridge to influence participation
	Expanded outside of faith-based organizations
5. Policy	Effect on the church and state and the relationship with the Internal Revenue Service laws
	Access to political leaders and polity

empowering each other, unlike past programs and ideas that have left them disenfranchised and further disengaged. The best outcome is to encourage participation and engagement through sustainable methods and the use of ideologies, such as spiritual capital, which are designed to assist leaders and their communities. Highlighting the importance of spiritual capital as a resource available (to all citizens) to be used to improve or better the conditions of communities may frame the way leaders perceive and use it with other resources to enhance engagement. A new challenge to community engagement includes building bridges across generations to maintain and expand leadership and engagement. According to Burgess and Martin-Jones (2018), spiritual capital is a tool that can support bridging the gap between generations and community engagement. If current leaders are able to recognize and accept the capital that younger generations bring, then they will not only accept but also seek room for them at the table to build greater capacity.

DISCUSSION QUESTIONS

1. Discuss how spiritual capital can be used for community engagement in communities where megachurches are located and the majority of church membership is from outside the local community.
2. Think about the chapter definition of spiritual capital. How do you use your personal spiritual capital for engagement and with whom?

3. Discuss how you think spiritual capital and community engagement can work outside of faith-based organizations. Provide examples.
4. What are some barriers to the effective use of spiritual capital in community engagement?
5. How might leaders think of ways to engage different generations in the community engagement process?

REFERENCES

Bruning, S. D., McGrew, S., & Cooper, M. (2006). Town-gown relationships: Exploring university-community engagement from the perspective of community members. *Public Relations Review, 32,* 125–130.

Burgess, S. W. (2011). *Spiritual capital: Relationship with civic engagement among faith-based leaders* [Unpublished doctoral dissertation]. North Carolina Agricultural and Technical State University.

Burgess, S. W, & Martin-Jones, K. M. (2018) Spirituality and value-centeredness. In J. Marques (Ed.), *The Routledge companion to management and workplace spirituality* (pp. 292–303) Routledge.

Carter-Edwards, L., Hooten, E. G., Bruce, M., Toms, F. D., Lloyd, C. L., & Ellison, C. (2012). Pilgrimage to wellness: An exploratory report of rural African American clergy perceptions of church health promotion capacity. *Journal of Prevention & Intervention in the Community, 40*(3), 197–207.

Centra, L., & McDonald, S. (1997). *Applying principles to the community engagement process.* Retrieved March 2013 from http://www.cdc.gov/phppo/pce/part3.htm

Crawford, S. E. S., & Olson, L. R. (2001). *Christian clergy in American politics.* Johns Hopkins University Press.

Ellison, C. (2010). *Challenges and opportunities of organizing faith-based leaders to lead* [Paper presentation]. Annual Meeting of the American Educational Research Association, Denver, CO, United States.

Goode, T., Dunne, C., & Bronheim, S. (2006). The Evidence Base for Cultural and Linguistic Competence in Health Care. The Commonwealth Fund.

Jackman, I. (2005). *The leader's mentor: Inspiration from the world's most effective leaders.* Random House.

King, C. S. (2008). *The words of Martin Luther King, Jr.* Newmarket Press.

Lloyd, C. M. (2010). *University relations* [Unpublished doctoral dissertation]. North Carolina Agricultural and Technical State University.

Putnam, R. D. (1995). Bowling alone: America's declining social capital. *Journal of Democracy, 6*(1), 65–78.

Sewell, S. (2001). African American religion: The struggle for community development in a southern city. *Journal of Southern Religion, 4.* http://jsr.fsu.edu/2001/sewellart.htm

Sewell, S. (2003). Lead me, guide me along the way: A study of the relationship between pastors' personal characteristics and their level of community participation. *North Star: A Journal of African American Religious History, 7*(1), 1–18.

Throop, J. R. (2008). The pastor as community witness: Prophetic call, public limits. *Clergy Journal* (July/August), 17–18.

Toms, F. D. (1997). *Communities in transition: Challenges and opportunities of community building.* Training Research Development, Inc.

Toms, F. D. (2010). Black elected officials and community/civic engagement [Paper presentation]. Annual Meeting of the American Education Research Association. Denver, CO, United States.

Toms, F. D., Glover, S., Erwin, A., & Ellison, C. (2008). Leadership and community engagement: A faith-based capacity building model. *Leadership Studies Magazine, 1,* pp. *13–15.*

Winseman, A. L. (2002). *In my congregation, my spiritual needs are met.* Gallup. http://www.gallup.com/poll/tb/religValue/20020723b.asp

Zohar, D., & Marshall, I. (2004). *Spiritual capital: Wealth we can live by.* Berrett-Koehler Publishers.

CHAPTER NINE

Engaging for Successful Community-Based Disaster Recovery

Myra Shird, PhD

DESCRIPTION OF THE PROJECT, ARGUMENTS

Background

This project proposes a grassroots community education program that empowers African American communities in local rural geographies to undertake community-based disaster management.

Studies document that racial and ethnic minorities may be at a disadvantage in terms of crisis preparedness (Spence et al., 2007). Why is this true? Lack of knowledge limits the ability of low socioeconomic groups to respond and recover from a disaster. Ethnic and racial minorities in rural areas are often at a lower socioeconomic level and may be excluded from preparedness and disaster-related messages and actions because of cultural or language barriers (Masozera et al., 2007).

A Disastrous Need

With the proliferation of natural disasters, local communities should be equipped to respond, mitigate against, and recover from their impacts. The federal government has provided disaster relief in the form of financial aid; however, communities should not rely solely on federal agencies. As was seen during the 2012 presidential campaign season, not all politicians support federal interventions on this level (Madhani & Kucinich, 2012).

Storms Keep on Coming

According to the National Weather Service, on average, each year, 10,000 thunderstorms, 5,000 floods, 1,000 tornadoes, and six named hurricanes literally take U.S. communities by storm. In addition, about 90% of all presidentially declared disasters are weather related, leading to almost 500 deaths per year and nearly $14 billion in damage.

When a community neglects to plan for the onslaught of a potential natural disaster or weather event, that community compounds the effect of the event because it has not properly planned. Disaster readiness is a continuous cycle of planning. Specific steps are necessary to mitigate against, respond to, and recover from natural disasters, acts of terrorism, and man-made disasters. Weather events are of special importance to this project's target group: African Americans living in rural communities in the southeastern region of the United States.

A Climate Change Discussion

Climate change directly correlates with the increased number of disastrous weather events experienced in the United States and the challenges to water resources and crop and livestock production, as well as human health.

According to the National Oceanic and Atmospheric Administration, 2012 marked the 36th consecutive year with a global temperature above the 20th-century average (NOAA National Climatic Data Center, 2012). The average annual temperature for the contiguous United States in 2012 was above the 20th-century average and was the warmest year in the 1895–2012 time frame. In addition, it was the 15th driest year on record. During 2012, the United States experienced its fourth warmest winter, a record warm spring, second warmest summer, and a warmer-than-average autumn. "The warmer-than-average seasons resulted in large percentages of the country ranking as 'very warm'" (NOAA National Climatic Data Center, 2012, para. 16). The southern region of the United States experienced some of the most widespread extremes during 2012 (NOAA National Climatic Data Center, 2012).

Vulnerabilities to climate change depend not only on where people are but also on their circumstances. Vulnerability to natural disasters is characterized as "the capacity to anticipate, cope with, resist and recover from the impact of a natural disaster" (Masozera et al., 2007, p. 300).

> In the future (as in the past), the impacts of climate change are likely to fall disproportionately on the disadvantaged. People with few resources often live in conditions that increase their vulnerability to the effects of climate change. (Karl et. al, 2009, p. 101)

Climate change effects on the southeast have lasting effects. Some of those mentioned in the following list highlight the adversarial impacts.

- Projected increases in air and water temperatures will cause heat-related stresses for people, plants, and animals.
- Decreased water availability is very likely to affect the region's economy, as well as its natural systems.

- Sea-level rise and the likely increase in hurricane intensity and associated storm surge will be among the most serious consequences of climate change.
- Quality of life will be affected by increasing heat stress, water scarcity, severe weather events, and reduced availability of insurance for at-risk properties.

Minority Impact

Natural disasters know no color, race, age, or socioeconomic background. Communities consisting of minorities are affected by disasters as frequently as majority communities. Disaster impacts may include a loss of housing stock, damaged infrastructure and transportation systems, and loss or limited access to energy sources, health, and social services. Impacts may not be visible; however, they may be felt. Bullard and Wright (2005) noted that black and white hurricane survivors also find themselves displaced from their homes. However, institutional discrimination cause blacks to have different experiences and challenges than whites in rebuilding their lives, homes, businesses, institutions, and communities after a hurricane.

"For people who cannot afford the costs of repair, reconstruction, relocation, it may take years to recover from the aftermath of disasters. The effects of a disaster may persist to the next generation because of lack of resources to recover" (Masozera et al., 2007, p. 300). This project is about leveling the playing field. It is a proactive effort that encourages and educates community members about taking charge of their own preparedness and becoming more self-reliant.

The Language of Preparedness Messaging

Current preparedness communications often do not speak to the individual. They speak to a faceless bureaucratic apparatus developed to respond to impending danger. As with other minority co-cultures, African Americans living in small rural areas are more in tune with the language of their community. The language of "the man," the oft-referenced powerful oppressor attributed to causing many of the negative conditions faced by the African American community, is not trusted. If this language carries with it the baggage of reprehensible racial injustice, distrust is understandable. The distrust that many African Americans feel toward power structures, such as the government, is about the lack of social justice.

God Talk as a Tactic for Disaster-Readiness Messaging

Katrina has exposed shortcomings in emergency preparedness, command and control, accountability, communication, and public trust. It is clear that if those directly affected by natural and manmade disasters don't have confidence in authorities, then it may be hard to get the public to take proper preventive steps.

> In order for homeland security programs—and related emergency preparedness programs for that matter—to be effective they must have the cooperation and trust of all Americans. (Bullard & Wright, 2005)

For the Christian community, the first preparedness message was delivered to Noah when God told him to prepare for the impending flood. He essentially communicated a preparedness message. From the beginning of biblical recordings of such crisis communications, naysayers have been reluctant to heed warnings. They have not believed, accepted, or acted upon crisis communication messages. Yet for the African American community, religious messages evoke a type of unifying strand.

The African American church has long been considered the nerve center of the African American community and the message hub for that which is important to the community. Political leaders and aspiring politicians use the church platform as a way of espousing their political agendas and aspirations. During election season, candidates compete for audiences with African American parishioners, so they may espouse the need for the community to come to action and to make choices for their future by getting out and voting for the candidate most likely to protect their interests. Church leaders often become enthralled in these calls for action and go as far as offering the use of church vans and buses as transportation so that community members can easily travel to various voting locations.

These political calls are quite frequently couched in the emotive language of religiosity—a language familiar to the parishioners. Drawing parallels between the injustice described in biblical works and the injustices the politicians purport a desire to eradicate (or at the least minimize) is a communication mechanism that draws parishioners into the politician's message. Because parishioners identify with "God"-infused talk, they are more likely to react favorably to these messages. Disaster-preparedness messengers in the African American Christian community would benefit from using this same strategy to relay their messages.

Cultural Perception of Messages About Impending Disasters

From a cultural standpoint, language is considered a "non-material component of culture. Non-material components of culture are intangible constructions that impact how we behave and think" (Shird, 2007, p. 72). "Language molds our perceptions of life, perceptions of ourselves, and our perceptions of ourselves in relation to others in the world" (Shird, 2007, p. 73). If disaster-preparedness messaging is packaged in a way that celebrates the culture of the people it is intended to educate, it is much more likely to achieve the end in which it is intended. Building the argument that African American churchgoers are members of a particular co-culture that embraces religious language, it would be beneficial to further explore the collectivistic nature of this group. Collectivistic cultures tend to focus on the group rather than the individual person (Shird, 2007, p. 73). In their approach to knowledge, which is how people come to know what is real and what is true, collectivistic cultures tend to focus on the subjective experience of a thing, in contrast to individualistic cultures that tend to know based on "what they can see, hear, feel, taste or smell" (Shird, 2007, p. 74). For collectivistic cultures, knowledge comes from the feelings associated with the thing. If African American Christians in the rural southeastern United States "feel" the preparedness message speaks to them, they are much more likely to embrace the call to action.

This proposed plan develops a structure for putting a community-based, disaster-readiness program in place. A strong characteristic of this project is that it is based in an already trusted and established institution within the African American community: the church. In addition, the project incorporates the church's already existing small groups (women's groups, choir, usher board) into the preparedness planning process, eliminating the need to initially create new groups. With guidance from disaster preparedness subject matter experts (SMEs), the church and its auxiliary groups can champion the preparedness education program, identify community risks, propose mitigation strategies, and develop recovery plans. There will be an organized outreach effort to community members not involved in the church to gain their participation and cooperation. A powerful component of this proposal is that it calls for the collaboration of all the churches within a targeted area to work toward self-sufficiency in terms of disaster preparedness. This community-based effort puts individuals in the community in decision-making roles concerning how they face imminent disasters.

PROJECT OUTPUTS: COMMUNITY ENGAGEMENT

The steps and proposals outlined here are designed to move the disaster-preparedness efforts forward and in the direction prescribed by the community's people.

Readiness Task Force Development

In the initial phase of the readiness project, African American churches are identified for participation. Churches will be asked to commit to a 90-day engagement process, where the readiness framework will be put in place. Once concurrence is reached, the church's auxiliary groups will be transformed into task forces that will facilitate the readiness agenda and manage the tactical aspects of delivery, including recruiting new members, setting up meetings, and advertising the readiness program. After an all-inclusive community visioning session is conducted by the SME, groups will be established as task forces representative of particular segments of the community. A task force is a temporary grouping under one leader for the purpose of accomplishing set goals. As the community develops its preparedness plans and activities, it may choose to identify task forces broken down by sector, responsibility, or subject matter expertise. Task forces will potentially focus on preparedness training, mitigation training and strategy development, recovery planning, and advocacy. Each community is responsible for identifying its own priority areas. These grassroots teams gather the community's ideas and begin developing those ideas into projects. The group will advance the preparedness message, formulate response activities, identify mitigation strategies, and propose recovery strategies. This framework provides a structured process for developing community-based preparedness, mitigation, and recovery project ideas. If the community undertakes this type of project development process, a completed project proposal is presented to the whole community for acceptance and incorporation into the preparedness plan.

Getting Ready for That Great Day: Tasks and Responsibilities

Task Force Members:

- Catalog community ideas
- Research and identify preparedness curricula to provide ongoing community education sessions
- Orchestrate preparedness, response, and recovery exercises
- Identify project champions

   Project champions are project advocates. Champions further research what needs to be done to bring the project idea to an implementation state. They develop timelines and identify partners that can assist in project implementation. Partners include funding resources, technical assistance, and community supporters

- Host four community open house events per year in the first year of engagement and two events each year thereafter. Open house sessions are informational and may include readiness exercises
- Hold regular open meetings (advertise)

Task Force Lead:

- Coordinates with other task force leads and identifies opportunities for collaboration on task force projects
- Determines how projects can be developed in a way that best leverages resources
- Identifies scribe/note taker to provide notes to the readiness facilitator
- Calls meetings and sets agendas

The task force lead and prospective project champion present the project to the steering committee.

Steering Committee:

- Determines if a group is composed of task force leads from churches in the network
- Analyzes programs/projects for feasibility

- Identifies opportunities where multiple task forces can collaborate
- Holds regular open meetings (advertises)
- Assures all projects are prioritized based on whether the project
  a. Supports the disaster-readiness vision
  b. Identifies the champion
  c. Identifies potential funding sources
  d. Contacts potential funding sources
  e. Gains commitments from potential funding sources

The steering committee represents projects to local emergency management agencies and municipal and state leadership for potential technical and financial assistance. Committee members have a keen understanding of funding sources and a demonstrated ability to raise funds for project implementation. The committee facilitates local-, municipal-, and state-level efforts to gain support for the community's preparedness agenda.

<u>Preparedness Facilitator:</u>

- Represents the community as a volunteer
- Acts as a member of the steering committee
- Acts as a scribe and administrative support to the steering committee
- Facilitates the organization of community open house events
- Manages project implementation
- Identifies readiness resources (technical assistance and funding)
- Facilitates the communication of the readiness activities to the community, media, steering committee, and municipal leadership
- Identifies the need for ad hoc committees and staffs those committees
- Communicates monthly with state and regional resources, inclusive of legislative and congressional representatives
- Serves as the media contact for preparedness efforts
- Catalogs task force minutes for web postings
- Facilitates the maintenance of the readiness website
- Attends task force meetings

Existing Terrain and Newness of Concept

This project furthers the work done by numerous preparedness efforts. Tools and resources are recommended by the National Consensus Panel on Emergency Preparedness and Cultural Diversity, Ready.gov, the National Preparedness Coalition, and the National Resource Center on Advancing the Emergency Preparedness for Culturally Diverse Communities. These resources provide tools and guidelines to aid minority communities in responding to risks, which include natural and man-made disasters. All of these resources catalog and demonstrate how to become disaster ready. Unfortunately, like much of the communication on preparedness, the messages rarely make it to rural African American communities. This knowledge is still bound, provided, and consumed by those historically deemed as the most privileged of the community. This proposed community education program is a proactive endeavor. The overarching goal is to use the tools provided by the aforementioned entities to educate individuals living in predominantly African American communities in rural parts of the southeastern United States.

IMPACT

The target community for this project is African Americans living in rural parts of the southeastern United States, especially unincorporated areas; however, the benefits extend to the larger composition of incorporated areas, inclusive of germane towns, cities, states, and the nation as a whole. When community capacity of these smaller areas is built so that individuals can prepare for, respond to, mitigate against, and recover from natural disasters, it minimizes the strain on the national economy. For fiscal year 2013, the Federal Emergency Management Agency requested $5,481,000,000 for major declared disasters (Federal Emergency Management Agency, 2013). Potentially, this dollar figure can be reduced if more communities plan and prepare.

DISASTER-PREPAREDNESS COMMUNICATION STRATEGY

Objective
To provide citizens with continuous information about disaster-preparedness messages and planning activities.

Recommendation

- Develop a community-wide newsletter
- Develop a computer-mediated social network
- Link the disaster-preparedness newsletter to existing community-based websites, including all church sites

Modes of Delivery
A hard-copy newsletter is distributed at the following locations:

- Churches
- Municipal buildings
- Community banks

- Local businesses
  a. Barbershops
  b. Grocers
  c. Hair salons
  d. Medical facilities
  e. Auto dealerships

Computer-Mediated Social Network

- Establish a Yahoo®/Google® group for task forces, steering committees, and church networks
- Establish a Twitter® account
- Newsletter web links
  a. Social media
  b. Church websites
  c. Community-based organizations' websites

Phone Tree

Task force members will be instructed to communicate the results of meetings to friends and to invite them to participate in upcoming meetings.

Assessment Method for Communication Strategy

- Measure the number of participants (guests—referring to community members in attendance but not *officially* on the roster) from week to week to determine if the number of attendees increases, decreases, or stays the same
- Survey weekly participants (guests) to determine how they heard about the meetings

REFERENCES

Bullard, R. D., & Wright, B. (2005). *Legacy of unfairness: Why some Americans get left behind.* Dr. Robert Bullard Father of Environmental Justice. Retrieved January 27, 2013, from http://www.ejrc.cau.edu/Exec%20Summary%20Legacy.html

Federal Emergency Management Agency. (2013, January 31). *About: Budget.* www.fema.gov/pdf/about/budget/11F_FEMA_disaster_relief_fund_dhs_FY13_cj.pdf

Karl, T., Melillo, J., & Peterson, T. (2009). *Global climate change impacts in the United States.* Cambridge University Press.

Madhani, A., & Kucinich, J. (2012, October 29). Hurricane puts spotlight on Romney's FEMA remarks. *USA Today.* http://www.usatoday.com/story/news/politics/2012/10/29/romney-fema-hurricane/1667059/

Masozera, M., Bailey, M., & Kerchner, C. (2007). Distribution of impacts of natural disasters across income groups: A case study of New Orleans. *Ecological Economics, 63*(2–3), 299–306.

NOAA National Climatic Data Center. (2012, December). *State of the climate: National overview for annual 2012.* Retrieved February 3, 2013, from http://www.ncdc.noaa.gov/sotc/national/2012/13

Shird, M. (2007). *Communication voices.* Kendall/Hunt Publishing Company.

Spence, P. R., Lachlan, K. A., & Griffin, D. R. (2007). Crisis communication, race and natural disasters. *Journal of Black Studies, 37*(4), 539–554.

PART III

Community/Civic Engagement in Action

CHAPTER TEN

Readiness and Preparedness for Civic Engagement

PRINCIPLES AND PRACTICES FOR COMMUNITY INSTITUTIONAL PARTNERSHIPS

Cheryl LeMay Lloyd, PhD, and Michael Palmer, CPA, CIA

CIVIC ENGAGEMENT AND institutions of higher education committed to research, teaching, and outreach are among the original properties of the participatory democracy that so uniquely frames the American experience. Universities find their future success framed by the effectiveness of not only their research and teaching but also the quality of the outreach and engagement that occurs with their communities of interest and place. Other governmental organizations, nonprofits institutions, and private businesses have come to the realization that engagement with people and communities benefits all interested parties. In the 21st century, communities, universities, and other institutions find sustainability in responding collaboratively to their most visionary interests. Success is tethered to the unbiased expertise and resources found in universities, profitable and nonprofit institutions, and community residents. The necessary partnerships between institutions and communities are most effective when both partners are prepared to face the challenges of celebrating mutual benefits, individual assets, and disparate interests.

This chapter explores the indicators of preparedness and readiness by both institutions and communities for sustainable engagement and the prerequisite leadership expectations. Much has been written of the structural prerequisites needed in effective partnerships (i.e., social capital, financial capital, and human capital). The reader is encouraged to consider the implications of interpersonal paradigms and relationships as benefits to developing sustainable partnerships. Community leaders and university partners found value in the concepts of learning in public and spiritual capital in our previous study. The exploration of social, fiscal, human, and interpersonal capital leads to critical questions for university and community leaders. We would suggest that other institutions would benefit from this exploration also. How might leaders assess structural readiness for civic engagement? What are the indicators and implications for leaders in accessing interpersonal readiness? Could these tenets imply a different way of leading?

PRINCIPLES AND PRACTICES FOR COMMUNITY INSTITUTIONAL PARTNERSHIPS

Community and civic engagement with universities and other nonprofit or for-profit institutions require communities and institutions to be prepared for the engagement, just as individual students and institutions must be ready for successful relationships. Preparedness and readiness can be interpreted as simply the capacity to access and develop the fiscal or physical attributes to produce the intended outcomes. Community leaders might inquire about the following: Is this a relationship or a transaction? Do you have what it takes to help us? Is there a resource to fund a community project? Is there a trustworthy person who will serve as the connection to funding? Institutional leaders inquire as to the ability of the community to meet the demographic requirement of their grants, or the fiscal capacity to address their needs, without excessive contributions from the institution. Engagement does require that these utilitarian questions of capacity be addressed, but there must also be emotional (relational) readiness. While there are structural prerequisites, and these are important, there are also interpersonal constructs that must be achieved in order for engagement to be sustainable and productive. Leadership for such partnerships will continue to be critical to the sustainability of both institutions and communities. This is particularly important in the 21st century's technologically dependent environment.

One might agree with the premise that our institutions of higher learning harbor a "high concentration" of this nation's intellectual capacity. One might also assume or agree that some of the most significant issues confronting this nation and the world are those "rooted" in poverty. Thus, it logically follows that if we as a nation are to optimize "our civilization" and serve as a beacon to the world, then it is imperative that we focus a significant portion of our "intellectual capacity" and "future leadership training" on solving poverty-related issues. Many of the nation's premier colleges and universities reside in or are proximate to economically challenged communities. This yields a fully equipped "low-wealth" socioeconomic "classroom" endowed with untold indigenous wisdom. Academic contributions that generate local workable solutions can initiate and inspire "portable" best practices to scale up by influencing public and economic policy. This challenge requires the innovative and visionary perspectives of entrepreneurs in public, private, nonprofit, and for-profit organizations as well. It is the engagement of all partners that promises benefits to the larger community.

This chapter discussion includes a set of common constructs or definitions, a case "story," not case study, and a series of introspective questions that will help you to better assess your personal and institutional readiness for engagement. Each component moves the community leader, the institutional partner, and the larger institution toward meaningful and sustainable engagement with *neighbors*.

Consider perspectives on the terms "community," "engagement," "leadership," and "spiritual capital." The rapidly changing world makes the defining of terms and constructs critically important to ensuring clarity for the development of new frameworks and the integration of old and new paradigms. Leadership without these shared meanings is doomed to implode.

As a term, *community* has both figurative and literal meanings that have evolved as our world has changed. Although locality or residency is the greatest predictor of community, relational proximity has become a more pronounced predictor of an individual's definition of community. This is perhaps one of many outcomes from the technologically advanced modes of communication that define the 21st century. Community residency can only be defined by community participants. Participants in the community determine the boundaries and have the authority to expand or contract those boundaries. Arbitrary designations of community, based on either physical proximity or relational correlations, can sabotage an engaged partnership prior to its inception. Communities of interest may be professionally, leisurely, or family focused, and they are group defined. Community will always be self-defined and engage the flexibility of its members and partners.

The Carnegie Foundation for the Advancement of Teaching describes *engagement* as collaboration between "institutions of higher education and their larger communities (local, regional/state, national, global) for the mutually beneficial exchange of knowledge and resources in a context of partnership and reciprocity. The purpose of community engagement is the partnership of college and university knowledge and resources with those of the public and private sectors to enrich scholarship, research, and creative activity; enhance curriculum, teaching, and learning; prepare educated, engaged citizens; strengthen democratic values and civic responsibility; address critical societal issues; and contribute to the public good" (Carnegie Foundation for the Advancement of Teaching, n.d.).

Carnegie, the noted authority on teaching and education, determined that engagement is so critical to the well-being of the academy that the foundation added two categories to higher education classifications in 2008 that denote a university's proficiency at such.

We would suggest that engagement is long term and reflects an internalization of the concepts of reciprocity and mutuality. Thus, engagement may not be collaborating on one project, or a grant, or even one community program. Institutions and communities benefit most from sustained relationships that create new solutions, incorporate the solutions in day-to-day living, and, eventually, generate new questions for the development of more new opportunities and new solutions. Although we visualize engagement as interactions between communities and institutions, sustainable engagement always reflects the relationships between individuals. Engagement is relational and requires interpersonal considerations.

Research consistently reflects engagement as associated with positive group socioeconomic outcomes, democratic processes, and improvements in educational and health outcomes. Communities and the people within communities are "better off" building skilled, knowledgeable citizens with the ability to prepare for a better future (Lloyd, 2010, p. 20).

Leadership is the ability to motivate individuals to select from among many life choices—one focus that they freely and enthusiastically give their best effort/resources to achieving. There are close to half a million other definitions according to Google®. The current environment of rapid change has produced a need for multidisciplinary thinking and suggests consistently that the 21st century requires collaborative leadership rather than the traditional leader-follower constructs (Drath et al., 2008). Leaders of engaged partnerships all reiterate the inability of one person's vision and agenda to achieve any traction in the journey toward boundary-spanning partnerships. This suggests the importance of self-confidence in one's own abilities prior to embarking on leading in an engaged partnership.

Colleges and universities are in the business of training tomorrow's leaders for government, industry, institutions, and communities. Human beings have their own unique combination of motives and triggers that must be discovered and incorporated in a leader's approach to optimizing individual and/or collective accomplishments. Consequently, leaders seek to comprehend and embrace the diversity of culture, learning style, philosophy, and thought orientation that motivates individuals to act strategically. There is no one-size-fits-all, cookie-cutter theory or approach to leading. A most relevant component, then, to educating future leaders who must be equipped to function in an ever-shrinking global economy is to provide them with "exposure or engagement" opportunities beyond their comfort zones. Urban institutions in particular offer a myriad of "controlled" exposure opportunities to provide carry-forward life referencing lessons and experiences for future leaders. The lesson from this construct is perhaps that you cannot effectively lead people you do not know, including yourself.

Spiritual capital is a unique construct that is critical to partners being engaged. It would suggest intentional relationships between individuals within a partnership—the relational connection that transcends the logical and contractual. It is representative of mutual faith that exceeds expectations of reciprocity. It is important to note that there is no reference to religion in this definition. Religiosity may lead to familiarity with the concept of spiritual capital, but it is not required for such relationships to develop. Most important is the need for the leaders in these relationships to exhibit self-confidence and maturity. This chapter offers a more extensive review of the concept of spiritual capital.

Preparedness for Engagement

What are the components needed for engagement to be successful from the very beginning? Similar to the personal relationships we build within our families, engagement begins with "commitment." To implement an effective engagement strategy, the institution must formally commit to the initiative. This key step is critical to readiness by an institution for engagement. Institutional leaders must contemplate personal commitment and the ability to lead their institution in dedication to a partnership and relationship. (Drath et al., 2008) suggested that commitment is the willingness to collectively subsume interest and benefits within the needs of the partnership. They further suggested that 21st-century leadership requires a unique tripod of direction, alignment, and commitment. How might a leader assess commitment? Consider the following questions as a starting point: Can you believe? What are the consequences of doing good? What do you feel when you see a smiling 4-year-old child who is of an ethnic group other than your own? Are you willing to search for the good? Do you have a vision? These may seem like unrelated thoughts, but they push leaders to recognize that commitment is more than participation. It requires one to engage emotionally. Institutions will have to consider with a critical eye similar questions. Institutions in search of grants or contracts alone must recognize that engagement is an institutional commitment important enough to require sacrifice. The sign outside the engagement door might say, "Grant and contract seekers—go home!" Consider the lessons one might learn from an engaged partnership.

Northside and the Jackson Center

A 20-year-old community center in Chapel Hill, North Carolina, offers a view into the work of a community with institutional partners that exhibit the tenets of sustainable and effective engagement. The center describes its work as inspiring generational change, inspiring intergenerational change, inspiring historic change, community-driven change and inspiring national change (Marian Cheek Jackson Center, 2020). The center works to create and protect ownership and economic opportunities for all in the community. Yet in a 2014 assessment of its purpose in the community, it describes it purpose as: "rooted in oral history listening and realized along three primary lines of creative community development: organizing and advocacy for livable neighborhoods, youth and education, and celebration and connection" (Marion Cheek Jackson Center, 2014, p. 2). The neighborhood of Northside was for many years a working-class minority community surrounded by the affluent college town within which it existed. Like many in this county, generational change and the struggles of gentrification gradually became the reality for the small neighborhood. Community members wanted desperately to hold on to their part of Chapel Hill. Business interests recognized the profitability that exists in the acquisition and sale or lease of the properties to more affluent town interests. Yet nonprofits and university students found an interest in helping to support this neighborhood and recognized the value of the skills and wisdom of the community to their organization. The Marian Cheek Jackson Center served a synergistic function in creating racially, ethnically, and economically diverse neighborhoods in the two communities of Northside and Pine Knoll. The center committed to hearing and carrying forward Northside and Pine Knolls history and promoting abundant community principles. This story of community-institution partnering is appropriate for our examination of preparedness for civic and community engagement.

How do we know if engagement can occur? How can we tell if a community, college, university, or any other institution is ready for engagement? Every successful opportunity for engagement begins with mature leaders who exhibit self-confidence, an ethical center, and the willingness to learn in public. A venerable leadership model more than 30 years old suggests that leadership requires one to first focus on personal development or "private victories" before one can address relationships with others (Covey, 1989).

The Jackson Center in its job announcement for an executive director described the ideal leader as (1) rooted in abundant community, (2) an adaptable shepherd, (3) humbled by and accountable to community power, (4) a creative connector, and (5) a responsible storyteller. Stop to consider what would exemplify such characteristics in a leader. Draw a mental picture of this individual and assess any resemblance to leaders you might know. Covey (1989) described the prepared leader as self-aware, proactive, capable of planning and preparation, and driven by prioritization of all aspects of life. Leadership matters. It matters in communities and institutions, and it enhances engagement when these characteristics are present.

Community leaders believe that universities must be prepared to contribute to authentic relationships, respect local interest and history, and recognize that as, often, the most financially endowed partner, they must dedicate effort and resources to the partnership (Burgess, 2011; Toms et al., 2011). There are also prerequisites for communities preparing for engaged partnerships. Effective community engagement begins in communities with the capacity to build trusting relationships internally. Communities ready for engagement are both process and product ready: There are indications of social efficacy, hope, social ties described as community capacity, leadership energy, social agency, and connections to neighborhood, family, and friends (Lloyd, 2010). Rev. Troy Harrison of St. Joseph CME Church and UNC Professor Della Pollock in 2007 began to listen to the oral histories of people in the Northside and Pine Knoll communities (Marian Cheek Jackson Center, 2020). Pollock is the current executive director of the Jackson Center. These individuals through their work, worship, entertainment, and housing made up the Jackson Center neighborhoods. Community historian,

Ms. Marian Cheek Jackson, provided guidance and history to this 20-year-old dream in Northside (Marian Cheek Jackson Center, 2020).

Community-University Civic Engagement

With appropriate leadership engaged, the community and institutions will need to focus on the continuous struggle to develop partnerships. Communities often view their engagement with institutions at both the macro- and microlevels. At the macrolevel, institutions dominate and appear overwhelming to vulnerable communities. Community needs are overshadowed by those of the university or organization. Communities have learned that when engaging institutions at this level, employing confrontational methods of social power results in some semblance of success. One can look through daily media reports for examples of communities, such as employee groups, disenfranchised workers, neighborhoods, and others, that choose to take the classic organizing model for social action to gain attention from and control over their more powerful or better-financed partners. Yet at the microlevel, within the context of a specific relationship, community leaders see opportunities for personal interaction. It is at this level that relational social power offers opportunities for both partners to employ interpersonal persuasion and influence relationships (Lloyd, 2010). The Jackson Center applies this principle as the "spirit of Beloved Community, focus especially on building connections, partnerships, and 'matchmaking' of all kinds: neighbor and neighbor, resource partners, eager community members and homes. Find what's in it for everybody. Co-labor" (Marian Cheek Jackson Center, 2020, para. 3). At this nexus, leaders may develop spiritual capital and partnerships that have the potential for mutual respect and the valuing of all partners.

The context of activities and the content to be developed in a partnership may or may not look at all like the outcome projected by an institution; however, the act of engaging in a sustainable partnership requires that all partners begin to see value in the needs of the whole. This is not always a reciprocal exchange; it is most likely built on the spiritual capital developed between the individuals in the community and in the institutions. Each unit works to complete necessary outcomes because of their faith in the interest and needs of their partners and the greater good.

Contemplate the following example from the Jackson Center and its partners.

Each week, the center shares recent achievements through its "Wakeup Everybody" update. During the early days of the 2020 COVID-19 pandemic, the townspeople and all of the country found themselves under stay-at-home ordinances. Many members of the Northside and Pine Knolls community were among those who would be in the greatest danger if they contracted the virus. Although faced with a legitimate option to close down, the Jackson Center proceeded with its community. The following is an excerpt from the weekly update: "It's been another powerful week to witness from all of you—thanks so much for continuing to be creative, loving, dedicated and strong in the midst of this crisis. Our team delivered 105 hot, delicious meals on Saturday to

176 of Lead the Way

elders and others across the community. Vimala's is calling it the 'Northside Beloved Community Meals.' This week will be a bit more of a challenge; Vimala's had said they can only do meals on Good Friday, so I will be looking for folks willing to deliver on Friday. ... She wants people to have a good Easter weekend meal! We continued our Wednesday walks through the neighborhood, keeping in small groups with lots of distance. ... Thanks to all for taking this seriously as we walk and sing."

Do you believe the center envisioned its function as one of delivering meals or participating in neighborhood walks in its inception? Given what we know about the Jackson Center, why would you believe these are critical to their mission? It is commitment that allows sustainable partnerships to develop macrolevel partnerships that have all the attributes and benefits of partnerships on the microlevel.

Empowerment Approach to Engagement

After crossing the commitment barrier, leaders and institutions begin the process of preparing for engagement and implementing partner efforts. We suggest a 12-step approach to preparing for sustainable community engagement.

Empowerment Model

1. Seek and share credible expertise	7. Find mutual goals and build interdependence
2. Search for the most effective individuals as community advocates	8. Participate in unbiased strategic planning and training
3. Search for the most important issues to the community	9. Attract investors
4. Openly develop relationships of trust and fellowship	10. Strategize for intentional maintenance of effort
5. Partner on programs that focus on commitment and community pride	11. Develop a practical view of the partnership
6. Invest in community ownership	12. Market and celebrate success

This 12-step process begins with the first eight steps focused on preparation and readiness for the partnership and the final steps, "the final four," focused on maintenance. These are the foundation of what we know as participatory democracy, and they are prerequisites, allowing individuals to play important roles in developing community-institution partnerships, developing new leadership skills, and experiencing empowerment. Institutions, universities, and communities will find themselves assessing their ability to accept and contribute resources in unique and challenging ways. Institutions must explore the expectations of the community and the university, the prerequisites for effective engagement, and the strategies for maintaining the partnership in an ever-changing environment.

The Jackson Center reflects the exploration of expertise and experiences that cross public and private institutions, communities of place and interest, and communities of thought. It merges empirical data and indigenous wisdom representative of the work of an engaged partnership.

Leaders preparing for effective community institutional engagement begin by learning to seek and share credible expertise. The literature might label this process "learning in public," while the Jackson Center calls it "learning in action." Institutions of higher education house some of society's best-trained minds covering a wide range of niche subjects. However, the requisite combination of sophisticated left-and right-brain skills needed to engage communities and their needs might not exist in current staff members. Thus, identifying and recruiting the "right leader" can be the most crucial component to fashioning the origins of a successful civic or community engagement initiative.

Community affairs involve creating very personal working relationships with a diverse range of people grounded in trust and transparency. Community development, civic engagement, community engagement, or whatever the town-grown effort or initiative; the work requires a leader to be a "compassionate hybrid." The leader must recognize and understand the cultural nuances of both the institution and the community and possess the patience, savvy, and spiritual endurance to reconcile that which makes for a vastly different world. The entrenched structure of the institution and the "volatility" that may exist in the perspectives of community folk toward the institution must be maneuvered. Nonprofit and for-profit leaders may find a place in this partnership but must also recognize their limited abilities and the community preconceptions that may exist. Experience reiterates; community folks can read your heart. They can easily detect bullshit; thus, the emissary of the institution must be "real" to them. Search for and start with a leader who has a proven "credible" record of accomplishment in the eyes or interpretation of the "people" who make up the community for a strong start to the relationship. A part of this early work is the identification of effective individuals as the community's advocates.

Leaders must identify issues and the appropriate individuals to both communicate with the new partner and earn the respect of the community. These leaders identify the issues that are important to the community. Such individuals are respected voices in the community, yet they may not be the loudest or most visible to outsiders. The term "real voices" fits them best. Real voices not only disperse local wisdom but also, like any great communicator, they are also intentional listeners, willing to investigate issues before they speak. They may draw a small audience, but their message is respected and distributed across the community. This is a challenging step for the institutional novice without credible connections in the community. Institutions are cautioned to ignore the "self-anointed." These are often the most vocal and ever present at public meetings. They are seldom the true voices of a community.

Identifying the most important issues is difficult without the appropriate pied pipers to share their insight. We will describe them as pet projects. These issues are the items that evoke passion and commitment from community members. They draw on the community's history and experience. Building mutuality and reciprocity in a sustainable effort requires that the ultimate goal be one that draws on the passion and interest of not only the campus researcher, student, or nonprofit advocate but also the majority of the community.

Review the Jackson Center Basic Operating Principles website to observe the tenants of these first empowerment steps (https://jacksoncenter.info/mcjc-operating-princi-ples/). Without the involvement of all partners in this initiative, driven by the basic operating principles, would the work on creating an oral history have surfaced as critical to the center's success?

The adherence to these first two steps results in the successful accomplishment of the third and fourth. Search for the most important issues in the community and openly develop relationships of trust and fellowship. The "pet project" is the issue most critical to the community. An institution's willingness to work and ability to see a place for such a pet project is important to the third step: establishing trust. Institutions committed to building community partnerships will find it important to identify and participate in a catalyzing project. Finding such a catalyzer not only evokes pride in a community but also a desire by community members to participate. Such a project may or may not be a compensated effort and may or may not have major benefits for the partner institutions. Commitment to projects and programs that build community pride help to build trust in these often financially unequal partnerships. This may not be a funded project but one that reflects the organization's commitment to making the community a better place to live and provides evidence that the partners care. Such activities reflect the value placed on the community by the institutions and the community's value of its partners.

One Jackson Center report of weekly accomplishments denoted heart-shaped bal-loons on the porch of elderly neighbors, interviews for the Oral History Museum, and the relocation of two houses into the community from the community home trust fund. These homes are available for community families to purchase. Each of these activities reflects the need or a pet project of a specific partner, but they also reflect the interest of all partners. Thus, the development of trust and fellowship require both intention and action.

Although a number of factors affect the institution's engagement, the capacity to develop trusting, authentic relationships between university faculty members, insti-tution members, and community members is critical in communities that have few individual or communal trusting relationships with agencies and institutions. Trust is the critical element in many social interactions that have an effect on the economic, health, learning, and emotional well-being of each of the partners (Foster-Fishman et al., 2007). While community and cultural norms are often the result of chance, accident, creativity, and, sometimes, genius, the knowledge and participation in such norms create a level of social trust that benefits all parties exponentially. Universities and community partners are rarely born with this bond. Cohen and Prusak (2001) in their study of organizations, concluded that social capital does not occur instantly. Thus, there is a need to work at the development of the trusting relationships needed to create social capital between partners. Finding common interests, seeking the understanding of others' perspectives, upholding one's commitments, and respecting and valuing partner attributes all contribute to the development of trust. Although there are differences, the groups find common interests and respect.

Achieving this level of trust is greatly affected by the individual development of spiritual capital—an individualized relationship that engenders a familial level of trust that embodies spirituality but not religiosity. Refer to Chapter 8 in this volume for a more in-depth review of spiritual capital. The individuals in the relationship empowered by spiritual capital are now capable of pushing the community-university relationship forward in ways that will benefit both partners based on the perceptions of social capital between the two. They become the pied pipers for the university and the community. The literature describes these individuals as boundary spanners (Lloyd, 2010).

There is a correlation between these individual perceptions of social capital and perceptions of organizational readiness for engagement. These initial correlations confirm that individuals who viewed their relationships with university faculty as responsive and frequent were significantly more likely to believe their organization's relationship with others to be strengthened by the university partnership. The data consistently suggest that community leaders' preferences for and valuing of inter-personal relationships are the foundation and framework for engaged organizational partnerships (Toms et al., 2011). We would suggest that this is also true of relationships of all institutions wishing to work in communities.

Social infrastructure is critical to generating tables of discussion and providing a sense of dignity for the community. Community crime watch organizations, churches, and other institutions help build social capital in communities, irrespective of the socioeconomic status. Social infrastructure may look different in different communi-ties. In some communities, they may take the form of the local golf clubs; yet in others, they may be the corner church or the community watch group. These social ties result in not only individual capacity but also community capacity (Toms et al., 2011). In diverse communities, these locations may be more challenging to discover. Building on these institutions validates community self-efficacy and self-determination.

Institutions prepared for engagement are also prepared for community self-own-ership. This requires institutions, faculty, and students to avoid the paternalistic inclinations that are pervasive among the resource-rich partner in such relation-ships. The community members have to feel like they are the owners of any project and recognize that they are a part of an equitable partnership in which each partner brings important attributes. Communities and universities cannot move to developing mutual goals until this level of self-worth and respect is achieved by the partners.

The Jackson Center delivered family activity bags to Northside families, including its Learning Across Generations Initiative. Their oral history team designed the community oral history archive, uploading hundreds of family photographs and documents from the center's history potluck. They hired local artists to help with the web design, and students joined the staff during the summer to serve as oral history fellows to assist with processing, accessioning, and increasing the accessibility of the more than 200 oral histories in the Jackson Center Oral History Trust. Consider activities and events that might encourage intergenerational investments in community dignity. How might leaders engender self-determination? Would you guess that the Oral History Trust might be a galvanizing program?

Well-facilitated strategic planning is core to the partnership and its activities. A sense of partnership and joint ownership enhances the subsequent work. A planning process should reflect the credible expertise, discussed previously, as it is important to the partnership. This chapter describes commitment to education and training prior to embarking on a project as "educating forward." Educating forward creates a basis on which the engagement can proceed. In 2010, when leaders participating in institution-community-engaged partnerships were asked their expectations from the partnerships, they consistently reported opportunities to grow, learn, and acquire technical expertise. Universities and communities have responsibilities for educating forward. This is the capacity to provide not only information or knowledge but also practice and application that result in higher level learning and, eventually, the capacity to evaluate and create new ideas. This acquisition allows partners to engage in problem solving as credible voices in decision making. This concept of educating forward requires the willingness to learn and to do so without the fear of failure. This readiness by institutions to participate in this concept of teaching and learning simultaneously reflects a similar paradigm shift in readiness in the community.

The Jackson Center encourages leaders to support, facilitate, and complement community leadership. This commitment is seen in the center's growth and employment practices over its 10-year existence. There are now a number of community members who have become staff members at the center and others who have become a part of its leadership. Consider the paradigms that must be present for institutional leaders and staff to begin to see community leaders as equals with valued assets to contribute to the work. Are there reflective actions that need to occur within an organization continuously to ensure that these paradigms remain a part of the organizational culture? These movements are exhibited in the sustained engagement of public and private universities across the nation. They are also reflected in the conversations with communities that describe their partnerships with universities and other institutions as effective.

The research suggests communities ready for engagement are both process and product ready. As organizations proceed through the empowerment movements, leaders will observe process and product readiness. There are indications of social efficacy, hope, social ties that are described as community capacity, leadership energy, social agency, and neighborhood, family, and friend connections. There is also evidence of preplanning by community leaders, initiation, infrastructure capacity, and collaboration (Toms et al., 2011). Not all communities will meet all criteria for readiness; however, the partner and the community will need to ask the following questions: Ready for *what*? Capable of *what*? We would suggest that partnerships separate the concepts of readiness and capacity. Capacity reflects the structural readiness often discussed in engagement literature—human capital, financial capital, and social connections. A community might have all the characteristics that reflect capacity. These include infrastructure, formal leadership, knowledge, and skills. If the community has little collective efficacy, hope for change, trust, and few social ties, there may be no evidence of readiness for engagement. These relational aspects contribute to readiness on the part of the institution and community. Institutions and communities must ask which of these is most important to the partnership and return to the beginning of the empowerment approach: commitment. Is civic engagement important enough to pursue the development of these attributes, and is the partner willing to commit the amount of time needed to proceed? The spiritual and social capital needed to begin this journey requires a commitment on the part of all partners.

Leadership for community engagement is reflected in the passion and ability to serve and learn by community, institutional, and university partners. There is much to be said about the requirements of effective engagement. Partnerships of any type often require more than the implementation of specific guidelines or rules. The same can be said for sustainable institution-community partnerships. Leadership will be important, but just as with effective partnerships, leadership requires more than the implementation of specific guidelines and rules. The works of noted sociology, psychology, and leadership scholars remind us of the importance of trust, self-efficacy, and social capital to the development of interdependent relationships and effective partnerships (Cohen & Prusak, 2001). Engaged organizations will need to build on the synergy of the team, redirecting it toward the vision, making changes and transitions as needed. Such leadership is needed to build sustainable systems. Leaders with the relational expertise needed for the crossing of institutional and community boundaries, the willingness to be learners, and the capacity to create and innovate collaboratively will serve both university and community partners well. These prerequisites will allow partnerships to proceed to what we describe as the final four.

The Final Four
These empowerment moves reflect the fundamental need for interdisciplinary knowledge and skills in the development of sustainable engagement. The previous movements reflect the humanity of engaged partnerships. The final four reflect the technical needs and structural prerequisites of the partnership.

The partnership must engage investors and supporters. This is only possible with viable and credible products. There is a fundamental need for projects to be financially buttressed, but money should not drive the goals of the partnership. A critical and key partner in the Jackson Center partnership is a regional financial institution. The credit union may see itself as an investor, but the success of the relationship is also built on commitment and trust. The identification of the most appropriate investors will allow the partnership to maintain its focus on the goals set in strategic planning. Appropriate investors are as important as appropriate partners.

Maintaining intentional effort is the next step in the development of strategies for maintaining the effort. This requires intentionality by both leaders and the partnership members. The presence of resources and the presumed success of an initiative will attract internal and external distractions and detractors. Partnerships must be prepared for these issues, as well as prepared for the supporters.

At the risk of limiting the vision of an engaged partnership, leaders must be able in the third of the final four movements to inject practicality. The planning and implementation of the work between the partners must reflect its investors, the broader community, and the broader university potential for success. Practical actions are often not as appealing as the grand vision upon which partnerships are formed; however, these actions are critical to sustainability. Achieving this movement will allow for the successful implementation of the last movement.

Marketing is a reinforcing movement and critical to the strengthening of the partnership and for preparation for future work within the partnership. This one movement allows for the reinforcement of the importance of the work completed in this engaged relationship. The Jackson Center describes it as inspiring change: generationally and historically in the community and nationwide. Marketing is the critical communication needed within the community and within institutions. Without marketing, partnerships can be sabotaged from within and from the outside.

Practice Makes Perfect and Lessons Learned

In a perfect environment, each of the empowerment movements occurs sequentially without challenges. Empirical data and indigenous wisdom would suggest that a perfect environment is seldom the reality. Experienced university and community leaders would suggest that there are lessons to be learned and taught to the next generation of leaders. The Jackson Center story of Northside and Pine Knoll not only reflects the empowerment approach in action but also highlights examples of the challenges that face communities and institutions in the implementation of such a model in a not-so-perfect environment. Consider how the partnership might address the following questions.

1. What are the benefits of partners who are prepared and ready for engagement?
2. What might be evidence in this partnership of mutuality, relational authenticity, and shared vision?

REFERENCES

Carnegie Foundation for the Advancement of Teaching. (2012). *Classification: Community engagement.* Retrieved February 27, 2013, from www.carneigefoundation.org/classification/index.htm

Cohen, D., & Prusak, L., (2001). *In Good Company: How Social Capital Makes Organizations Work.* Boston: Harvard Business School Press.

Drath, W. M., McCauley, C., Palus, C., van Velsor, E., O'Connor, P., & McGuire, P. (2008). Direction, alignment, commitment: Toward a more integrative ontology of leadership. *Leadership Quarterly, 19,* 635–653.

Burgess, S. (2011). S*piritual capital: The relationship with civic engagement among faith-based leaders and universities.* North Carolina Agricultural and Technical State University.

Carnegie Foundation for the Advancement of Teaching. (n.d.). *Classification: Community engagement.* Retrieved February 27, 2013, from http://www.classifications.carnegiefoundation.org/methodology

Covey, S. (1989). *The seven habits of highly effective people.* Simon & Schuster.

Foster-Fishman, P., Cantillon, D., Pierce, S., & Van Egeren, L. (2007). Building an active citizenry: The role of neighborhood problems, readiness and capacity for change. *American Journal of Community Psychology, 39,*91–106.

Lloyd, C. L. (2010). *Indicators of Community-Land Grant University Readiness for Engagement from the Community Perspective.* Greensboro: North Carolina A&T State University.

Marian Cheek Jackson Center. (2014). *Historic and Vibrant Rogers Road-Extensive Community Engagement Findings.* Town of Chapel Hill NC. Retrieved August 10, 2020 from http://www.townofchapelhill.org/home/showdocument?id=25227

Marian Cheek Jackson Center. (2020, May 8). *Basic operating principals, or what's in the sauce.* Retrieved May 8, 2020 from https://jacksoncenter.info/mcjc-operating-principles/

Marian Cheek Jackson Center. (2020). *MCJC community justice. Our Story.* Retrieved August 1, 2020 from https://jacksoncenter.info/our-story-1/

Toms, F., Lloyd, C., & Ellison, C. (2011). Improving health and health care advocacy through engagement: A faith-based community view. *Practical Matters,* 1–13.

CHAPTER ELEVEN

Historically Underutilized Businesses

AWARENESS, ACCESS, AND EMPOWERMENT

Tanya Ayscue, PhD, Rochelle Cook, PhD, and Lonnie Cockerham, PhD

INTRODUCTION

Objectives

This chapter addresses the distribution of funding to historically underutilized businesses (HUB) in North Carolina. The primary focus of this chapter is to address the disparities in the distribution of funds between nonminority businesses and minority-owned businesses. It reveals the connections between the complexities of entrepreneurship and its effect on access, empowerment, and engagement for HUBs for all minority groups in North Carolina. In addition, it outlines the HUB certification process, limitations, and opportunities. Lastly, it provides a narrative of practical applications for awareness, access, and actions for policy makers, practitioners, and community partners.

Frames of Entrepreneurship

Recent history in the United States has been marked by a decade of significant increase in entrepreneurial activity. According to a report from the Global Entrepreneurship Monitor, more than 14% of adult Americans are entrepreneurs (Buchanan, 2015). Even during periods of high unemployment, entrepreneurship has remained a preferred career option, just as it was during the recession period of 2007–2009 (Lange et al., 2018/2019).

Along with its growth, the complexity of American entrepreneurship has changed. For instance, while there is significant research about small businesses and entrepreneurs in general, the number of nonemployer business owners (i.e., independent contractors) increased more than 12% nationwide in 2002 (Barbato et al., 2009). People age 55 or older own over half of the privately-owned companies. As a result, ownership is transferred to the next generation (Wiefek et al., 2019). While this practice leads to generational wealth for nonminorities, it creates disparities, inequalities, and barriers for minority business owners—disadvantages that are rooted in a lack of capital and collateral to invest in their businesses, primarily because "wealth levels among whites are 11 to 16 times higher than for minorities" (Fairlie & Robb, 2010, p. 6).

According to Fairlie and Robb (2010), in the United States, more than 10% of the total workforce are business owners. However, business ownership rates differ substantially by race and ethnicity. The number of minority firms increased between 1997 and 2002. However, when compared to the number of minorities in the workplace and the percentage of the minority businesses as a percentage of the minority workforce, the numbers were significantly less than those of nonminority business owners. White business owners make up 11.3% of businesses. Asians own 10.3%, Native Americans own 7.6% of businesses, Hispanics own 7.9%, and Black businesses make up the lowest at 5.5%. Overall, minority business ownership is small relative to the size of the minority workforce (Fairlie & Robb, 2010, p. 9).

It is also important to note that, according to the American Express® 2019 *State of Women-Owned Businesses Report*, women-owned firms recently generated $1.9 trillion in annual revenue and represented more than 40% of all U.S. businesses. The report further states that women of color made up the largest portion of new women-owned businesses, with African American women far outpacing all other female groups by race (American Express, 2019, p. 15). However, when it comes to access to opportunities for women business owners at the federal, state, and local levels, Black women owners and other minority groups still face similar barriers or inequities.

Small businesses play a vital role in the economy. What is the definition of a small business? According to Formoso-Suralta (2017), a *small business* is defined as a privately-owned company in the legal form of a corporation, partnership, or sole proprietorship. The Small Business Administration (SBA) defines a small business as one that typically makes a maximum of $750,000–$38.5 million in annual revenue and has less than 100–1,500 employees, depending on the industry (Formoso-Suralta, 2017). According to Census.gov, more than four million small businesses are microbusinesses, compared to 125,000 midsized businesses. Whereas a small business can be considered a sole proprietorship or a microbusiness, a *sole proprietorship* is owned and operated by one person, and the owner is responsible for profits and losses. It is not a legal entity, and it is the easiest way to start a business. It can operate under the owner's name or a trade or business name. The owner can also be an independent contractor, and a sole proprietor is not required to register with the state; however, a business license is required. A *microbusiness* is a business that employees six or fewer people (W2 or 1099) and requires less than $35,000 in working capital (Murray, 2019).

The U.S. Chamber of Commerce Foundation described small businesses as 'the heart of America's economy' because of job creation and innovation" (Hendrix, 2017, para. 1). According to a 2017 U.S. Chamber of Commerce Foundation study, small businesses are responsible for the employment of more than 50% of the workforce in the private sector and are responsible for more than 400,000 jobs created in 2013. Ironically, 98% of small businesses have less than 100 employees. Yet because of federal regulations, small businesses are financially affected the most, especially those with less than 50 employees, because they pay almost 20% more than the average for all firm.

History has shown us that small businesses are vulnerable to any type of societal or economic disruption. In 2008, Jessica Gordon Nembhard stated in the Black Enterprise "Recession Survival Guide," "For black people, economic downturns often cut deeper, in terms of job losses and business survival. We're the first to fall back when a recession comes and the last to recover when it ends" Polyak, 2008, para. 7).

The coronavirus disease 2019 (COVID-19) pandemic is a prime example of a disruption that has devastated the global economy and especially the small business community. Many businesses were forced to shut down across the world. Over 3 short months, in the United States, African American business ownership fell by 41%, Latinx ownership dropped by 32%, and Asian business ownership fell by 26%—compared to 17% of their white counterparts (Fairlie, 2020, p. 7). In North Carolina, between March 15, 2020, and April 15, 2020, more than 598,000 unemployment claims were filed, including small business owners (American City Business Journals, 2020). U.S. small businesses, considered the "heart of America," sustained a sudden, harsh, and long-impacting blow because of COVID-19. As a result, the world economy has again faced widespread uncertainty, and the struggle to stay afloat amid general uncertainty and financial setbacks became a "new normal" for businesses and consumers alike.

North Carolina Entrepreneurship

In 2007, there were an estimated 821,189 small businesses in North Carolina and approximately 551,040 self-employed workers (North Carolina Small Business and Technology Development Center [SBTDC], 2020). Among those small businesses, more than 225,000 were women-owned businesses, which generated an estimate of $32 billion in revenues. Self-employed women totaled 155,000 and represented 32.8% of self-employed workers in North Carolina. In addition, in 2007, North Carolina reported a total of 132,000 minority-owned businesses, which generated more than $16.4 billion in revenue (SBTDC, 2020). In 2018, the U.S. Small Business Administration Office of Advocacy reported 97.9% of North Carolina businesses were small businesses, and 46% of North Carolina employees worked for small businesses. Further, according to the U.S. Census Bureau Quick Facts, as cited by the U.S. Small Business Administration Office of Advocacy, in 2012, there were 282,058 women-owned businesses and 183,380 minority-owned businesses (p. 7).

Uzialko (2019) suggested that the state of North Carolina has more than 900,000 entrepreneurs, representing more than 44% of the private sector. In 2018, North Carolina ranked in the top 25 as the best place to start a business (Treece, 2018) based on critical metrics, such as taxes, labor market, start-up costs, and access to capital.

Small businesses help drive the economy through dedication, creativity, resourcefulness, and growth. Even during economic downturns, there are several opportunities for small businesses to flourish. The SBA and government contracting are just two avenues with resources to help launch and grow small businesses. Another channel, the North Carolina Office of HUB, primarily focuses on minority-owned businesses.

AWARENESS

HUB

On April 20, 1999, the North Carolina Office for HUB formed the Office of Administration to increase opportunities for historically underutilized businesses and promote diversity and inclusion in state government procurement and contracting (North Carolina Department of Administration [NCDOA], 2020). This Executive Order (No. 150, 1999)—Support for Historically Underutilized Business—was signed into law by Governor James B. Hunt, Jr.

The HUB Office of Administration serves as an advocate to promote and increase diverse participation of HUB firms when state-supported institutions purchase goods and services. In addition, the office advocates for state-supported construction spending according to the Purchasing Policy, which was set by the NC General Assembly and defined by General Statutes §143–48 (2007). The HUB Office of Administration monitors and ensures compliance with Article 3 of the statutes—Purchases and Contracts. The state invites and encourages participation in the procurement process by businesses owned by minorities, women, disabled, disabled business enterprises, and nonprofit work centers for the blind and severely disabled. The state encourages the use of HUB-certified vendors as subcontractors on state contracts.

Recipients of HUB dollars include the following minority groups: Black, Hispanic, Asian American, American Indian, female, disadvantaged, and disabled populations. Before 2016, minority business enterprises (MBEs) were included in the reporting. The MBEs consisted of the total amount allocated to Black, Hispanic, Asian American, and American Indian minority groups collectively. The nonprofit work centers and disabled business enterprises (DBEs) are considered self-identified categories and are not certified by HUB (NCDOA, 2020).

The HUB Process

According to the Department of Administration certification registration instructions, published by the Office for Historically Underutilized Business (2017), the Statewide Uniform Certification application (SWUC) process consists of three applications:

(1) SWUC, also known as the HUB certification application, (2) North Carolina Department of Transportation/North Carolina HUB reciprocity application, and (3) North Carolina HUB reciprocity application. Although applicants must ultimately select the most appropriate application for their case, the scope of discussion in this chapter will be limited to the SWUC/HUB certification application process.

ELIGIBILITY

Eligibility for the HUB Statewide Uniform Certification (SWUC) is available under North Carolina General Statutes § 143–48.4—the Statewide Uniform Certification of historically underutilized businesses. Approved vendors must meet and maintain the following criteria to be classified as a historically underutilized business as outlined in § 143–48(a)—state policy; cooperation in promoting the use of small contractors, minority contractors, physically handicapped contractors, and women contractors; purpose; required annual reports.

This is also outlined in 143-128.4. Historically Underutilized business defined; statewide uniform certification.

1. At least 51% is owned by one or more persons who are members of at least one of the following groups: (1) Black, (2) Hispanic, (3) Asian American, (4) American Indian, (5) female, (6) disabled, (7) disadvantaged.
2. The management and daily business operations are controlled by one or more owners of the business who are members of at least one of the groups outlined in subsection (1a).
   a. To qualify as a HUB, a business owned and controlled by one or more citizens or lawful permanent residents of the United States who are members of one or more of the following groups: (1) Black, (2) Hispanic, (3) Asian American, (4) American Indian, (5) female, (6) disabled, (7) disadvantaged.

The simplified application process for obtaining HUB certification has opened doors for more minority businesses.

The Application Process

The application process for HUB certification under the Statewide Uniform Certification Program consists of the following three steps, which can take up to 90 days to be approved.

1. Register electronically in the electronic Vendor Portal (eVP).
2. Complete, sign, and date the SWUC application.
3. Submit the required documents located at https://vendor.ncgov.com/vendor/login.

The HUB application (SWUC) consists of six sections:

Section 1: General information, including information about the business: name of the firm, contact name, owner title, phone, address, legal name of the firm, federal employee identification number, DUNS number, and method of acquisition.

Section 2: Company information/business structure (i.e., corporation, limited liability, partnership, sole proprietorship, or joint venture) and the firm's relationship with other businesses.

Section 3: Ownership information, including business owners' identities based on ethnicity (Black, Hispanic, Asian American, American Indian), gender, disability, and citizenship.

Section 4: Officers and board of directors' information and daily management functions (i.e., who controls the firm in different areas of the business).

Section 5: References. Provide two business references, including business names, addresses, and phone numbers.

Section 6: Other certifications and signature. Check any agency or certifications currently held by the firm. Sign and date the application. Make sure all the following supporting documents are included in the package:

Supporting Documentation:

- ✓ Signed SWUC application
- ✓ Work experience resumes for all owners (make sure all places of ownership/ employment with dates)
- ✓ Proof of citizenship or permanent residence (copy of birth certificate, passport, voter's registration card, green card, military ID, or driver's license)
- ✓ Provide proof of ethnicity (copy of passport, green card, or birth certificate). You can also complete and submit the ethnicity affidavit, which is also available online if none of the above prove ethnicity
- ✓ Copies of professional licenses, if required (i.e., certified public accountant, project management professional)
- ✓ Schedule of salaries paid to all officers, managers, owners, or directors of the firm
- ✓ A copy of a signed lease for office or storage space
- ✓ Provide a list of equipment (leased or owned) along with signed lease agreements, titles/proof of ownership, and equipment needed to operate your business (i.e., computers, printers, vehicles)

✓ Provide home state certification (for out-of-state businesses)
✓ Proof of disability, if applicable
✓ Business structure
✓ **Corporations must provide copies of the following:**
  o Official articles of incorporation (signed by a state official)
  o Both sides of all corporate certifications and stock
  o Transfer ledger
  o Assumed name certificate
  o Shareholders agreement
  o Minutes of the first and most recent stockholder and board of directors' meetings
  o Corporate bylaws and any amendments
✓ **Limited liability corporations (including PLLC) must provide the following:**
  o Articles of organization (LLC)
  o Operating agreement (LLC)
✓ **Partnerships (including LLP) must submit the following:**
  o Partnership agreement
✓ **Franchises must provide the following:**
  o Franchise agreement

The process diagram is available in Appendix A.

ACCESS

Access to Training

The North Carolina HUB Office partnered with North Carolina community colleges to provide the training course "How to Become HUB Certified." The training provides a high-level overview of the HUB certification process: "How to Get Started." An overview of the process, tools, contacts, and links to other resources to help business owners navigate the HUB process is covered during the training. This is an all-day class that is held during core business hours from 9:00 a.m. to 3:00 p.m. Registration in the eVP is encouraged before attending the HUB certification training. Once certified, vendors receive an invitation to the "HUB Vendor Orientation Training."

The HUB vendor orientation is specifically for HUB certified vendors and/or staff members. The training consists of the following modules: purchasing, construction, supplier diversity, access to capital, and projected outcomes. The purchasing module covers the rules and regulations that govern the state procurement process and outlines the step-by-step bidding process and how to submit a good proposal. The construction module includes subcontractors, suppliers, bidding, and estimating, as well as good faith efforts. The access to capital module addresses financial programs that are available to small businesses.

Web-based training is available to vendors to inform them on how to register for the eVP. The training courses also educate vendors on how to manage contacts and navigate the North Carolina e-Procurement billing information. The e-Procurement training includes understanding the billing process and how to view and download invoices. Online videos are available for instructions on how to search for registered vendors. Training is available for vendors on the NCDOA website. Additional links to training resources are available in Appendix B.

Access to Contract Opportunities

The "Contractors College" is a HUB Office education program that has provided growth opportunities for the state's small and minority business owners. The primary objective of this program is to help participants develop relationships with industry leaders, state agencies, universities, and local governments to gain access to the many construction opportunities available across the state (North Carolina Historically Underutilized Businesses, 2015).

There are different term contacts available for vendors, which include (1) the standard term contract, (2) the statewide term contract, and (3) the agency-specific contracts.

- The *standard term contract* is an agreement between the purchaser and the vendor to buy and sell certain commodities, printing, or services at negotiated prices based on specific terms and conditions.
- The *statewide term contract* was established by the Division of Purchase and Contracts for use by all agencies unless exempted by statute, rule, or special terms and conditions specific to the contract. Other contract opportunities include service contracts.

There are two types of service contracts: (1) contractual service and (2) consultant service.

- The *contractual service contract* involves an independent vendor who performs work or tasks requiring specialized knowledge, skills, and experience. Some examples include landscapers, medical/lab assistants, security guards, training instructors, and so forth.
- The *consultant service contract* involves work or tasks performed that require specialized knowledge, experience, expertise, and professional qualifications to investigate assigned problems or projects and to provide counsel, review, analysis, or advice by formulating or implementing improvements in programs or services. The governor's office must approve this type of contract.
- The *agency-specific contract* is used by a selected agency for a specific amount of time.

Access to Tools

The *North Carolina Electronic Vendor Portal (eVP)* is one place to register and gain access to all the Department of Administration's systems. The eVP is the first step in the SWUC certification process. Registration is free, and it is required to conduct business with the state. The following are required to register:

1. Internet access
2. The owner's federal tax ID/employer identification number
3. A valid email address to initiate the eVP HUB certification process

The *Interactive Purchasing System* is the heart of the contracting process and a free tool for vendors to search and review bid opportunities. The bids are available by category, by department, and by bid number. The tool also allows vendors to search for open bids. It is available at www.ips.state.nc.us.

North Carolina e-Procurement is North Carolina's purchasing system for vendors and suppliers.

NC BIDS is the new electronic billing system that allows vendors to access and respond to bids electronically. This electronic billing process saves time and money for vendors.

Access to Information

The HUB website is the center of information for minority businesses. Information regarding the mission, vision, general statutes, reporting, and resources are located on the HUB website. In addition, certified vendors receive weekly newsletters from the Office of HUB Department of Administration and updates from the City of Durham Department of Equity and Inclusion, which provides information on construction bids, notices, and requests.

HUBSTER is a monthly newsletter published by the North Carolina Office of Administration of the HUB. This publication includes highlights about the HUB Office and vendors, upcoming events, and webinars, as well as a list of the newly certified vendors.

The *City of Durham Equity and Inclusion* is a weekly newsletter that provides links, training opportunities, town hall meetings, SBA updates, links to construction bids, requests for proposals/qualifications and services, etc. Appendix C contains additional resources for small businesses.

GAPS/DISPARITIES

Access to Contracts

Inequities in securing corporate or government contracts for minority businesses have always been a factor, despite a sharp increase in the number of minority owned businesses from the time a major U.S. recession ended in 2009 until the negative social and economic impacts a global health crisis took effect in 2020. According to the *Washington Post* (2013), the demographics of the U.S. population have changed. The Hispanic population now represents 17% of the total U.S. population, and Blacks represent 13%. Even with the shift in population toward a browner America, limited access to state-level government contracts still exist for minority owned businesses. In 2013, Hispanic companies commanded 8.4% ($8.2 billion) of a total of $98.2 billion in contracts awarded to small businesses, while Black owned businesses received $7.1 billion (7.2%). However, the number of contacts assigned remain in single digits for both minority groups.

Access to Capital

Capital access continues to be a key constraint for the establishment, growth, and sustainability of minority businesses. According to Fairlie and Robb (2010), disparities to capital access include access to loans, equity, and financial investment. There are several barriers and obstacles that exist for establishing loans for minority businesses: (1) "minority-owned firms are less likely to receive loans than non-minority firms, (2) minority firms are more likely to be denied loans, (3) minority firms are less like to apply for loans due to fear of rejection and (4) those minority firms that apply pay a higher interest rate on the business loan" (p. 5).

In addition, Fairlie and Robb (2010) revealed that minority businesses are awarded smaller loans and have less money to invest in their own companies. This is primarily driven by the inequalities faced when it comes to access to funding. Minority businesses are also often discriminated against because of limited financial resources, less business experience, and based on geographic locations, which restrict their ability to raise funding (p. 5).

As previously stated, the COVID-19 pandemic has taken the world by storm on many levels. The heavy toll on the world psyche shifted to areas that no one could imagine. Although the Coronavirus Aid, Relief, and Economic Security (CARES) Act was enacted to provide aid for small businesses, the funding ran out less than 2 weeks after the application process opened. On March 27, 2020, the CARES Act of 2020 was signed into law to respond to "the COVID-19 (i.e., coronavirus disease 2019) outbreak and its impact on the economy, public health, state and local governments, individuals, and businesses" (Congress.gov, 2020, para. 1). The bill provided more than $376 billion in aid for Americans and small businesses as a result of the devastating effect of the outbreak. The SBA and other agencies implemented programs to assist small businesses during this economic downturn.

The *Paycheck Protection Program* was designed to help employers keep employees on their payrolls. Employers with less than 500 employees (small businesses), sole proprietorships, and independent contractors were eligible to apply. The application process began on April 3, 2020, for corporations, S-corps, and partnerships, while sole proprietors and independent contractors could apply beginning April 10, 2020. Under the program, the business loan would be underwritten by SBA lenders under the existing SBA 7(a) programs with the assumption that a portion of the loan would be forgiven if employees were kept on payroll or brought back to work for an 8-week period. According to an article in *Forbes* magazine, "Section 1102 of the CARES Act provide[d] that PPP loans [were] only available during the 'covered period' of February 15–June 30, 2020, and during that time, [could] only be used to pay payroll costs, mortgage interest, rent, utilities, and interest on other debt" (Nitti, 2020, para. 10). Because of an overwhelming response and greed on the part of many of the larger "small" businesses, the initial funding was quickly depleted. Many smaller businesses were left with no access to this capital meant to help pay for rent, employees, or other debt. In response, the U.S. Congress approved additional funding to assist small- and microbusinesses and qualified smaller banks to lend under the program, while some of the larger businesses returned the funding under fierce public scrutiny. On April 22, 2020, an additional $349 billion in funding was approved by the U.S. Congress for the Paycheck Protection Program (Smith, 2020). For a period, the SBA would find itself unable to accept new applications for the Paycheck Protection Program or its long-standing Economic Injury Disaster Loan Program, which was modified to classify COVID-19 as a "disaster" similar to those more closely compared to weather-related events. North Carolina's initial portion for eligible payroll was 51.8%, with a total of 39,520 loans approved out of the $8 billion (Mider & Sam, 2020).

The *Community Advantage Loan Program*, initiated in 2011, was established to help secure loans for small businesses in underserved communities. The program was introduced to provide up to $250,000 in funding for small businesses, with the SBA securing up to 85% of the loan. Lenders cannot charge more than 6% of the prime interest rate. The pilot program is scheduled to end in 2020 (Reed, 2020). Lastly, in 2016, the SBA guaranteed more than $770 million in small business loans in North Carolina (U.S. Small Business Administration Office of Advocacy, 2020).

Access to Insurance

Small businesses usually face the most difficult challenges in obtaining insurance; they often have the smallest amount of options when it comes to providers and pay the highest for the minimum amount of coverage. Many people who would like to start new businesses are stuck in jobs because they cannot afford to give up the health insurance they receive from their current employer. Alternatively, small business owners have to pay expensive premiums or depend on a spouse's health coverage to have affordable health coverage.

According to a *Forbes* contributing editor, Newtek Business Solutions Company (2012), there are several different types of insurance that small businesses should have in place. The following are a few of the recommended policies:

- *General liability insurance* protects business owners if their employees or products or services cause injury or property damage
- *Business owner's policy* provides coverage for property, vehicle coverage, liability, and crime insurance

- *Commercial auto insurance* provides protection for company vehicles. If employers allow employees to drive their own cars on company business, a nonowned auto liability policy is recommended to protect the company in case the employee does not have adequate insurance
- *Professional liability insurance*—also known as errors and omissions insurance—protects against damages for failure to provide or improperly executing professional services
- *Data breach policy* protects against the loss of data (client or employees' sensitive information)
- *Bonding insurance* comes in several forms, depending on the type(s) of services provided. Companies may obtain a bond if they intend on doing business with government entities, such as city and county libraries or schools

ENGAGEMENT

HUB Participation

The HUB Office has engaged and partnered with several organizations to help minority businesses receive equitable opportunities to bid for government (state and local) contracts. According to SBA.gov (2008), the SBA provides resources for small businesses to establish and grow their business. The SBA also provides free counselors to assist business owners with creating business plans, and it offers access to resource partners to assist with finding and securing guaranteed business loans for small businesses. In addition, the SBA provides opportunities for small businesses to bid on federal contacts. Certify.SBA.gov offers several programs to help small enterprises to become certified, which opens additional opportunities to bid on federal government contracts. The programs include the Women-Owned Small Business HUBZone Program, also known as the 8(a) Business Development Plan (Small Business Administration, 2008). The website outlines eligibility requirements for each of the programs.

The North Carolina HUB Office also partners with the Minority Enterprise Development Corporation. The mission of this organization is to educate and assist minority business owners with professional growth and development through tools, networking, workshops, and access to key business contacts in corporations and municipalities. On the federal level, the U.S. SBA HUBZone Program provides contracting opportunities for small businesses in high unemployment and low-income areas to promote job growth, capital investment, and economic development. To qualify, the following must be met:

- Must be a small business defined by SBA guidelines
- Must be owned and controlled at least 51% by U.S. citizens, a community development corporation, an agricultural cooperative, or an Indian tribe

- The main office must be located within a "HUB Zone," which includes lands considered "Indian country" and military facilities closed by the Base Realignment and Closure Act
- At least 35% of its employees must live in a HUBZone at least 180 days or be a current registered voter in that area

On June 28, 2016, the SBA announced the launching of a new HUB Zones map (via Google Chrome) at www.sba.gov/hubzone-maps. The HUBZone map is the first transformative step in developing the SBA's federal contracting programs. The partnership between SBA and the U.S. Digital Service streamlines and enhances online services for small businesses (Clements, 2017). What does this mean for minority business owners? How does the creation of these maps empower minority business owners? How does this affect community engagement for small businesses?

The HUBZone program was passed into law as a part of the Small Business Reauthorization Act of 1997. The SBA manages programs and determines that companies are eligible to receive HUBZone contracts. In addition, the SBA maintains a list of qualified HUBZone small businesses that federal agencies can use to locate qualified vendors. The government established a goal of 3% of the prime contract dollars that can be awarded to HUBzone businesses (sba.gov/hubzone). The computer mapping software can determine if vendors are in a qualified HUBZone area. Additional resources are available in Appendix C.

HUB Spending

The North Carolina Office of HUB is responsible for reporting the distribution of HUB dollars to minority businesses in North Carolina. The data is available online in the North Carolina Office of HUB annual reports and was taken from the NCDOA Office for Historically Underutilized Businesses *HUB Participation Report, Purchasing (Goods and Services) and Construction Projects* (2015, 2016, 2017, 2018, 2019).

According to statute §143-128-2 (State Budget, 2007), the minority participation goal in North Carolina is to obtain a 10% minority participation rate for the purchase of goods and services and construction spending.

The definition of a minority business (includes ethnic minorities and White women) was expanded to include "socially economically disadvantaged" individuals (Bluestein, 2001, p. 30). The law defines socially disadvantaged individuals as "those who have been subjected to racial or ethnic prejudice or cultural bias because of their identity as a member of a group without regard to their individual qualities" (Bluestein, 2001, p. 31). The annual reports depict the distribution of funds among the following minority groups: Black, Hispanic, Asian American, American Indian, female, disadvantaged, and disabled. However, before 2016, the HUB *Purchases of Goods and Services Annual Report* included MBE, Black, Hispanic, Asian American, American Indian, female, disabled, nonprofit work center for the blind, and DBE as separate categories in the report. MBEs include Black, Hispanic, Asian American, and American Indian minority groups. The MBE column reflects the sum of each of the minority businesses, as well as the individual minority groups.

OVERALL SUMMARY OF HUB DISTRIBUTION DATA

The NCDOA Office for Historically Underutilized Businesses *HUB Participation Report, Purchasing (Goods and Services) and Construction Projects* (2015, 2016, 2017, 2018, 2019) shows the distribution of HUB dollars allocated to minority businesses with the percentage of the total of HUB dollars for the following categories: *council of state agencies* (Administration, Commerce, Department of Military, Environmental Quality, Information Technology, Public Safety, Transportation, Natural and Cultural Resources and Revenue). *Public entity categories* include council of state agencies, community colleges, public schools, public universities, and support agencies and council of state agencies (Agriculture, Auditor, Insurance, Justice, Labor, Lieutenant Governor, Public Instruction, Secretary of State, and Treasury).

Since 2015, female businesses have been awarded most of the HUB dollars in both construction spending and the purchase of goods and services in all categories. According to the NCDOA Office for Historically Underutilized Businesses *HUB Participation Report, Purchasing (Goods and Services) and Construction Projects* (2016), female businesses were awarded 62% of the total HUB dollars across cabinet agencies in construction spending, 53.8% of the dollars allocated for HUB spending across public entities, and 42.5% of the total HUB dollars across the council of state agencies.

The NCDOA Office for Historically Underutilized Businesses *HUB Participation Report, Purchasing (Goods and Services) and Construction Projects'* (2016, 2017, 2018, 2019) allocation of HUB dollars for state universities, community colleges, and public school systems shows that the distribution of funds were primarily allocated to female businesses (Table 11.1- Appendix D). Public school systems were awarded $72.6 million (52%) to female business, community colleges were awarded $28 million (65%), and state universities were awarded $47 million (57.8%). This allocation was more than all the MBEs combined. MBEs received a total of $48.9 million (34%) for the purchase of goods and services, and of that total, Black businesses only received $29 million (21%). The trajectory and the inequities in distribution continued for the distribution of HUB dollars for the purchase of goods and services from 2015 to 2019. The NCDOA Office for Historically Underutilized Businesses *HUB Participation Report, Purchasing (Goods and Services) and Construction Projects* also reflects the same trend from 2015 to 2019 (see Tables 11.1a–11.4a) as it relates to the allocation of HUB dollars for minority businesses. Female businesses continue to receive a majority of the funds, as reflected in the distribution of funding for construction spending from 2018 to 2019 for community colleges, public school systems, and state universities (see Table 11.4a). The data reveals inequalities in female business owners receiving 66.5% of the total percentage of HUB dollars from state universities, 87% from community colleges, and 67% from public school systems, while American Indians received less than 1% (0.57%), Asian Americans received less than 2% (1.73%), Hispanics received less than 5% (4.73%), and Black businesses received slightly more than 25% (26.7%).

EMPOWERMENT

The Rev. Martin Luther King Jr. once said, "Power properly understood is nothing but the ability to achieve purpose. It is the strength required to bring about social, political and economic change" (Schiffer, 2008, para. 1). What are some practical applications that minority business owners in North Carolina can use to ensure that their business needs are known, acknowledged, and included in decisions such as funding and distribution? Let us consider the following factors: capacity building, information sharing, and intellectual continuity.

Capacity Building

When it comes to having the ability to support the mission of your business today and in the future, identify relationships, processes, and information that can be leveraged. For instance, the HUB Office partners with several agencies to help break down barriers for small businesses in North Carolina. The link to all strategic partners and resources are available at https://ncadmin.nc.gov/businesses/historically-underutilized-businesses-hub/hub-business-resource-links. Also, there are multiple training opportunities available. Free training can be accessed in person and online. Links to training are available in Appendix B.

Information Sharing

Information sharing continues to evolve and can inform and equip entrepreneurs when presented, socialized, and promoted adequately. For instance, the HUB website is the central location for the latest developments and information. A monthly newsletter is published to keep stakeholders informed. As multiple generations participate in the HUB processes, communication preferences vary. Contact the HUB Office and inform them about how minority businesses in this state expect communication to be disseminated and challenge them to transform your requirements into information that is easily shared.

Intellectual Continuity

There are three different term contacts that entrepreneurs can pursue, depending on their needs. Connect with the HUB agency for seminars and other resources that will help you identify which contract aligns with your needs. Stay connected through local and state civic organizations that promote socioeconomic equity. Also, seek volunteer opportunities with organizations that can benefit from your business based on the causes they represent.

Practical Application: Gap Analysis

To be equipped to engage with HUB and other sources for training, funding, and infrastructure, business owners must take what information is available and compare it to their particular needs. One way to apply the information, resources, and relationships is by performing a gap analysis of business needs on an ongoing basis. Kubiak and Benbow (2017) defined a gap analysis as "a tool used to identify a performance difference between a current state and a desired or future state using metrics implied by the states" (p. 485).

HUB data suggest that female businesses receive the most funding, far exceeding MBEs (Black, Hispanic, Asian Americans, and American Indians). A gap analysis can assist in identifying areas of focus as one prepares to engage in capacity building, information sharing, and intellectual continuity. It can also identify opportunities for HUB to narrow or close the gap.

Imagine that you are an entrepreneur who is interested in HUB certification. While the current HUB application process is clear, if you live in rural North Carolina and lack broadband access, completing the application may prove to be a challenge. This gap is significant because it can be a contributor to other disparities, such as HUB dollar distribution by county. A GAP template with an example is in Appendix E.

SUMMARY/CONCLUSION

This chapter focused on the North Carolina minority small business owner. When comparing existing HUB processes, tools, and resources for this subgroup, three major takeaways emerge. First, women, particularly women of color, have recently made up the largest percentage of startup entrepreneurs. However, while North Carolina HUB distribution data reveal that female businesses receive most of the funding for the purchase of goods and services and construction spending, these data do not delineate women by race/ethnic group. For example, a Black female business owner cannot classify as both. She must select one or the other.

Second, while HUB currently provides various sources of information to connect minority small businesses with certification, participation, and bidding opportunities, there is still a need to align the processes with the current needs of these businesses. Such a case raises some important questions. For instance, which counties in North Carolina tend to have the greatest challenge in accessing these resources because of infrastructure disparities? What is the relationship between technological limitations (i.e., cell phone towers, access to WI-FI, hardware) by county and opportunities to bid for HUB funding? When external disruptions have a sweeping and negative economic impact on a business of color (social, physical, technological, etc.), what role should agencies such as HUB play in recovery and sustainability efforts? What contingency plans exist for North Carolina agencies, such as HUB, that are designed to inform, aid, and equip small (especially micro-minority) businesses in times of crisis?

Minority entrepreneurs have an important and significant role in driving the economy in North Carolina. As the world changes and evolves, and one generation transfers wealth to the next, the need to effectively engage people, systems, and processes for the mutual benefit of all citizens will remain. Although critical to the survival of agencies and businesses, federal- and state-level policies that bridge the gap between financial health and minority inclusion continue to be scant. Policies and processes that enable data transparency and representation will help leaders understand where they are and forge an environment of access and empowerment for them and the communities they serve.

REFERENCES

American Express. (2019). 2019 State of women-owned businesses report. https://s1.q4cdn.com/692158879/files/doc_library/file/2019-state-of-women-owned-businesses-report.pdf

American City Business Journals. (2020). *Here are statewide resources for small businesses in North Carolina.* https://www.bizjournals.com/triangle/news/2020/03/30/here-are-statewide-resources-for-small-businesses.html.

Barbato, R., DeMartino, R., & Jacques, P. (2009). The entrepreneurial motivations of nonemployer entrepreneurs. *New England Journal of Entrepreneurship, 12*(1), 33–43.

Bluestin, F. S. (2001). Changes affecting construction, purchasing, and conflicts of interest. *School Law Bulletin, 32*(4), 26–39.

Buchanan, L. (2015, September 2). The U.S. now has 27 million entrepreneurs. *Inc. Magazine.* https://www.inc.com/leigh-buchanan/us-entrepreneurship-reaches-record-highs.html

Clements, T. S. (2017). SBA launches new HUBZONE maps and partners with U.S. Digital Service to streamline and enhance online services for small businesses. Retrieved March 30, 2020, from https://www.sba.gov/about-sba/sba-newsroom

Coronavirus Aid, Relief, and Economic Security (CARES) Act of 2020, Public Law 116–136 (2020). https://www.congress.gov/bill/116th-congress/house-bill/748

Disparities in Capital Access Report. (2002). Retrieved from: https://theinstitutenc.org/wp-content/uploads/2018/03/DisparitiesinCapitalAccessReport.pdf

Exec. Order No. 150, Support for Historically Underutilized Businesses. (1999).

Fairlie, R. (2020). The impact of COVID-19 on small business owners: Evidence of early-stage losses from the April 2020 current population survey. The Stanford Institute for Economic Policy Research. https://siepr.stanford.edu/sites/default/files/publications/20-022.pdf

Fairlie, R. W., & Robb, A. M. (2010). *Disparities in capital access between minority and non-minority-owned businesses: The troubling reality of capital limitations faced by MBEs. U.S.*

Department of Commerce, Minority Business Development Agency, 1–59. Minority Business Development Agency. https://theinstitutenc.org/wp-content/uploads/2018/03/Disparitiesin-CapitalAccessReport.pdf

Formoso-Suralta, B. (2017). *What is a small business?* Fit Small Business. https://fitsmallbusiness.com/what-is-a-small-business/

Hendrix, M. (2017). *Regulations impact small business and the heart of America's Economy: Complex. Cumbersome. Costly.* U.S. Chamber of Commerce Foundation. https://www.uschamberfoundation.org/blog/post/regulations-impact-small-business-and-heart-americas-economy

Kubiak, T. M., & Benbow, D. W. (2017). *The certified Six Sigma Black Belt handbook* (2nd ed.). ASQ Quality Press.

Lange, J., Brush, C., Corbett, A., Kelley, D., Kim, P., Majbouri, M., & Vedula, S. (2019). *Global Entrepreneurship Monitor 2018/2019 United States Report.* Babson. https://www.babson.edu/media/babson/assets/blank-center/GEM_USA_2018-2019.pdf

Mider, M., & Sam, C. (2020). *Small-business rescue shows not all states are created equal.* Bloomberg.com https://www.bloomberg.com/graphics/2020-sba-paycheck-protection-program/.

Murray, J. (2019). All about sole proprietors and sole proprietorship. The Balance Small Business. https://www.thebalancesmb.com/sole-proprietorship-398896

Newtek Business Solutions Company. (2012). 13 types of insurance a small business owner should have. *Forbes.* https://www.forbes.com/sites/thesba/2012/01/19/

Nitti, T. (2020). Ten things we need to know about Paycheck Protection Program loan forgiveness. *Forbes.* https://www.forbes.com/sites/anthonynitti/2020/04/15/

North Carolina Department of Administration (NCDOA). (2020). https://ncadmin.nc.gov/

North Carolina General Statute. (n.d.). *Historically underutilized business defined; statewide uniform certification.* https://www.ncleg.net/EnactedLegislation/Statutes/HTML/BySection/Chapter_143/GS_143-128.4.html

North Carolina Historically Underutilized Businesses. (2015). *2015 annual report.* Retrieved May 3, 2020, from https://files.nc.gov/ncdoa/hub/documents/reports/2015AnnualReport.pdf

Office for Historically Underutilized Businesses Annual Report. (2016). *HUB Purchasing report, purchasing (goods and services)* 2015–2016.

Office for Historically Underutilized Businesses Annual Report. (2016). *HUB Purchasing report, - Construction Spending* 2015–2016. https://files.nc.gov/ncdoa/documents/files/FY-15-16-Construction-Spending.pdf

Office for Historically Underutilized Businesses Annual Report. (2017). *HUB participation report, purchasing (goods and services) and construction projects,* 2016–2017. https://files.nc.gov/ncdoa/documents/files/FY%2016-17%20HUB%20Purchasing%20Detail%20Report.pdf

Office for Historically Underutilized Businesses Annual Report. (2017). *HUB Construction report, purchasing (goods and services) - construction,* 2016–2017. https://files.nc.gov/ncdoa/documents/files/FY%2016-17%20Construction%20HUB%20Participation%20Report.pdf

Office for Historically Underutilized Businesses. (2018). *HUB participation report, purchasing (goods and services) projects,* 2017–2018. https://files.nc.gov/ncdoa/documents/files/FY_17-18_Annual_Report_Goods_and_Services.pdf

Office for Historically Underutilized Business Annual Report. (2018). *HUB Construction report, 2017–2018*. https://files.nc.gov/ncdoa/documents/files/FY_17-18_Annual_Report_Construction.pdf

Office for Historically Underutilized Businesses Annual Report. (2019). *HUB participation report, purchasing (goods and services), 2018–2019*. https://files.nc.gov/ncdoa/documents/files/FY-18-19-Annual-Report-Goods-and-Services.pdf

Office for Historically Underutilized Businesses. (2019). *HUB participation report, Construction, 2018–2019*. https://files.nc.gov/ncdoa/documents/files/FY-18-19-Annual-Construction-Report.pdf

Polyak, I. (2008, June 1). Recession survival guide. *Black Enterprise*. https://www.blackenterprise.com/recession-survival-guide/

Purchases and Contracts, General Statute 143–48 (2007). https://www.ncleg.gov/EnactedLegislation/Statutes/HTML/BySection/Chapter_143/GS_143-48.html

Reed, E. (2020). *The SBA community advantage loan program*. Smart Asset. Retrieved April 30, 2020, from https://smartasset.com/financial-advisor/sba-community-advantage-loan-program

Schiffer, E. (2008). *Martin Luther King about power and love*. Net-Map Toolbox. https://netmap.wordpress.com/2008/07/09/martin-luther-king-about-power-and-love/

Small Business Administration. (2008). Federal contracting opportunities for HUBZone entrepreneurs. https://www.treasury.gov/resource-center/sb-programs/Documents/HUBZone%20FINAL%20Fact%20Sheet.pdf

Smith, K. A. (2020). Congress approves more funding for the Paycheck Protection Program. Here's what you need to know. *Forbes*. https://www.forbes.com/sites/advisor/2020/04/22/the-senate-approved-more-funding-for-the-paycheck-protection-program-heres-what-you-need-to-know/#6feaedee4084

State Budget, Minority Participation Goal, Statute §143-128-2. (2007). https://www.ncleg.gov/EnactedLegislation/Statutes/HTML/BySection/Chapter_143/GS_143-128.html

State of Small Business and Entrepreneurship. (2018, August). http://sbtdc.org/wp-content/uploads/SSB

Treece, K. (2018). *Best states to start a business in 2018: Definitive ranking of all 50 states*. Fit Small Business. https://fitsmallbusiness.com/best-states-to-start-a-business/

Triangle Business Journal. (2020). *Here are statewide resources for small businesses in North Carolina*. https://www.bizjournals.com/triangle/news/2020/03/30/here-are-statewide-resources-for-small-businesses.html

U.S. Census Bureau, Wealth and Asset Ownership. (2008). http://www.census.gov/hhes/www/wealth/2002/wlth02-1.html.

U.S. Small Business and Technology Development Center (SBTDC). (2020). NC business statistics. Retrieved May 3, 2020, from http://www.sbtdc.org/resources/nc-business-statistics/

Uzialko, A. (2019). How to start and run a business in North Carolina. *Business News Daily*. http://businessnewsdaily.com/9577-doing-business-in-north-carolina.html

Washington Post. (2013). *Minority contracting doesn't match population's numbers*. https://www.washingtonpost.com/politics/minority-contracting-doesnt-match-populations-numbers/2013/08/08/bba9cec8-005a-11e3-9711-3708310f6f4d_story.html

Wiefek, N., Rosen, C., & Garbinsky, T. (2019). Promoting employee ownership: A look at the states. *Journal of Participation and Employee Ownership*, 2(3), 183–189.

Figure Credit

Fig. 11.1: Source: https://ncadmin.nc.gov/businesses/hub/hub-certification.

APPENDIX A

The Historically Underutilized Businesses (HUB) Certification Process

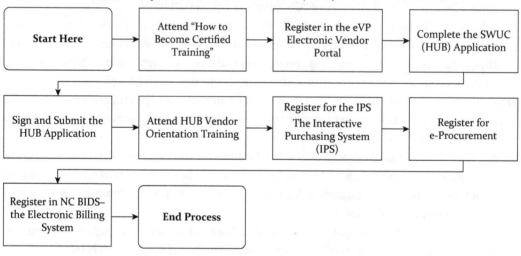

FIGURE 11.1 Source: https://ncadmin.nc.gov/businesses/hub/hub-certification

APPENDIX B

Link to Training Resources

NC BIDS: https://ncadmin.nc.gov/about-doa/divisions/purchase-and-contract/nc-bids

Interactive Purchasing System: www.ips.state.nc.us

e-Procurement: http://eprocurement.nc.gov/

HUB Certification: https://ncadmin.nc.gov/businesses/hub/hub-certification

Statewide Purchase and Contact—Provides a list of current statewide contracts
https://ncadmin.nc.gov/government-agencies/procurement/statewide-term-contracts

APPENDIX C

Small Business Resources

Business Registration—Register your business and file annual reports
https://www.sosnc.gov/corporations/

North Carolina Department of Secretary of State—Oversees the business activities of the state
https://www.sosnc.gov/corporations/

U.S. Small Business Administration—Helps small businesses acquire business loans and provides free counseling
https://www.sba.gov/

Capital Opportunities for Small Businesses—Provides education and financial resources for small businesses
http://www.sbtdc.org/pdf/capopps.pdf

North Carolina Department of Commerce—Provides grant incentives, data, tools, and job training resources and information
https://www.nccommerce.com/

Small Business and Technology Development Center
http://www.sbtdc.org/

Resources for Market Research Data—Provides links and market data
https://www.ncsbc.net/DocumentMaster.aspx?doc=1011

SCORE—Provides mentoring and education for small businesses
https://www.score.org/

Business Plan Guide for Small Business Start-Up
https://www.ncsbc.net/images/Biz_Plan_Start_Up_Guide.pdf

Introduction to Federal Government Contracting
https://www.usa.gov/government-contracting-for-beginners

NC Cooperative Extension
https://www.sba.gov/

Licenses and Permits
https://www.sba.gov/business-guide/launch-your-business/apply-licenses-permits

How to File Annual Report
https://www.sosnc.gov/divisions/business_registration/annual_report

USA.gov—Provides resources on how to research and bid on government contracts
https://www.usa.gov/business

Small Business Resources   (Continued)

Intellectual Property Guide
http://www.sbtdc.org/pdf/intellectual-property-guide.pdf

Economic Development Partnership of North Carolina—*Focused on recruiting new businesses and helping small businesses get started*
https://edpnc.com/about-the-edpnc/

Rapid Recovery Lending programs—Helps small businesses and farmers recover from economic impacts
https://ncrapidrecovery.org/

Golden LEAF Foundation—Helps provide funding for small businesses in North Carolina
https://www.goldenleaf.org/

The Small Business Center Network—Helps increase the success of small businesses
http://www.cccti.edu/smallbusiness/

*These links are subject to change

APPENDIX D

TABLE 11.1 *Office for Historically Underutilized Businesses* HUB Participation Report, Purchasing (Goods and Services) and Construction Projects *FY 15–16 ($M)*

MINORITY GROUP	HUB $ PUBLIC SCHOOLS	% HUB PUBLIC SCHOOLS	HUB $ COMMUNITY COLLEGE	% HUB COMMUNITY COLLEGE	HUB $ STATE UNIVERSITY	% HUB STATE UNIVERSITY
MBE	$48.9M	34.86	$8.7M	20.14	$13.2M	16.19%
BLACK	$29M	20.72	$5.5M	12.71	$9.9M	12.22
HISPANIC	$4.7M	3.33	$368K	0.85	$846K	1.04
AMERICAN ASIAN	$12.5M	8.90	$2.4M	5.58	$2.3M	2.92
AMERICAN INDIAN	$2.7	1.91	$436K	1.01	$1.5M	1.88
FEMALE	$72.6M	51.75	$28M	65.30	$47M	57.81
DISABLED	$7.7M	5.54	$1.4M	3.35	$232K	0.28
DBE	$5.3M	3.81	$58K	0.14	$229K	0.28
NPWC	$4.0M	2.86	$623K	1.44	$1.2M	1.44
SED	$1.67M	1.19	$4.1M	9.63	$18M	22.11

Legend:
MBE-Minority Business Enterprise (Black, Hispanic, Asian American, American Indian), B-Black, H-Hispanic, AA-Asian American, AI-American Indian, F-Female, D-Disabled, DBE-Disabled Business Enterprise, NPWC-Nonprofit Work Center for the Blind, and Severely Disabled SED-Disadvantaged
Source: Office for Historically Underutilized Businesses HUB Participation Report, Purchasing (Goods and Services) and Construction Projects, *2015–2016.*

CONSTRUCTION SPENDING: TABLE 11.1A *Office for Historically Underutilized Businesses* HUB Participation Report, Purchasing (Goods and Services) and Construction Projects, *2015–2016.*

MINORITY GROUP	HUB $ PUBLIC SCHOOLS	% HUB PUBLIC SCHOOLS	HUB $ COMMUNITY COLLEGE	% HUB COMMUNITY COLLEGE	HUB $ STATE UNIVERSITY	% HUB STATE UNIVERSITY
MBE	$48.9	34.86%	$8.7	20.14%	$13.2	16.19%
BLACK	$29.0	20.72%	$5.5	12.71	$9.9	12.24%
HISPANIC	$4.67	3.33%	$.368	0.85%	$.846	1.04%
AMERICAN ASIAN	$12.5	8.90%	$2.4	5.58%	$2.4	2.93%
AMERICAN INDIAN	$2.68	1.91	$.436	1.01%	$1.54	1.88%
FEMALE	72.6%	51.75	$282	65.30%	$47.2	57.81%
DISABLED	$7.7	5.54%	$1.45	3.35%	$.233	0.28%
DBE	$5.3	3.81	$58.8	0.14%	$.229	0.28%
NPWC	$4.01	2.86%	$.623	1.44%	$1.18	1.44%
SED	$1.66	1.19%	$4.17	9.63%	$18.06	1.44%

*MBE includes Black, Hispanic, American Asian, and American Indian.
Source: *Office for Historically Underutilized Businesses* HUB Participation Report, Purchasing (Goods and Services) and Construction Projects, *2015–2016.*

TABLE 11.2 *Office for Historically Underutilized Businesses* HUB Participation Report, Purchasing (Goods and Services) and Construction *FY 16–17 ($M)*

MINORITY GROUP	HUB $ PUBLIC SCHOOLS	% HUB PUBLIC SCHOOLS	HUB $ COMMUNITY COLLEGE	% HUB COMMUNITY COLLEGE	HUB $ STATE UNIVERSITY	% HUB STATE UNIVERSITY
BLACK	$31.7	21.5	$2.1	4.93%	$14.8M	16.4%
HISPANIC	$5.07	3.43	$.473	1.08%	$1.83	3.11%
AMERICAN ASIAN	$12.7	8.62	$2.7	6.35%	$1.53	1.70%
AMERICAN INDIAN	$9.7	6.56	$1.23	2.91%	$1.23	1.37%
FEMALE	$60.5	41.00	$34.5	78.84%	$51.9	57.5%
DISABLED	$12.1	8.22	$1.17	2.66%	$.542	0.6%
DBE	$2.2	1.48	$.27	0.06%	$1.0	1.11%
NPWC	$9.9	6.69	$.821	1.87%	$1.02	1.13%
DISADVANTAGED	$3.7	2.52	$.563	1.29%	$16.2	18.0%

Source: *Office for Historically Underutilized Businesses* HUB Participation Report, Purchasing (Goods and Services) and Construction Projects, *2016–2017.*

CONSTRUCTION SPENDING: TABLE 11.2A *Office for Historically Underutilized Businesses* HUB Participation Report, Purchasing (Goods and Services) and Construction Projects, *2016–2017*

MINORITY GROUP	HUB $ PUBLIC SCHOOLS	% HUB PUBLIC SCHOOLS	HUB $ COMMUNITY COLLEGE	% HUB COMMUNITY COLLEGE	HUB $ STATE UNIVERSITY	% HUB STATE UNIVERSITY
BLACK	$31.7	$21.47%	$2.2	4.93%	$14.8	16.46%
HISPANIC	$5.1	3.43%	$.473	1.08%	$1.83	2.03%
AMERICAN ASIAN	$12.7	$8.62%	$2.79	6.35%	$1.54	1.70%
AMERICAN INDIAN	$9.69	6.56%	$1.23	2.91%	$1.23	1.37%
FEMALE	$60.5	41%	$34.7	78.84%	$51.9	57.56%
DISABLED	$12.1	8.22%	$1.2	2.66%	$.542	0.60%
DBE	$2.2	$1.48%	$.27	0.06%	$1.01	1.11%
NPWC	$9.88	3.71%	$.822	1.87%	$1.02	1.13%
SED	$3.7	2.52%	$.563	1.29%	$16.3	18.04%

Source: Office for Historically Underutilized Businesses HUB Participation Report, Purchasing (Goods and Services) and Construction Projects, *2016–2017.*

TABLE 11.3 *Office for Historically Underutilized Businesses* HUB Participation Report, Purchasing (Goods and Services) and Construction Projects *FY 17–18 ($M)*

MINORITY GROUP	HUB $ PUBLIC SCHOOLS	%HUB PUBLIC SCHOOLS	HUB $ COMMUNITY COLLEGE	% HUB COMMUNITY COLLEGE	HUB $STATE UNIVERSITY	HUB% STATE UNIVERSITY
BLACK	$35.9	23.42%	$2.5	6.20%	$13.3	13.24%
HISPANIC	$7.4	$4.83	$.360	0.88%	$.715	0.71%
AMERICAN ASIAN	$13.4	8.73%	$3.45	8.44%	$1.81	1.81%
AMERICAN INDIAN	$8.73	5.73%	$1.59	3.91%	$.807	0.81%
FEMALE	$56.7	37.01%	$30.67	74.99%	$55.5	55.46%
DISABLED	$11.4	7.43%	$1.37	3.34%	$.115	0.11%
DBE	$8.9	5.78%	$.40	0.10%	$.284	0.28%
NPWC	$7.5	4.89%	$.788	1.93%	$2.02	2.02%
DISADVANTAGE	$3.4	2.22%	$.89	0.22%	$.25	25.55%

Source: Office for Historically Underutilized Businesses HUB Participation Report, Purchasing (Goods and Services) and Construction Projects, *2017–2018.*

CONSTRUCTION SPENDING: TABLE 11.3A *Office for Historically Underutilized Businesses* HUB Participation Report, Purchasing (Goods and Services) and Construction Projects, *2017–2018*

MINORITY GROUP	HUB $ PUBLIC SCHOOLS	% HUB PUBLIC SCHOOLS	HUB $ COMMUNITY COLLEGE	% HUB COMMUNITY COLLEGE	HUB $ STATE UNIVERSITY	% HUB STATE UNIVERSITY
BLACK	$5.2	9.23%	$.234	10.38%	$11.1	12.9%
HISPANIC	$3.2	5.66%	$.162	7.17%	$4.2	4.60%
AMERICAN ASIAN	$99.6	0.18%	$0	0%	$.978	1.07%
AMERICAN INDIAN	$.234	0.41%	$.264	11.71%	$.50	0.05%
FEMALE	$47.8	84.17%	$1.59	70.74%	$74.7	$81.95
DISADVANTAGED (SED)	$.199	0.35%	$0	0%	$117	0.13%
DISABLED	$0	0%	$0	0%	$0	0%

Source: Office for Historically Underutilized Businesses HUB Participation Report, Purchasing (Goods and Services) and Construction Projects, *2017–2018*.

TABLE 11.4 *Office for Historically Underutilized Businesses* HUB Participation Report, Purchasing (Goods and Services) and Construction Projects *FY 18–19*

MINORITY GROUP	HUB $ PUBLIC SCHOOLS	% HUB PUBLIC SCHOOLS	HUB $ COMMUNITY COLLEGE	% HUB COMMUNITY COLLEGE	% HUB STATE UNIVERSITY	HUB $ STATE UNIVERSITY
BLACK	$30	19.30%	$5.7	12.89%	$10.7	13.55%
HISPANIC	$10.	6.56%	$.646	1.47%	$1.17	1.49%
AMERICAN ASIAN	$20.9	13.45%	$4.6	10.49%	$4.79	6.06%
AMERICAN INDIAN	$5.1	3.30%	$2.4	5.46%	$1.4	1.74%
FEMALE	$59.7	38.42.	$28.4	64.63	$55.9	70.63%
DISABLED	$10.5	6.77%	$1.3	2.95%	$.159	0.20%
DBE	$11.7	7.52%	$.830	1.89%	$3.8	4.78%
NPWC	$4.6	2.96%	$.78	0.18%	$.737	0.93%
DISADVANTAGE	$2.8	1.72%	$.15	0.04%	$.499	0.63%

Source: Office for Historically Underutilized Businesses HUB Participation Report, Purchasing (Goods and Services) and Construction Projects, *2018–2019*.

CONSTRUCTION SPENDING: TABLE 11.4A *Office for Historically Underutilized Businesses* HUB Participation Report, Purchasing (Goods and Services) and Construction Projects, *2018–2019*

MINORITY GROUP	HUB $ PUBLIC SCHOOLS	% HUB PUBLIC SCHOOLS	HUB $ COMMUNITY COLLEGE	% HUB COMMUNITY COLLEGE	HUB $ STATE UNIVERSITY	% HUB STATE UNIVERSITY
BLACK	$6.67	18.63%	$86.3	7.60%	$7.5	26.71%
HISPANIC	$4.1	11.50%	$58.7	5.17%	$1.3	4.53%
AMERICAN ASIAN	$.16	$0.04	$.19	0.17	$.482	1.73%
AMERICAN INDIAN	$.844	2.36%	$0	0%	$.161	0.57%
FEMALE	$22.9	64.11%	$.988	87.06%	$18.6	66.46%
DISADVANTAGED (SED)	$77.8	0.22%	$0	0%	$0	0%
DISABLED	$1.1	3.14%	$0	0%	$0	0%

Source: Office for Historically Underutilized Businesses HUB Participation Report, Purchasing (Goods and Services) and Construction Projects, *2018–2019.*

APPENDIX E

Gap Analysis Template

CURRENT STATE	DESIRED STATE	DIFFERENCE	OPPORTUNITIES TO ADDRESS THE GAP
Access to bid for three different term contracts	Bid for term contract	Don't know which one to bid for	Seek HUB resources for more information

CHAPTER TWELVE

Building and Sustaining Leadership and Capacity for Civic/Community Engagement

A LONGITUDINAL CASE STUDY OF THE CORE (LEADERSHIP) GROUP IN CLEVELAND COUNTY, NC (1999–2020)

Forrest D. Toms Sr., PhD, Richard Hooker Sr., BA, Forrest D. Toms II, BA, Marcus Bass, BA, and Masonya Ruff, EdD

OPENING THOUGHTS OF OUR CURRENT REALITY (TOMS ET AL., IN PRESS)

> What one? What many? Organized by what ethos, creating what kind of social and political system, giving what substance to the shared groups identity call American? What is to be the relation between whatever continues to mark us apart, by race, religion, heritage, and what we all hold in common? (Harold Isaacs, 1975, 1997)

Isaacs's statement poses two critical questions. The first centers on the issue of "power to define." That is, which group's values, beliefs, and ethos will be used as the standard measuring stick for defining what it means to be American. The second question relates to a need to focus on the similarities (those things we have in common) versus the differences (those things that separate and create conflict) (Toms, 1997).

The unfolding events in the United States beginning in March 2020 with the coronavirus disease 2019 (COVID-19) pandemic and its devastating and ravishing effect on our citizens' health, particularly African Americans, and the nation's economic health. COVID-19 has become a magnifying apparatus of the historical social ills of this country and their continued effect on the quality of life for Black, Brown, and poor people. The virus and its subsequent effects have pushed all our systems to the extreme: ecosystems, economic systems, social systems, environmental systems, health systems, and racial inequity systems. Which raises the question, how do we handle the health of our democracy?

Just as the nation was coming out of a "stay-at-home order" that closed the country down, resulting in the largest unemployment rates and stock market drops since the Great Depression, a 17-year-old girl captured George Floyd's murder by a Minnesota police officer on a cell phone camera, our digital equalizer, and shared it on the Internet for all to see. The assaulting officer threatened the girl with mace, but she refused to stop filming. The killing of George Floyd was preceded by the killings of Ahmaud Arbery and Breonna Taylor weeks before. The combination and short time frame of these three murders resulted in the largest ongoing protests, riots, and unrest in cities across the country that we have ever witnessed, mainly because of the diverse and inclusive makeup of those participating stateside and worldwide; they represented the broadest spectrum of diversity across racial, ethnic, economic, and class lines ever witnessed. Right before our eyes, we are seeing a "national consensus of outrage" building and sustaining from large cities to small rural communities in the United States to protests worldwide, with the same messages: "Justice for George," "Black Lives Matter," and "End Structural and Systemic Racism." As one of the two "OG" authors, I can say that we are both reminded of the irony of author, poet, and spoken word artist Gil Scott-Heron's depiction of life in the late 1960s in his poem "The Revolution Will Not Be Televised."

The power in the atmosphere, the climate, and the psychosocial space that we are all experiencing as human beings right now in the United States, and seemingly the world, has forced our attention to and conversations about the marginalization and undervaluing of Black, Brown, and poor people's lives; to examining and challenging deep historical and structural inequities in legislation, governance, policies, and practices undergirding the preconditions for protest; and to moving from a protest movement to political action and from political action to political change.

While seen as an exercise of democracy for America, the political process in this country has historically and contextually marginalized African American sovereignty. Political gains made in the short span of emancipation has been met with the same if not greater violence as physical emancipation, resulting in a trauma-informed political analysis that undermines not only Black voters but also the political process in its entirety—that is, a decade or more of expansion of the White franchise for political gain, the Reconstruction era, and Jim Crow legislation [...].

INTRODUCTION

This research provides an understanding of the circumstantial power/influence created by a group of local Black leaders in a small rural community, despite systemic barriers and a practicing philosophy of a restrictive, conservative, racist, southern strategy. The study examines the dynamics of interpersonal/inter-organizational relationships, the ebb and flow and transitions involved over 2 decades, and the tangible and intangible effects of sustained civic/community engagement of African American leaders and citizens, internally as a group and externally through sustained engagement while battling social/political resistance on the local and state levels.

Toms et al. (2014) discussed this notion of the ideal versus the reality of participatory democracy:

> There appears to be a general agreement that citizens should be able to act on their own behalf and have the power and right to participate in decisions that impact their quality of life and well-being (White, 2009). These ideals and discussions can be heard daily in workplaces, homes, classrooms, and even on various media mediums throughout the day. Yet, the practice of this philosophy and set of ideals by private, public, nonprofit, government agencies, and human service agencies in their attempt to address everyday social, civic, and political challenges in our communities, more often than not fail to be actualized. (p. 9)

They went further and suggested,

> If, in fact, there is a general belief in participatory democracy (the will of the people to act on their own behalf), then why do institutions and organizations struggle to "engage" communities in collaborative partnerships, work effectively with citizens in community-building efforts—particularly citizens from low-income and ethnically and culturally diverse groups? (Toms et al., 2014, pp. 9–10)

The ideal versus the reality of justice and equality for all is clearly being tested, challenged, and extended in ways never before seen in our country's history. This new and younger generation of American citizens have seen over and over again that justice is not blind; it is not equal; it is, has, and continues to disproportionately place Black, Brown, and poor people at risk: educationally, economically, politically, and socially. Yet the ideal remains on display in mainstream institutions (schools, businesses, government, human services, law enforcement, to name a few) that we participate in every day as employees, customers, and citizens. These overt/covert organizational policies, procedures, and practices, not to mention the lack of diversity and inclusiveness in the workforce and leadership, continue as the primary vehicles and tools through which systemic racial inequalities survive and thrive today.

In Chapter 3 of this book, Toms et al. (2014) point out that there remain persistent themes in many dialogues about the nature of African American leadership that must be identified, planned for, and addressed:

1. The lack of visibility and participation of African American leaders and organizations in the public discourse in school boards, city councils, county commissioners, and public health board meetings
2. Why participation and involvement in these decision-making arenas remain limited to nonexistent
3. What could and should be done to prepare citizens for more substantive, consistent, and persistent engagement and involvement in civic/community decision

making. Such activity explicitly affects policies and resource distribution. At the community level, many citizens believe that this lack of representation and participation in the civic process directly affects the consistent and mounting disparities in African American communities. These disparities are most evident in data reflecting early educational achievement and performance, health-care outcomes, employment compensation and access, gaps in employment with livable compensation, and, ultimately, declining individual economic net worth and collective access to capital

In addition, the authors discussed how the continued lack of participation in civic/community activities affects overall quality of life:

> The lack of participation in civic/community activities at the local level translates into the development of policy and distribution of needed resources that ultimately can, and do, negatively impact children, families, and communities. At the least, the lack of policy development and resource distribution compounds the already historic disparities impacting African American communities. (Toms et al., 2014, p. 49)

It is the historical and continued effect of this lack of participation in civic/community affairs that we will address through the lens of a case study of a small rural community in western North Carolina.

Methods

A longitudinal case methodology was used to capture the inner thinking, planning, and operations of a group of community leaders for more than 2 decades. The study methods included primary data sources, such archived data, firsthand accounts, video interviews, review of meeting notes, programs and events, newspaper articles and reports, a chronology of activities from 1997 to 2020, and a completed questionnaire from five of 10 members of CORE's ongoing executive team. (Note: CORE is not an acronym or abbreviation for another word.)

The authors will (1) describe the genesis of a group of African American leaders in a small rural community who organized, planned, and implemented a community engagement strategy and process centered on "closing the achievement gap" that has spanned 20 years; (2) provide a chronology of CORE's more than 20 years of civic/community engagement activities and events; (3) provide an analysis of interviews and questionnaires from five of the group's core planning team members; and (4) provide a discussion and reflective analysis of the observation, transitions, and lessons learned over the past 2 decades. The information collected and analyzed provides insight into the experiences, perceptions, practices, and reflections of CORE's civic/community engagement activities and processes.

LONGITUDINAL CASE STUDY: CLEVELAND COUNTY CORE LEADERSHIP GROUP

Who We Are

Cleveland County has had a long history of minority leaders who have served their communities, county, and state in numerous and noteworthy capacities. In 1999, African American leadership was again on display when a group of concerned citizens came together in response to a need to build leadership capacity in solving critical problems facing their community. The CORE Group of Cleveland County emerged as a self-motivated team of professional community-based advocates working to make the academic journey of African American students a successful path. The collective group was also working in concert with community partners to address social, economic, and educational issues, including closing the achievement gap.

The group was active in sponsoring a variety of activities. Among these are male and female forums, Distinguished Image Awards and Scholarship Program, the Annual Education Summit, faith-based forums, high school advanced placement programs, Community Math Academy, and the Leadership Academy.

Mission

The group's mission centered on the belief that increasing achievement and closing the gaps in education would be the top priorities.

Shelby native and diversity and community engagement consultant Dr. Forrest Toms designed a blueprint (framework) for community organizing to identify and bring key community leaders to the table. The group further recognized that failing to educate all students has a long-range social and economic effect on our state and community. The mission of the CORE Group of Cleveland County was to pull together a self-motivated team of professional community-based advocates who work to make the academic journey of African American students a successful path. The group originated from numerous efforts made by organizations in the past to address the issue of "closing the academic achievement gap" in Cleveland County. The group also began to expand its focus and involvement to affect education disparities by holding high expectations for all students, community engagement, and having clearly defined goals for student achievement. The group also advocated for policy change, workforce development, data driven decision making, and collaboration.

Key Players

The group of concerned citizens came together in response to a need to build leadership capacity in solving critical problems facing their community. The CORE Group was composed of local pastors, college professors, retired educators, elected officials, banking executives, and school administrators. Efforts to intentionally recruit community leaders with credible voices and respectability were strategic.

They included community stakeholders, a National Association for the Advancement of Colored People (NAACP) president, local pastors, retired educators, school administrators, school board members, county commissioners, city council members, a bank executive and historian, college professors, community college instructors, and business professionals. The development of this local think tank was periodically benefited by the establishment and connection to statewide networks of organizations focused on collaborative models of coalition building as a means to strengthen the infrastructure necessary to execute political demands and assist in the coordination of objectives and goals for the CORE Group. Organizations with statewide reputations for social justice and racial equity, such as the North Carolina Black Alliance, the North Carolina Justice Center, and the Southern Coalition for Social Justice, provided opportunities to bring to scale several efforts during the process.

"Silent Partners"

Key partners or "conductors" in the movement were largely the NAACP, Committee on Closing the Achievement Gap, and CORE Group. Because the group did not have a bank account, there were other silent partners that provided support and resources. Palmer Grove Baptist Church was a key resource. Located in Kingstown, North Carolina, in western Cleveland County, the church provided a safe haven to meet, strategize, coordinate, and organize the group's grassroots efforts. Meetings were scheduled and held monthly for several years. On a typical Saturday morning, once a month, the group would meet in a church classroom in Kingstown, North Carolina, for 4–6 hours of strategic planning, organizing, processing, and collaborating. It was a contagious atmosphere of ideals, sharing, group dynamics, and interactions with a singular focus: improving the outcomes of minority students. Occasionally, meetings would rotate to other area churches. Team members would also be greeted with a hot breakfast provided by the church members prior to a Saturday meeting.

Cleveland County Business Development Center (CCBDC)

The CCBDC was another integral partner. CCBDC provided the administrative support, including managing communications, drafting agendas, providing copies, designing programs, supplying certificates, writing emails, and gathering mass mailings and postage.

The cofounders of the organization were local business leaders, Harold Ramseur and Richard Hooker Jr. According to Hooker, "It was the late Troy Watson, area director of the Charlotte Minority Business Center, however, that provided the vision and framework to help foster strategic alliances and support for this initiative." With the assistance and guidance of Mr. Watson, the center was successful in promoting local collaboration and assisting several local businesses with a variety of services, including loan packaging, business plans, and feasibility studies. More than $200,000 business loans were acquired by several local small businesses with technical assistance from the Charlotte Area Business Minority Business Center within the first 5 years of the organization's existence. Participating financial institutions included First National Bank, First Union Bank, BB&T, and Shelby Savings and Loan. Other strategic partners included CCC, Gardner-Webb University, Cleveland County Schools, Cleveland County Chamber, and North Carolina Institute for Minority Economic Development.

"We certainly have a rich history of engagement over the years," says Hooker. The CCBDC, for example, has facilitated more than 150 education workshops; hosted numerous Minority Enterprise Development Week (MED) events, leadership forums, youth outreach, and education enrichment; and cosponsored other events. Our business model also included recognizing small business, hosting trade fairs and elected officials' summits, and collaborating with numerous business partners. They include Gardner Webb University, Cleveland Community College (CCC), Cleveland County Chamber, Cleveland County Schools, financial institutions, faith-based groups, and churches, as well as participation in statewide executive conferences.

In 1999–2008, CCBDC provided communication support to the CORE Group. Administrative support was provided in the form of mailings, meeting announcements, coordinating events, and supplies. Further, during the formative years of the Community Math Academy in 2008, CCBDC provided administrative support for fundraising and other operational assistance.

In keeping with its mission to support entrepreneurship through capacity building, education, and networking, the CCBDC reached a new milestone in 2017. It marked the 25th anniversary of CCBDC. Founded in 1992, CCBDC was introduced initially as the "Small Cities Program" at CCC. The objective of the initiative was to facilitate a public/private partnership to promote economic development, inclusion, and entrepreneurship through a series of programs, projects, and networking.

To create a new cadre of emerging leaders, CCBDC is currently serving as an incubator for talent development to support and aid the evolution of the next generation of civic and business leaders. The Cleveland Emerging Leaders Academy (CELA) seeks to create a first-class leadership model for business and public service, capacity building, and transformative leadership. The academy graduated its first class in 2018. Other signature programs include Minority Enterprise Development Week, the Women in Business Series, and the Lecture Series.

"Building for the Future ... Celebrating the Past."
Each year, CCBDC events bring together small business owners, local officials, and community stakeholders to honor and commemorate the accomplishments of small business owners, local citizens, and community partners.

Chronology of Community and Civic Engagement Actions and Outcomes (1999–2020)

The chronology entails events that transpired that caused concern for the African American residents of Cleveland County from which emerged the CORE Group.

1997 NAACP Retreat—June 7, 1997

The Cleveland County Branch of the NAACP hosted a retreat at CCC that would prove to be a precursor to the Close the Gap movement. The one-day retreat, held at CCC on June 7, 1997, attracted 70–80 participants. Eight major areas were discussed in small groups: (1) community health awareness, (2) education, (3) economics, (4) community safety (crime), (5) youth, (6) motivation, (7) discrimination, and (8) injustice. After addressing all eight topics, participants identified "education" as the top issue.

1997 Student Suicide—September 7, 1997

The NAACP event preceded another pivotal incident that would propel the community into a call to action around education. On September 7, 1997, a 12-year-old middle school student committed suicide after being suspended from Shelby Middle School. This tragic incident set into motion a series of community reactions, responses, and school policy changes. Following passionate and pointed questions concerning the handling of the suspension from Rev. James Smith, pastor of Palmer Grove Baptist Church, at the Shelby City School Board Meeting, Superintendent Steve Curtis set out to address the racial and cultural divide within the school district and community.

"School Officials Hope to Raise Cultural Awareness"—Shelby Star, Friday, October 10, 1997

The article reflects when teachers and principals, cops and counselors, parents and people from health and social service agencies—even a couple of judges—got together to talk about Shelby's climate and culture. Concerned about about the social, emotional and cultural climate being experienced in the schools and throughout the community, more than 50 people showed up at the At-Risk Task Force meeting.

1997 Cultural Diversity Training—October 1997

Fueled by the 12-year-old's suicide, officials from Shelby City Schools pushed for more training and understanding of cultural differences, academic disparities, disciplinary behaviors, and out-of-school suspensions. Subsequently, Dr. Forrest Toms, an education consultant and trainer, was selected to lead both this uncomfortable discussion and cultural training. In October 1997, a kickoff meeting of the At-Risk Student Task Force brought together teachers, principals, counselors, social service agencies, clergy, and court judges. The goal was to encourage self-examination and cooperation. A series of school training and cultural awareness forums continued for almost a year.

1998 Student Family Advocacy Coalition

The dialogue addressing community and family concern succeeded the diversity training. Dr. Toms continued to meet with community stakeholders to help develop an action plan for more intervention and family support.

1999 Formation of Core Group/Concerned Citizens

In 1999, two events would transform North Carolina's educational trajectory for the next 20 years, especially for minority students.

On February 1, 1999, Governor James B. Hunt addressed the North Carolina General Assembly and the people of North Carolina with a bold and calculated vision. In his State of the State Address, the governor proclaimed that the goal for North Carolina's schools was to be "first in America" by 2010. Following the governor's challenge, educators were met with another reality: the facts about the educational condition of minority students across North Carolina and in Cleveland County would require not only a bold vision but also bold and sustainable leadership.

The Close the Gap Initiative in Cleveland County also began in February 1999 with a group of committed leaders and concerned citizens organized for the purpose of making the academic journey for all students successful and led by the CORE Group, an inner group of self-motivated community stakeholders within the Black community. Again, the group's mission centered on the belief that raising achievement and closing the achievement gaps in education would be their top priorities (see the description of the CORE Group noted earlier).

1999 Cosponsor of the First Education Summit—June 19, 1999

On June 19, 1999, the inaugural Education Summit was held at CCC. Cosponsored with the NAACP, the event was highlighted by the presentation of disaggregated data from the three school districts within Cleveland County.

1999 Gathering of the People (September 1999)

Early strategies were implemented, including holding crucial meetings with county commissioners and school administrators, making presentations at local churches, disaggregating data, and hosting the inaugural Education Summit in June 1999. In September 1999, "A Gathering of the People: A Call for Commitment" document prepared by the group brought to the community's attention the significant achievement gaps and disparities among minority students and at-risk students. The document also provided a summary of recommendations, best practices, benchmarks, high expectations, and measurable goals as a pledge of making those goals a reality. A county-wide task force, consisting of school personnel, local agencies, community college, United Way agencies, GWU, and Chamber of Commerce, was formed. A memorandum of understanding (MOU) between the Committee on Closing the Achievement Gap, Cleveland County Schools, the faith community, and other community-based organizations was also drafted to provide a written commitment to action and to enlist support from community stakeholders.

1999 Distinguished Image Awards (DIA)

In recognition of their strong academic achievement, leadership, and community involvement, African American students are showcased on an annual basis to highlight efforts to close the achievement gap in Cleveland County Schools. The program was conceived by CORE member and county commissioner Mary Accor.

2000 Raising Achievement and Closing the Gap Conferences, Greensboro, North Carolina

Marvin Pittman also spearheaded the successful Closing the Gap and Raising Achievement Conferences held annually in Greensboro, North Carolina (1997–2017). The CORE Group was a frequent presenter and long recognized for disaggregating data years before it was popularized by the national and state governments.

2000 Formation Close the Gap Committee

In 2000, a town hall meeting was organized. The group invited Marvin Pittman, who is perhaps best remembered as the guru of Close the Gap in North Carolina. For several years, he served as the community liaison for the North Carolina State Board of Education and the Department of Public Instructions. He would often acknowledge Cleveland County as a leader in the state regarding this issue. Pittman would often compliment local leaders on their dedication to lead a county-wide effort that was community driven and not sanctioned or controlled by the school districts. Pittman was universally recognized for his passion and commitment concerning this issue. He demonstrated an extraordinary commitment to student success and passionately believed that all children can learn and invested his life in helping to make that happen. He was a tireless advocate for ensuring educators had the tools and resources they needed. He felt that test scores did not tell the whole story. The cornerstone of Pittman's philosophy and career was his deep-seated belief that all students in our state, including Cleveland County, had a right to be taught well by educators and that gaps in achievement were inextricably linked to our collective well-being.

2000 MOU

An MOU provided a written commitment to action and support. After the formation of the Close the Gap Committee in 2000, an MOU document was drafted to ensure connectivity among the faith community, public schools, families, and civic and community organizations. The purpose was to develop and implement strategies that promote student success and family cohesiveness and to work collectively to eliminate the achievement gap in Cleveland County.

2000 Black Male and Female Forums

Shelby Star: "Straight Talk from Forums": Black leaders hit schools. Focus on Black males. Black males represent a demographically identifiable subgroup. They face unique barriers, require gender and culturally responsive strategies, and necessitate a specific focus within school communities to increase their levels of academic achievement, high school graduation, reduction of the school-to-prison pipeline, better health outcomes, and improve college enrollment.

Male and female forums are designed to create informal mentoring sessions that allow gap members the opportunity to engage in dialogue and conversations for emotional support and enhance social and relationship skills. The goal is to promote positive youth outcomes by influencing a child's academic success with role models and lifetime coaches.

2000 Leadership Academy

The Leadership Academy of Cleveland County began as a result of a NAACP retreat in 1997 to address community issues, build capacity, and cultivate leadership development in the minority community. Founded in 1998, the program has graduated more than 40 new and emerging leaders in the African American community. Other sponsors included Cleveland Regional Hospital, CCBDC, GWU, Alliance for Health, and NAACP.

2000 School Merger Approved by County Commissioners

Shelby Star, March 3, 2000—"So Much for Merger Referendum"
Shelby Star, March 5, 2000—"Studying Merger Gets New Support"
Shelby Star, March 9, 2000—"Shelby Board Favors Merger"
Shelby Star, March 8, 2000—"Courts Will Decide Merger"

2001 No Child Left Behind (NCLB) Legislation

The No Child Left Behind Act of 2001 represented one of the most significant expansions of the federal role in K–12 education. In Cleveland County, the Close the Gap and CORE Group began disaggregating data as early as 2000. Congress passed the NCLB legislation in 2001, which mandated a focus on subgroups, and signed it into law on January 2, 2002. The law grew out of the goal to advance American competitiveness and close the achievement gap. The law grew out of concern to hold schools responsible for academic progress and boost performance of certain subgroups, including English learners, special education, racial minorities, and children from low-income families. Under the law, states must test students in reading and math in grades 3 through 8 and once in high school.

2004 School Merger Passes

Cleveland County is a county of 100,000 residents. In 1999, there were three school districts (KM School District, Shelby City Schools, and Cleveland County Schools).

The county commissioners voted to merge the three districts in 2000. After a lengthy court battle, the three school districts merged into one in 2004. During the public debates and discussions, it was the position of the CORE Group not to advocate for or against the merger. The group members were steadfast in their position that closing the achievement gap for all students would remain their top priority.

The past 2 decades saw unprecedented demographic shifts nationally and in North Carolina. Cleveland County, not unlike other areas of the state and country, faced many challenges, such as a slow economy, loss of jobs, and high unemployment. These challenges have produced significant problems for school systems and other human service agencies, with more students qualifying for free lunch and placed at risk for underachievement. Educational attainment is fundamentally linked to future economic and social mobility. Therefore, unless marginalized learners are achieving at expected levels, an inordinate number of minority and economically disadvantaged children will remain trapped in a social and economic caste system that severely limits their job prospects, curtails economic prosperity, and impedes quality of life.

2005 "Closing the Achievement Gap: Then, Now, & the Future"

In 2005, a second "Gathering of the People" initiative brought together educators and community and faith-based leaders to present several recommendations for strengthening families and schools. The group also began to expand its focus and involvement to address education disparities by holding high expectations for all students and having clearly defined goals and benchmarks for student achievement. A second document, "Closing the Achievement Gap: Then, Now, & the Future" was published by the committee in collaboration with Cleveland County Schools. The report highlighted goals, measurable benchmarks, endorsements, initiatives, programs, and recommendations as guideposts for continued progress and future goals.

2008 Established Community Math Academy

According to school data, far too many students in the county continued to struggle in the area of math. In response to growing community concerns, the Community Math Academy was founded in 2008 with the purpose of helping students develop positive feelings toward mathematics, understand math concepts, and improve their math skills. The scope of the program is to provide quality instruction to rising third to rising sixth graders. A new partnership emerged as key community stakeholders joined with area churches, pastors, and school leaders to mobilize community support and ownership of the Community Math Academy.

The goal of the Community Math Academy is designed to equip students with rigorous academic coursework and new kinds of knowledge and enrichment that will position promising students to meet academic success through high expectation, nurturing, and community engagement. Since its establishment in 2008, the Community Math Academy has served more than 200 students for a 3-week period each summer at two designated sites. Highlights of the program also included the staffing of highly qualified teachers and volunteers, an effective parent support group, transportation services, and daily meals.

The Community Math Academy is funded entirely from community support. An enrichment coordinator was also assigned to provide non-instructional enrichment and interactive learning opportunities, including field trips, arts and crafts, and computer exercises. The daily average attendance of students was 90%. More than 70% of parents attended weekly support meetings. Professional staff training, technology lab support, special church programs, full scholarships, and an assigned principal per site were other invaluable resources that further enhanced the Community Math Academy. With access to a quality education, increased achievement, and improved opportunities for student success as top priorities, the Community Math Academy has expanded its reach and collaboration with several community groups, organizations, area ministers, and Cleveland County Schools resources.

The Community Math Academy, through a collaborative network of programs and initiatives, is further committed to implementing research-based strategies and best practices to meet 21st-century demands and challenges. The Community Math Academy and community stakeholders continue to share a deep commitment to raising achievement and closing gaps in achievement among all students. Failing to educate all students has a long-range social and economic effect on our community and nation. The global workplace continues to demand and require future learners and workers who possess skills and the ability to think interpretively and analytically. The extent to which all children achieve and perform to their potential is the extent to which they add to the overall vibrancy and value of our community and the world.

2009 Diversity Presentation to the School Board
A lingering issue that continued to manifest was the lack of adequate representation of diversity in the school system. Members of the CORE group, with the support of school board members, made a presentation to the board of education. The team was led by Rev. Lamont Littlejohn, Ron Harrill, Larry Corry, and Rev. Ray Lockhart. The presentation set forth several community concerns about the issue of the lack of workforce diversity and the effect on the community, data analysis, and forecast for the future.

2010 Formation of Diversity Committee (External)
Following the presentation to the Board of Education, leaders of the Core Group prepared a Diversity Committee Organizational Plan for Cleveland County Schools. The plan was in response to public concerns, rising expectations, accountability, and a forecast for the future. The recommendation to establish a Diversity Committee was endorsed and approved by the board to address hiring and employment practices, leadership development, policy development, data collection and actions steps for better student outcomes and equity impact.

2014 New Superintendent/Restructure Diversity Committee

Following the transition of a new administration within the school system, the Diversity Committee was expanded to include a broader representation of community members and school leaders. An initial Diversity Plan was drafted with recommendations, a work plan and community outreach strategy that included the following actions: the development of a recruitment plan, cultural competency training, community and business outreach, measures of progress, professional development, develop faith-based partnerships, increase community awareness, mentoring, and an equity impact.

2015 School Board Presentation/Moving From Diversity to Inclusion

The Diversity Committee returned to the Board of Education to present updated recommendations and data analysis. The discussion expanded to a more robust approach that included equity, inclusion, and diversity. A review of hiring data was a primary focus as well. Additionally, the group continued to hammer at student performance, workforce diversity, professional development training, and a review of policy, programs, and processes.

2016 Introduction of Diversity Plan/Emerging Leaders Planning

As Cleveland County Schools continued to respond to a shift in system's thinking, the need to address ongoing and systematic barriers and practices within the school system became a top priority. The expansion of Cleveland County Schools system-wide Diversity Plan introduced a cultural competence framework that includes series of training, planning, and understanding how to lead, with and through a frame of diversity, inclusion, equity, cultural competence, and community engagement. The process would also include building an inclusive school system, a process of co-construction, community engagement, the formation of an internal and external team, experiential and interactive activities, strategic planning, and personal reflections. The reentry of Dr. Forrest Toms and Dr. Burgess also ushered in a unique understanding of the dynamics of organizational change and systematic approach to dealing with a changing school climate that would focus on high expectations, academic rigor, and leadership engagement.

2017 Emergence of CORE 2.0

The emergence of CORE 2.0 was in response to a need to reinvigorate and regenerate a sense of action in the group. The goal was to ignite and give more impetus to the CORE Group. Efforts to recruit and attract generational leaders were also intentional and aspirational. Several meetings and presentations were conducted. Meetings were also arranged with congressional representatives and speakers of the house. Goals and objectives the group intended to address include the following:

- Relationship and trust
- Data review: Where are we?

- Diversity training
- Impact strategy
- System engagement
- Organized political awareness
- County voter analysis
- Meeting with Patrick McHenry
- Hub update
- CCS hub plan update Hooker
- Community preference plan
- Support resolution
- Capacity-building overview
- Mobilization
- Leadership training

2018 Graduation of CELA—Class I

After 2–3 years of planning and preparation, the first class of the CELA met their requirements for graduation services in May 2018. The demand for more generational leadership presence was continually emphasized and eventually realized. Recognizing that leadership is an essential component of sustaining communities and improving the quality of life for communities, the CELA was official.

Leadership Perspective

Cleveland County has a long history of minority leaders who have served their communities as elected officials and volunteers, as well as through community-based programs and services. As we view the landscape for the next generation of leaders in minority and underserved communities, we recognize that the leadership pool is aging and narrowing and that no organized effort to identify and prepare the next generation is currently in place.

The CELA is designed to identify and prepare a cadre of local leaders to serve on community and civic boards and committees to ensure representation of the issues and concerns of their communities. We acknowledge a need to intentionally seek out and identify younger generations of prospective leaders who have the "will" and "desire" to serve and work to improve the quality of life for everyone in the community. The CELA includes skill-building sessions, self-assessments, 360-degree feedback, and one-on-one coaching with an external professional coach to help equip promising leaders for greater responsibility. The main focus includes (a) creating a legacy of transformative leadership within and beyond Cleveland County that affects the African American community; (b) producing a cadre of informed, socially conscious public servants; and (c) developing a first-class leadership model of public service, capacity building, and collaborative problem solving. The following sections will describe the vision, mission, values, and program framework for the CELA.

Vision
Provide community and civic organizations or initiatives with effective and willing leaders with shared values who will in turn work to sustain, build, and expand community engagement efforts.

Mission
To develop a first-class leadership model that produces a cadre of informed public servants from the minority and underserved communities.

- Inaugural class September 2017
- Twelve to 15 professional men and women selected
- Six-month program
- Meetings are once a month on Saturdays
- Civic engagement activity twice a month
- Local, state, and national speakers
- Participation in statewide programs and conferences

2018 Resume Diversity Training
After an almost 20-year absence of a formal diversity training program in Cleveland County Schools, the Cleveland County Board of Education and Administration refocused its efforts and attention to equity, inclusion, and systems change in response to changing demographics as more and more students entering public schools were nonwhites. An updated diversity plan was adopted, which included assessment, technical assistance, building an operational framework for capacity building, community engagement, team building, and cultural competency.

2019 20th Anniversary of the Close the Gap/Education Summit
The 20th Anniversary of the Close the Gap movement highlighted a unique and enduring legacy in the history of Cleveland County education. The Education Summit continued to push the limits while challenging both the community and school system to embrace a new reality of building capacity to engage all families and stakeholders. Moving forward, the hope was that this community would continue to plant the seeds of greatness in every child through a culture of high expectations, a relentless pursuit of excellence, and a renewed sense of community partnerships to close the achievement gap.

2020 Creation of the Internal Diversity Team
A cross-section of CCS employees committed to equity and systems change was assembled, trained, and coached as part of the district's team to build the internal capacity of personnel to assess, plan for, and operationalize policies and practices reflective of a diverse and inclusive community.

Summary (1997–2020)

The past 2 decades (1999–2020) saw unprecedented demographic shifts nationally and within North Carolina. Cleveland County, not unlike other areas of the state and country, faced many challenges, such as a slow economy, loss of jobs, high unemployment, and declining school population. These challenges have produced significant problems for school systems and other human service agencies, with more students qualifying for free lunch and placed at risk for underachievement. Educational attainment is fundamentally linked to future economic and social mobility. Therefore, unless marginalized learners are achieving at expected levels, an inordinate number of minority and economically disadvantaged children will remain trapped in a social and economic caste system that severely limits their job prospects, curtails their economic prosperity, and impedes their quality of life.

For Cleveland County to have a vibrant and productive future, leaders must commit to fully educating all children. As we embark on a new decade, it is clear that the realities of the global economy challenge our schools to leave no child behind. Therefore, at the local level, we must intensify our efforts to support achievement at high levels for all students and expand efforts to close the achievement gap. Through various partners, there has been noticeable success, including the Education Summit, student forums, Community Math Academy, DIA, and leadership academy.

Over the past 20 years, there have been numerous challenges, conflicts, and a test of leadership will. The lack of system thinking also factored into community disenchantment and impatience, especially in the African American community. After nearly 20 years without any substantive or sustainable diversity and cultural training, school leadership began to make an intentional and gradual acceptance to more training and professional development. The emergence of new groups eager to command the attention and space once fully occupied and embraced by the CORE Group has added to the new challenges and opportunities. Moreover, to reach our goals during the next 5 years, school and community leadership will need to make strong and persistent efforts to work collaboratively and cohesively in the same space. As CORE leaders begin to reconstruct a new and revised mission and vision, the following principles need to be adhered to.

Strategic Imperatives

- Organized political awareness
- Diversity to improve student performance
- Create economic leverage and inclusion
- Continue the legacy of leaders and leadership
- Build a community infrastructure

The Role

- Persistent leadership and commitment to community
- Data driven and results orientated

- Community collaboration
- Leading-edge community initiatives and willingness to stay at the table

Analysis of the CORE Group Questionnaire

Participants were invited to offer their honest thoughts and observations about the many challenges to building and sustaining leadership. The following is the synthesis of the CORE Group surveys over the years. The responses are broken into three main time periods: (1) 0–5 years, (2) 5–10 years, and (3) 10–20 years. Participants were asked to provide responses to each of the three categories—observations, transitions, and lessons learned—by time period. The following represents the synthesis of five participants' responses to the questionnaire.

a. Early challenges (0–5 years) internal to the CORE/African American community
    1. Observations
        Formation of CORE
        Developing plans and goals
        External awareness of CORE
        Internal awareness of CORE
        Led by an inner group of concerned citizens
        Egos and in-group conflict
        Group dynamics—positive, excited, good
    2. Transitions
        Ministers, laymen, and laywomen identified
        Importance of faith-based community
        Gathering of people, MOUs
        Community organizing (CORE)
        Community presentations (CORE)
        Taken more seriously as a collective African American community
    3. Lessons learned
        Different, multiple approaches needed to address issues in the community
        Build a blueprint
        Work smart
        Consistency and persistence are key
        Trust and teamwork are essential
        Focus on minority achievement, education specialty

b. Early challenges (5–10 years) internal to the CORE/African American Community
    1. Observations
        Underrepresentation of African American students in higher level courses

Set benchmarks and goals
CORE strength focuses on data
Closing the Gap Forum
Trust issues emerge in the group
Changes in-group dynamics, as some do more, and others do less
Some group members "highlighted" more than others

2. Transitions
Merger finalized (2004)
Demographic shifts
More time demanding activities
Lack of participation from some members
Youth summits
Community Math Academy emergence
Parent training and engagement
Loyal to the goal of education

3. Lessons learned
Positive media coverage
Presentations on the road (state, regional)
Community interaction and support
Many issues intersect/interact/intertwine with one another
School visits prove to be beneficial
Mentoring emphasis
Readiness and preparation are key

c. Early challenges (10–20 years) internal to the CORE/African American Community
   1. Observations
   Sustainability
   In-group conflict increase
   No meetings and functions
   Decreased communication
   Loss of interest among members
   In search of next generation(s)
   CORE 2.0 did not work
   Unit dismantling
   Formation of the Community Math Academy
   CORE sets standard(s) for African American organizations
   2. Transitions
   From "closing the gap" to "equity" discussions
   Commitment to persistence
   Expand reach and depth of presentations

Shift in Community Math Academy focus

Meetings with political leaders (local, state, and federal)

3. Lessons learned

Transparency and frequent communication important

Lack of rapid response

Obtain verbal and written commitments for specific tasks and actions

Establish clear and focused priorities—cannot do it all

Consistency and persistence are key

Introduction of systems thinking

Important to create a sense of inclusiveness to maintain effort and sense of group

Summary of Findings

(0–5 years) The "Energy" Phase

The CORE Group, being composed of community "stakeholders," helped to create a sense of pride and confidence within the group and the community. Goal setting, talent identification, talent development and talent utilization, and subsequent capacity building proved to be essential in keeping CORE focused. Collaboration with other entities, such as law enforcement and community leaders, was integral in communicating necessary information to the community. In Cleveland County, the ministers, laymen, and laywomen were able to use church spaces for workshops, self-help sessions, and community forums. Consistency and persistence helped to change perceptions of CORE's effectiveness within and outside of the community. Managing group dynamics was listed by numerous participants. It was noted that group dynamics are good. Trust and open communication were listed as ways to combat issues of ego and encourage teamwork. Lessons learned in these first years helped in establishing a blueprint for leadership in Cleveland County.

CLOSING THE GAP PLANNING COMMITTEE	GATHERING OF THE VILLAGE
ADDITIONAL ENGINES	
Community in schools, colleges, Cleveland County	Partnerships
Schools, Parents, the Chamber, NAACP	Advocacy
Summit 2000	Commitment Process
Published Report	MOU
Action Plan	Feedback via Written Reports and Presentations
Creative Activities	
Planned Feedback Process	Movement Validated
Develop Goals	Benchmarks

(5–10 years) The "Bond" Phase

Education, especially the numerous disparities among African American students (particularly males), poor, and other minority students, was established as the primary focus of CORE. An underrepresentation of students in higher level classes, inability of teachers to interact with minority students, and lack of cultural competency in the schools were identified as the main challenges facing poor and minority students in Cleveland County. An action plan was developed, emphasizing mentoring that focuses on the areas of recruitment, retention, and promotion of African Americans in the administration and classrooms. The in-group excitement and enthusiasm slowed, but productivity did not. Members gained experience while engaging in community forums and summits (see the chronology of events for further reference). Communication and teamwork continued, as there were weekly multihour planning calls among members. Further emotional and spiritual capital was built by continuing to partner with community and faith-based organizations. Human capital and technical assistance from statewide organizations, such as the North Carolina Black School Board Association (NCABSBM), the Alliance of Black Elected Officials, and the North Carolina Institute for Minority Economic Development through Richard Hooker, who at the time was the president (NCABSBM) and vice chair of two of the organizations. The establishment of the Community Math Academy was noted by multiple surveys as a "benchmark" for what CORE could accomplish. The constant communication, challenging conversations, and persistent effort from group members in Cleveland County helped forge a trust between community members and CORE.

(10–20 years) The "Sustaining" Phase

The scope and effectiveness of CORE continued to grow by getting meetings with local, state, and federal political leaders. The tenor of conversations changed from "closing the gap" to "equity," showing the progress of persistent community engagement. Some surveys noted a significant drop in meetings/frequency of meetings and an increase in in-group conflicts. It is important to note that while communication slowed between some members, others often increased their involvement. Rates of participation were said to be due to personal differences, territorial power issues, egos, and, often, a lack of effective communication strategies. Nightly and weekly planning and coordinating meetings were essential in continuing CORE activities. Building sustainability into the process became more of a conscious undertaking as findings indicate that some CORE members' energies strayed from the group. The trust and communication that was previously known to CORE as a "bonding strength" was slowing evolving into a major weakness.

Surveys noted the creation of CELA as another key component. Biweekly themed meetings of concerned community members of all ages centered on diversity, capacity building, and community engagement. More recently, because of COVID-19, meetings have transitioned to digital format. This digital format has, in fact, increased participation and involvement.

DISCUSSION/REFLECTIONS AND SUGGESTIONS

A review of CORE's history, chronology of engagement practices, and analysis of the survey questionnaire affirms earlier research indicating the importance of interpersonal relationships in building trust among leaders and, ultimately, influencing performance (Zaheer et al., 1998). Findings reveal the ebb and flow of the engagement work over the years, transitions of leader capacity, transitions of organizational leadership capacity, and transitions in community participation rates. Researchers have defined the nature of these interactions as relational context and relational social power.

This relational capacity is based on fostering a positive working climate, developing a shared vision, and promoting power sharing. The characteristics and outcomes of these partnerships for civic engagement depend on several factors: prior relationships, motivation, trust, ability of the partner to serve as a leader, and management of competing institutional demands. Partnerships that emerge from such an orientation are better equipped to achieve targeted outcomes and sustain community support (Toms et al., 2011).

Toms et al. (2011), in a study of 150 African American church and community leaders, found that the following capacity-building strategies and practices helped to develop new mental models and build organizational capacity: (1) monthly training sessions, (2) bimonthly site-based meetings, and (3) information transfer through reading, discussion, and reflection. Encouraging the modification of existing paradigms and practices became the salient challenge for the partnership. Respondents addressed the challenges faced in getting pastors and communities to think regionally in terms of (a) addressing disparities through community/civic engagement, (b) intentionally addressing health disparity issues through local health department boards and meetings, and (c) opening up to new ideas and concepts that could then be communicated to parishioners to encourage change.

The documented, sustained engagement process and activities of CORE, for 20 years, inside (the community) and outside (with city/county leaders, agencies, and officials) demonstrate what some researchers have labeled as building "spiritual capital." It is not a religious construct but more of a relational connection between people and groups that transcends the logical, rational, dependence on faith in individuals (Lloyd, 2010; Toms et al., 2011; Toms et al., 2014).

Burgess et al. (2014) suggested that "it lies in the relational engagement among and between partners that permits individuals to develop a degree of faith in each other that goes beyond just dependability to perform a task. Leaders in such partnerships mutually allow for the acceptance of risk that accompanies the establishment of new relationships and innovations. Spiritual capital shared by individuals is critical to building sustainable leadership processes and practices for civic community engagement" (p. 113). See Chapter 8 for more on spiritual capital.

As the nation and the world continue to grapple with the aftermath and residuals of the COVID-19 pandemic and ongoing protests to dismantle the existing structural and systemic inequities of racism, institution after institution—public, private, for-profit, and not-for-profit—have publicly released statements announcing sweeping legislative, policy, and organizational practice changes in response to public outcries and demands. Demands from protesters witnessing, and at the same time experiencing, their involvement in what Dr. Michael Eric Dyson (Corden, 2015–present) described as "a time when COVID-19 was introduced to COVID-1619."

In this moment, it is uniquely evident that a complement to the political and social justice movement of African Americans has always been the advancement of technology. From the utilization of the sounds of the river bed to insulate the abolitionist organizing freed slaves to the hashtag activism that held the movement for Black Lives Matter through two presidential cycles, five generations removed from slavery, modifications of modern technology have historically afforded advantages for liberation and elevation of strategy for the global Black south. Our ability to use fragments of social evolution to strategically engineer our movement should be significantly credited for the swift movements of social and political actions of Black citizens in America. Spurred recently by the issue of police brutality in the throes of a global pandemic, the soapbox has elevated to a 21st-century social media strategy that has amplified and nurtured a social justice ecosystem that has not been televised. Several looming questions remain about the nature of this moment and the space at this time in history: What has the COVID-19 pandemic and the killing of Black people released into the 21st-century American psyche? What has COVID-19 released that made it the change agent? What did the imagery of George Floyd's killing release into the "psyche of White Americans" and the world? Jeffrey Prager's (1982) analysis of American racial ideology provides insight.

He said, "[It] is not the mere fact that Blacks hold a dual identity in this country which has constrained achievement, to one degree or another, every ethnic group and racial group has faced a similar challenge. The Black experience in America is distinguished by the fact that the qualities attributed to Blackness are in opposition to the qualities rewarded in society" (Prager, 1982).

Prager (1982) continued by stating, "The specific features of Blackness as 'cultural imagery' are, almost by definition, those qualities which the dominant society has attempted to deny in itself, and it is the differences between Blackness and Whiteness that defines, in many aspects, American cultural self-understanding."

And, lastly, did COVID-19's cessation of everything normal reset our "being" on some "humanity" scale or continuum? Did it cleanse our palates so that we might be readily open to the tastes of old spices in new combinations: "justice and equality for all"?

We suggest that we are witnessing a social learning experiment in action as individuals, institutions, and the country take undeveloped "concepts" of a "new reality" to developed and defined concepts that are spoken into new legislation, policies, and practices that live on national TV in a matter of days and/or weeks. Examples of this include defunding the police and how from one pronouncement of the concept to 1 week later having fully defined parameters of what defunding can be and should be springing up in different parts of the country. Or the recent college graduate who petitioned *Webster Dictionary* editors to change their definition to better reflect racism in society today. The editors responded in 2 days and plans for changes were released within a week. Toms defined this process as "learning in public" (LIP), where individuals are able to learn, process, and make cognitive and psychological adjustments in the moment in the midst of chaos and using the ongoing and growing dynamics of energy and synergy of that moment to process and birth a new reality (Toms et al., 2011; Toms et al., 2014).

For context, Toms et al. (2011) suggested that "this new paradigm for knowledge flow requires that institutions, communities and individuals become far more adept at the process of "learning in public (LIP)" (p. 61). Toms noted that LIP for a local context includes the history of engagement, nature of local protocol (overt/tacit), psychocultural context, types of intentional collaborations, communication skills, understanding of the metrics of engagement, and capacity to plan, develop, and innovate (Toms et al., 2011).

In lieu of the power in the atmosphere and climate for change and change now, the following question seems timely and necessary: *How, and in what ways, will leaders and leadership processes and practices in African American communities, from local municipalities to statewide organizations/associations, assess, rethink, plan for, and implement sweeping reforms in how we collectively work to ensure more participation in and engagement of governing bodies and their policies and practices?*

We suggest that a top-to-bottom framework to prepare African American leaders and communities for the challenges in the post-pandemic United States is necessary and required. Also required will be what Toms et al. (2011) described as a need to create "capacity-competent leaders and leadership processes" (p. 63) grounded in building contextual leadership. Capacity-competent leadership demonstrates skills in planning, developing, and implementing shared visions. Competent leadership is also accepting of the shared responsibility for the workload and the shared recognition of achievement (Toms et al., 2011; Toms et al., 2014). We offer the following lens as a frame for thinking about capacity-competent leaders and leadership processes.

CENTRAL COMPONENTS OF CAPACITY-COMPETENT LEADING AND LEADERSHIP PRACTICES

- Readiness/preparedness
- Strong relationships critical to building trust and inclusive climate

- Systems-level thinking and planning
- Adaptable/flexible in thinking and interactions with others
- Consistency
- Persistence
- Presence
- Saturation and maturation of leadership engagement processes and practices
- Accountability
  - o Self
  - o Leadership group
  - o Community

Starting points of capacity-competent contextual leadership and leading may vary depending on the following: local psychosocial history of African American leadership, demographics and intergenerational changes, self-efficacy and attitude, access to and participation in decision-making bodies, and the community's propensity to think, innovate, and act as a global and local dynamism.

OTHER COMPONENTS OF CAPACITY BUILDING FOR LEADERSHIP SUSTAINABILITY

Grooming or Sharing the Wealth. Identify key people who can take the organization to the next level without compromising the mission and vision. This is important because you want to leave a legacy. It is hard to leave a legacy if all the information dies when the key players leave.

Do Not Miss the Gap, or Everyone Has Something to Contribute. There are people who have skills and knowledge but are not considered "key players." We often look at the more polished and refined "folk" as people who have something to contribute. However, there are "unpolished"-looking people who may not be "well-spoken" but who have a wealth of knowledge and skills to contribute. Oftentimes, once these individuals are connected, they remain loyal to the organization (maintain a sense of inclusiveness).

Realize That Change Is the Only Constant. You have to be willing to change or modify what you are doing to be more effective. This does not mean that you change who you are but are willing to change your mode of doing things.

Develop a Strategic Plan. The importance of a detailed strategic plan cannot be understated. The who, how, what, when, and why of the group's mission will be identified and explicated. It will ensure that the group maintains a focus on its previously stated goals.

Focus on the Data. Data is inherently empirical in the sense that data reports the facts without feelings or emotions. While emotions are important to effective engagement and leadership, they could also skew thoughts and decision making.

Others Before Self. Getting members of the group to forgo the idea of self for the idea of the group.

Capacity Building. Related to the topic of "talent identification." The process of finding and implementing different methods of further improving the skills of your group members. This will also further improve the overall reach, scope, and effectiveness of your leadership.

Partnerships and Collaboration. If there are other individuals, groups, or organizations that are working effectively in an area of civic engagement, explore partnerships and collaboration with them. Partnerships can increase effectiveness, reach, and scope of the group, as well as individual members.

Keep Your Story Relevant. Be specific. Be concise. Be direct. Stay focused on the narrative at hand. Getting too distracted or off topic with too many examples serves to confuse and conflate any message you are trying to communicate. Develop a communication strategy.

High Degree of Commitment. When soliciting the help and participation of others, it is important to communicate the level of commitment needed to build and maintain leadership. The higher the commitment level and the longer it is maintained, the better for your organization.

The 21st-century, capacity-competent leader in African American communities will need to (a) negotiate and embrace an insider-outsider role (Boykin & Ellison, 1993) as a leader in their own community and as a representative of the community's voice in public discourse (Toms et al., 2014), (b) be open to and endorse boundary-spanning competencies (personally and as a leader), (c) master the art of communication strategies, and (d) embrace the rules of effective decision making and the ability to engage in robust discussions without internalizing responses as personal affronts—that is, leaders who have developed the psychosocial maturity and skill sets to lead themselves and their communities of "place" into a new era of intentional participatory engagement (Toms et al., 2011; Toms et al., 2014; see Chapter 3 this book).

SPECIAL ACKNOWLEDGMENT TO CORE GROUP OF CLEVELAND COUNTY

Ms. Mary S. Accor, human resources, director of recruiting and retention, Cleveland County Schools, Cleveland County Board of Commissioners; *Mr. David Banks*, retired, PPG Industries; *Ms. Claytenna Camp*, site manager, Communities in Schools; *Mrs. Deborah Corry*, Title I director, Cleveland County Schools; *Mr. Larry Corry*, chairman of CORE, "Closing the Gap" Committee, chairman of Cleveland County, Healthcare Systems Trustee Council, former member of the Cleveland County Board of Education; *Ms. Mary Degree*, teacher, Cleveland County Schools; *Rev. Robert E. Devoe*, former NAACP president in Cleveland County; *Mrs. Mary Evans*, Cleveland County Board of Education; *Mr. Henry Gilmore*, media and communications coordinator Cleveland County Schools; *Mr. Phillip Hager*, retired educator, Kings Mountain; *Mr. William Hager*, former principal and community leader, Kings Mountain; *Mrs. Gloria Harper*, Communities in Schools, Cleveland County; *Mr. Ronald S. Harrill*, VP Wachovia, author of the children books and play *Makeda—Queen of Sheba*; *Ms. Stephanie Herndon*, Shelby Police Department; *Mr. Richard Hooker*, cofounder and executive director of Cleveland County Business Developmental Center, Cleveland County Board of Education; *Mr. Andrew Hopper*, former and current city councilman; *Dr. Linda Hopper*, assistant superintendent for School Improvement and Administrative Services, Cleveland County Schools; *Rev. Billy D. Houze*, pastor, First Baptist Church-Lawndale; *Dr. Kevin T. James*, surgeon/Miller Orthopedic Clinic, Shelby; *Mr. James King*, director, Kingsport Academy; *Mr. Bill McCullough*, director of Student Services, Cleveland County Schools; *Mr. Willie B. McIntosh*, former county commissioner and chair; *Dr. Cindy McKinney*, professor of Education, director of field experiences and student teaching, coordination of elementary education in the School of Education, Gardner-Webb University; *Mrs. Tropzie McCluney*, principal of Township Three Elementary School; *Mr. Robert Miller*, retired assistant principal, Cleveland County Schools; *Dr. Anthony Negbenabor*, dean of Gardner-Webb Business School, director of Gardner-Webb Graduate School of Business, former Olympic athlete; *Mr. Curtis Pressley*, Axle Alliance, Inc., Cleveland County African American Caucus; *Ms. Joy Scott*, *Shelby Star*; *Rev. James L. Smith*, pastor, Palmer Grove Baptist Church; *Rev. William Thompson*, pastor, St. Peter Missionary Baptist Church; *Mrs. Janet Walker*, director of testing, Cleveland County Schools; *Mrs. Cassie Watkins*, accounting executive, Wachovia Insurance Services

SPECIAL ACKNOWLEDGMENT TO THE CELA PLANNING TEAMS

Early Planning Team & Founders
Al Adams, Curry Transmission, customer service; *Bob Campbell*, retired engineer; *Larry Corry*, CORE Group, retired plant executive; *Gaye Devoe*, past board chair, CCBDC;

Dr. William C. Dixon Jr. (deceased), assistant superintendent, CCS School Board; *Haywood Homesley*, CCBDC board member, retired educator; *Richard Hooker Jr.*, school board; *Dr. Linda Hopper*, retired assistant superintendent; *Angela Jeter*, nonprofit consultant; *Angela Leach*, administrator, CCBDC; *Bruce Mack*, vice president Cleveland County Community College; *Robert Miller*, CCBDC board chair, retired educator; *Scott Mitchell*, CCBDC board member, Purolator Plant executive; *Dr. Masonya Ruff*, vice principal, CCS; *Dr. Forrest Toms Sr.*, retired professor, senior consultant, One Step at a Time Consulting

Class I
Tonya Arrington, school counselor, CCS; *Velvet Briscoe*, Wells Fargo account representative; *Brenda Crawford*, assistant clerk, Cleveland County Clerk of Courts; *Felicia Degree*, adult student; *Chris Gash*, pastor, New Ellis Baptist Church; *Titus Hopper*, principal, Shelby Intermediate School, CCS; *Jeff Ross*, logistics clerk, Kendrio, adjunct instructor, CCS; *Dennis Toms*, mental health professional

Class II
Amia Briscoe, mental health professional; *Tiqeece Davis*, administrative support, NVR; *Kristen Downs*, assistant principal, CCS; *Nancy Hillman*, director, Common Ground café; *Alexandria Massey*, self-employed exercise instructor; *Keeynan Pharr*, youth director, Cleveland County Boys & Girls Club; *Christiana Taylor*, social worker, DSS; *Forrest Toms Jr.*, technical writer, project manager

REFERENCES

Boykin, A. W., & Ellison, C. (1993). The multiple ecologies of black youth socialization: An afrographic analysis. In R. Taylor (Ed.), *Black youth* (pp. 93–127). SAGE Publications.

Burgess, S. W., Ellison, C., & Scott, J. (2014). Spiritual capital and community engagement. In F. Toms & S. W. Burgess (Eds.), *Lead the way: Principles and practices for community and civic engagement* (pp. 113–124). Cognella Publishing.

Corden, J. (Producer). (2012, June 12). *The Late Late Show With James Corden.*

Isaacs, H. (1975, 1997). *Idols of the tribe: Group identity and political change.* Harvard University Press.

Lloyd, C. L. (2010). *Indicators of community-land grant university readiness for engagement from the community perspective.* North Carolina A&T State University.

Prager, J. (1982). American racial ideology as collective representation. *Ethnic and Racial Studies, 5,* 99–119.

Toms, F. D., (1997). Challenges and opportunities of communities in transition. In F.D. Toms & A. D. Hobbs (Eds.), *Who are we?: Building a knowledge base of ethnic, racial, and cultural groups in America* (pp. 41–52). Diverse Books.

Toms, F., Burgess, S., & Bass, M. (pending publication). A time to download.

Toms, F. D., Lloyd, C. L., & Burgess, S. W. (2014). Leadership and engagement in African American communities: A psychosocial framework. In F. D. Toms & S. W. Burgess (Eds.), *Lead the way: Principles and practices in community and civic engagement* (pp. 49–65). Cognella Publishing.

Toms, F., Lloyd, C. L., Carter-Edwards, L., & Ellison, C. (2011). A faith-based community view of improving health and health care advocacy through engagement. *Practical Matters, Spring 2011*(4), 1–13.

White, B. P. (2009). *Navigating the dynamics between institutions and their communities. A study for the Kettering Foundation.* Kettering Foundation.

Zaheer, A., McEvily, B., & Perrone, V. (1998). Does trust matter? Exploring the effects of inter-organizational and interpersonal trust on performance. *Organization Science, 9*(2), 123–251. https://doi.org/10.1287/orsc.9.2.141

CHAPTER THIRTEEN

Hispanic/Latino Leadership and Engagement

Fiorella Horna-Guerra

I. **Overview of Hispanic/Latino Culture**
   1. What's in a Name? Hispanic Versus Latino
   2. Diversity Within the Hispanic/Latino Community
   3. Cultural Clues—Key Elements of Hispanics/Latinos
   4. Unique Challenges Faced by Hispanics/Latinos

II. **Leadership and Community Engagement Within the Hispanic/ Latino Community**
   1. Community Brokers/Navigators; the *Promotora* Model
   2. Mentorship and Coaching Approaches
   3. Advocacy and Social Activism Methods
   4. Politics and Civic Representation

III. **Working With and Reaching the Hispanic/Latino Community**
   1. Building a Relationship of Trust
   2. Incorporating Outreach Strategies
   3. Creating Environments of Acceptance and Inclusion
   4. Developing and Supporting Leaders

Engaging members of the Hispanic/Latino community through outreach and leadership opportunities can be easily achieved, as long as one takes the time to understand key components of the culture, its history, and the challenges, as well as opportunities experienced by this community.

OVERVIEW OF HISPANIC/LATINO CULTURE

What's in a Name? Hispanic Versus Latino

Often, individuals ask themselves what is the correct term to use when referring to members of the Hispanic/Latino community, particularly when so many of those labeled as such do not respond to or identify with the term "Hispanic/Latino." Traditionally, government agencies, educational institutions, and marketing companies have used the term Hispanic/Latino to capture information—particularly racial/ethnic data—on a group of people who seem to share in common aspects of culture, language, and life experiences.

Hispanic

Edward Retta and Cynthia Brink in an article titled "Latino or Hispanic Panic: Which Term Should We Use?" explained that "the term Hispanic as used in the USA, was coined by the U.S. Census Bureau in the 1970s to describe people of Spanish-speaking origin. It is not a term that originated from within the culture. Primarily people who have been formed and educated in the USA use Hispanic. They are accustomed to the term by education or by family custom. Latin American nationals, recent immigrants to this country, will not self-identify as Hispanic" (Retta & Brink, 2007, para. 4). This term has also been used to represent people with roots or origins in Spain.

Latino

Retta and Brink (2007) further explained that the term "Latino most often refers to people of Latin American descent, as distinct from Spanish descent (people from Spain). This term is used frequently in South America to describe people on the continent as a whole, including Portuguese-speaking Brazilians. Latino is more likely to be used by first or second-generation Latin Americans who have closer cultural ties to Latin America than to the USA." (para. 8).

It is important to note that some individuals of Mexican or Central American descent, as well as those who are U.S. born in past generations and do not speak Spanish, may not identify as Latino. Yet there are those, particularly foreigners, who accept the term Latino as being more inclusive when referring to this group (Retta & Brink, 2007).

Individuals with origins or a heritage related to Mexico, Central America, the Caribbean, South America, or Spain, and who identify with the people and culture of these nations, may prefer to be recognized by their country of origin or by terms accepted, created, or used within their communities to represent themselves, such as Chicano, Boricua, or Neorican.

Individuals of Mexican origin have been known to further identify by the district in Mexico where they are from, such as Distrito Federal, Oaxaca, Guerrero, just like a U.S.-born Mexican American may identify by the southwestern state they are from, such as Texas, Arizona, or New Mexico.

Hispanic/Latino

Being Hispanic or Latino is a matter of cultural identity, heritage, language, and national origin (Retta & Brink, 2007). This term, Hispanic/Latino (where the term Hispanic and Latino are joined together by a hyphen or forward slash), may be combined in this way to represent a category used to gather ethnic information about the population. However, to gather ethnic data accurately, an inclusive list of nationalities should follow (i.e., Mexican, Salvadorian, Colombian, Puerto Rican, Dominican, Jamaican) for individuals to select from. There should also be a list of languages (i.e., Spanish, Portuguese, Creole, Nahuatl, Mayan) that adequately represent origins for each term. This would provide a better description of the population (Horna-Guerra, 2006).

Based on formats presently used by the U.S. Census Bureau to gather ethnicity, the Census Data for 2007–2011 shows that of the 16.7% of the population reported to have Hispanic or Latino origins, 12.8% were foreign born, and 20% of the U.S. population ages 5 and over speak a language other than English in the home (U.S. Census Bureau, n.d.).

While the term Hispanic/Latino may be used to help capture the ethnic background of a population, it cannot be used to capture racial data. It is common to see on some forms racial data listed as White, Black, Hispanic/Latino, American Indian, and other. To list the term Hispanic/Latino to capture racial data is incorrect. The Hispanic/Latino term captures ethnicity, not race.

To capture racial data on the Hispanic/Latino population, racial selections must include "White," "Black," "Indígena" (the Spaniards' term used for Native Americans in the Americas), "mestizo" (European and Native American mix), "mulatto" (European and African mix), and the selection of "other," to name a few. The "other" category allows for individuals to self-identify and build awareness of the racial diversity that may exist in a community (Horna-Guerra, 2006).

It is important to interject here that the issue of race is not as important in nations of Latin America since many of these nations experience homogeneity of race. Identification of race is a U.S. practice, and as such, people learn to identify by race. However, when their racial category is not represented on a form, individuals who would identify as Indigenous or mestizo would probably select "White" or "other."

In conclusion, while the census, health-care agencies, educational institutions, marketing companies, and other groups may use the term Hispanic/Latino to describe or capture information on a group of people who may speak Spanish (keeping in mind that individuals of Hispanic/Latino origin speak languages other than Spanish, which may be overlooked); have origins from countries of Spanish, Central American, Caribbean, or South American descent; and may share some cultural similarities, this term is not widely used or accepted by those labeled as such. It is best to not make assumptions about the background of individuals; rather, it is best practice to ask people about their origins or how they identify. Most individuals of Hispanic/Latino background will appreciate the interest in them and the expressed desire to learn more about their culture.

Diversity Within the Hispanic/Latino Community

The Hispanic/Latino culture in itself is very diverse. In addition to diversity of race and ethnicity, Hispanics/Latinos come from different national origins, socioeconomic levels, and cultural backgrounds. Most Hispanic/Latino community members refer to their place of national origin when identifying who they are, whether born in or outside of the United States. The longer the individual has resided in the United States, the less likely they remain 100% true to their core cultural values and beliefs.

Many Hispanic/Latino immigrants may assimilate into the U.S. mainstream culture, while many others may function within two cultures: that of the United States and that of their country of origin or ancestry. This is particularly so for children who migrated to the United States as infants or toddlers, were reared in the States, and whose families did not reinforce the language and culture in the home. However, it is important to note that there is a greater number of children of new immigrants who have grown up learning to function within two cultures and who speak a language or languages other than English.

National Origin

"Where is America?" "Who is an American?" Often, the term "American" is used loosely by those born in the United States to represent their nationality. However, many individuals of Hispanic/Latino descent not born in the United States identify as Americans since their nations of origin are a part of what is geographically called "the Americas," made up of countries in North, Central, and South America. Furthermore, they take much pride in identifying as Puerto Rican, Haitian, Salvadorian, Brazilian, Peruvian, and Mexican, among others.

Nationalism is a big part of the Hispanic/Latino culture, and it is not uncommon for new immigrants to stay strongly connected to the culture of their countries of origin, even while adopting culture elements of the United States. However, in the early 1960s and 1970s, some immigrants chose to renounce some of their cultural elements and even their languages to assimilate into the United States, although they were never fully seen as equals by their then European immigrant counterparts (Gonzalez, 2000).

It is important to know a bit of the history behind the relationships of Latin American nations and the United States to better understand cultural backgrounds and migration patterns. The book *Harvest of Empire: A History of Latinos in America* by Juan Gonzalez (2011) does a great job outlining some of these histories and how they affect worldviews and relationships with individuals from various nations.

For example, at times when someone identifies as a Mexican, the assumption may be that the person is an immigrant and, even further, an undocumented immigrant. To do this is to negate the fact that much of the southwestern part of the United States was once Mexico and that many of the native people of what are now called California, Arizona, Nevada, Utah, Colorado, and Texas are of Mexican origin. These individuals are citizens of the United States.

After the Mexican–American War of 1846–1848, the United States and Mexico wrote the Treaty of Guadalupe Hidalgo, which compensated Mexico with $15 million for its territories and gave Mexicans living in those territories American citizenship, as well as the right to keep their language, religion, and culture (Gonzalez, 2000). These "natives" of the area, many generations later, are now commonly known as Mexican Americans.

Socioeconomic Differences

Rather than identifying by race, socioeconomic status is a big factor in most Latin American nations. You are either poor or well-off. Individuals on a higher socioeconomic level in nations of Hispanic/Latino people may have achieved that status because of inheritances, education, political positions, or successful entrepreneurism. Social status is a thing of great pride and informs their cultural etiquette; formality is seen as a social grace when interacting with others and represents respect and the keeping of a person in high regard.

Hispanics/Latinos are found in different socioeconomic levels in the United States, ranging from the working poor to successful business owners. Socioeconomics may be influenced by the same factors that influence most U.S. citizens: income, education, literacy levels, and social networks. Hispanics/Latinos work as contractors, shop owners, housekeepers, maintenance workers, teachers, doctors, lawyers, engineers, scientists, military personnel, government workers, and much more. Like the general population, income levels may vary according to educational attainment, occupation, and financial literacy.

Education

Not everyone can afford to go to school in many Latin American countries, and attending college is a privilege of the rich. In some nations, to get a good high school education, you have to be able to pay for it, leaving those who cannot to rely on community schools, often taught by less-skilled teachers or government workers.

If a person of Hispanic/Latino descent had limited access to education or did not graduate from college, chances are they will have a lower income level. If an individual is fluent in the English language and is able to communicate effectively both in speech and in writing, then they may have access to greater information, resources, and opportunities that may place them ahead, compared to others with limited English proficiency.

In addition, if a person came from humble beginnings from their country of origin and did not have proper schooling or any schooling at all, then the person may have low literacy and may even lack the ability to read and write in their own language of origin, let alone English. Because of these experiences, some individuals have a high regard for education and reinforce getting an education to their children. However, there are also others who do not see the value in getting an education but rather encourage their children to just get a job and contribute to family finances. This experience will vary by family and should be looked at carefully.

Ironically, individuals of an upper class in their countries of origin and/or who attained a university degree in their homelands find themselves at a disadvantage when they come to the States, where their financial wealth may not translate equally when measured by the U.S. dollar or when their university degrees may not be recognized, even that of doctors and nurses. Some professionals have to seek revalidation of degrees through boards, commissions, or educational institutions, and may even have to go back to school altogether. This is further hampered by English proficiency and tuition costs.

Cultural Clues—Key Elements of Hispanics/Latinos

What is culture? Culture refers to "the integrated pattern of thoughts, communications, actions, customs, beliefs, values, and institutions associated, wholly or partially, with racial, ethnic, or linguistic groups, as well as with religious, spiritual, biological, geographical, or sociological characteristics" (U.S. Department of Health and Human Services, Office of Minority Health, 2013, p. 10). It is passed on from one generation to another. It is learned and reinforced by the society or surroundings one is in. National origin, race, geographic locations, or socioeconomic status may define it. Individuals may have a core culture that was taught in their homes and reinforced by their surroundings, yet they may also often participate in a subculture defined by their professional groups, religious groups, hobbies, and other affiliations. Cultural beliefs, practices, and experiences may inform thinking and interactions with others (Toms & Lopez, 1998).

It is important for U.S.-born citizens to not make assumptions when interacting with individuals of Hispanic/Latino origins based on their experience with their neighbors south of the border—namely, Mexico. It may be offensive to some people of different nations to be called a Mexican or to assume their food, music, and histories are that of the Mexican experience. While national origin may greatly influence cultural behaviors, such as food preferences and preparation, music, artifacts, and communication styles, there are a few key elements of the culture that are common across the board: family, a sense of community, communication preferences, and tradition.

Family

In general, individuals of Hispanic/Latino descent follow traditional family roles and structures, which consist of the husband as the head of the household, father, and provider of the home and the wife as the support to her husband, mother, and primary caretaker of children and the home. Children are cherished and actively participate within the family. Siblings are to watch over and care for one another. Teens may be expected to assist with chores, care of children, and even work to help with finances (Horna-Guerra, 2005). In the United States, it is difficult for families to continue following the traditional family structure and roles since the economy requires a two-income household. More women are entering the workplace to follow careers and other professional endeavors, thus depending on day-care services to care for their children.

However, the family structure is not limited to the husband, wife, and children. Hispanics/Latinos encompass an extended family, where grandparents, aunts, uncles, and cousins are a great part of the family structure. Elders are respected, and often their opinion and counsel will override that of a husband or wife. This is especially true when family is nearby and there are strong family ties. It is not uncommon for grandparents, aunts, and uncles to take the place of a missing mother or father when helping to care for and rear children.

When family members are far away or missing, it is not uncommon to adopt a family member. These are usually close friends or neighbors with whom there is a deep level of trust, to the point where they are like family. They may be called "aunt" or "uncle" with no blood relation and may even gain the title of "godmother" (madrina/comadre) or "godfather" (padrino/compadre) as part of the baptismal ceremony of an infant in the Catholic religion. These terms may also be loosely used to refer to someone who is a very close friend.

Community/Group Orientation

Hispanics/Latinos are social creatures and prefer to participate in, or be a part of, groups. There is a preference to do things as a group and/or that benefit a group. The mere fact that someone relates to individuals of other Hispanic/Latino origin already gives them an affinity for this group, even if they are from different nations or from nations that may have had struggling histories with each other. The stronger element is that of Hispanic/Latino descent, and that will work to benefit the group as a whole.

One-on-one relationships are also important and highly valued. Relationships of a personal nature are based on trust and mutual respect. Relationships are with individuals, not institutions. It is not uncommon when seeking services for individuals to ask specifically for an individual within an agency that they trust and have built a relationship with. Individuals may often be referred to by terms of endearment, and it would not be uncommon for a service provider who is trusted and respected to be invited to family affairs, such as baptisms, weddings, and/or family events. Respect is particularly demonstrated to those considered elders and those in a position of authority, such as doctors, teachers, and law enforcement. One should address other individuals with formality and social etiquette. For those Hispanics/Latinos who speak Spanish, they may refer to someone by the formal pronoun of "you," *usted*, and only use the informal "you," *tu*, when two individuals have achieved a sense of familiarity and friendship.

Children and teens are expected to address an adult with respect and to heed to and care for the elderly. Other adults are to consider the position of authority of a person and not to question it. This causes many individuals to be taken advantage of, and even victimized. These practices may subside the longer an individual is in the United States.

Communication

There is a diversity of languages spoken by individuals of Hispanic/Latino origin. New immigrants may find affinity with those individuals who speak the language of their homelands, particularly Spanish, Portuguese, and Creole. Most individuals who speak a Native American tongue understand some form of Spanish, and Spanish-speaking individuals may understand those who speak Portuguese because of common Latin roots of words.

However, individuals who come from Spain take great pride in their Spanish language, similar to how the British are with English. If a person is not known to speak *castellano*, or Castilian Spanish, they are viewed as uneducated. Many Mexicans and South Americans claim they speak Castilian Spanish, but many Spaniards would say that they do not speak good Spanish. This may be because there are many Native American terms found within the Spanish spoken by Mexicans and because of the many different dialects incorporated by the Spanish speakers in Latin America. It is not uncommon for a Spanish word to be pronounced differently and/or have a different meaning, depending on the country of origin. It is a good practice to become familiar with the nationalities of a community and any differences in terms or words spoken in Spanish. For example, in Mexico, the word used to refer to a turkey is *guajolote*, while in most South American countries, it is called *pavo*. Cubans call it *guanajo*.

In addition to verbal communication, Hispanics/Latinos rely heavily on nonverbal cues for communication. It is not uncommon for someone to have received a message from facial expressions, mannerisms, and posture. Spoken communication is further enhanced by facial expressions that reflect attentiveness, emotion, and curiosity. In some Caribbean cultures, pointing the lips in a certain direction may give directional cues without even saying a word.

There is a preference for oral communication rather than print/written communication. Many Latinos are storytellers and will spend time sharing their experiences as they unfold rather than cutting to the chase or to the point of the matter. Taking time to visit and interact with one another is highly valued. Short "doctor" visits or speeding a conversation along to get to the point of the matter may be seen as disrespectful or distant.

Visuals also enhance written communication for many Latinos. The assumption should not be made that this preference is due to low literacy levels, although this method does help relay information for those with low literacy levels. Pictures, graphs, flow charts, maps, and other visuals aids are preferred for instruction, to generate discussion, and/or to follow directions.

Tradition

Tradition is a great part of Hispanic/Latino culture, whether rooted in nationality, religious beliefs, indigenous practices, or social etiquette. Because of nationality, traditions may be practiced the most during special events or holidays, such as a *quinceañera*, *El Dia de los Muertos*, *Dia de la Virgen de Guadalupe*, or *La Corrida de Toros*. Rallying around sports events fueled by national pride is often seen at events such as soccer tournaments, particularly the World Cup and the Olympics.

Some traditions based on religion may depend on the religious beliefs of a community. Historically, Hispanics/Latinos have followed traditions based on the Catholic Church. Religious values and beliefs greatly influence decision making among devout followers of religions and should be taken into consideration when interacting with this population.

Likewise, there is a great influence of indigenous practices, particularly in the form of folk healers (*curanderas/curanderos*) and folk remedies. There is great reverence toward natural elements of the sun, moon, earth, and water. Manifestations and guidance may be sought through astrology and the supernatural. Some Latin American cultures practice *Santería*, which is a merge of Catholicism, Native American beliefs, and African practices.

There are many cultural traditions and beliefs that influence the views of health and sickness. Often, references are made to elements of cold or hot diseases experienced by the human body or elements of balance or imbalance with natural elements. These traditions and beliefs are mostly found among Hispanic/Latino communities that are still deeply rooted in the culture of their homeland (particularly of an indigenous nature) and whose members continue to practice and reinforce those traditions while living in the United States (Deeb-Sossa, 2006).

Unique Challenges Faced by Hispanics/Latinos

Legal Status

Can a person be illegal? A person cannot be illegal but may have performed an illegal act, such as entering the United States without proper documentation, making the individual an "undocumented" person.

In the 2005 Pew Hispanic Center report titled "Estimates of the Size and Characteristics of the Undocumented Population," the author of the report, Jeffrey S. Passel, stated,

Undocumented or unauthorized migrants are those who do not fall into any of the US legal categories. Two groups account for most undocumented migrants:

those who entered the country without valid documents, including people crossing the Southwestern border clandestinely; and

those who entered with valid visas but overstayed their visas' expiration or otherwise violated the terms of their admission.

Some "undocumented" migrants have legal authorization to live and work in the United States. Such groups include those with temporary protected status and asylum applicants; these groups represent as much as 10% of the total estimate.

Documented or authorized residents are

a. legal permanent residents, meaning individuals who have resident alien cards ("green-card holders"), including amnesty recipients under the Immigration Reform and Control Act of 1986;
b. refugees, asylees, and parolees; and
c. legal temporary residents, which include students, professors, high-tech workers, and a number of other temporary visa categories, such as the H-2A Agricultural Guest Worker visa.

Because of their undocumented status, unauthorized residents experience greater challenges in securing employment, housing, and health care. A greater number of undocumented individuals live in poverty, are uninsured, and are not often eligible for medical assistance and social service programs. They take advantage of health services offered through health departments, community health centers, and free clinics (Passel, 2005, p. 4).

The question of one's citizenship or legal status is often asked of those who identify as Hispanic/Latino, even those who are U.S.-born citizens. This became more prevalent after 9/11. There was a great rush to protect our borders, particularly the southern border, and to reform the U.S. Department of Immigration and Customs Enforcement. In spite of free-trade agreements and immigration laws focusing on family reunification, the United States worked to keep certain nationals out of the country in an effort to deter "terrorists" from entering. During this time, many of those found in the United States who were undocumented were considered possible terrorists and immediately deported.

Under the Immigration and Nationality Act Section 287(g), some states chose to deputize law enforcement personnel as Immigration and Customs Enforcement agents (U.S. Department of Homeland Security, Immigration and Customs Enforcement, n.d.). A sheriff's deputy or police officer could stop a person for a minor traffic violation, search for a person's name in a national database, and if they were found to be undocumented or wanted, they could detain them until federal officials arrived—or even go as far as starting a deportation process. It is not uncommon to hear stories among undocumented immigrants about family members or friends who went to a courthouse to appear before a municipal court for a parking or speeding ticket and paid for the ticket, but before they could leave the courthouse, they would be passed on to an Immigration and Customs agent; if they could not produce documentation to prove their legal status, they would be taken in for deportation.

Many individuals of Hispanic/Latino descent, particularly Mexicans, have been overly targeted by these efforts, fueling the idea that most Hispanics/Latinos are undocumented immigrants. Even U.S.-born citizens of Latino origin and naturalized citizens are affected by these biases, having to prove their citizenship or defend their affiliation to the United States—something most citizens of European origin are not asked to do.

Guest worker programs, particularly for migrant farmworkers, were adversely affected, with fewer H-2A visas being granted. H-2A visas are granted to individuals who are recruited in their country of origin to work in agriculture in the United States for a season. Many farmers found themselves with little to no farm labor to help harvest crops, often having to turn over unharvested crops back into the ground as compost, at a loss to the farmer and to the American public, who ended up paying higher prices for produce.

Minority Status

The term "minority" is not limited to the Hispanic/Latino population. Many groups fall under the category of minority. This term often implies that those who fall under this category are somehow less than, uneducated, or of a lower socioeconomic status.

In spite of their social etiquette and status, these people are suddenly placed in a situation in which they are seen as minorities and expected to identify with individuals of a lower social status and economic level. Some may even take offense when referred to as a minority.

Most individuals who make up the upper class in their countries have no need to migrate to the United States other than for purposes of tourism. However, there are times when a person of higher social status is forced to migrate to the States, whether because of political unrest in their countries of origin, downward economic upheavals, globalization, or humanitarian purposes.

Unfortunately, when persons of higher social status come to the States, their status is not recognized, nor can they retain the social status they came with; rather, they are seen by their racial makeup or citizenship status. If such individuals had to leave behind their financial wealth or business endeavors and networks, they—who once had housekeepers, gardeners, nannies, or chauffeurs in their homelands—may end up working in these jobs in the United States, particularly if they do not speak English. This is a very humbling and frustrating experience for some Hispanics/Latinos who came from an upper class status in their countries of origin.

LEADERSHIP AND COMMUNITY ENGAGEMENT WITHIN THE HISPANIC/LATINO COMMUNITY

Community Brokers/Navigators; the *Promotora* Model

A *promotora* is a kind of lay health adviser or community broker, navigator, or peer educator. This model involves the identification of and building upon the knowledge and skills of community members who are natural helpers, known and trusted by their peers to function as health promoters.

The model builds upon existing social networks within a community to prevent disease, promote health, access health and human services, and enhance the quality of life. *Promotoras* may also function as cultural brokers to facilitate communication and build relationships with providers and key community leaders and/or navigators to maneuver health and human services delivery systems. *Promotoras* may even take on the role of advocate and speak on behalf of the community before agencies, service providers, and decision makers to influence organizational policy and practice.

The *promotora* model is a mechanism to help get the word out about specific issues or concerns, link individuals to needed services/resources, and/or to model healthy behaviors. It is grounded in the culture, language, and real-world experiences of a community. The model fosters a helping attitude to bridge community members to service providers, community leaders, and decision makers. It provides volunteers with a sense of accomplishment and of making a contribution in their community (Ayala & Horna-Guerra, 2006).

Mentorship and Coaching Approaches

Since many Hispanics/Latinos value relationships, it is not uncommon for individuals who have achieved some level of success to share information and assist others who are trying to get ahead academically or professionally, particularly when it comes to helping youth. Youth and young professionals may be taken under the wings of older professionals or community leaders to be taught how to communicate with individuals within the mainstream culture and to function with institutions and systems. They may connect individuals to key people and resources, particularly those that lead to career opportunities or job advancements.

This is a reciprocal relationship, founded in gratitude and recognition of the mentor, as well as of the mentored person. It is based on mutual respect and admiration. Examples of mentorship and coaching approaches are programs that prepare youth as early as middle school to follow a track toward a college education or fellowships that guide teens and young adults into specific professions, such as health care and engineering, or that position them for political involvement and service.

Advocacy and Social Activism Methods

Many Hispanics/Latinos are passionate when it comes to fighting for social causes or issues that affect their communities. However, their efforts are not self-centered. Often, when fighting for some form of social justice, they will also fight on behalf of other racial/ethnic minorities. There are many social activists who have supported civil rights, workers' rights, equality, and inclusion of Hispanics/Latinos. Some well-known activists are César Chávez and Dolores Huerta, who worked on behalf of laborers and the human rights of farmworkers.

Activists may bring groups of people together to discuss an issue affecting their lives, identify the root causes of the issues, and find the decision makers behind the concern. They may discuss possible solutions and seek to influence change. When change cannot be achieved through conversation and more diplomatic approaches, movements may be organized in the form of protests, marches, and campaigns to influence change among policy makers. On occasion, activists may organize sit-ins, boycotts, and visits with legislators.

Politics and Civic Representation

It is common knowledge that political representation is the best way to voice concerns and advance the efforts of a community. Traditionally, minority populations—especially Hispanics/Latinos—have been underrepresented in political positions. Agency boards, city councils, county commissions, and legislative seats lack adequate representation.

As Hispanics/Latinos evolved in the United States, and as second and third generations reared in the States began to get involved in the political process and parties, one can start to see young political representatives emerge. Further, as teens and young adults are mentored and coached about political issues and representation, there is a generation that is growing more comfortable and savvy within the political arena.

In addition, as voting campaigns educate community members on the power of the vote, there is a greater opportunity for Hispanic/Latino representatives to be voted into office. It is important to mention that, while there may be great pride in selecting a Hispanic/Latino representative, it is not uncommon for Latinos to vote in African Americans or other minority representatives, particularly if they feel the candidate understands, furthers efforts for, and maintains an alliance with Hispanic/Latino community members.

Political parties in the United States are limited to two dominant parties, whereas there may be a great variety of political parties in Hispanic/Latino nations. New voters often find themselves limited in the selection, particularly if they do not align with either party—to the point that they may not cast a vote at all. In addition, rather than voting because of an alliance to a political party, Hispanics/Latinos tend to vote in accordance with the issues being discussed, selecting a candidate based on their alignment to the issues.

WORKING WITH AND REACHING THE HISPANIC/LATINO COMMUNITY

Building a Relationship of Trust

Trust is an import component when building relationships with Hispanic/Latino community members. It is best to identify those within the community who are already trusted and respected. Such individuals may be identified by simply asking community members who they go to for information or assistance with problems. Once these individuals are identified, approach them by letting them know that others have identified them as trusted community leaders and that you wish to get to know them. The desire to get to know a community leader must be sincere and honest. There must be no hidden agendas.

If community leaders are being contacted for a particular purpose, that purpose should be revealed early on. An open mind should be kept when discussing approaches or possible solutions to certain issues. Community leaders should be seen and treated as equal partners in decision making and as a way to access other community members.

Because community members rely and depend on peers and community leaders for information or to voice concerns, one must be careful of community gatekeepers who may limit access to the community because of personal reasons or issues of control. To avoid gatekeepers, it is best to identify many different types of trusted individuals in a community.

Trust is further built when agency leaders or decision makers participate in and immerse themselves within the community they wish to get to know. As one participates in events and festivities and aligns with movements around issues affecting the population, the community will begin to embrace the individual and consider them part of the community.

Incorporating Outreach Strategies

There are many ways to reach out to individuals within the Hispanic/Latino community. Again, working with and through natural leaders, those respected and recognized by the community as peer leaders, is the primary strategy. Another already mentioned strategy is having a presence in and helping to further causes that benefit the community, which helps build trust and acceptance.

In addition, one may further reach the Hispanic/Latino community through local TV channels, radio shows, and newspapers. One can also frequent locations and events that individuals attend, such as soccer games, church meetings, festivals, and community gatherings. However, one must remember that, given the post-9/11 anti-immigrant sentiment, some community members may no longer frequent these open events out of fear of sudden raids; even home visits by representatives of government agencies are not as accepted, so relying on a trusted community leader and cultural broker to connect with certain community members is preferred (Horna-Guerra, 2007).

Creating Environments of Acceptance and Inclusion

Government agencies and community organizations seeking to work with Hispanic/Latino community members must create an environment that reflects acceptance and inclusion of community members. This may be done by employing individuals who reflect and understand the cultural background of the population and are able to interact with them.

If language is a barrier, one may seek to enlist individuals who speak the language and are able to communicate effectively in it. It is best to find bilingual and bicultural individuals who have good interpersonal skills. One should avoid English-only attitudes and policies and seek to reach individuals where they are, particularly if limited English proficiency is a concern. Signs, forms, and educational materials should be available in the different languages spoken by the community members being served. In addition, decor may reflect elements of the cultural background of the communities served. Remember not to make assumptions and to check in with community members about what items may represent their cultural background and/or make them feel welcome.

Developing and Supporting Leaders

Agency representatives seeking to further maintain relationships and effectively reach Hispanic/Latino communities should maintain both formal and informal communications and involvement with community leaders. This may be done through telephone calls, letters, emails, home visits, lunch meetings, and networking events.

When communicating with community leaders, inquire about them as individuals, give and ask for advice, provide encouragement, discuss what types of things are occurring within the community, determine their needs, and share information. When needed, offer training, share resources, and recognize volunteers.

Remember that as volunteers, community leaders are giving of their time and talents without any financial compensation. Yet the services they render provide a great benefit to the community. It is important to provide recognition in a way that is meaningful to the volunteer. This may include giving a certificate of achievement, holding an awards ceremony, or dinners.

Summits, celebrations, and other similar activities help bring together all *promotoras* and community leaders to recognize their efforts and highlight achievements. It is preferable to celebrate goals that the group as a whole has helped achieve rather than highlight only the contributions of one individual or a select few. If one decides to recognize individuals, make sure that all individuals are recognized for whatever they have contributed, even if it seems to be the most insignificant thing—everything from securing resources, to most hours worked, to always being available with a smile are just a few examples (Garland & Horna-Guerra, 2006).

In conclusion, engaging members of the Hispanic/Latino community through outreach and leadership opportunities can be easily achieved when consideration is given to the diversity within the community; the different cultural elements that influence behavior and decision making; the historical events of the different nations, particularly as they relate to U.S. relationships; and the challenges, as well as opportunities, experienced by this community.

REFERENCES

Deeb-Sossa, N. (2006, September). *A word on curanderas: Hispanic/Latino community in North Carolina: A lay health adviser train-the-trainer curriculum.* (Note: this is not a book—personal curriculum she developed)

Garland, B., & Horna-Guerra, F. (2006, September). Supporting and maintaining lay health advisers: A lay health adviser train-the-trainer curriculum. (Note: this is not a book—personal curriculum she developed)

Gonzalez, J. (2011). *Harvest of empire: A history of Latinos in America.* Penguin Books.

Horna-Guerra, F. (April 2005). *Feeling invited: Listening, learning about Latinos* [PowerPoint presentation]. 7th Annual Wide Awake Forum. Raleigh, NC, United States.

Horna-Guerra, F. (2006, September). *Hispanic/Latino community in North Carolina: A lay health adviser train-the-trainer curriculum.* (Note: this is not a book—personal curriculum she developed)

Horna-Guerra, F., (2007, April). *Hear our voices: Communities united to eliminate health disparities* [PowerPoint presentation]. Raleigh, NC, United States.

Horna-Guerra, F., Ayala, G. X., Garland, B., Duarte Sauls, K., Triantafillou, S. A., Siman, F., Clifford, S., & Billings, D. (2006, September). *A lay health advisor train-the-trainer curriculum.* North Carolina Department of Health and Human Services, Office of Minority Health.

Horna-Guerra F., Bender, D., Lynch S., Morgan G., Rowehl K., Adams D., McLeod C., McKeithan K., & Murchison S. (1999). *A community's gift: Ways of working with us.* Lee County Health Department.

National Council of la Raza. (n.d.). *Latino Empowerment and Advocacy Project (LEAP).* http://www.nclr.org

Passel, J. (2005, March 21). *Estimates of the size and characteristics of the undocumented population.* Pew Hispanic Center.

Retta, E., & Brink, C. (2007). *Latino or Hispanic panic: Which term should we use?* Cross Cultural Communications. www.crossculturecommunications.com

Toms, F., & Lopez, L. (1998). *Nosotros: Latino culture and public health.* North Carolina Office of Minority Health and Health Disparities.

U.S. Census Bureau. (n.d.). *American community survey, 5-year estimates.* http://quickfacts.census.gov/qfd/states/00000.html

U.S. Department of Health and Human Services, Office of Minority Health. (2013, April). National standards for culturally and linguistically appropriate services in health and health care: A blueprint for advancing and sustaining class policy and practice. https://www.thinkculturalhealth.hhs.gov/pdfs/EnhancedCLASStandardsBlueprint.pdf

U.S. Department of Homeland Security, Immigration and Customs Enforcement. (n.d.). *Fact sheet: Delegation of Immigration Authority Section 287(g) Immigration and Nationality Act.* Retrieved March 31, 2013, from http://www.ice.gov/news/library/factsheets/287g.htm

CHAPTER FOURTEEN

An American Indian Leadership Perspective

A CONCEPTUAL FRAMEWORK FOR THE EMERGENCE OF A NORTH CAROLINA AMERICAN INDIAN TRANSFORMATIONAL LEADERSHIP TRAINING SUCCESSION ALLIANCE INSTITUTE

Barry Harding, EdD, and Gregory Richardson, BS

INTRODUCTION

Over the course of the past hundreds of years, missteps, deliberate wrongs, and mistakes have been made in the treatment of American Indians. There is a long history chronicling these atrocities and indefensible acts. It would be desirable for all contributory parties to admit that such errors have been made and pledge by demonstrated action that upon reflection, we have increased in wisdom and are ready for a long-overdue course correction. Such an action would serve to acknowledge what has historically happened in America and perhaps reduce the historic trauma affecting many American Indians.

This chapter is not intended to disrespect any person or race but is a call for a method to purposely produce, include, and satisfactorily recognize American Indians' leadership contributions and talents. It is not a chapter on the chronology of American Indian history based on a list of the order of events in history. It is intended to suggest that significant emotional experiences, historic trauma, and fairness issues continue to shape and affect the lives of North Carolina's American Indian people. It is also our hope to open a serious dialogue with the American Indian people and political leadership, seeking avenues for advancing creative leadership thinking, workforce development, job opportunity promotion, and inclusion for a proud and intelligent people.

The authors of this chapter seek to offer thought-provoking facts, observations, and suggestions for establishing an innovative North Carolina American Indian Transformational Leadership Training Succession Institute. In the following words, Harding and Richardson define a framework and passionately call for meaningful collective dialogue and inclusionary action from tribal governments, councils, commissions, communities, and state officials.

Train a leader in the way they should go, and when they are faced with systemic opposition and oppression, they will not quit, but soar toward the mark of success.

> —Dr. Barry Harding, Former North Carolina State-Recognized Superintendent of the Year and CEO Harding Parker & Associates Consulting

American Indians who lead with commitment, lead with passion, lead with honor and respect will be embraced by many followers and other leaders!

> —Gregory Richardson, Executive Director, North Carolina Commission of Indian Affairs, Member, National Congress of American Indians, Member, United Tribes of North Carolina

The American Indians have a rich history; they have had great leaders who have made many outstanding contributions. The American Indian people can claim a distinct identity but believe it is important to respect all people who have contributed to humanity. We do not believe that leadership evolves from any one person. We believe that leadership is an asset that each of us summons from within. In this respect, the same qualities we seek in one person can be found distributed among many people who learn in communities to exercise this "leadership" at appropriate moments. Leadership occurs when people are vitally concerned about issues or when executing their responsibilities. Leadership thus becomes a philosophy, focusing on those behaviors that propel the work of individuals, groups, and communities. A philosophy of American Indian leadership, found in leadership development programs of the past, may no longer adequately be effective for dealing with the complex problems inherent in North Carolina American Indian communities and in Indian tribes today.

THE PURPOSE

The purpose of this chapter is to describe a leadership void and to identify the causes that hold back American Indians from having an opportunity to serve in top leadership positions in local, state, and federal government and to begin a dialogue for growing American Indian transformational leaders for community, state, and national service by removing obstacles and barriers that prevent inclusion.

Performance management is a large part of the team-building process because it lets management (in this case, American Indian communities and tribal leaders) look at their performance and see how it is affecting the whole community. In this way, effective, positive change can be realized. The rationale for developing such a transformative leadership approach that integrates ethics and critical thinking are fourfold: (1) communities benefit from having a purposeful framework and vehicle for intentionally grooming and identifying their own transformational future leaders; (2) American Indian tribes, tribal governments, tribal councils, and urban Indian leaders make decisions on a daily basis; these entities must exercise diligence in teaching, modeling, and mentoring the next generation if North Carolina's American Indian communities expect to be relevant in contributing to the decisions that affect the lives of their youth and tribal members; (3) to focus attention on the reality that there are internal and external pressures to accomplish more with fewer resources and why investments in American Indian youth matter; and (4) to extend a challenge appeal to appointed and elected state officials to help correct the imbalance of American Indian representation in top leadership positions in state government. Data have been collected from archives, newspapers, and published reports that reveal huge disparities in representation exist. State personnel data also reveals that the great majority of state employees are employed in low-level, low-paying, non-policy-making positions.

> No discussion about improving the quality of American Indian Communities or political inclusion can omit the critical role of followers or constituents who inevitably can affect even an autocratic system's behavior. "State and Community Leaders are almost never as much in charge as they are pictured to be, followers are almost never as submissive as one might imagine." (Burns, 1978, p. 7)

TRIBES OF NORTH CAROLINA

According to the 2010 U.S. Census, North Carolina is home to the largest American Indian population east of the Mississippi River, with eight tribes, four urban Indian associations, and a population of 183,000 (American Indian in combination with other populations, 122,000 American Indian alone) and with citizens with a median age of 28 years old. The North Carolina American Indian community is a young population, where thousands of young Indian students become educated in all areas of modern disciplines. These students are the resources that the state of North Carolina and the American Indian community can use to implement transformative and sustainable change. They are eager to learn; they have young minds, and their thoughts can contribute to the leadership maturing of the North Carolina American Indian community population (U.S. Census and Source Data, 2010).

VACUUM DOMICILE IN SEARCH OF RELEVANCE

The term "vacuum domicile" means "lacking habitation or empty land not used." This metaphor can be compared to the struggle by the American Indian people of North Carolina. American Indians have worked diligently and tirelessly in search of a place of inclusion, fair justice, acceptance, and validation, and they have long sought relevance as a people. Even in 2020, the search continues.

Often, when an Indian leader or community suggests or recommends actions or dialogue to correct a real or perceived injustice, they most certainly will be perceived by the system as defiant, disgruntled, hard to work with, or other such descriptions to marginalize their serious intent. American Indian people have become accustomed to and know that non-Indian people often do not understand how a lack of inclusion in state and national representation symbolizes something controversial. Too often, these individuals—and perhaps because of their lack of understanding—fail to grasp the offensiveness of noninclusion or why it is emblematic of the need for peaceful political and cultural insurgence intervention. To American Indian people, this pervasive lack-of-understanding mentality construct and thinking is a powerful reminder of the long history of mistreatment of the American Indian people. In many instances, when an American Indian is hired into a policy-making position, agency officials will dismiss their policy recommendations and proceed to focus their discussions on issues affecting African American, Hispanic, or even the Asian populations. These are certainly important discussions; however, a quick review of most publications produced by local, state, and federal agencies excludes information about American Indians, even though American Indians are the citizens of county, state, and United States.

SYMBOLISM MATTERS

The symbolic intent and result of noninclusion have created politically and socially perverse frustration felt by American Indian citizens, who see an all-too-familiar and perpetual future of facing the same fate as their parents and ancestors. This is all the more reason for tribal governments, community leaders, and politicians and elected officials to work together to set a course correction for a new direction. This is also a reason to hold public officials, legislators, congressional representatives, etc., accountable to the American Indian community.

It is time for American Indians to regain their proud position and return to being the master of their situation.

—Paul Brooks, Former North Carolina Indian Commission, Tribal Chairman of the Lumbee Tribal Nation

HISTORICAL EXCLUSION: A WAY OF LIFE (AI-ROI)

Historically, within but over the last several decades, American Indian communities in North Carolina have felt more disenfranchised as a people—not less. American Indians have traditionally been told that if they would just become better educated and more politically active, or if they could just wait their turn, good things would surely soon come their way. Very few of these promises seem to have materialized or brought to fruition the magic bullet for fighting poverty, gaining federal recognition, accessing promotional advancement opportunities, or generating greater inclusion or representation in North Carolina's top government leadership positions in significant and measurable ways. A first natural question, one that is not part of the quagmire of often disingenuous political rhetoric, one might ask is, "Why does such disproportional American Indian representation leadership exist in the upper echelons of the North Carolina state government?"!

Why have state American Indian tribal leadership allowed such disparities to continue to exist? Similar questions are increasingly being asked by American Indian stakeholders in formal, informal, and tribal government meetings around the state and nation. Such questions as where are the American Indian people's promised returns on their investments in their state (American Indian-return on investment [AI-ROI]), or when will it be their children's turn to reap the fruits of their labor and sacrifice? It is difficult to explain this anomaly of noninclusion or the proud symbolic affirmation statement from politicians that "our organization has one" (tokenism). American Indians, or anyone else who cares to examine the data that clearly exist, are aware that other non-Indigenous minority groups have opportunities, access, and inclusion, while American Indians continue to be excluded and are treated as less relevant, marginalized, etc. Asking legitimate questions and expressing genuine concerns must not be defined, viewed as, or represented as an "America Indian victim mentality seeking pity." If we believe evidence is important, then we must conclude that these questions simply present the facts based on the evidence of data.

Some state representatives (the reader can decide the party), when presented with irrefutable facts, say, "Just wait. We will convince the authorities to right these wrongs, past isolationist practices, unfair governance, and dismissive procedural frameworks so that we may finally advance the American Indian cause of ensuring that fair recognition and inclusion are achieved." They say, "Just give it time and trust us; the next administration of political leaders will act decisively and make sure that the American Indians' concerns are on the top agenda of priority." They further maintain, "I know that if we can continue to work together, we can significantly impact this wrongful injustice and disparity." However, there is almost always a caveat that seems to include a "but"—"given the complexity of the problem in the organizational environment, internal tensions, and rather unique organizational situation, right now is just not the best time to address this issue." Some view these comments as "code talk" for

"American Indians already give us a block vote, and this has not changed for decades, so why should we give the American Indian any consideration except for a big smile, nice pat on the back, and another promise we do not intend to keep, which the American Indians seem to like because it works every time."

History should have long taught American Indian leaders that the right question that asks to be honestly answered is, "Mr. Politician, if not now, when?" Many American Indian stakeholders suggest that what has been labeled as "hope, commitments, good words, and pledges" sure seems a lot like more broken promises that they, unfortunately, have heard too many times before. In other words "people that speak with forked tongues," what American Indians are asking is, "When will our local, state, and federal leaders allow our children to be included in the American Dream? When will we get our role models hired in top-level local, state, and federal leadership positions?" American Indian citizens are asking, "What can our country/North Carolina do for us to right these wrongs?" Unfortunately, political authorities respond and demonstrate by their actions by asking the proverbial question, "What can the American Indians do for your state leaders to help their cause?"

By their nonaction, political leaders convey to the American Indian people, "I see your confusion, but you must agree that we as a government must do what is best for every other priority or culture of people except for Indigenous American Indians."

Indian voices ask, why? Maybe, just maybe, if someone could rally the collective soul, consciousness, and spirit of the American Indians and convince them to not be so predictable—and just once vote en masse for another political party—perhaps that strategy could make a difference for the seemingly forgotten first American Indians.

Nothing is so thin that it only has one side.

—Dr. Barry Harding, National Indian Educator

A Historical View That May Contribute to the Leadership Void in State Government and American Indian Communities

Many voices have expressed similar sentiments that when elementary, middle, and high school students are taught American history, it usually begins with Christopher Columbus and the discovery of the New World. Never mind that the Americas were already inhabited by highly advanced civilizations during this time period. With the arrival of Columbus, history books tell us that America's official history begins. It should come as no surprise that great American Indian leaders are, for the most part, ignored in history class discussions or textbooks; most often, they are relegated to a brief mention or a passing footnote about the contribution of these great American Indian leaders or how they were leaders of "war" rather than men and women of principle. In fact, some believe that the American history taught in our public educational institutions today has contributed to the decline of real American Indian identity and pride and is the beginning of the indoctrination of American Indian youth. Sadly, many youth today cannot recite any meaningful or factual contributions from the few American Indians who are the rare exceptions appearing in history books or even today look at the upper echelons of our state and national government agencies and see a leader who looks like them or represents the American Indian heritage. Why? To many American Indian youths, this void of capable role models in leadership positions has created a fatal belief that their own chances or aspirations to reach such lofty leadership positions are impossible. Why such a void in American Indian leadership representation exists today can only be described as complex and very complicated to explain. Often, non-American Indian individuals elected to state government leadership office with decision-making authority attempt to explain this void by saying, "We cannot find any qualified American Indians, but we would love to have our government represented by all citizen groups of our great state." The information that follows reveals some contrary information.

The following information was sourced from the 2010 U.S. Census and Source Data (American Community Survey 2009–2011):

- Bachelor's degree: 5,762
- Graduate degree (not broken down by MS and PhD): 2,636
- Lawyers, judges, magistrates, and other judicial workers: 185
- Physicians and surgeons: 110
- Engineers: 149 (includes multiple categories of engineers)
- Hundreds of business owners, entrepreneurs, and contractors
- Hundreds of other skilled professionals

Many American Indians represented in the previous categories reside within miles of the heart and confines of our state government operation. Given the chance to serve in top North Carolina government leadership positions, American Indians would be proud to serve its citizens (U.S. Census and Source Data, 2010).

Some political leaders explain this void by proudly pointing to one or two American Indian individuals who are appointed to lower level paid government positions or those who serve on a nonpaying committee or task force as evidence of their worldview of inclusion. Most experts believe that, unless an individual is in charge of budgets, the supervision of personnel, or has hiring authority, they are truly not in a top-tier leadership position. Still, others maintain that the low inclusion rates of American Indians are due to a lack of involvement in political support and election systems, or their failure to effectively network and develop relationships, or that they are inactive in significantly contributing financially to the state's political organizations. Consequently, American Indians are not considered for upper level state cabinet positions.

Part of the problem, it seems, is that a systemic effort has propagated the myth that American Indians cannot lead. The mind control of the American Indians' oppressors has ingrained this disgustingly blatant lie. Unfortunately, in some instances, this has been reinforced by American Indian people. This is a dishonest, insulting lesson that has been difficult to deprogram. It has been said that when you control a person's thinking, you do not have to worry about their actions. If an individual or race has not historically been afforded equal opportunity to advance, they will find their "proper place" and not aspire. You need not tell them not to apply for top state leadership jobs—they will not apply or aspire without being told. In fact, others in the race will often help reinforce this belief and readily assist in applying more discouragement. American Indian tribal communities must find a way to undo this myopic thinking among Indian people and political leaders. Whatever the reasons are for this noninclusionary void, the end result can only be described as patently unfair, shameful, and a total disservice to capable, intelligent, educated American Indian people and to the state of North Carolina's citizens, who are denied the contributions and services of these capable individuals.

SNAPSHOT OF INDIAN EDUCATION IN NORTH CAROLINA

In the late 1800s on into the 1900s, many American Indian leaders took the lead to assure that American Indians received an education when counties and the state of North Carolina failed them. Schools were provided for other citizens, but none were provided for American Indians during an era when there were separate or segregated publicly funded school systems in North Carolina. There is far too much history, and there are far too many historical citations to include in this document; nevertheless, we will cite a few:

1887 The Croatan Normal School at Pembroke, North Carolina (Virtual Museum of University History, 2020)

Hamilton McMillan, a representative of Robeson County, sponsored a bill for a Native American school in his home county in the late 1880s. Lumbee Indians who lived in the region had requested an academic institution for educating Native American teachers. McMillan's bill passed the North Carolina legislature on March 7, 1887, and the Croatan Normal School was soon constructed in Robeson County.

Beginning humbly, the Croatan Normal School enrolled 15 students in its first year, and classes were taught by one teacher. The school's first students earned their diplomas in 1905, and by 1909, the school moved to Pembroke. From 1911 to 1913, the Croatan school underwent two name changes, becoming the Indian Normal School of Robeson County (1911) and then the Cherokee Indian Normal School of Robeson County (1913).

Beginning in the early 1930s, the Normal School added college classes to its curricula. The school added its first undergraduate degrees in 1939. Two years later, the general assembly changed the name of the school again to Pembroke State College for Indians. Other degrees were added, and the student body grew when the college was opened to all recognized Native American tribes. Until 1953, the Pembroke State

College "was the only state-supported, four-year college for Native Americans in the nation" (Powell, 2006, p. 1153). It is now the University of North Carolina at Pembroke.

1859 East Carolina Indian School, Sampson County, North Carolina (Coharie Tribe, 2020)

Throughout the 1800s, the Coharies built a political base in Sampson County. This allowed the tribe to establish their own small subscription school for Coharie children since 1859. This was accomplished with the tribe's own funds and teachers. In 1911, the North Carolina legislature gave the Coharies their own school system. While the state legislature rescinded its permission for the school system in 1913, it reinstated the separate Coharie school system 4 years later as a result of tribal activity, which included a published book on the tribe's history. The Coharies were given the East Carolina Indian School (ECI) in 1943. This was a high school for tribal members that also serviced Native American students from several surrounding counties. Governor Melville Broughton gave the main address during the dedication services. The original ECI building now serves as the current Coharie Tribal Administrative Building.

Haliwa Indian School—Now the Haliwa-Saponi Tribal Charter School Hollister, North Carolina (Haliwa-Saponi Tribal School, 2020)

The school was constructed in 1955 as a one-room structure for tribal meetings and expanded to house the tribal school in 1957. The building was constructed without state or federal funding and paid for out of funds donated by tribal members. Tribal members also donated their time and labor to construct the building. The Haliwa Indian School was operated as a private Indian school beginning in 1957. Tribal leaders lobbied the local school and state officials to gain public funding for the school. The Haliwa Indian School operated until 1969, when desegregation policies required the school to close and public funding was terminated. The students who resided in Warren County were bussed 17 miles away to Warren County Public School. The student who resided in Halifax County were bused 17 miles away to Aurelian Spring, near Littleton, North Carolina. The old Haliwa Indian School has since been expanded into a larger campus, where it currently houses the Haliwa-Saponi Tribal Charter School.

There are many other schools that were established as a result of American Indian leaders who had a vision for Indian education in North Carolina; however, because of limited space, we will only list them for future reference and study:

- Wide Awake Indian School, Columbus County, North Carolina, located in the Waccamaw-Siouan Indian Community
- High Plains Indian School, Person County, North Carolina, located in the Sappony Indian Community, which, back in time, was legally referred to as the Indians of Person County Community

- Hawkeye Indian School, Hoke County, North Carolina, located in the Lumbee Indian Community
- Less Maxwell Indian School, Cumberland County, North Carolina, located in East Fayetteville and served Coharie and Lumbee Indians

The road has been long for recognition, success and inclusion for America's NC First People, but filled with monumental Indian Education successes!

—Greg Richardson, Executive Director of the North Carolina Indian Commission

Note: Many of the teachers who taught in these schools were educated at the Coratan Normal School in Pembroke, Pembroke State College for Indians, which is currently the University of North Carolina at Pembroke! One other important historical point to make is that most of these schools evolved as a result of American Indian church leaders who worked through a network of American Indian churches to establish American Indian schools!

THE AMERICAN INDIAN PEOPLE'S CHALLENGE FOR THEMSELVES

In North Carolina, great American Indian tribes can disagree and separate at an angle of two roads, but for their communities and emerging leadership to evolve and become productive, they must eventually arrive at mutually respectful and agreed-to common goals.

Today, much of the traditional American Indian culture has been abandoned, destroyed, or forgotten, but we are seeing a strong resurgence of this culture through our youth! Many communities have succumbed or been conquered because of a lack of funding and decline of political access and have been forced into adapting to contemporary social and cultural practices to survive. The road has been long for recognition of America and North Carolina's First People. Many changes have been followed by a major rift in cooperation between tribes, creating jealousy and barriers of contemptuous protectionism. There is no way to prevent discussing this sensitive subject or having an open dialogue about differences if a new paradigm shift is to be realized. Having this conversation may be the best cleansing discussion and ambition for the internal life of tribal communities and American Indians. There needs to be an understanding that no single tribe or community is superior to another. American Indian leadership should conclude that the only real difference between most American Indian tribes is often in regard to how to shape the methods and procedures for producing the best outcome. What do we lose by admitting that all tribes and leaders have good ideas for improving the American Indians' communities?

If we have learned anything from the rear-view lenses of history, we should know that there is no way this controversial subject will be resolved perfectly for everyone.

We know that different people have different beliefs, opinions, and biases based on their experience with life and past interactions with others. Maybe now is the time to put aside (bury the hatchets of) animosity and distrust because our collective future survival depends on a unified voice and a clear vision. Maybe now is the time we need to say to our children that we are willing to do our best to reset the course of history for the benefit of their future. We repeat what so many great American Indian leaders have repeated in the past—it is time for a new generation of great leaders to arise and demonstrate courage and leadership. The question for American Indian leaders is whether they have the will to come together. Unfortunately, some are pessimists, saying we have never been able to work together; this is the way it has always been and always will be. However, many also believe that at this point, the future is calling for the American Indians to turn the pages of distrust and divisionism and to seek and explore the possibilities of mutual cooperation for our common good.

Peace and happiness are available in every moment. Peace is in every step we shall walk hand in hand. There are no political solutions to spiritual problems. Remember: If the Creator put it there, it is in the right place. The soul would have no rainbow if the eyes had no tears.

—Indian proverb

A HISTORICAL PERSPECTIVE, NOW AND THEN (HONOR TO ELDERS)

American Indian leadership development planners today can learn from their past. The traditional tapestry of leadership development in American Indian communities may not be a truly representative mirror in some regards to history. Today, like in the past, individuals and tribal communities often long for their representatives, keepers of the spirit, fire keepers, and cultural traditions to step up and save them. In the past, communities were social constructs that had close ties on multiple levels. There were leaders of the community, village advisers to the leaders who looked out for the welfare of the people, those who protected the community's best interests, and those who enforced the will of the people. Acceptable leadership candidates in the past were identified, sought out, groomed, and trained to assume leadership roles. This process allowed for a seamless succession and leadership transition (French & Raven, 1959).

Giving all due respect, honor, and appreciation to our countless past tribal and community ancestral leaders for their contributions, their visionary leadership has served the American Indian communities very well. But today, many tribal communities find themselves in a declining leadership cycle. Unfortunately, to reverse this cycle, survive, thrive, and participate in civic government, many tribal stakeholders and their leadership believe that they must now shift to embrace a new paradigm focus with a transformative global economic perspective–style leadership vision.

In many North Carolina Indian communities, there is a need, a desire, and a call for a movement to identify a new generation of young leaders who can be trained and mentored to act as effective agents of positive change from within their local tribal communities. Many believe that these new leaders must understand and be skilled in business and economic development; tribal, state, and federal government processes and civic responsibility, as well as cultural issues; and communication and negotiation skills; they must also be engaged and well rooted in their culture and in politics and education. Others think the need is greatest for concerned, caring, positive, forward-thinking individuals with a heart and love for their community and people. They believe these characteristics are the basic first attributes needed for growing the next generation of American Indian transformative leadership.

AMERICAN INDIAN TRANSFORMATIONAL LEADERSHIP DEVELOPMENT FOR NORTH CAROLINA TRIBES, GOVERNMENTS, AND COMMUNITIES: THE CHALLENGE

The challenge of turning theory into practice when trying to forge a new paradigm shift must address the question, How can we develop the minds, hearts, spirits, and bodies of students into leaders of transformative change for their state and communities?

American Indian tribes and stakeholders in North Carolina are living with enormous and challenging issues, such as the will—or at least a clear agreement—to work together and how leadership can refocus their vision to be guardians of the torch for the sustainability of their communities and tribes. How can we encourage our political leaders to include American Indian representatives in meaningful positions in top local, state, and national policy-making positions? How do we address our elders' physical, safety, and housing needs, and how do we attract industry to our communities to employ our people? How do we educate the hearts, minds, and souls of our youth to wear the mantle and press forward? Are we prepared to address natural disasters, pandemics, and other national challenges?

In North Carolina, the Indian Commission supports the establishment and development of an American Indian Transformational Leadership Institute. The commission seeks to identify and encourage students and candidates to become future leaders in their communities, using internships and youth leadership through the North Carolina Native American Youth Organization, which holds an ad hoc seat on the commission. The question becomes how to do it when 12 independent Indigenous communities and tribes have their own distinct philosophies and global views as it relates to leadership. It is an enormous challenge. It is a reality that each tribal government's goals, mission, and vision will be fundamentally different, resulting in very distinct ideas and beliefs for grooming leaders.

As there should be, there will be debates and some fundamental disagreements regarding professional development curriculum, process, and professional training needs. Many tribes may want to educate students/candidates on the history of American Indian leadership. Others, no doubt, will want to train and develop students who know the practical needs of their communities and tribes. However, what is needed is to transform an ideology away from competition into cooperation, to promote group harmony, to promote tribal partnerships and collaborative agreements, to facilitate unity of purpose, and to understand and work with tribal leaders and individual talents to sustain and identify community commonalities of social, cultural, and spiritual frameworks!

Tribes, no doubt, will want to identify students and candidates who want to lead their communities and tribal councils to transformative and sustainable change. This reality should be understood up front. Such a leadership model should allow individuality for accountability to the philosophical principles set forth by their respective tribal entities. In addition, what is needed is discussions centered on cultivating a paradigm for transformative American Indian leadership development as it relates specifically to North Carolina tribes and their cultures but could be applicable or similar to local and national tribes as a whole by way of some collaborations. Identifying transformative leadership development theories for specific Indian tribes can be the first building block in educating students to become the visionaries and protectors of their tribal governments and communities. The North Carolina Commission of Indian Affairs' strategic plan addresses a summary for integrating tribal philosophies into a pathway for leadership and can be used as the basis for identifying a collective and mutually respected achievable agreement.

The focal point of this debate should be to analyze the ideas set forth by all tribal representatives through surveys, open dialogue, and community focus groups to balance the old dichotomy of assimilation versus traditionalism, which may no longer be applicable regarding how best to educate student candidates and how to be transformative and productive leaders for their tribal communities and governments. North Carolina tribal governments, perhaps, may all agree that to solve American Indian problems and uphold their common values, they must learn and agree on how to govern themselves rather than allowing outsiders, especially, non-Indian agencies, to dictate what is in the best interest for the American Indian people. An open dialogue and focus on transformational ideas and thoughts will hopefully create a theoretical framework for problem solving and leadership development.

The North Carolina American Indian population is approaching 200,000 citizens. These older and younger citizens can be the answer to implementing transformative and sustainable change. The minds and thoughts of our seniors, elders, and young students can be invaluable contributors to the maturing and grooming of the North Carolina Indian tribes' next generation of leaders.

Traditional individual American Indian governance and leadership are distinct from the present. As a wise elder once said, "Times are a changing." Until recently, many American Indian communities and tribes never had an elected tribal chief, chairman, or unified elected government system, although traditional mechanisms of recognizing and acknowledging leaders are still in place in many North Carolina tribal communities. Today, in many communities, democratically elected leaders have replaced the traditionally recognized informal community leadership. However, still in existence are highly respected ministers, elders, community power brokers, respected wise counselors, and key influencers. The effect of a new governing system for some North Carolina tribes is helping to establish and identify protocol. Although some communities are struggling with the growing pains of a new government—politics, policy influence issues, and shared governance—this can be expected for new governments if we consider how long it has taken the United States to evolve as a nation. Today, tribal chiefs, chairmen, and council leaders must interact with many community people to be known and eventually elected. Prior to this type of governance, no single individual represented an entire district or community of Indian tribal people. For some tribes, the collective body has decided to establish mechanisms and governing systems for their people to develop and mature into leaders of their communities. What is missing is a formalized process for training this next generation of transformative leaders who will be beneficial to all governments and communities.

Traditional American Indian tribal values support education, hard work, the belief in a heavenly Creator, strong moral values, and a willingness to succeed, which reflects their global view and way of life. American Indians want their children to aspire to become upper- and middle-class successful citizens. At the same time, many still promote living and believing in the traditional values system and lifestyle of honesty and integrity. They advocate that their people should engage in self-determination and recognition initiatives. Many tribes today see no contradiction between being an American Indian and wanting to aspire to serve in local, state, and federal government positions and other leadership roles, even in the private sector. Indian youth are better educated, ambitious, and want to become leaders. Unfortunately, in many situations, these avenues have been closed to American Indians. To be an American Indian in North Carolina often means, sadly, that you can "aspire, but you must remember your place." What is needed is a North Carolina state task force to determine why this explicit cultural model is still in existence in 2020, and *immediate action needs to be taken to rectify this unfair reality.*

An honest and good-faith effort by elected officials who are interested in inclusion and fairness for all people would be to publicly support and appoint highly qualified American Indian leadership to serve in government positions at the highest cabinet levels. Why not let American Indians assist in recruiting and drafting the advertisements and job descriptions and allow them to serve on interview teams to select candidates. We have many highly qualified experts in the human resource field and organizational development, along with CEOs and educators who would be willing to participate in a selection process.

In the past, American Indian communities helped to identify great community leaders who are responded to and respected by the people today. Religion plays an important role in the lives of most American Indians.

> *We should treat all people as our Brothers.*
>
> —Bill Hardin, American Indian leader, Baltimore, MD

Often, when a well-respected preacher supports an unjust issue, the community will follow their recommendation. However, no one individual is viewed as the main chief or leader for all American Indian tribes. It is important, though, for tribal and community leaders to come together with other leaders, respecting them for their work, although there are differing views on how to go about helping Indian people.

Tribal leaders need to encourage and embrace the concept of a unified voice when they speak with politicians regarding issues that affect areas of commonality. American Indians should seek equal progress; a uniformed, well-funded education system; uniformed treatment; and uniformed progress when possible. It is believed that the whole North Carolina American Indian community would advance as a collective unit if these issues could be embraced and followed.

Many American Indians would not want to return to the traditional cultural ways of living, simply for the reason that they are acculturated and/or assimilated into the American lifestyle. Yet many would agree that there is a need to reclaim, relearn, and hold on to their rich American Indian culture while acting and living based on traditional philosophies. Traditional American Indian philosophy allows for the ability to incorporate and align itself with other philosophies. The paradigm of American transformative leadership development should be based on commonalities and a sustainable future for all American Indians. It requires more than the idea of balancing traditional cultural values with contemporary ways of living or for espousing only living in the present day that benefits communities in isolation. These manipulative tools and mentalities have been used as a wedge instrument to divide and conquer Indian people for generations. We are intelligent and must demonstrate out-of-the-box thinking, not out-of-body or out-of-mind tired, philosophically myopic thinking.

> *The function of American Indian transformational leadership is to produce more leaders, not more followers.*
>
> —Dr. Barry Harding, Retired School Superintendent/CEO Harding Parker & Associates Consulting

A NEED FOR AMERICAN INDIAN COMMUNITY LEADERSHIP SUCCESSION AND INCLUSION DYNAMICS

De facto means "in fact" and is usually used to distinguish between those who are legally something (de jure or based on laws) and those who are not named as such but effectively are that.

North Carolina American Indian tribes and communities share some similar dynamics and elements that most believe are needed for effective leadership. The need for shared values, the power of a vision, the ability to rally people to action are all commonalities shared in American Indian communities. These core beliefs are the way in which American Indians have exercised leadership for generations and how they have become a divergent people. In the context of American Indian communities today, effective leadership is one of the most often cited voids.

Frequently, when people in American Indian communities are asked who their leaders are, they typically list elected officials and members of various boards. These individuals may or not be de facto leaders (in the absence of truly recognized leaders) because, quite often, these individuals are recognized as elected local officials but are often ignored by the people of the American Indian community as their spokespersons.

True American Indian leadership must be for the benefit of all concerned and the followers, not the enrichment of the leaders!

—Greg Richardson, American Indian leader, Haliwa-Soponi Tribe, North Carolina

In many American Indian communities, leadership is often given by the members of the community to individuals they best trust. It seems today that many in the American Indian communities believe that we have lost our core ability to embrace or identify individuals among us whom the masses respect and are willing to follow as spokespersons for them.

A strong local community economy, good local schools, healthy families, a sense of hope, a sense of future—these do not altogether come from the outside, they do not come totally from the government they originate from; they come from the people, and leaders with a commitment for service to their communities.

—Dr. Barry Harding, National Indian Educator for the USA

The capacity of American Indian communities and tribal governments to fill their unique leadership needs is not consistent in many cases. Our members are often heard asking, "Where are all our leaders, jobs, and role models?" This leadership cultural construct perceptual void is extremely critical to the debate of whether American Indian communities and tribal governments have an expectation of fairness, inclusion, and cultural survival. Many American Indian communities and tribal governments are struggling with an unprecedented leadership challenge to create internal succession strategic unity without creating an increased chaotic environment of despair, distrust, and irrelevance. The struggle for societal relevance has been caused by hundreds of years of mistreatment and the exclusion from many mainstream society opportunities and equal access.

A CALL FOR A NEW APPROACH AND COOPERATION AMONG AMERICAN INDIAN TRIBES

Voices from American Indian communities are calling for a new paradigm shift—one that includes a transformative leadership training and succession process to help grow the next generation of American Indian leaders. It was due to such a strong American Indian community outcry for advocacy and inclusion in 1971 that the North Carolina Commission of Indian Affairs was created by the North Carolina General Assembly, shortly after the civil rights movement in the '60s. The purpose of the commission was to serve as a voice for American Indians. In addition to the statutory responsibilities, the commission identified in its 2012 *Strategic Plan* the "need to train the next generation of tribal community leaders as a means to preserve a way of life and to insure that American Indians have a voice in the state, when decisions are being made at the state level." The philosophy of the commission is the best first step in providing American Indian youth and others with the tools, skills, and support necessary for filling this leadership void by establishing an American Indian Transformational Leadership Alliance Succession Institute in North Carolina. Ultimately, the Indian Commission believes that a strong core of educated, committed community leaders is the most valuable resource an Indian tribal community can possess (NCCOIA, 2012).

> *Some American Indians are born leaders, but a good leader must first become good servants and understand that it is not about me, it is about the people!*
>
> —Greg Richardson, Executive Director of the North Carolina Commission of Indian Affairs

> *Establishing an American Indian Leadership Institute framework will contribute a promising analytical perspective for future generations. Such an institute could promote guiding practitioners and future leadership mentee students into making decisions based on ethical analysis and critical thinking.*
>
> —Harding and Richardson

A TRUE AMERICAN INDIAN LEADERSHIP DEVELOPMENT TRAINING: AN UNDEFINED PATH

In the corporate world, leadership development programs are standard operational practices. Such programs often include well-defined competencies and performance metrics, as well as regularly scheduled feedback and mentoring sessions, especially for those employees designated as blue-chippers or high-potential performers. This is not usually true in American Indian communities. Often, there are no defined paths or standardized curricula for future leaders to follow and few written policies in this area. Leadership development in the American Indian community can best be achieved by providing activities that enhance the quality of leadership within individuals, organizations, or the community. It will be extremely difficult to overcome the ideology of comfort, custom, and tradition to accommodate new realities unless efforts have been made to establish trust.

American Indian people often think of leadership as a position and therefore don't see themselves collectively as leaders with power.

—Leroy Scott, Community Indian Leader, Lumbee Tribe

AMERICAN INDIAN TRANSFORMATION LEADERSHIP INSTITUTE

If an American Indian Transformational Leadership Institute program is to emerge, it should not be decided based on trial-and-error methods in the application of a successful process in dealing with future events. Impartation of information is not within itself education. The successful efforts of an American Indian Transformation Leadership Institute must result in training leaders to think and do for themselves, despite a feeling of unfair universal persecution.

In estimating the results obtained from having a North Carolina American Indian Transformation Leadership Institute, there is no need to increase leadership for the sake of numbers. This would be the wrong kind of increase and could serve as a disadvantage rather than an advantage. The goal for seeking an American Indian Transformational Institute in North Carolina is to produce right-thinking leaders who are actually equipped to face the challenges before them and not to unconsciously contribute to their own undoing by perpetuating the current oppressive noninclusion. It is fair to ask if such an institution is different from one race to another. The answer is yes; the difference is in the method of attack. Although some methodology may be similar, we need to consider that American Indians have for so long been inconveniently denied

Without proper transformational leadership, American Indian communities will not thrive or reach their highest expectations.

—Dr. Barry Harding, National Indian Educator

opportunities for advancement, so they are naturally afraid of anything that sounds like discrimination. Classroom education training is an antiquated process that will not alone hit the mark when measured by transformational standards. A mentorship, an executive coaching internship-experience-based model, must also be a part of this training.

THEORY INTO PRACTICE: DEFINING AN AMERICAN INDIAN TRANSFORMATIONAL LEADERSHIP APPROACH

Transformational Leadership Definition

There are literally thousands of theoretical behavioral authors, psychologists, and practitioners who espouse a particular method, trait, theory, or style as the one best method for leadership development. There is a seemingly infinite number of leadership styles as well. Is it any wonder that defining leadership can be confusing?

We seek to use an old concept defining leadership by applying the transformational leadership theory to a new framework for examining a training methodology and visionary American Indian leadership needed for the 21st century. To our knowledge, the term "American Indian Transformational Leadership" has not been introduced by this name or applied to identify the essential skills necessary for developing a community leadership succession program approach. We believe that if this approach is implemented in the proper context, American Indian communities and tribal governments can help sustain and preserve a way of life for the next generation.

There are lots of different transformational leadership definitions around. The term has evolved over the years. Originally, "transforming leadership" was popularized by Burns in his book *Leadership* (Burns, 1978). Bass (1985) used the term "transformational leadership."

Transformational leadership definitions are presented below:

> "Transformational leadership is defined as a leadership approach that causes change in individuals and social systems."—Wikipedia

> "Transformational leadership: Motivating people by using energy, enthusiasm, and passion to sell a vision."—Businesstermsdictionary.com

> "Transformational leadership is a type of leadership style that leads to positive changes in those who follow."—Psychology.about.com

> "A leadership style that involves generating a vision for the organization and inspiring followers to meet the challenges that it sets. Transformational leadership depends on the leader's ability to appeal to the higher values and motives of followers and to inspire a feeling of loyalty and trust."—Encyclopedia.com

"A style of leadership in which the leader identifies the needed change, creates a vision to guide the change through inspiration, and executes the change with the commitment of the members of the group."—BusinessDictionary.com

According to Bass (1990), transformational leadership includes four key elements: (1) individualized consideration, (2) intellectual stimulation, (3) inspirational motivation, and (4) idealized influence.

Elements of an American Indian Transformational Leadership Definition

American Indian transformational leadership is a leadership style that promotes change focused on a tribal government, council organization, commission, or an American Indian individually. Transformational Indian leaders are change agents who do not march to the drumbeat of the status quo.

American Indian transformational leaders are men and women of action who understand that "good enough" never is. And what works could always be made better. They believe having standards and making progress are not dirty words to be resisted in the name of tradition, routine, or because some embrace and cling to the "we-have-always-done-it-this-way mentality."

Lack of information and ignorance are great tools of oppression.

—Dr. Barry Harding, Former nationally recognized School Principal of the Year

Children need exposure to caring leaders and mentors who are driven by a passion of the heart and a clear vision for student success.

—Dr. Anthony L. Parker, Former School Superintendent and Principal of the Year

In a proactively involved American Indian family, the parents teach their children everything that they should do to become adults—and what they should not do. Traditionally, American Indian parents tell their children, "You must be honest, follow the rules, work hard in school, and one day, you will achieve the American Dream." This hope is the vision American Indian parents have for their children and grandchildren. It is a hope that has not yet been fully realized, but it is a hope that Indian parents and communities must not give up on. It is the desire that transformational leadership will lead American Indian communities from hope to successful achievement.

American Indian Transformational Leader Defined

An American Indian transformation leader is an individual who can get through the storms of life, corporate organizational structure, and political meandering channels when it seems no one else can. An American Indian transformational leader is one who doesn't falter when everyone else does. They are individuals who provide encouragement when the tribe or team is discouraged. They encourage their fellow brothers to fight the good fight of perseverance. An American Indian transformational leader uses words so that everyone knows they are a part of the same family. An American Indian transformational leader says what is in the people's hearts. They are gatekeepers; they keep the vision alive; they remind followers what the vision means to them, their communities, and their people. They challenge followers collectively to press toward the mark and to not give up. American transformational Indian leaders have a nondefeatist mindset when it comes to understanding and identifying the men and women they serve, and not their own selfish goals. American Indian transformational leaders have the compassion, courage, endurance, and skills to ensure the well-being and prosperity of the American Indian people and that their goals are realized.

> *It is not enough for a man to depend upon himself; I have found that he becomes stronger when he has the backing of a good community support systems.*
>
> —Dr. Johnny Hunt, Former
>   Superintendent and Principal
>   of the Year

PERFORMANCE OF AN AMERICAN INDIAN TRANSFORMATIONAL LEADER

Performing successfully as an American Indian transformational leader requires characteristics above and beyond those of leaders who function within the status quo. It requires a great deal of courage and quite a lot of wisdom—both of which will be essential if an individual is elected or aspires to serve their people.

According to John C. Maxwell (2001) in *The 17 Indisputable Laws of Teamwork*, the single biggest way to affect an organization is to focus on the leadership. There is almost no limit to the potential of an organization that recruits good people, raises them up as leaders, and continually develops them.

American Indian transformational leadership is a communal responsibility—one that shares concern for the welfare of the people, tribes, organizations, and the next generation. American Indian transformational leadership is based on skills and abilities. Leadership shares responsibility and promotes people's well-being. It is authentic, selfless, courageous, contagious, and free of hidden self-agendas. True

> *American Indian transformational leadership establishes the vision for the future and sets the strategy for getting there: They cause change. They motivate and inspire others to go in the right direction and they don't mind sacrificing along with others to achieve the organizational or community goals.*
>
> —Dr. Barry Harding, North Carolina
>   State University Adjunct Professor

American Indian leadership must be for the benefit of the followers, not the enrichment of the leaders.

A significant premise of American Indian transformational leadership engages us in the lives of others, which requires us to first know how to lead our own lives. This premise is nurtured in the belief that an American Indian transformational leader must first grow as a person. As a beginning point, this involves understanding their essence and becoming balanced in the heart, mind, and soul. A servant's mentality has to focus on a commitment to serve others. Then, people will sense their essence and honesty and choose voluntarily to follow.

An American Indian transformational leadership vision is "to teach and inspire." Without question, many believe that all individuals, whether they are elected tribal officials, commission representatives, community workers, or other, have the opportunity to develop their leadership skills to more effectively contribute in a positive manner to their family, tribe, church, community, state, and place of work. The old adage "if they are not qualified, they are qualifiable" is based on the context in which they provide opportunities to interact and learn, are exposed to good external skills and guided relationships with mentors, and taught best training practices. As John Dewey once wrote, "One learns by doing."

> *American Indian transformational leadership is "a communal responsibility with a concern for the welfare of the 'people' or tribe, and then sharing the work that needs to be done based on skills and abilities. Leadership is shared responsibility and promoting people's well-being."*
>
> —Dr. Barry Harding, National and International Speaker and Author

American Indian Transformational Leadership Principles and Practices

American Indian transformational leadership evolves from having a healthy character within and by applying positive external skills to guide relationships with others. This approach allows individuals to better realize their leadership potential and to make meaningful contributions to their communities and society. It's a desire from inside reflection to outside action with relationships with their heritage. American Indian transformational leadership is developed through a thoughtful process that helps Indian people discovering a deeper sense of values and purpose. This thinking is fostered by a set of American Indian transformational leadership principles and practices organized around the following:

1. Having a global visionary perspective
2. Possessing high moral character
3. Demonstrating relationship-building skills
4. Practicing truth and honesty
5. Seeking fairness, peace, and compassion when dealing with others

6. Communicating and conveying truth with words
7. Living by a high ethical code of personal responsibility and professional integrity
8. Encouraging unity of purpose for achieving common causes (Harding, *American Indian Transformational Leadership*, 2020)

Developing a transformational American Indian leader's inner capacity involves a number of perspectives that will help individuals to understand one's essence.

—Dr. Barry Harding, National Indian Educator and Mr. Greg Richardson

Eight Beliefs of an American Indian Transformational Leader (Harding, 2013)

1. The belief that central to understanding is dialogue—a process that encourages open engagement with others (mutual respect).
2. The belief that an environment where people feel safe and comfortable to interact and share their deeper feelings and concerns is the best path to create new ideas (trust building).
3. The belief that being receptive to "respectful conversations" and allowing the wisdom that naturally resides within groups or individuals can be very powerful tools for progress (group collaboration).
4. The belief that the function of transformational leadership is to produce more leaders, not more followers (the power of people).
5. The belief that good leaders must first become good servants (humility).
6. The beliefs that people often think of leadership as only a position and therefore don't see themselves as leaders (shared decision making and governance).
7. The belief that successful communities begin with strong leadership (integrity).

American Indian transformational leadership acts as a catalyst for innovation in tribal communities and governments and for change in individuals and groups.

—Barry Harding, The American Indian Transformational Leader, 2020

8. The belief that leaders must be incorruptible in public affairs and sincere in their private lives—in contrast to the often hypocritical, self-serving ethics of contemporary politics. Do they truly serve the people (self-analysis and understanding)?

AMERICAN INDIAN TRANSFORMATIONAL LEADERSHIP SUPPORT SYSTEM

The learning curve for an American Indian Transformational Leader Institute can be steep and fraught with many potential land mines. The business of running a tribal government, or American Indian Transformational Leadership Institute, or serving in a top state leadership position is like anything else: The more a leader is exposed to leadership, the better they get. There are lessons that need to be communicated in an identifiable written form and will be useful to know for aspiring leaders. Some refer to these lessons as policies and procedures, the "how-we-do-things-around-here" organizational building blocks.

Some researchers suggest that individuals are born with leadership abilities, but others believe it is something learned over time. An American Indian Transformation Leadership Institute can be compared to a race between expectations and capability. When an aspiring American Indian transformational leader is presented with challenges, they will rise to the occasion and soar like an eagle, or they will seek wise advice from mentors who have traveled the hard-knock roads of adversity. If an aspiring American Indian transformational leader commits to receiving training with their whole heart, the team, community, and tribal leaders will lift them up and see that they will not falter, fail, or faint. We can all learn a lot from the geese and how they protect, support, encourage, and take care of their own.

There are activities that tribes and leadership coaches should use that are unique challenges and approaches to help American Indian transformation leaders build a road map for supporting their people. Identifying, developing, and retaining leaders with the right talents and effective management skills are prerequisites for organizational growth and success.

What one believes inside is about heart—it's where character is built.

—Brian Wallwork, American Indian Supporter of Youth Programs

15 Features of an Emergent/Exemplary Transformational Leadership Institute Model

At a minimum, an effective American Indian transformational leadership preparation development program must include features that address the following:

1. A highly credible identified recruitment and selection process for emerging candidates and expert instructors with specific attributes and skills in an array of talents
2. A professionally aligned, coherent, rigorous curriculum identifying standards and expectations that are developed based on program goals, measurable learning, rigorous assessments, beliefs, values, and knowledge, and skills of highly effective best practices for leadership
3. Simulative reflections involving students in simulated (and real) reflective processes and procedures. (Students can learn from the experiences of their peers. Examining others' practice, comparing it with their own, and considering how to build on both can be a useful activity for the individual learner. Student or

learner reflections can also provide feedback for discussion in a study group or other professional development setting)

4. Competent, knowledgeable faculty, staff, and practitioners who have experience in leadership and administration, as well as organizational development
5. Collaborative coordination and relationships with Indian communities, public schools, and universities that create a pipeline for the recruitment, hiring, and induction processes
6. Clear funding sources that do not compromise the ability of the program administrators to operate the program
7. Identifiable centrally located facilities and technology
8. Social and professional support systems, with formalized mentoring, advising, and evaluation of personnel and program effectiveness
9. Competent, sustainable lay, professional, administrative staff
10. Adequate time for planning evaluation to support, implement, and reinforce the sustainable change
11. Finding critical pathways for Indian youth to participate in civic leadership at the local and state governmental levels
12. Identifying individuals who are not afraid to seek the counsel of those deemed as wise and serving the good of the people
13. Teaching individuals how and where the people want our leaders to lead them
14. Evaluating the effect of leadership
15. Being able to communicate effectively, which includes the ability to not only speak but also listen to others as they speak in their own words and to understand what is being conveyed

A strong, local community economy, good local schools, healthy families, a sense of hope, a sense of future—these do not come from the outside; they do not come totally from the government; they originate from within. They come from the people and leaders with a commitment of service to their communities.

—Dr. Barry Harding, National Indian Educator

TRANSFORMATIVE AMERICAN INDIAN LEADERSHIP CAN BE A DIRECT LINK TO TRIBAL ECONOMY

The key to sustainable economic development in American Indian communities lies in how our communities and transformational leaders govern themselves. Tribal governments and communities need to seek out and work with community entrepreneurs to develop opportunities that promote and encourage tribal business members to establish opportunities in their communities. North Carolina American Indian communities need to participate in research, examining the most progressive American Indian and non-Indian regional political best practices in the nation and both traditional and contemporary successful government examples. With a well-developed plan, American Indian tribes in North Carolina can help eliminate high unemployment and create high-paying jobs for their people. This will take visionary leadership from highly developed American Indian transformational individuals committed to their people.

There are models of successful tribal government entrepreneurship, so communities do not have to reinvent the wheel. Successful tribes are the ones that are assertive and proactive about planning for the generations to come. This future requires leadership, cooperation, inclusion, shared resources, and a belief that we are all in this together. We must stop accepting excuses, believing in broken promises, and apologizing for who we are. We need to embrace our uniqueness and talents and stop cannibalizing our own through endless infighting that leads to dysfunction. American Indians can do great things. We should never underestimate our own resolve. It has been said that it is amazing what can be accomplished when no one cares who gets the credit. The reality of it all is that no hero on a white horse is coming to save Indian communities. North Carolina American Indian tribes must look within to save themselves and their communities.

> *"Riches, poverty, and mediocrity begin in the mind." Indian people need to embrace their uniqueness and turn from the fragmented dysfunction of past separated voices.*
>
> —Dr. Barry Harding, American Indian Transformational Leader, 2020

SUMMARY

The American Indian community and culture are becoming increasingly more complex. Although it is rooted and grounded in tradition, in reality, it must adapt and learn to interact in a fast-paced contemporary society driven by globalization, technology, and a need to access the political culture to have equal access and inclusion. With the erosion of tribal community cohesion and advancement opportunities in state government leadership positions, American Indian people must broaden their strategic view to thrive and survive in a capitalist society immersed in the pursuit of materialism.

Tribes are facing historical challenges with the onset of natural disasters, such as

> *Respect, inclusion, and fair treatment describe some sources of one's dignity. It is hard to describe, but as an American Indian, you just know you are different. You are not white, black, Hispanic or other, you also know that you are better than ("other").*
>
> —Harding and Richardson

floods, hurricanes, and now pandemics. Therefore, leadership must move forward with the required education and knowledge to protect our land and people and have the ironclad drive to hold local, state, and nationally elected officials accountable to tribal communities and their citizens.

As a mirror to what is happening in society today, American Indian communities must address the infusion of greed, materialism, and destructive competition that has some leaders—and, often, whole communities—moving in the wrong direction. Like contemporary society, American Indian culture is, unfortunately, producing many people who are largely self-centered and think of the common good as something for themselves, their families, and their tribes and no one else. Some communities rationalize their behaviors by saying they are only seeking what those in the greater community and society are seeking, while some de facto leaders push to do whatever it takes because "it's just business." Regrettably, the record shows that no American Indian community in North Carolina is producing the transformational leadership needed to propel their tribes and circumstances from the status quo of the past.

If American Indian communities, which are a part of the democratic, free-market system, are going to prevail in this world, tribal governments and communities will need—and expect—more from their leaders. The common good must be balanced with group and individual achievement and success. The positive potential of an American Indian Transformational Leaders Institute must be more fully developed through tribal collaborative alliances.

Developing a collective strategic plan for reaching the American Indian community's best-interest goals is best made when decisions are healthy and whole—and when decisions evolve from the head and the heart.

American Indian communities and tribal government leaders must set their own example on theorizing what a transformation leadership development program will mean for their mission. It can mean a "better life for their people as a whole." An American Indian transformational leadership development program can fulfill the dreams of our ancestors for fairness and inclusion. An American Indian transformational leadership program is a lofty and challenging goal, but it is one that needs to be created to meet and ensure sustainability, dignity, and inclusion for all American Indian people in North Carolina and to afford opportunities, hope, and service to tribal communities and their youth.

Movements are not inconsequential. If new American Indian Transformational Leadership Training Institute and succession processes are to be realized, it will be extremely difficult to overcome the ideology of comfort, customs, and traditions unless American Indian tribes and state-elected officials work together and embrace the necessary changes, seek the resources, and insist on fair policy change to accommodate this reality. May honorable men and women have the courage of an American Indian transformational leader.

REFERENCES

Bass, B. M. (1985). *Leadership and performance beyond expectations*. Free Press.

Bass, B. M. (1990). *Learning to share the vision: Organizational dynamics*. Harper and Row.

Burns, J. M. (1978). *Leadership*. Harper and Row.

Coharie Tribe. (2020). Welcome to the Coharie Tribe. http://coharietribe.org/

French, J. P., & Raven, B. (1959). *The bases of social power* (D. Cartwright, Ed.). Studies in Social Power.

Haliwa-Saponi Tribal School. (2020). Haliwa-Saponi School. https://www.hstsedu.org/

Harding, B. (2013). *The transformational American Indian leader*. https://hardingparker.com/

Maxwell, J. C. (2001). *The 17 indisputable laws of teamwork*. Christian-Press.

North Carolina Commission of Indian Affairs (NCCOIA). (2012). Strategic plan.

U.S. Census and Source Data. (2010). American community survey, 2009–2011.

Powell, W. S. (2006). University of North Carolina at Pembroke. *Encyclopedia of North Carolina* (University of North Carolina Press: Chapel Hill, NC . https://northcarolinahistory.org/encyclopedia/the-university-of-north-carolina-at-pembroke/

Virtual Museum of University History. (2020). The Croatan Normal School. https://museum.unc.edu/exhibits/show/american-indians-and-chapel-hi/the-croatan-normal-school-pem

** *Data from local sources for other business owners and multiple state and municipality data banks.*

KEY TERMS: FOR THE CHAPTER

AI-ROI—American Indian-return on investment. An investment into a system or process with an expected return on the contribution.

American Indian transformational leadership—A leadership style that promotes transformative change focused on a tribal government, council organization, commissions, or an American Indian individually.

American Indian tribal elders—In American Indian communities, within each tribe, elders are repositories of cultural and philosophical knowledge. They are the transmitters of history and wisdom.

American tribal vacuum domicile—Lacking habitation or empty land not used.

Indian stakeholders—An entity, or tribe, of Indigenous people that can be affected by the results of that in which they are said to be stakeholders—that in which they have a stake.

Indian voices—American Indian individuals who can identify with the generational struggles of a proud Indigenous people, whose life experiences have helped them gain wisdom and insight regarding fairness and truth.

Leadership—Described as a process of social influence in which one person can enlist the aid and support of others in the accomplishment of a common task.

Leadership void—Containing no matter; empty, not recognized as occupied; unfilled based on credible authority. Completely lacking; devoid: void of understanding or trust.

Significant emotional experiences—A group or individual's emotional life experiences that have significantly influenced their actions or belief system.

Transformational Indian leaders—Defined as change agents who do not march to the drumbeat of the status quo. American Indian transformational leaders are men and women of action who understand that "good enough" never is. They are visionaries and leaders of exceptional insight and leadership quality.

Tribal council—The governing body of an Indian tribe. As elected representatives, the council exercises all legislative authority, except that vested in the general council.

CHAPTER FIFTEEN

Engaging Faith-Based Communities

A PUBLIC HEALTH LEADERSHIP PERSPECTIVE

Lori Carter-Edwards, PhD, Barbara Pullen-Smith, PhD, Melicia Whitt-Glover, PhD, Cheryl Emanuel, BA, Forrest D. Toms, PhD, and Chevella Wilson, PhD

This chapter will

- provide a historical summary of the roles of faith-based organizations in service, support, and health promotion, with an emphasis on Black communities;
- present a multidimensional leadership framework for faith-based organizational engagement in health promotion;
- present two illustrations of engagement in Black faith-based organizations, which integrate concepts of capacity building, organizational change, and leadership theories/frameworks; and
- discuss next steps for faith-based, community-engaged leadership in health promotion.

INTRODUCTION

Faith-based organizations (FBOs) have been the hallmark of service in communities for centuries, providing spiritual care and support, resources, outreach, and health care for their congregations and beyond. With the uncertainty of the repeal of the Affordable Care Act of 2015, as well as the effect of and the impending "new normal" emerging from the coronavirus disease 2019 (COVID-19) pandemic (Yancy, 2020), coupled with the nation's civil unrest because of systematic racism (Jones, 2020; Hawkins et al., 2020), addressing health-care reform through FBOs will need to be even more strategic than ever as a leading sector for addressing public health needs in disparate populations among different geographic regions, racial and ethnic groups, socioeconomic status, and cultural practices.

The nation's current efforts to address health disparities and achieve health equity at the federal level highlight the importance of the role and influence of community organizations, such as FBOs. For instance, while the White House Office of Faith-Based and Neighborhood Partnerships no longer exists in President Trump's administration, there is an established White House Faith and Opportunity Initiative designed to "provide recommendations on the Administration's policy agenda affecting faith-based and community programs; provide recommendations on programs and policies where faith-based and community organizations may partner and/or deliver more effective solutions to poverty; apprise the administration of any failures of the executive branch to comply with religious liberty protections under law; and reduce the burdens on the exercise of free religion" (White House, 2018, para. 1). The nation's first National Prevention Strategy remains an important blueprint for leaders to align partners in prevention across the country to implement directions and priorities to improve the health of Americans across the life course (National Prevention Council, 2011). The National Office of Minority Health (OMH) provides a series of resources, including the Partnership for Action to End Health Disparities 2010 Toolkit for Community Action, a relevant tool to help individuals, communities, and organizations from public and private sectors work together to implement policies and programs to help eliminate health disparities (U.S. Department of Health and Human Services [U.S. DHHS], 2010). Also, within its Resource Center, the OMH has a Knowledge Center Online Catalogue of the nation's largest repository of information dedicated to the health of minority populations, as well as capacity building and technical assistance for minority community organizations to conduct health equity programs (OMH Resource Center, 2020). FBOs and their leadership should be at the forefront of all of these strategies and resource usage. It is recommended that they convene and engage diverse partners to plan, implement, and evaluate community efforts and implement processes to help ensure that people actively participate in the decisions surrounding their health and improving the systems in which they receive services and care.

Community engagement is "the *process* of working collaboratively with groups of people who are affiliated by geographic proximity, special interests, or similar situations with respect to issues affecting their well-being" (CDC, 1997, p. 9). This comprehensive construct is rooted in community organizing, capacity building, development of coalitions and partnerships, and community-based participatory research (Wallerstein et al., 2015). Collaborative building on community strengths is fundamental to this process and the ability to make sustainable changes that improve the health of underserved communities. Most disparate populations are communities of color—with more challenging health problems than majority populations, often because of social and environmental determinants, such as adequate education, job opportunities, affordable housing, transportation, and access to quality, basic resources, including food, recreational facilities, and preventive care. With community development at the forefront of sustainable social change, and with the increased reliance on faith communities to bridge the gap for the citizens they are proximally destined to serve, FBOs provide a unique opportunity for engaged leadership and social action that are centered on principles of spiritual well-being and support grounded in empowerment from a Higher Being. Their sustained structures serve as the basis of capacity building rather than deficit-driven approaches to better health.

There is an ever-increasing national emphasis on FBOs' partnerships in addressing social concerns, in daily living and during public health emergencies. As a result, FBO leaders and their institutions are being challenged to be more innovative, proactive, and even transformational in providing vision, leadership, and strategies to meet the needs of people in their communities through capacity-building programs and processes. While many FBO leaders and churches are engaged in various types of service programs on a daily basis, there remains a need for increased leadership and engagement around civic, governmental, political, and economic issues that continue to negatively impact the quality of life in their communities. Just as important is a need to identify the common assets present in the communities served and replicate them. Leadership, by definition, requires a greater understanding of self and the core values that determine individual actions. Therefore, leadership for community engagement enlists a focus on how leaders of communities perceive their roles in building capacity within the church and communities to promote equity in the areas of health, education, and economic opportunities.

This chapter will provide a historical overview of the role of FBOs in health promotion, with an emphasis on Black FBOs and communities. This is followed by a discussion of a multidimensional leadership approach for engaging FBOs in health promotion. This approach will be illustrated through the Community Empowerment Network (CEN), as well as Village HeartBEAT as an evolution example where community engagement principles are applied through Black FBOs, integrating concepts from capacity building, organizational change, and leadership development. We conclude the chapter with a discussion of future efforts in faith-based engaged leadership in health promotion, with implications for the application of Public Health 3.0 (DeSalvo et al., 2017) in other community-engaged organizations.

Historical Perspectives

Social Activism and Civic Support

FBOs, or churches, have a long history of service provision to their congregations and the community at large (Braithwaite et al., 2000; Koenig et al., 2012). They are the oldest organizations within most Black communities (Braithwaite et al., 2000). Rooted in the period of the Great Awakening (1790–1840s) (Foster et al., 2004), Black churches served a chief role as cultural nurturer, social emancipator, political organizer, business innovator, and educator, and they have continued in varying degrees up to the present (Billingsley, 2003; Brown et al., 2017; Cavendish, 2000; Cené et al., 2011; Frazier, 1963; Harris, 1999; Meier & Rudwick, 1978; Powdermaker, 1968; Wilmore, 1983). As an institution, the church has been the primary "force" with which the majority of Blacks in America have affiliated, contributed most of their resources—both monetary and nonmonetary—and, most importantly, sought help (Dilulio, 1999; Harris, 1999; Reid et al., 1990; Sernett, 1999). As a result, Black churches, according to Dilulio and others, have historically served as a "second safety net" to governmental programs that were often too slow or unresponsive to the needs of the Black community. Therefore, among low-income and minority communities, churches are often the first source of support (Goldmon and Roberson, 2004; Olson et al., 1988).

In his investigation of community engagement and the relationship between pastoral community participation and background traits, Sewell (2003) reported that many scholars have illustrated how and why Black churches responded to the needs of the Black community. Slaves formed their own underground churches, which E. Franklin Frazier called the "invisible institution," where slaves were able to gather for community support and spiritual renewal. Black churches fostered self-worth, particularly during slavery, by allowing Blacks to turn to each other for support and collective action (Powdermaker, 1968). In addition to the psychological effects, Black churches produced numerous sub-institutions (e.g., mutual and benevolent societies, as well as educational facilities) that were effective in meeting the practical needs of the Black community. These groups were primarily designed for providing communal aid to enslaved and freed Blacks who were facing traumatic situations in their lives (Frazier, 1963; Lincoln & Mamiya, 1990; Sernett, 1999). For instance, when an enslaved Black family was split up because of the institution of slavery or death, it was these mutual aid and benevolent societies that assisted the remaining family members with necessities, mainly moral support and material support, such as food and money. As Sewell (2003) reported, in terms of empowerment and resilience, Carter G. Woodson (1972) concluded that each organization that was birthed out of the Black church was revolutionary because they were testaments to how Blacks pulled their meager resources together to help meet the needs of their communities.

Since the turn of the 21st century, in terms of church affiliation, the 2001 American Religious Identification Survey of 50,000 Americans reveals that an estimated 81% of the population identifies with a religious group; 77% reported being Christian (Kosmin & Keysar, 2009). Women, Blacks, and older adults are still most likely to describe themselves as religious compared to other subpopulations, with 81%–82% of Blacks reporting a religious affiliation. For several reasons, Blacks tend to be more religiously engaged than Whites (Barna Group, 2007; Taylor et al., 1996), including the aforementioned necessity for cultural preservation and social support resulting from historical discrimination.

Even with the current rapid decline in religious affiliation with Christianity, particularly among the youth, and an increase in nonorganized or no religious affiliation (Pew Research Center, 2019), a greater percentage of Blacks report a religious affiliation than other racial and ethnic groups. While the level of engagement of Blacks through the church—particularly since the 1960s civil rights movement—has varied among and between members, organizations, and leaders, social activism, now more than ever, has been reignited to address current social, political, and environmental needs, including health and public health emergencies.

Health Promotion
Churches represent one of the ideal settings for health education and health-promotion efforts (Resnicow et al., 2000; Wimberly, 2001), particularly among Blacks, because of their central role in spiritual guidance, communication, social support, and networking in Black communities (Kumanyika & Charleston, 1992; Lasater et al., 1986). Churches often serve as the first source for health promotion and disease prevention in low-income and minority communities. Churches tend to be situated in communities to connect with hardly reached populations (Goldmon & Roberson, 2004). Since churches are concerned about health and health outcomes, most of them encourage and promote holistic health and are often seen as a place for comfort, guidance, and inspiration in Black communities, offering a variety of resources that can be beneficial for health-promotion efforts (e.g., health ministries) (Goldmon & Roberson, 2004). To be successful, many church-based community health programs strive to focus on an all-encompassing approach to healthy living, as opposed to fear of dying, serving in a position that embodies relationships between physiological, psychological, and spiritual health (Sanders, 1997).

Since the 1990s, Black churches have launched a growing number of chronic disease prevention interventions, with a surge of studies published in the past decade. Most of these interventions focused on an increasing awareness of behaviors that address chronic disease management for conditions such as hypertension, diabetes, and cancer—mainly through healthy eating and increased physical activity (Coughlin & Smith, 2017; Whitt-Glover et al., 2014).

Others focused on the human immunodeficiency virus and acquired immune deficiency syndrome (HIV/AIDS) (Cené et al., 2011; Pichon and Powell, 2015; Ransome et al., 2018); factors that may impact chronic disease outcomes, such as sleep (Baron et al., 2019); and even more system-level factors that address drivers and determinants of health (Cené et al., 2011; Scott & Wilson, 2011). Some interventions and programs were specifically designed to train members of the community as lay health professionals (Campbell et al., 1999; Faridi et al., 2010; Holt et al., 2017; Morales-Alemán et al., 2018; Rose et al., 2008; Scheirer et al., 2017), which is an important strategy for establishing both reach and sustainability. There are also observational studies that provide feedback from pastoral leadership on their perceptions of FBOs' roles in promoting health, revealing the necessity of their expertise in strategic planning and decision making (Brown & McCreary, 2014; Carter-Edwards et al., 2012; Corbie-Smith et al., 2010; Ford, 2013; Gross et al., 2018; Stewart et al., 2019; Story et al., 2017).

Several studies in the past 2 decades have examined the association between spirituality/religion and health-related behaviors among Blacks. Overall, the data suggest a strong association between spirituality/religion and health. For instance, an exploratory study of cancer-screening behaviors among Blacks showed an association between religion and spirituality and communication with health-care providers, personal health assessment, and dietary behaviors (Underwood & Powell, 2006). Focus group interviews conducted with Black women who reported being active participants in health ministry programs within a faith community revealed that prayer, pastoral support, and trust in the congregational nurse were among the factors that influenced their engagement in healthy lifestyles (Drayton-Brooks & White, 2004). Cross-sectional data among 260 Black, Caribbean, and Hispanic-Black women examined associations between spirituality, diet, and exercise and showed a positive association between spiritual growth and physical activity and diet (Chester et al., 2006). Black women who participated in a weight-loss intervention in a church setting reported less disordered eating attitudes and less personal distrust at baseline and higher weight loss at follow-up than Black and White women who participated in the same intervention in a university setting (Sbrocco et al., 2005). More recent studies reveal mixed results. Holt and colleagues (2017), using a national probability sample for a longitudinal study among 565 Blacks, found that religious coping was not associated with a change in health behaviors over a 5-year period, despite positive findings in previous cross-sectional assessments. However, the results imply that religious beliefs may be protective against declines in positive religious coping over time. Cozier and colleagues (2018) found an association between religious and spiritual coping and incidences of hypertension among Black women, particularly among women reporting higher levels of stress. In a qualitative study of religion, spirituality, coping, and resilience among Blacks with diabetes, Choi and colleagues (2019) found that spirituality, religious beliefs, and coping strategies were all important to diabetes self-care, and understanding the contextual balance of treatment with religion and spiritual practices was germane to health outcomes.

In implementing health-promotion interventions in Black church settings, influential components include the teaching of faith tenets and biblical principles, collaboration, and cultural sensitivity. *Faith-based* interventions, which are emerging, incorporate tenets of FBOs (e.g., religious beliefs, scriptural references) and involve FBOs in the planning of the intervention from beginning to end (Campbell et al., 2007; Lancaster et al., 2014). *Faith-placed* interventions, which are more common, are developed outside the FBO and simply carried out within the church but do not attempt to incorporate elements of the FBO (Campbell et al., 2007; Lancaster et al., 2014). Collaborative programs implemented in churches, or ones that involve multiple partners and resources, have had the most potential for success; programs that are not collaborative may limit program acceptability, sustainability, fidelity, and, ultimately, program success. Cultural sensitivity, viewed in two distinct dimensions—surface structure and deep structure—can be useful for effective program implementation (Resnicow et al., 1999). Surface structure is described as matching intervention materials and messages to observable characteristics of the population of interest, such as commonly used products, behavior patterns, and environmental and social contexts in which behaviors occur. Deep structure refers to programs that reflect ways by which cultural, social, psychological, environmental, and historical factors and values can influence behavior and, particularly, how these factors influence behaviors across different population subgroups. For health promotion in Black churches, attention to deep structure involves understanding and recognition of how religion and faith-influenced behavior in the population of interest (Campbell et al., 2007; Ard et al., 2004). Two reviews have highlighted additional essential elements for successful health-promotion programs in churches (Campbell et al., 2007; Peterson et al., 2002). These elements include a focus on positive health values, community-focused interventions, changing health behaviors, supportive relationships through existing social systems, interventions that incorporate the sociocultural environment and can be delivered by the community, and ongoing plans for program sustainability.

An Engaged Faith-Based Organizational Leadership Framework

The key to successfully promoting health in Black churches and the surrounding communities most often begins with its leadership—namely, the senior pastor. Although denominations may differ in procedures and approach, when connecting with a church to conduct any program, whether faith-based or faith-placed, the pastors are often the central decision makers (Gross et al., 2018; Sewell, 2003; Stewart et al., 2019; Story et al., 2017). It is their perspective that can affect the level of engagement of a church (Corbie-Smith et al., 2010; Dash & Rasor, 2002; Lincoln & Mamiya, 1990; Story et al., 2017). However, their leadership role must be viewed from the standpoint of the church as a whole institution, not simply as the pastor as decision maker or the congregation as a target for health-promotion interventions devoid of faith tenets and principles. Churches should be seen as organizations composed of multiple levels of leadership—e.g., pastor, other clergy, deacons, auxiliaries (health ministry, kitchen committee), congregation—serving as a collective body that meets the spiritual, as well as the social and economic, needs of its members and those it serves in the greater community, particularly in Black communities. Faith-based leadership should not be viewed as an individualized approach but rather as a contextually integrated, dynamic network. Furthermore, engagement with other partners and stakeholders who can provide human, financial, and material resources to address these needs helps enhance the role of the church as a leading agency in Black populations. From the perspective

Trust	Cultural Competence
Faith-Based Community Engaged Leadership in Health Promotion	
Community Organizing	Capacity Building

FIGURE 15.1 Core Community Engagement Principles for Faith-Based-Led Promotion

of church leadership, community engagement to bring about social, political, and/or environmental change is anchored in a set of common integrated principles, four of which are germane to building a framework around improving population health: (1) trust, (2) cultural competence, (3) community organization, and (4) capacity building (see Figure 15.1).

Building trust is fundamental to collaboration and partnership building (Alio et al., 2014; Frerichs et al., 2017; McCloskey et al., 2011). Tied closely to culture, trust is often an outcome from shared ideas in a partnership or group. Culture is defined as "a complex integrated system of thought and behavior shared by members of a group—a system whose whole pattern allows us to understand the meanings that people attach to specific facts and observations" (Kiefer, 2007, p. 10).

Establishing an understanding of the cultures in Black churches should lead to increased trust. While trust takes time to build, it can take an even greater period of time to build if lost through a lack of respect or when mutual respect and co-learning are absent. In addition, resources (time, material, and human in nature) and efficiencies are also lost when a culture is not respected (Henry, 2011; Miller & Shinn, 2005; Minkler et al., 2004; Wallerstein et al., 2015). Thus, recognizing the importance of the role of pastors in church leadership as trusted resources and how they operate from a position of strength and empowerment within their organizational body is essential.

Culture is a dynamic and complex construct, even within the constellation of Black churches. Cultural competence, or the ability to have knowledge of a group's cultural differences and typical behaviors or beliefs, is heavily based in the contexts of cultural meaning of norms, beliefs, and practices within a community (Carpenter-Song et al., 2007). Using a "meaning-centered approach can also help reveal how community conditions are determined by social, economic, and political forces rather than simply by individual choices" (Carpenter-Song, et al., 2007, p. 1364). From the perspective of Black churches, cultural competence means understanding, for instance, how these institutions serve their populations in ways other agencies may not and what they feel are the resources needed to help them improve health conditions in their communities. This is a critical approach to engagement such that it not only helps to build trust between groups but also sets the stage for mobilizing and organizing to promote change.

Community organizing, which is grounded in the principle of social action, involves bringing people together for a commonly shared interest (Braithwaite et al., 1994). It recognizes that, in order to change, we all must feel a need for change and that we are more likely to do so when we are involved in group learning and decision making (Minkler, 1990). Dahl's work on pluralism (1967) posited that through collective action, people formed community organizations to influence decision makers to advance the group's agenda. These organizations had a fundamental desire to influence government, either indirectly or directly, by capitalizing on the sociological need of people to belong to such groups, as well as the political concept of "strength in numbers" (Berry, 1989; Lindsey & Beach, 2002), or they would respond to the community's needs themselves without waiting for the government to react (Herson & Bolland, 1998). Community organizations, including Black churches, often serve in this capacity. The fundamental tenets are principles of empowerment, community competence, and active participation, and, as Nyswander stated, it is "starting where the people are" (Nyswander, 1956, as cited in Minkler, 2005, p. 27). As discussed earlier in this chapter, Black churches have been at the forefront of community organizing simply because of people's common interest in civil rights. While this remains a prevailing issue today, there are now more competing, complex layers of priorities, such as the right to adequate access to health care compared to the quality of existing care, or the marketing of unhealthy food and beverages in Black communities by large corporations compared to the needed jobs these same corporations provide in Black communities, or the post–civil rights heterogeneous needs of the Black middle-class population compared to the needs of a growing class of impoverished Blacks, just to name a few. This means that more than ever, community organizing needs to be designed to help communities—including faith-based ones—identify the primary causes of problems while "selecting issues that are 'winnable, simple, and specific' and that can unite members of the group, involve them in achieving the solution, and further build community" (Minkler, 1990, p. 27). Black churches, building off their long-term history as a sustainable force in Black communities, are in a unique position to provide leadership, guidance, and spiritual support that can successfully motivate a collective body of people to act (Fry & Egel, 2017). However, once that occurs, skills must be developed and fostered to bring about change.

Capacity building, particularly in terms of health promotion, involves the "development of sustainable skills, resources, and organizational structures" in the impacted communities (McCloskey et al., 2011). This includes promoting shared knowledge, leadership skills, and the ability to represent the interests of the body of constituents (Maxwell et al., 2019). An understanding of the specific environment must take place (Eng & Parker, 1994). According to prior research, seven key elements are required to establish successful church-based community health programs: (1) partnerships, (2) positive health values, (3) availability of services, (4) access to church facilities, (5) community-focused interventions, (6) health behavior change, and (7) supportive social relationships (Carter-Edwards et al., 2011; Petersen et al., 2002). To successfully establish and maintain these critical elements, particularly in today's resource-constrained environment, requires *lateral capacity building*, which involves investments in the training of church leaders and in facilitating strategic alliances with other key community stakeholders who can play a pivotal role in improving health promotion and disease prevention (McCloskey et al., 2011).

In summary, four principles— (1) trust, (2) cultural competence, (3) community organizing, and (4) capacity building—provide a foundation for understanding the role of faith-based engaged leadership in health promotion. With respect to Black communities as described, pastors as decision makers are empowered through congregational trust, and the actions the collective body chooses to take within FBOs and their surrounding communities require multiple levels of engaged leadership and external partnerships. The collaborative approach to promoting health requires a clear understanding of the dynamic cultural norms, beliefs, and practices of the faith-based communities, and community organizing provides the basis for identifying the common goal that advances the communities' specific agendas. Once the collective body has assembled to pursue the same goal, capacity building can occur, developing and/or enhancing the skills needed for successful and sustainable change in population health.

Based on these principles, a framework is proposed for conducting faith-based engaged leadership programmatic activities to promote health. Table 15.1 displays a health-promotion capacity logic model. While the *inputs* include the pastor and other levels of leadership within FBOs, it also includes various external partners and sectors that help provide resources, materials, and support for the health-promotion mission (including health and government agencies). The *activities* are designed to prepare FBOs by fostering organizational change through baseline needs assessments (which will vary across FBOs and regions) and skills building and training. Activities such as partnership development strategies indicate that to build capacity within and between FBOs, there must be collaborative and bidirectional growth for those entities that support the FBOs in this effort. It should also be noted that it is these types of activities that help build or enhance infrastructures needed for sustainable change. The *outputs* involve process measures that help indicate that the activities conducted by the FBOs and other stakeholders have taken place. These include the completion of reports and organizational work plans, assessment of increased knowledge by the FBOs (as indicators of skills building/enhancement), and outreach activities necessary for change (e.g., disseminated health messages and health-promotion tips). *Outcomes*, defined as short term, intermediate, or long term, provide incremental evidence along the health-promotion capacity continuum on whether the engaged leadership activities have had an impact. By implementing the logic model, FBOs and their partners can identify where there are gaps or limitations (e.g., additional stakeholder involvement needed, shift in FBO leadership responsibility) so that activities and work plans can be modified to maximize success. The model can also help them identify the strengths and key successes to replicate in different settings. The following section is an illustration of this logic model in action.

TABLE 15.1 *FBO Leadership Engaged Health-Promotion Capacity Logic Model*

INPUTS	ACTIVITIES	OUTPUTS	OUTCOMES
Within FBO Leadership Pastor/clergy Health ministry Food/culinary ministry Congregation Transportation ministry Benevolence committee Missionary department	Organizational needs assessments Faith network needs assessments Plan development for building leadership and organizational capacity	Report on organizational capacity and readiness to implement health activities Organization work plan (goals, objectives, action steps, time lines, and partners)	*Short Term* • Increased health-promotion capacity of individual churches • Increased network of health advocates/ partners engaged in health promotion
FBO Network FBO collaborative	Organizational development training • Board development • Budget management	Informed board of directors regarding roles, responsibilities, meeting protocols, etc.	*Intermediate* • Increased number of FBOs in the network promoting health
Partnering Sectors Community-based organizations Private agencies Public agencies Academic institutions Health departments Clinics/hospitals Private providers Social services Mental health Social/civic groups	• Fund-raising, grant resources, development Health education/ health-promotion workshops and training sessions Material resources development • Health-promotion messages for bulletins and announcements • Health messages for pastors/clergy	Increased knowledge of sound fiscal practices and organization protocols Increased knowledge of resources • Funding opportunities • Community resources Increased health awareness • Chronic diseases • Prevention strategies • Disease management Disseminated health messages and health-promotion tips	• Expanded relationship with local government *Long Term* • Increased volunteer workforce • Engaged coalition of faith leaders • Increased social networks between the coalition of faith leaders and other stakeholder sectors • Improved health outcomes
Federal Government Resources National Office of Minority Health Resource Center			
Local Government Resources County commissioners Mayor's office Law enforcement	Faith network capacity-building strategies Community organizing/partnership development strategies	Increased knowledge of stakeholder partnerships Increased community organizing skills	

Using the health-promotion capacity logic model as a framework (see Table 15.1), the following two interrelated illustrations highlight the series of collaborative steps taken to develop a faith-based leadership collective to ultimately reach its congregations and the communities it serves.

Illustration 1: The Community Health Ambassador Program (CHAP)

Preparing Faith-Based Leaders as Partners in Health Promotion in Eastern North Carolina

The North Carolina Office of Minority Health and Health Disparities (NCOMHHD), established in 1992 by the general assembly to lead statewide efforts to advocate for the elimination of health disparities among all racial/ethnic minorities and underserved populations in North Carolina, has five major focus areas: (1) advocacy, (2) culture and language, (3) partnership development, (4) policy and legislation, and (6) research and data dissemination. In 2005, the NCOMHHD targeted Eastern North Carolina (ENC) as a geographic area of the state in which to invest resources, work with community partners, and, ultimately, eliminate health disparities. ENC is a region covering 41 counties that are predominantly rural, with reported high rates of poverty and mortality (ECU, Center for Research and Health Systems Development, 2011). Significant disparities were observed for heart disease, cancer, cerebrovascular disease, chronic lower respiratory diseases, and all other injuries, and the NCOMHHD understood that a complex set of socioeconomic, educational, cultural, lifestyle, and occupational factors have contributed to these burdens in some way.

In an effort to focus on health-promotion and disease-prevention strategies rather than disease management and to involve the faith communities in these areas—a sector that had not been organized around such issues—the NCOMHHD staff reached out to faith leaders in ENC. To initiate this partnership, the NCOMHHD sought to identify a faith-based leader and organization that could serve as a local champion concerning health priorities, lead community-based efforts, and help build a foundation of leadership in communities in ENC while the office provides technical assistance and resources. At that time, NCOMHHD reached out and identified Dr. Calvin Ellison, then pastor and executive director of a 501(c)(3) community development corporation called Success Dynamics. His organization's mission aligned with that of the office, and he was open to learning more about health disparities, their links to poverty, and the burden among racial/ethnic minorities in North Carolina and nationwide. Together, NCOMHHD and Success Dynamics worked to mobilize faith-based efforts to promote health in ENC. All faith leaders contacted had health ministries that provided some common types of service (routinely visiting the sick, praying for families in hospitals, assisting the congregants and communities with paying for medications through benevolent ministry funds, and transportation to provider visits). They were interested in being engaged with this health-promotion partnership rather than the common reaction to problems because, as one pastor stated, "We are tired of preaching funerals." Since the types of services varied across churches, there was an apparent need for collaborative activities so that all churches were ready with basic health ministries and services.

Development of the CEN

The NCOMHHD and Success Dynamics worked with the initial faith leaders to organize, mobilize, and gain understanding of the baseline capacities of their organizations. Using active listening and cultural competence strategies, NCOMHHD and Success Dynamics implemented a three-phase approach to the development of the CEN: (1) organizational assessments, (2) capacity building, and (3) coalition development.

For the first phase, *organizational assessments*, informal surveys were administered to approximately 25 faith leaders in ENC over a 4-month period. Information was collected on faith leaders' knowledge of health disparities issues, perceptions of health priorities in their area, priorities for their church and community, organizational capacity to promote health and available resources, and proposed leadership roles regarding the community's health.

Data from the assessments guided the second phase, *capacity building*, which involved NCOMHHD's provision of consultation services, technical assistance, training, and skills development for the faith leaders and their organizations. Pastors and other faith leaders were trained first since as identified stakeholders (i.e., community leaders), they must seek avenues to provide intentional representation of the issues, needs, and concerns of their groups within the fabric of mainstream institutions, programs, and service delivery vehicles (Toms et al., 2011). Training and skills-building activities included the following:

- *Public Health Information Training.* NCOMHHD and other state agency partners provided training on topics, including Public Health 101, leadership skills, accessing local systems of care, basic information on health-specific topics, and program evaluation and reporting. Individual-level and group-level consultation and training sessions were tailored based on faith leaders' levels of knowledge and experience.
- *Organizational Capacity Building.* Strategies included training in board development, grant writing, fundraising, strategic planning, organizational readiness, fiscal management, operational and reporting procedures, and establishing a nonprofit 501(c)(3) for community outreach. NCOMHHD continued to work with churches on an individual basis until a regional strategy was employed.

Over the 8-month period that these trainings occurred, faith leaders worked to develop a feasible leadership model. Despite being a financially constrained effort, this grassroots, human resource–intensive undertaking was necessary for setting the foundation for practical, effective, and sustainable strategies toward improved community health.

In the third phase, *coalition building*, steps were implemented over a 6-month period to increase the visibility and advocacy organizing faith-based leaders as partners in health. Since the faith leaders had increased their knowledge of the health challenges facing their region through their training, they found new ways to access potential services and resources. Success Dynamics, through Dr. Ellison's leadership, assisted in organizing meetings and referred to its own social capital to bring a diverse group of faith-based leaders to the stakeholder table. Ongoing communication strategies—conference calls, email updates, and face-to-face meetings—were put into place to encourage participation; keep community leaders informed of key trends, policies, programs, and services; and outline action steps for engagement around local health issues.

In 2006, approximately 18 months after the initial communications between the NCOMHHD and Dr. Ellison, the CEN, was formally established. Serving as a statewide initiative, the CEN's mission was to advance member communities through partnerships that thrive on economic development, superior education, and elimination of health disparities. The goal of this social action network was to build administrative capacity, develop nontraditional outreach programs, collectively leverage resources, and empower the people in the various communities served by its partners. At that time, the eight-region coalition included 150 churches in 20 counties in ENC. In 2007, through a collaboration with Dr. Forrest Toms and the North Carolina Agricultural and Technical State University Leadership Studies Program, the Leadership Enhancement Engagement Project (LEEP) and Participation Engagement Practice Project were designed to develop the CEN's capacity to promote health. Capacity building focused on three primary areas:

1. Enhance CEN's organizational capacity to plan, develop, implement, and sustain ongoing community engagement efforts;
2. Develop and enhance the knowledge and skills of CEN churches to intentionally engage public officials and agencies around policy and resource distribution in the areas of health, educational, and economic disparities; and
3. Provide CEN members with the training, multimedia educational tools, and community-building skills to organize and engage citizens to get involved and participate in the civic and political processes (Toms et al., 2008).

Through discussions and experiential learning opportunities, the framework included participation in monthly leadership and advocacy training institutes, bimonthly site-based team meetings, observations of civic government agencies, and completion of observation forms (Toms et al., 2011).

Implementing the CHAP

CHAP was established in 2006 by the NCOMHHD, in partnership with the CEN, as an initial response to a need for health-promotion programs and services for church congregants that complement the skills and training received by faith leaders (Pullen-Smith et al., 2008). The emphasis was on building a network of "willing workers" within congregations so that basic health information, screenings, and referrals could be offered in FBO settings. CHAP was a unique, statewide lay health adviser model involving multiple sectors and partnerships, including training approved and offered by the North Carolina Community College System. Informal leaders or natural helpers trusted by the community receive training as candidate community health ambassadors (CHAs), conducting volunteer community outreach activities with individuals or groups, advocacy, and community resource-driven patient navigation. Candidate CHAs completed a 22-hour course offered by one of the 17 community colleges at the time, receiving 2.0 continuing education units after completing course requirements. Coursework included in-class sessions on the definition of diabetes, diabetes prevalence, nutrition, physical activity, and strategies for reaching out to clients in one's social network. Fieldwork included identifying resources clients can use to promote their health (e.g., transportation sources, diabetes information, referral locations for the uninsured). CHAP initially focused its attention on diabetes; however, the model was designed to subsequently address the series of chronic diseases identified by the state as having high rates of health disparities. Through a grant from the NCOMHHD, 11 CEN FBO-based community wellness and resource centers served as pilot programs. Each FBO site was equipped with diabetes health education materials, blood pressure monitors, glucose meters, and weight scales. The wellness centers were maintained by the CHAs from each FBO. In terms of the initial 6-month feedback on the program and its reach, the NCOMHHD conducted a brief survey with a small sample of 53 CHAs on their awareness of their role, number of organizations reached to provide outreach services, and general "yes/no" questions on the types of outreach activities they conducted. A total of 81.1% reported using their CHA training to work with others. Among these ambassadors,

- activities included such actions as health fairs, diabetes and blood pressure screenings, trainings within their FBOs on chronic disease self-management, exercise and nutrition programs, connections with health-care providers, and outreach to members in nursing homes;
- the median volunteer time spent working with others during the 6-month period was 20 hours (range: 4–100 hours), or approximately 3.3 hours per month;
- all provided information about diabetes, felt they were knowledgeable about providing diabetes information to their communities, spoke comfortably in front of an audience, and worked one-on-one to educate individuals; and
- approximately two thirds referred individuals to community resources, providers, and human services or health agencies.

More than 400 volunteers in North Carolina successfully completed the training from 2006 to 2010. A 2010 assessment conducted in partnership with NCOMHHD and the University of North Carolina at Chapel Hill revealed that approximately 200 CHAs across 22 counties remained active in their outreach efforts in their communities.

Broader Use of the CHAP Framework

The use of the CHAP framework has extended beyond faith communities at the local and state levels. In 2009–2010, a pilot program was conducted with a local public health department and public housing authority (PHA) in southeastern North Carolina. A CHAP coordinator (who was key in maintaining program activities), 17 CHAs (predominantly Black), and 62 clients within the PHA engaged in activities to promote better health and diabetes-related awareness. At 6 months post-baseline, health assessments using the CHAP evaluation tools were collected from 32 participants, five of whom had diabetes. Focus groups were subsequently conducted to contextually supplement the results from the health assessments. The findings were as follows:

- The primary outreach services provided by the CHAs included the distribution of health education materials, referrals to community services, and recommendations to see a physician.
- There was an increase of 6% and 7% in the proportion of clients meeting the recommended amount for vegetable intake and physical activity, respectively.
- The participants experienced a mean weight loss of 9.6 pounds.
- The participants experienced a mean reduction in glucose of 4.3 mg/dL.
- Healthy cooking demonstrations, community gardens, and Zumba® exercise sessions spawned from CHAP outreach activities.
- CHAs felt that they met their goals to improve clients' health and those around them.
- Participants felt empowered and respected by the CHAs as they provided them with information and resources.

The results from this pilot program indicate that a multilevel program involving a coordinator from the community, CHAs, clients, and partnering sectors (community colleges, an academic institution, community vendors, businesses, health-care facilities) is feasible to implement CHAP in public housing communities. Implementing community-led health programs may empower public housing residents, improve their community's health, and promote a sustainable approach that is cost-effective to our health-care system.

Currently, at the state level, CHAP is one of the frameworks used to advance the certification and accreditation processes for the North Carolina statewide Community Health Worker (CHW) Initiative (NC Department of Health and Human Services [NC DHHS], 2018). The CHW Initiative is designed to establish a sustainable infrastructure to support the development, training, and maintenance of CHWs within the state. The recognition of CHWs "provides an opportunity to impact population health, reduce disparities and integrate their roles into a new healthcare delivery model" (NC DHHS, 2020, para. 1). The initiative began in 2014 with a NC DHHS team exploring statewide CHW opportunities, reviewing programs in other states, and examining the landscape within North Carolina. From 2015 to 2017, the team coordinated a road series of stakeholder and leadership meetings, statewide summits, community listening sessions, ad hoc competencies group and certification group meetings, strategic recommendations, and survey administration. In 2018, NC DHHS published a report describing the core competencies and a proposed plan for certification. Standardized statewide training will cover nine core skills as part of the certification process. These include skills in (1) communication, (2) capacity building, (3) service coordination, (4) interpersonal relationships, (5) advocacy, (6) personal development, (7) outreach, (8) education and facilitation, and (9) knowledge base. An accreditation and certification committee has been formed, which includes a CHAP developer on the committee (Dr. Carter-Edwards), and training protocols are currently being developed. Using the CHAP training framework, trainings will be conducted through the community colleges. Lessons learned from CHAP, including the development of community tools for working with participants, will continue to be shared with the leaders of the CHW Initiative. This connection to CHAP is important given that many ambassadors trained across the state have the skills to serve as CHWs within the initiative. Their familiarity with the process may serve a useful role in building sustainable capacity to maintain community partnerships and promote better health.

Illustration 2: Village HeartBEAT—Establishing Deep Roots With the Community

The Village HeartBEAT (Building Education and Accountability Together) Initiative (VHB) evolved from the underlying development of strategic relationships that were deeply rooted within the community. These long-standing relationships with local clergy and community stakeholders, coupled with the understanding of local community history, led to a series of leadership efforts to reduce the racial/ethnic health disparities in Mecklenburg County, North Carolina. This award-winning initiative, built from an established coalition, includes stakeholders from a wide array of sectors committed to promoting better health through a faith leadership framework. The following section highlights the series of partnerships that led to the VHB community model, followed by a description of VHB's purpose and how its partnership between the faith community and Mecklenburg County Public Health (MCPH) (formerly the Mecklenburg County Health Department) illustrates a sustainable leadership collaboration to address persistent chronic diseases in the region.

In 2000, NCOMHHD's executive director met with the Mecklenburg County health director to get buy-in and commitment. This strategic move positioned Mecklenburg, the county with the largest population in North Carolina, as a leader by aligning its vision and mission with the nation and state to address health disparity issues, diversity, and inclusion. MCPH embraced the national and state public policy agenda to eliminate health disparities and took proactive steps. To build its internal capacity, MCPH created a community health administrator position in 2000 held by Ms. Cheryl Emanuel, who coordinated the conceptualization, design, development, and implementation of community interventions targeting disparities in heart disease and diabetes. Guided by the vision that "everyone in Mecklenburg County will enjoy good health regardless of their race/ethnicity, disability or socioeconomic status," MCPH redesigned its policies, programs, and resource allocations with a greater emphasis on health equity. One top priority was to establish partnerships with external community-based leaders and organizations from the neighborhoods with the highest rates of morbidity.

Creation of the Faithful to the Call Network of Churches

After a review of demographic data, MCPH identified public health priority areas (PHPAs) as locations within the county that had high rates of morbidity and mortality. In response, MCPH sought to engage the community, specifically faith leaders, as partners in health in new ways. To do so, MCPH reached out to pastors to initiate conversations about the disturbing trends in health status data for racial/ethnic minorities in their zip codes. MCPH shared what they understood about the public health data, which led to a short survey of the pastors. Their responses to key questions laid the foundation for the partnership:

1. What do you understand about public health data?
2. Do you know how to access public health data?
3. Are you interested in partnering to set up a health ministry in your congregation?
4. What would your health ministry look like?
5. What resources do you currently have in place?
6. What factors would impede your ability to start a health ministry?
7. What are the taboo public health topics in your church?
8. Can you designate three to five members to serve as the "health cabinet" to plan, coordinate, and implement your health ministry?

With permission from the pastors, a more detailed survey of their congregations was conducted to identify health-specific priorities and concerns.

Bishop Wade Ferguson III was one of the first pastors who committed to the effort by engaging in the process of addressing the community's health. Under his leadership, a core group of 12 pastors became active partners with MCPH to promote health and reduce disparities in their communities and formed the Faithful to the Call Network of Churches. This network aligned with the CEN, an existing church network organized by NCOMHHD in the eastern part of the state. NCOMHHD and the CEN offered the LEEP training to a group of 26 ministers in Mecklenburg County. This training focused on building capacity to engage in local civic forums, understanding the policy-making process, and influencing policies on resource distribution. Health empowerment zones—communities that experience disproportionate disparities in health status and health care (Health Empowerment Zone Act, 2009)— were formed to bridge faith-based leaders, community partners, and health and human resources.

Evolution of the Partners in Eliminating Health Disparities (PEHD) Coalition

From 2000 to 2004, MCPH held a series of *neighborhood think tanks* to engage a diverse group of partners, including health-care providers, minority organizations, civic groups, community and faith-based organizations, private-sector partners, educational institutions, NCOMHHD, and other stakeholders with a strong interest in and commitment to addressing health disparities. Faith leaders served as the foundation for the PEHD. All the *neighborhood think tank* sessions were held at churches in the priority neighborhoods.

In collaboration with Johnson C. Smith (a historically Black college/university), Pfeiffer University, and the University of North Carolina at Charlotte, MCPH held a county-wide think tank called "The Education Collaborative to Eliminate Health Disparities in Mecklenburg County" (Aluko, 2007). Discussion, which included more than 250 participants, led to the formation of the PEHD in 2004. The stated mission and charge of the Mecklenburg County PEHD coalition was to "eliminate health racial and ethnic health disparities through collaboration, education and partnerships." Its overarching goal was to unify community representatives around minority health disparities and address them systematically and cooperatively. Given that county-wide community health assessment continued to reveal inequities, and the inherent challenges of addressing social determinants of health, no single agency or organization could expect to contribute significantly to the elimination of health disparities without a broad base of partners. However, developing meaningful and well-integrated involvement in a complex community intervention is a time- and labor-intensive process (Plescia & Emanuel, 2014).

In 2005, the county manager declared eliminating health and mental health disparities a priority for Mecklenburg County. He charged MCPH to serve as the county lead for developing its Call to Action to Eliminate Health Disparities. As such, Mecklenburg County became the first county in North Carolina to have a Board of County Commissioners adopt a Call to Action Strategic Plan for Eliminating Health Disparities. The county Call to Action provided a strategic framework to identify, monitor, and address health disparities in Mecklenburg County. Specifically, aligning several strategies to advance its goal of eliminating health-care disparities, including (1) building a community network to identify early interventions and provide timely health care, as needed; (2) improving minority health care and access to care that cuts across traditional barriers and draws from resources of the entire health-care market; and (3) developing standards of quality health care and culturally appropriate responses to health-care needs. As one partner stated,

> Eliminating health disparities in Mecklenburg County will take more than one well-crafted program. It will take unprecedented collaboration among public and private healthcare providers. It will take an enormous public health education effort aimed at specific and diverse populations. And it will take creative partnerships between government agencies and private entities. But, most of all, it will take the realization that public health is essential to a healthy society and healthy economy. It will take the realization that a healthy population is essential to the growth and prosperity of our region. (Algire, 2005)

The NC DHHS and NCOMHHD provided pivotal leadership, technical support, and resources to MCPH. For example, in 2001, in her newly appointed role, Carmen Hooker Odom, secretary of the NC DHHS, declared eliminating health disparities as a priority for the state department (OMH, 2003). The OMHHD was charged to lead the development of a state plan and the DHHS Steering Committee for Eliminating Health Disparities was formed. The 2003 *DHHS Call to Action to Eliminate Health Disparities* reported the health statistics and demographics for the state and aligned the strategies for eliminating health disparities with the Healthy People 2010 conceptual framework. Activities included focus groups, regional meetings on health disparities issues, and a Disparity Program Assessment. A set of perspectives internal and external to DHHS were identified, and a set of nine recommendations were developed:

1. Increase awareness of health and service disparities, especially disparities related to race/ethnicity, disability, and socioeconomic status.
2. Communicate, document, and champion best practices for eliminating health disparities.
3. Promote, develop, and enhance communities' capacity to engage in healthy living and the elimination of disparities in health status.
4. Monitor progress toward the elimination of health disparities.
5. Promote customer-friendly services that meet the needs of underserved populations (i.e., the poor and minority groups).
6. Increase resources and investments to eliminate health status gaps.
7. Build, support, and fully use a diverse workforce capable of working in cross-cultural settings.
8. Identify and advocate for public policies that aid in closing the health status gap.
9. Demonstrate accountability and ownership of health outcomes.

The Call to Action recommendations served as the blueprint for Mecklenburg County to shape PEHD's engagement and strategies to eliminate health disparities.

To help accomplish this work, MCPH engaged in an *intentional partnership* with NCOMHHD involving the training and support of lay health advisers (CHAs) and opportunities for community empowerment through capacity building and resource sharing so that MCPH could receive state-level support to address local health disparities.

The coalition used community-based participatory approaches at all stages of work to successfully promote large-scale, sustainable changes in health through the deliberate inclusion of multiple partners. All these efforts supported MCPH's 2005 development of a county-level plan for building an infrastructure to help eliminate health disparities adapted from the state-level plan generated through the recommendations of the DHHS Call to Action. MCPH's plan was successfully approved for funding by the county commissioners. PEHD's priorities included the following:

- *Improved access to health care* (connecting people and health-care services to one another),
- *Improved quality of health care* (educating consumers to identify lower quality health care and advocate for better quality care),
- *Improved cultural and linguistic competence in health care* (increased minority representation in health care and health-care administration), and
- *Education, research, and science in health care* (health disparities education and training through an interdisciplinary academic community research partnership).

The PEHD coalition positioned MCPH for county, state, federal and private funding. For example, from 2005 to 2012, capacity building grant funds from NCOMHHD were used to advance the PEHD infrastructure development to address the key health indicators, access to health care, preventive screenings, referrals, and expansion of the Faithful to the Call Network in PHPA (high morbidity/mortality zip codes). These efforts evolved into the Village HeartBEAT Initiative.

Development of the Village HeartBEAT Initiative

In 2012, MCPH and the PEHD coalition developed VHB. From the outset, VHB was designed to work in collaboration with governmental, academic, business, civic groups, hospital systems, community organizations and FBOs, and federally qualified health centers. The main themes in this process revolve around studying the community, understanding health data, growing accountability partners, and putting promising models into practice to affect positive change. The acronym BEAT describes our approach to community engagement:

- **B**uilding community capacity
- **E**ducation to increasing awareness and understanding of cardiovascular disease prevention

- **A**ccountability for success, including monitoring individual and partner adherence to program objectives, and working
- **T**ogether in collaboration with participant input in all aspects of the program

The goal of VHB is to prevent cardiovascular disease through the overall strategy of adopting healthy behaviors (reduced tobacco use, improved nutrition, and increased physical activity) in PHPAs.

A central component of VHB is to *empower faith-based and minority communities as engaged stakeholders.* We are intentionally engaging our priority community partners and stakeholders, including African American and Latino residents and FBOs in PHPA communities, in changing health behaviors at the individual, policy, system, environmental, and community levels.

The VHB Initiative implemented programs to reduce heart disease and the related risk factors (e.g., obesity, poor nutrition, physical inactivity, and diabetes) in partnership with FBOs. A yearly program conducted through churches, VHB uses trained CHWs, called "ambassadors," to work in targeted census tracts with adults who have self-identified chronic disease risk factors.

Innovations of the Village HeartBEAT Initiative

The VHB initiative has four key innovations that have supported sustainability and growth:

1. **Use of the Concept of "Health as a Shared Value."** This framework is used to identify and recruit FBOs within high-risk neighborhoods. Our team intentionally identifies FBOs that are working independently to improve the health of their congregants and/or the neighboring community. This framework allows the public health team to partner with the FBO and improve health-related outcomes through use of the health ministries and trained health ambassadors.

2. **Intention to Have Multilevel Impact on Individuals as Well as on Policy, Systems, and Environment.** For this approach, we work with FBOs to assist members in institutionalizing locally tailored evidence-based strategies. Specifically, we ask FBO partners to implement policies directed toward tobacco usage, nutrition, and physical activity. For example, a church partner would implement a nonsmoking policy prohibiting tobacco use within their facilities.

3. **The Thereasea Clark Elder Community Health Leadership Academy.** It is a community-engagement strategy to support cardiovascular disease prevention, deliver chronic disease prevention education, and provide access to health and human services programs in high-risk communities. The academy is named after Ms. Elder, the oldest living public health leader in Mecklenburg County.

4. **Challenge and Competition.** Perhaps most importantly, we use friendly competitions to engage FBO teams in the VHB program. The 16-week competition

is aimed at lowering cardiovascular risk factors and obesity among competing FBOs.

Three educational phases are employed during the challenge to (1) improve healthy eating, (2) increase physical activity, and (3) promote weight loss. All members are required to provide a full set of key pre- and post-program measures, including weight, blood pressure, and blood glucose levels. Members also participate in intermediate weigh-ins to monitor progress. A community celebration recognizes their health improvement accomplishments.

VHB has won numerous local, state, and national awards, including the grand prize winner of the Healthiest Cities & Counties Challenge and received $500,000 in grants and prizes to help combat cardiovascular disease in the community. A global partnership with the World Council of Churches recognized VHB as a best practice model and has developed a guidebook (Jones, 2018; World Council of Churches, 2018). With a global fellowship of 350 churches in 110 countries and territories, the council represents more than 500 million members.

SUMMARY

FBOs are in a unique position as prominent leaders in facilitating community-based health promotion among their citizens and raising consciousness around the social determinants of health that drive the systems responsible for service delivery and care. This cannot be more apparent than in Black communities given the persistent chronic health disparities juxtaposed with the current global public health crisis and national civic unrest regarding race relations. The collective process of working together and with others toward a common goal is an inherent characteristic of FBOs. Demonstrated through the framework and the illustrations described in this chapter, a multilevel leadership approach to community engagement that involves traditional and nontraditional partnerships, organizational change strategies, and core principles of trust, cultural competence, community organizing, and capacity building are necessary elements for socioecological change (Frieden, 2010). Faith leaders are very central to these efforts and should *collectively* extend their contributions to their congregations and greater communities beyond decision-making responsibilities and engage in social action through strong strategic partnerships and advocacy.

Public Health 3.0 centers on partnerships across multiple sectors and "leveraging data and resources to address social, environmental, and economic conditions that affect health and health equity" (DeSalvo et al., 2017, para. 1). Building on the prior progress in advancing public health, Public Health 3.0 seeks to foster an inclusive systems-level approach to respond to present health issues while promoting health for the future through new funding streams, as well as resource-constrained settings. The five recommendations for conditions that support the transformation of public health departments and public health systems are (1) chief health strategists for communities, (2) structured cross-sector partnerships, (3) accreditation, (4) actionable data and clear metrics, and (5) enhanced, sustainable funding (DeSalvo et al., 2017). Faith communities and their leaders are essential partners in this transformation. Just as the field of public health has made considerable progress over time, so has FBOs in Black communities in building partnerships, capacities, and skills. However, more is needed if faith communities intend to rely on their collective networks to sustain the advancement of health for their citizens. While networks exist, there is not a clear understanding of how they operate; how to systematically evaluate their connections, assets, and challenges; or how to develop broad plans to address gaps within the networks to strengthen their collective abilities to provide services alongside public health departments and other agencies. Recommendations for next steps in building FBO network capacity to promote health in the era of Public Health 3.0 include the following:

- Asset mapping to document the strengths within and between the networks that can be used for planning future programs and initiatives
- Ensuring that all FBOs regardless of size have the tools and resources to promote health
- Training members of FBOs to build a sustainable volunteer and paid workforce of CHWs or ambassadors
- Scaling up existing FBO programs so that their reach can help transform a broader community base
- Engage in innovative strategies for securing funding efforts led by FBOs
- Use new and existing criteria to identify the next set of leaders who can push forward community engagement in health promotion

By making the effort to build individual, small group, and network capacity to better serve communities, faith leaders and the FBOs will be better equipped to not only address a common health goal identified but also multiple goals with greater reach. In an ever-changing health, social, economic, and political climate, building on strengths that promote health equity will be critical for establishing lasting impact.

Acknowledgments for the Village HeartBEAT Initiative Illustration 2: Public Health Consultants Mr. George Hill and Dr. Lisa Hodges; the NCOMHHD; Bishop Wade H. Ferguson III, pastor of the 15th Street Church, Charlotte, North Carolina; Harry Jones, Mecklenburg County manager, Charlotte, North Carolina; Consultant Frank Parker; Dr. Helen Caldwell, dean of social work, Johnson C. Smith University; Chaplain Harry Burns, Novant Health; Dr. Diane Bowles, vice president, Government Sponsored Programs, and research director, Smith Institute for Applied Research, director, Title III Programs, Johnson C. Smith University; Ms. Thereasea Clark Elder; and all the churches and organizations who initiated VHB and made this award-winning work possible.

REFERENCES

Algire, J. (2005). Community Health Services. https://www.careringnc.com/

Alio, A. P., Fields, S. D., Humes, D. L., Bunce, C. A., Wallace, S. E., Lewis, C., Elder, H., Wakefield, S, & Keefer, C. (2014). Project VOGUE: A partnership for increasing HIV knowledge and HIV vaccine trial awareness among House Ball leaders in Western New York. *Journal of Gay Lesbian Social Services, 26*(3), 336–354. https://doi.org/10.1080/10538720.2014.924892

Aluko, Y. (2007). Carolina Association for Health Equity—CACHE: A community coalition to address health disparities in racial and ethnic minorities in Mecklenburg County, North Carolina. In R. A. Williams (Ed.), *Eliminating healthcare disparities in America: Beyond the IOM report.* (pp. 417–421). Humana Press Inc.

Ard, J. D., Coffman, C. J., Lin, P. H., & Svetkey, L. P. (2004). One-year follow-up study of blood pressure and dietary patterns in dietary approaches to stop hypertension (DASH)-sodium participants. *American Journal of Hypertension, 17*, 1156–1162.

Barna Group. (2007). *Church attendance.* http://www.barna.org/FlexPage.aspx?Page=Topic&TopicID=10

Baron, K. G., Gilyard, S. G., Williams, J. L., Lindich, D., Koralnik, L., & Lynch, E. B. (2019). Sleep-related attitudes, beliefs, and practices among an urban-dwelling African American community: A qualitative study. *Sleep Health, 5*(4), 418–425.

Berry, J. (1989). *Interest group society.* Little Brown Press.

Billingsley, A. (2003). Mighty like a river: The black church and social reform. Oxford University Press.

Braithwaite, R. L., Bianchi, C., & Taylor, S. E. (1994). Ethnographic approach to community organization and health empowerment. *Health Education Quarterly, 21*(3), 407–416.

Braithwaite, R. L., Taylor, S. E., & Austin, J. N. (2000). *Building health coalitions in the black community.* SAGE Publications.

Brown, A. G., Hudson, L. B., Chui, K., Metager, N., Lebron-Torres, N., Seguin, R. & Folta, S. (2017). Improving heart health among black/African American women using civic engagement: A pilot study. *BMC Public Health, 17*(1), 112.

Brown, J. Y., & McCreary, M. L. (2014). Pastors' counseling practices and perceptions of mental health services: Implications for African American mental health. *Journal of Pastoral Care and Counseling, 68*(1), 1–14. https://doi.org/10.1177/154230501406800102

Campbell, M. K., Demark-Wahnefried, W., Symons, M., Kalsbeek, W. D., Dodds, J., Cowan, A., Jackson, B., Motsinger, B., Hoben, K., Lashley, J., Demissie, S., & McClelland, J. W. (1999). Fruit and vegetable consumption and prevention of cancer: The black churches united for better health project. *American Journal of Public Health, 89*(9), 1390–1396.

Campbell, M. K., Hudson, M. A., Resnicow, K., Blakeney, N., Paxton, A., & Baskin, M. (2007). Church-based health promotion interventions: Evidence and lessons learned. *Annual Reviews in Public Health, 28*, 213–234.

Carpenter-Song, E. A., Nordquest Schwallie, M., & Longhofer J. (2007). Cultural competence reexamined: Critique and directions for the future. *Psychiatric Services, 58*(10), 1362–1365.

Carter-Edwards, L., Hooten, E. G., Bruce, M. A., Toms, F., Lloyd, C. M., & Ellison, C. (2012). Pilgrimage to wellness: An exploratory report on clergy perceptions of church health promotion capacity. *Journal of Prevention and Intervention in Community, 40*(3), 194–207.

Carter-Edwards, L., Johnson Jr., J. H., Whitt-Glover, M. C., Bruce, M., & Goldman, M. V. (2011). Health promotion for the elderly: Training black clergy in entrepreneurial spirituality. *Journal of Religion, Spirituality, and Aging, 23*, 139–154.

Cavendish, J. C. (2000). Church-based community activism: A comparison of black and white congregants. *Journal for the Scientific Study of Religion, 39*(1), 64–77.

Cené C. W., Akers, A. Y., Lloyd, S. W., Albritton, T., Powell-Hammond, W., & Corbie-Smith, G. (2011). Understanding social capital and HIV risk in rural African American communities. *Journal of General Internal Medicine, 26*(7), 737–744. https://doi.org/10.1007/s11606-011-1646-4

Centers for Disease Control and Prevention (CDC). (1997). *Principles of community engagement* (1st ed.). CDC/ATSDR Committee on Community Engagement.

Chester, D. N., Himburg, S. P., & Weatherspoon, L. J. (2006). Spirituality of African- American women: Correlations to health-promoting behaviors. *Journal of the National Black Nurses Association, 17*(1), 1–8.

Choi, S. A., & Hastings, J. F. (2009). Religion, spirituality, coping, and resilience among African Americans with diabetes. *Journal of Religion Spiritual Social Work, 38*(1), 93-114. https://doi.org/10.1080/15426432.2018. 1524735

Corbie-Smith, G., Goldmon, M., Isler, M. R., Washington, C., Ammerman, A., Green, M., & Bunton, A. (2010). Partnerships in health disparities research and the roles of pastors of black churches: Potential conflict, synergy, and expectations. *Journal of the National Medical Association, 102*(9), 823–831.

Coughlin, S. S., & Smith, S. A. (2017). Community-based participatory research to promote healthy diet and nutrition and prevent and control obesity among African-Americans: A literature review. *Journal of Racial and Ethnic Health Disparities, 4*(2), 259–268.

Cozier, Y. C., Yu, J., Wise, L. A., VanderWeele, T. J., Balboni, T. A., Argentieri, M. A., Losenberg, L., Palmer, J. R., & Shields, A. E. (2018). Religious and spiritual coping and risk of incident hypertension in the black women's health study. *Annals of Behavioral Medicine, 52*(12), 989–998. https://doi.org/10.1093/abm/kay001

Dahl, R. A. (1967). *Pluralist democracy in the United States: Conflict and consent.* Rand-McNally.

Dash, M., & Rasor, S. (2002). ITC/Faith factor project 2000: An affirmation for the journey inward and outward. *Journal of the Interdenominational Theological Center, 29*(1 & 2), 9–25.

DeSalvo, K. B., Wang, Y. C., Harris. A, Auerbach, J., Koo, D., & O'Carroll, P. (2017). Public health 3.0: A call to action for public health to meet the challenges of the 21st century. *Preventing Chronic Disease, 14*. http://dx.doi.org/10.5888/pcd14.170017external icon.

Dilulio, J. (1999). Living faith: The black church outreach tradition. *Jeremiah Project Report,* 1–9.

Drayton-Brooks, S., & White, N. (2004). Health promoting behaviors among African American women with faith-based support. *ABNF Journal, 15*(5), 84–90.

ECU Center for Research and Health Systems Development (2011). *North Carolina Health Data Explorer.* https://www.ecu.edu/cs-dhs/chsrd/InstantAtlas/IA-FAQs.cfm

Eng, E., & Parker, E. (1994). Measuring community competence in the Mississippi Delta: The interface between program evaluation and empowerment. *Health Education and Behavior, 21*(2), 199–220.

Faridi, Z., Shuval, K., Njike, V. Y., Katz, J. A., Jennings, G., Williams, M., Katz, D. L., & PREDICT Project Working Group. (2010). Partners reducing effects of diabetes (PREDICT): A diabetes prevention physical activity and dietary intervention through African American churches. *Health Education Research, 25*(2), 306–315.

Ford, C. D. (2013). Building from within: Pastoral insights into community resources and assets. *Public Health Nursing, 30*(6), 511–518.

Foster, D. A., Blowers, P. M., Dunnavant, A. L., & Williams, D. N. (2004). *The encyclopedia of the Stone-Campbell Movement.* Wm. B. Eerdsman Publishing.

Frazier, E. F. (1963). *The Negro church in America.* Schocken Books.

Frerichs, L., Kim, M., Dave, G., Cheney, A., Hassmiller, L. K., Jones, J., Young, T. L., Cene, C. W., Varma, D. S., Schaal, J., Black, A., Striley, C. W., Vassar, S., Sullivan, G., Cottler, L. B., Brown, A., Burke, J. G., & Gorbie-Smith, C. (2017). Stakeholder perspectives on creating and maintaining trust in community-academic research partnerships. *Health Education & Behavior, 44*(1), 182–191. https://doi.orgt/10.1177/1090198116648291

Frieden T. R. (2010). A framework for public health action: the health impact pyramid. *American Journal of Public Health, 100*(4), 590–595. https://doi.org/10.2105/AJPH.2009.185652

Fry, L., & Egel, E. (2017). Spiritual leadership: Embedding sustainability in the triple bottom line. *Graziadio Business Report, 20.*

Goldmon, M. V., & Roberson, Jr., J. T. (2004). Churches, academic institutions, and public health: Partnerships to eliminate health disparities. *North Carolina Medical Journal, 65*(6), 368–372.

Gross, T. T., Story, C. R., Harvey, I. S., Allsopp, M., & Whitt-Glover, M. (2018). "As a community, we need to be more health conscious": Pastors' perceptions on the health status of the black church and African-American communities. *Journal of Racial and Ethnic Health Disparities, 5*(3), 570–579.

Harris, F. C. (1999). *Something within: Religion in African American political activism.* Oxford Press.

Hawkins, D., Kornfield, M., Taylor, A., Copeland, K., Flynn, M., Shepherd, K., ... Bella, T. (2020, June 8). 9 Minneapolis city council members announce plans to disband police department. *Washington Post.* https://www.washingtonpost.com/nation/2020/06/07/george-floyd-protests-live-updates/

Health Empowerment Zone Act of 2009, H. R. 2233. (2009). https://www.govtrack.us/congress/bills/111/hr2233

Henry, S. G. (2011). The tyranny of reality. *Journal of the American Medical Association (JAMA), 305*(4), 338–339.

Herson, L., & Bolland, J. (1998). *The urban web: Political, policy, and theory* (2nd ed.). Nelson-Hall Publishing.

Holt, C. L., Shipp, M., Eloubeidi, M., Fouad, M. N., Britt, K., & Norena, M. (2017). Your body is the temple: Impact of a spiritually based colorectal cancer educational intervention delivered through community health advisors. *Health Promotion and Practice, 12*(4), 577–588.

Jones C. (2020, April 7). Coronavirus discriminates: Health care doesn't have to. *Newsweek.* https://www.newsweek.com/2020/04/24/coronavirus-disease-discriminates-our-health-care-doesnt-have-opinion-1496405.html

Jones, R. (2018). *Getting healthy the ecumenical way.* Presbyterian Church USA, Office of the General Assembly. https://www.pcusa.org/news/2018/11/6/getting-healthy-ecumenical-way/.

Kiefer, C. W. (2007). *Doing health anthropology: Research methods for community assessment and change* (1st ed.). Springer.

Kleinman, A., & Benson, P. (2006). Anthropology in the clinic: The problem of cultural competency and how to fix it. *PLoS Medicine, 3*(10), e294.

Koenig, H. G., King, D. E., & Carson, V. B. (2012). *Handbook of religion and health* (2nd ed.). Oxford University Press.

Kosmin, B. A., & Keysar, A. (2009). *American religious identification survey (ARIS 2008) summary report.* Trinity College. http://commons.trincoll.edu/aris/files/2011/08/ARIS_Report_2008.pdf.

Kumagai, A. K., & Lypson, M. L. (1992). Beyond cultural competence: Critical consciousness, social justice, and multicultural education. *Academic Medicine, 84*(6), 782–787.

Kumanyika, S. K., & Charleston, J. B. (1992). Lose weight and win: A church-based weight loss program for blood pressure control among black women. *Patient Education and Counseling, 19*(1), 19–32.

Lancaster, K. J., Carter-Edwards, L., Grilo, S., Shen, C., & Schoenthaler, A. M. (2004). Obesity interventions in African American faith-based organizations: A systematic review. *Obesity Review, 15*(4), 159–176. https://doi.org/10.1111/obr.12207

Lasater, T. M., Wells, B. L., Carleton, R. A., & Elder, J. P. (1986). The role of churches in disease prevention research studies. *Public Health Reports, 101*(2), 125–131.

Lincoln, C. E., & Mamiya, L. (1990). *The black church in the African American experience.* Duke University Press.

Lindsey, L., & Beach, S. (2002). *Sociology* (2nd ed.). Prentice Hall.

Maxwell, A. E., Santifer, R., Chang, L. C., Gatson, J., Crespi, C. M., & Lucas-Wright, A. (2019). Organizational readiness for wellness promotion—a survey of 100 African American church leaders in South Los Angeles. *BMC Public Health, 19*(1), 593.

McCloskey, D. J., McDonald, M. A., Cook, J., Heurtin-Roberts, S., Updegrove, S., Sampson, D., ... & Eder, M. (2011). Community engagement: Definitions and organizing concepts from the literature. In *Principles of Community Engagement* (2nd ed., NIH Publication No. 11–7782). U.S. Government Printing Office.

Meier, A., & Rudwick, E. (1978). *From plantation to ghetto* (3rd ed.). Hill and Wang.

Miller, R. L., & Shinn, M. (2005). Learning from communities: Overcoming difficulties in dissemination of prevention and promotion efforts. *American Journal of Community Psychology*, 35(3–4), 169–183.

Minkler, M. (1990). Improving health through community organization. In K. Glanz, F. M. Lewis, & B. K. Rimer (Eds.), *Health behavior and health education: Theory, research and practice* (pp. 257–287). Jossey-Bass.

Minkler, M. (2004). *Community organizing and community building for health* (2nd ed.). Rutgers University.

Morales-Alemán, M. M., Moore, A., & Scarinci, I. C. (2018). Development of a participatory capacity-building program for congregational health leaders in African American churches in the US South. *Ethnicity & Disease*, 28(1), 11–18. https://doi.org/10.18865/ed.28.1.11

National Prevention Council. (2011). National prevention strategy: American's plan for better health and wellness. Office of the Surgeon General. http://www.surgeongeneral.gov/initiatives/prevention/strategy/report.pdf

NC Department of Health and Human Services (NC DHHS). (2003). "From disparity to parity in health": Eliminating health disparities call to action. Retrieved June 5, 2020, from https://www.ncminorityhealth.org/data/documents/NCDHHSImplementationPlan.pdf.

NC Department of Health and Human Services (NC DHHS). (2018). Community health workers in North Carolina: Creating and infrastructure for sustainability. Retrieved June 1, 2020, from https://files.nc.gov/ncdhhs/DHHS-CWH-Report_Web%205-21-18.pdf.

NC Department of Health and Human Services (NC DHHS). (2020). About the NC community health worker initiative. Retrieved June 1, 2020, from https://www.ncdhhs.gov/divisions/office-rural-health/community-health-workers/about-nc-community-health-worker-initiative

Nyswander, D. (1956). Education for health: Some principles and their applications health education monographs. *Journal of Public Health, 14*, 65–70.

Office of Minority Health (OMH). (2020). *Resource center*. Retrieved May 31, 2020, from https://minorityhealth.hhs.gov/omh/ browse.aspx ?lvl= 1&lvlID=3.

Olson, L. M., Reis, J., Murphy, L., & Gehm, J. H. (1988). The religious community as a partner in health care. *Journal of Community Health, 13*(4), 249–257.

Petersen, J., Atwood, J. R., & Yates, B. (2002). Key elements for church-based health promotion programs: Outcome-based literature review. *Public Health Nursing, 19*(6), 401–411.

Pew Research Center. (2019). *African Americans and religion*. The Pew Forum on Religion and Public Life. http://www.pewforum.org/African- Americans-and-Religion.aspx.

Pichon, L., & Powell, T. (2015). Review of HIV testing efforts in historically black churches. *International Journal of Environmental Research and Public Health, 12*, 6016–6026. https://doi.org/10.3390/ijerph120606016.

Plescia, M., & Emmanuel, C. (2014). Reducing health disparities by addressing social determinants of health: The Mecklenburg County experience. *NCMJ, 75*(6), 417–421.

Powdermaker, H. (1968). *After freedom: A cultural history of the deep south*. Viking Press.

Pullen-Smith, B., Carter-Edwards, L., & Leathers, K. (2008). Community health ambassadors: A model for engaging community leaders to promote better health in North Carolina. *Journal of Public Health Management and Practice, 14*(Suppl: S), 73–81.

Ransome, Y., Bogart, L. M., Nunn, A. S., Mayer, K. H., Sadler, K. R., & Ojikutu, B. O. (2018). Faith leaders' messaging is essential to enhance HIV prevention among black Americans: Results from the 2016 National Survey on HIV in the black community (NSHBC). *BMC Public Health, 18*(1), 1392.

Reid, D. R., Shelley, L. B., & Stout, H. (Eds.). (1990). *The dictionary of Christianity in America.* Intervarsity Press.

Resnicow, K., Baranowski, T., Ahluwalia, J. S., & Braithwaite, R. L. (1999). Cultural sensitivity in public health: Defined and demystified. *Ethnicity and Disease, 9*(1), 10–21.

Resnicow, K., Wallace, D. C., Jackson, A., Digirolamo, A., Odom, E., Wang, T., ... Baranowski, T. (2000). Dietary change through African American churches: Baseline results and program description of the "eat for life" trial. *Journal of Cancer Education, 15*, 156–63.

Rose, M. A., Arenson, C., Harrod, P., Salkey, R., Santana, A., & Diamond, J. (2008). Evaluation of the chronic disease self-management program with low-income, urban, African American older adults. *Journal of Community Health Nursing, 25*(4), 193–202.

Sanders, E. C. (1997). New insights and interventions: Churches uniting to reach the African American community with health information. *Journal on Health Care of the Poor and Underserved, 8*(3), 373–375.

Scheirer, M. A., Santos, S. L., Tagai, E. K., Bowie, J., Slade, J., Carter, R., & Holt, C. L. (2017). Dimensions of sustainability for a health communication intervention in African American churches: A multi-methods study. *Implementation Science, 12*(1), 43. https://doi.org/10.1186/s13012-017-0576-x

Scott, A. J., Wilson, R. F. (2011). Social determinants of health among African Americans in a rural community in the deep south: An ecological exploration. *Rural Remote Health, 11*(1), 1634.

Sbrocco, T., Carter, M. M., Lewis, E. L., Vaughn, N. A., Kalupa, K. L., King, S., Suchday, S., Osborn, R. L., & Cintrón, J. A. (2005). Church-based obesity treatment for African-American women improves adherence. *Ethnicity and Disease, 15*(2), 246–255.

Sernett, M. (1999). *African American religious history: A documentary witness.* Duke University Press.

Sewell, S. (2003). Lead me, guide me along the way: A study of the relationship between pastors' personal characteristics and their level of community participation. *North Star, 7*(1), 1–18.

Stewart, J. M., Hong, H., & Powell, T. W. (2019). Strategies to promote African-American church leadership engagement in HIV testing and linkage to care. *Journal of Racial and Ethnic Health Disparities, 6*(2), 319–326.

Story, C. R., Gross, T. T., Harvey, I. S., & Whitt-Glover, M. C. (2017). Pastoral perceptions of the learning and developing individual exercise skills (L.A.D.I.E.S.) intervention: A qualitative study. *Health Education Research, 32*(1), 81–95.

Taylor, R. J., Chatters, L. M., Jayakody, R., & Levin, J. S. (1996). Black and white differences in religious participation: A multisample comparison. *Journal for the Scientific Study of Religion, 35*(4), 403–410.

Toms, F. D., Glover, S., Erwin, A., & Ellison, C. (2008). Leadership and community engagement: A faith-based capacity building model. *Leadership Studies Magazine, 1,* 13–15.

Toms, F., Lloyd, C. L., Carter-Edwards, L., & Ellison, C. (2011). A faith-based community view of improving health and health care advocacy through engagement. *Practical Matters, 4,* 1–13.

Underwood, S. M., & Powell, R. L. (2006). Religion and spirituality: Influence on health/risk behavior and cancer screening behavior of African Americans. *ABNF Journal, 17*(1), 20–31.

U.S. Department of Health and Human Services. (U.S. DHHS). (2010). *National partnership for action to end health disparities: Toolkit for community action.* http://minorityhealth.hhs. gov/npa/files/Plans/Toolkit/NPA_Toolkit.pdf.

U.S. Department of Health and Human Services. (U.S. DHHS). (2012). *About faith-based and neighborhood partnerships.* http://www.hhs.gov/partnerships/about/index.html.

Wallerstein, N., Sanchez, V., Carter-Edwards, L., Avila, M., & Minkler, M. (2015). Using community engagement, community building, and social action to improve health. In K. Glanz, B. K. Rimer & K. Viswanath (Eds.), *Health behavior: Theory, research and practice* (5th ed., pp. 277–300). Jossey-Bass.

Wilmore, G. (1983). *Black religion and black radicalism: An interpretation of the religious history of Afro-American People.* Orbis.

Wimberly, A. E. S. (2001). The role of black faith communities in fostering health. In R. I. Braithwaite & S. E. Taylor (Eds.), *Health issues in the black community.* Jossey-Bass.

White House. (2018). *Faith and opportunity initiative office.* HUD. https://www.hud.gov/ program_offices/faith_based

Whitt-Glover, M. C., Keith, N. R., Ceaser, T. G., Virgil, K., Ledford, L., & Hasson, R. E. (2014). A systematic review of physical activity interventions among African American adults: Evidence from 2009 to 2013. *Obesity Reviews, 15,* 125–145. https://doi.org/10.1111/obr.12205

Woodson, C. G. (1972). *The history of the Negro church.* Associated Publishers.

World Council of Churches. (2018). Momentum grows for health promoting churches. https://www. oikoumene.org/en/press-centre/news/momentum-grows-for-health-promoting-churches

Yancy, C. W. (2020). COVID-19 and African Americans. *JAMA, 323*(19), 1891–1892. https://doi. org/10.1001/jama.2020.6548

CHAPTER SIXTEEN

The Community Reinvestment Act and Civic Engagement

Irvin Henderson, BA

CONSUMERISM AND BANKING: A RICH HISTORY

The first mention of lenders and money changers in the Bible is not a kind one, as Jesus threw them from the temple for their usurious rates and their wicked ways. The irony did not escape President Bill Clinton when he called on the reinvestment advocates of our country to revamp the Community Reinvestment Act (CRA) regulations to make them more effective. He said, "I have it on good authority that what we are doing today, Irvin, will make a difference." This was immediately after he held an event on the South Lawn of the White House in which he had asked advocates, regulators, and bankers to work together to get scarce capital to our neediest neighborhoods. President Clinton was concerned about something that his comptroller of the currency, Eugene Ludwig, called "the democratization of credit" and something that we now refer to more broadly as the "democratization of capital."

The day was July 15, 1993, and the president and vice president stood for 10 minutes behind me as I spoke. President Clinton introduced me. The audience was all of the Capital Beltway nonprofits and reinvestment advocates from around the country, the Congress, the cabinet, and the banking lobby. And there I stood, representing the everyday Jane and Joe, the lowly nonprofit—the small businessman who could not get a loan if his or her life depended on it. On that bright, shining day, President Clinton and Comptroller Ludwig were leaning forward toward a color-blind, opportunity-forged financial democracy where the content of your ideas and the strength of your ability to carry out your plan were the only criteria for access to credit, and, yes, even capital. This is the "opportunity society" that President George W. Bush would later talk about, and its origins are grounded in the art and science of civic engagement.

The CRA was a relatively benign law that the banks did little toward compliance with from 1975 until 1989. The regulators were largely agnostic about the law, and many politicians felt that it was wrong for community advocates and regular citizens to have a say in how the banks operated and made their billions. However, the advocates, supportive politicians, and forward-thinking bankers, such as Cathy Bessant of NationsBank (now known as Bank of America®), were beginning to understand the civic and public hook that the banks could not ignore. All banking success is built on the deposit insurance provided by the U.S. government. We, the people, are the representatives and trustees of the full faith of the government, as we, the people, stand behind the banking industry in times of crisis. No other industry owes as much to the people for its ability to make money. Without the perception of the full faith and credit of the country standing behind the banks, there would be no relatively low cost of funds (their deposits) to use to lend to consumers and businesses to make their interest dollars. In other words, roughly half of all banking revenue flows from this unprecedented support and backstopping by the citizens, people like you and me.

During the banking crisis of 2007–2012, there was graphic evidence of how sacrosanct that support and backstopping could be, as between the Troubled Asset Relief Program, the Federal Reserve discount window lending, and the make-whole, dollar-for-dollar payments from risky investments of AIG and Lehman Brothers, the U.S. government, and you and I as citizens, delivered more than $7 *trillion* to save the industry. It is this realization that got advocates, seriously committed community bankers, and politicians to say that there is a public obligation on the part of the banks to provide services, credit, and capital to all aspects of their communities. This obligation is enforceable through all banking laws, but specifically, the CRA and the Community Benefit Agreement statutes allow for a comprehensive plan, addressing the credit needs of a defined community and providing special and specific outreach to the underserved consumers and businesses on a neighborhood-by-neighborhood basis. When organized, these neighborhoods become the poster children for civic engagement through many ways. Advocates and activists organized their neighborhoods, and in many cases, the first action and first victory was a citywide agreement by a bank (or several banks) to only place public deposits in institutions that had received high marks from public watchdogs, such as the Pittsburgh Community Reinvestment Group (PCRG), which publishes a report card every year on all of the banking institutions in their metropolitan statistical area (MSA). Through civically engaging their political leadership, they were able to get control of all of the public asset deposits by the city and guarantee that there would be no deposits of public funds in institutions that had not been judged highly responsive to community credit needs.

At PCRG, Stanley Lowe had a vision for his community, which is a historically Black neighborhood with lots of historic housing stock. He fought for access to the top leaders of the banking community by holding street protests and contesting meetings, political briefings, editorial board briefings, and city- and county-wide encounter sessions. Stanley and his civic partners, such as Aggie Brose of the Bloomfield-Garfield neighborhood, held sessions in which they educated their constituents about the laws, their rights, and the kinds of responses from the banks that others were able to generate by using these tactics. They analyzed credit needs and met with the banks, asking for specific products that would address the needs that had been forgotten or redlined. They devised and published their inaugural report card and got national media because some of the institutions with failing grades had satisfactory and out-standing ratings under the public file for CRA. The regulators and grade inflation became twin apologists for the failings of the industry. However, Stanley and PCRG persisted. Through their meetings with hundreds of constituents and the banks, they were able to get changes from the banks in everything from their lending criteria and policies to the types of low-income, low-cost deposit accounts offered to consumers. They got special mortgage products designed to work with the people who were the neediest, such as the first-time home buyer and special business lending products for the small business owner and the small farmer, and they got the ability to monitor on a quarterly basis all aspects of the bank.

All of this occurred because they engaged themselves to organize, train, learn, and motivate the civic community in Pittsburg. They then took the tenets of civic engagement and used them to attack a far stronger adversary and won because they organized and created the perception that many thousands would descend upon the institutions in protest if their requests (demands) were not met. Very often, they had to show force before the institutions would listen to reason, but over the years, PCRG developed good relations with most lenders, as is evidenced by the fact that they just had their 25th anniversary and their third annual summit, both broadly supported by the banking community.

Their process and tactics were as follows:

- Organize the constituents
- Disturb them with education and information
- Get the attention of the potential advocacy target—use protests, meetings, letters, media
- Determine what the needs are
- Design programming and responses to eliminate the needs and increase the flow of capital, credit, and banking services

The "Gale" Force: Gale Cincotta

The community reinvestment movement was started by a housewife from Chicago who refused to accept that she and her neighbors did not deserve the same access to credit and banking services as their suburban neighbors. Cincotta may have been the single-most effective example of civic engagement in action that became more relevant nationally than its origins locally. Within any civic engagement case model, we first find the common ground to organize and disturb; we develop the rationale for the case; we engage the powers that be to determine where there may be resolution.

Cincotta used the linked-deposit scenario and the CRA to frighten the Chicago banks into the following:

- Complying with community benefit standards developed by Cincotta and her committee of community folks
- Establishing lifeline accounts for low-income residents
- Providing affordable mortgages with terms that were user-friendly
- Increasing small business lending

In the biography of this American hero, *Gale Force*, written by Michael Westgage with Ann Vick-Westgate, the author describes her as passionate about her community and its credit needs. Cincotta watched the foreclosures that were spurred by massive Federal Housing Administration lending and concentration of mortgages in working-class neighborhoods, but as the recession of the late 1970s and early 1980s became a reality, more and more neighborhoods seemingly had been targeted by lenders as "redlined neighborhoods," which meant that no lending would be sanctioned in those areas. Not only were the foreclosures decimating the neighborhoods but also no new lending meant no new investment, which meant that the decline was accelerated. Cincotta also noticed the connection between the lack of access to capital and credit for small businesses and the dearth of job creation in her neighborhoods. But it was the sheer arrogance of the banks to willingly take deposits from working-class families, pay them a pittance, and then refuse to lend them their own capital for projects, businesses, and homes in those very same neighborhoods that moved her to act. She used many different tactics but found that the protest was the most effective. Cincotta formed an entity known as National People's Action. Through this organizing arm, she recruited reinvestment advocates from around the country. The national staff provided technical assistance to local groups. They encouraged people in other locales to take a stand and fight for their rights and to make their cities accountable through linked-deposit programs and access to capital programs.

The key was to use the city's clout with the banks to get the banks to treat the residents and their credit and capital needs better and to realize the potential market value of the customer base that these neighborhoods represented. The cities during this period were some of the largest and most predictable depositors. Banks love predictable, large depositors because it allows them to invest the capital in more complex investments, such as derivatives and long currency trades because they know when they will need the money to service the deposit accounts. This arbitrage allows banks to increase their return on equity (their own cash value) and their return on capital as well. Cincotta would call a protest when the bank was having a shareholders' meeting and use the bully pulpit, the press conference, and the media coverage to shine a spotlight on their activities. She discovered the concept of "reputational risk," which means that a bank or any large corporation runs the risk of losing its entire book of business if it makes too many decisions or actions that can be exploited in the press in a negative manner. Banks were extremely sensitive to this concept because what does a bank really sell other than banking services and money with interest? Banks sell stability and confidence, so a lack of regard for a major hit to their reputation could end up creating a run on the bank and destabilizing its reserve position (the amount of capital a bank must hold to be safe).

Cincotta's tactics of protests and challenges to banks helped establish the community reinvestment movement as a force in consumerism and financial services. All of the industries associated with financial services, including the Wall Street brokerages and investment banks, are all concerned about the Dodd-Frank Act that laid out the new rules for financial services companies after the great financial meltdown of 2007–2008. The Consumer Frauds and Protection Bureau was established nationally, with Richard Cordrey as the inaugural chief executive. The first entity that he chose for a policy speech was the National Community Reinvestment Coalition, the organization that has made CRA and civic engagement its main tactics for progress, equality, and empowerment for low-wealth people and low-to-moderate-income neighborhoods and communities.

The establishment of Dodd-Frank and the Consumer Fraud and Protection Bureau was the institutionalization of all of the efforts in the arena of community reinvestment that had begun with civic engagement. The initial conversations with banks, city treasurers, municipal officials, mayors, and council representatives have led to resolutions and ordinances throughout the land, indicating that a bank's performance will be considered when the decision is made as to where the city's millions—and in some cases billions—will be held and distributed. This decision was set up as the major tool to use civic engagement to get some accountability to the banks. The results are as follows:

- Special accounts for low-income and elder residents
- Small business capital access programs
- Affordable mortgages with nonpredatory terms
- Better rates of return for cities and counties
- Branch placement in low-income and central-city locations
- Bank investment in nonprofit infrastructure
- Bank investment in financial literacy training and materials
- Large bank commitments to multiple areas of finance and banking services—totaling more than $8 trillion

The Community Reinvestment Association of North Carolina

Early in 1985, Debbie Warren, a legal services professional and community reinvestment organizer, began working with several prominent North Carolinians to use a relatively new law known as the "CRA" of 1977 to hold banks more accountable to all aspects of their communities, including low-to-moderate-income neighborhoods.

The law had been passed with sponsors Senator William Proxmire, a famous liberal lion of the Senate, and Congresswoman Barbara Jordan, whose combative but effective tenure in the House is surpassed in import only by her blunt oratory about the civil and economic rights of minorities and women.

This law was preceded by another gem of legislation by Senator Proxmire, the Home Mortgage Disclosure Act of 1975. This act provided the evidence that was required to convince banking regulators and the banking industry of the widespread discrimination and fair lending violations that were prevalent in the United States during the '50s, '60s, and '70s. As was mentioned earlier, the term "redlining" refers to the process of lending supervisors at financial institutions taking a map of a given community or MSA and drawing red circles around certain areas of town that were marked as unfit for lending because of perceptions about housing stock, the character of the residents, the desire to honor obligations, and the ability to maintain steady employment. Although these perceptions were found to be stereotypes and atypical of many borrowers in these neighborhoods, years later—and, in fact, even today—the problem of racial and gender discrimination in lending still exists, especially in business lending.

The Home Mortgage Disclosure Act (HMDA) provides data on all mortgage lending by covered institutions such as community banks, mortgage companies, and commercial banks. It indicates the address of the borrower and the loan, their income, race, interest rate, fees paid, gender, employment tenure, and type of loan—the terms and the policies and procedures. Before this data was available, community reinvestment advocates had to use interviews and counseling sessions to ferret out potential discrimination and fair lending violations. With the analysis of the data, advocates and their researchers were able to spot trends in fields such as loan declination ratios when compared to race and when compared to gender and pricing of the loans. They found that African American borrowers were twice as likely to end up with a subprime mortgage with a higher interest rate, predatory practices (such as prepayment penalties and extra commissions paid to get the borrower into a high-cost loan), and exorbitant fees. With this information, for every HMDA loan, activists were able to compare institution to institution and to the field and determine who was doing a very good job and which institutions were doing a very poor job and may have been, in fact, discriminating.

One of the overarching tenets of civic engagement is that to motivate a group of people to action, you must have a set of information with the following characteristics:

- The information must be accurate.
- The information must be verifiable.
- The two facts above must be printed or published by a reliable source.
- The information must be relevant.
- The information must be of a serious enough nature that it disturbs the target audience.

- The information must not counter the conventional wisdom that has led the target audience to its level of disturbance.
- The target audience must be disturbed enough to spur action to make changes.

This point of information is referred to as the "catalyst," named after the agent in a conflagration that starts the fire. With these new tools, Debbie Warren; Andrea Harris, executive director of a regional nonprofit; Lewis Myers, government consultant and gubernatorial aide; and Julian Brown, executive director of the North Carolina Association of Minority Businesses established the statewide Community Reinvestment Act Committee.

It became important to organize concerned citizens from different areas, and the most effective method was to organize them city by city. Most of the groups were aware of the act but did not understand it fully. So education became very important to progress. Seminars were developed to expose new recruits to the language and philosophy that buttressed the act and the case studies of successful engagement. The city model worked well because of the way that banks themselves were organized. Most institutions had established a "city executive" as their top representative in medium-to-large cities. Very often, this individual was tied into the political fabric and framework, which made it difficult to advocate for change and progress in that the city executive felt that the politicians protected them. Most local politicians had received loans and favors from the banks, and there was a covenant of protection.

This made for the first organizing action in a lot of places—the disturbance of the relationship between the mayor, city council, county council, and other elected officials, perhaps a city treasurer and the banks. It was necessary to establish an analysis based on HMDA data, which showed exactly where the loans were or were not going. When some civic leaders began to get a peek under the kimono of the banks, they realized in many cases that banks were taking deposits out but were not making loans back to the same communities. During this period, banks were trying to make loans to their large corporate customers, developers, and others that needed large-scale lending. Character-based lending for small businesses became a thing of the past. All commercial lending was now based on credit scores, which were skewed against small businesses and clearly favored larger businesses, even though sometimes a large business may have been in default within the last 5 years.

Inside the CRA movement, the regulators were dealing with two concepts that dictated the tactics of the advocacy community: (1) the assessment areas and (2) a measure known as factors.

Civic Engagement and the Payday Lending Industry

Creativity is an essential element in civic engagement. One of the leading examples of creativity is the advocacy directed at the payday lending industry by advocates in North Carolina, California, and Ohio. Peter Skillern, the executive director of the Community Reinvestment Association of North Carolina (later renamed Reinvestment

Allies), spearheaded the effort after doing an analysis of payday lending to military personnel in the state of North Carolina. The study found that the average number of rollovers for the payday loans were 7 times, and as high as 11 times, for many people. So, a customer may have borrowed only $255 but paid more than $300 in interest within 1 year. This showed that the loans were predatory and a way to get people to always owe some interest to the lender and never pay the principal. It was largely a wealth transformation tool that took scarce resources from those who could least afford it with a promise of immediate relief but also deferred greater need.

Skillern organized from one end of the state to the other using organizational contacts to reach people but also developing a series of news reports to educate the public on how the payday lenders were violating the public trust. He then enlisted Alan Fisher from the California Reinvestment Committee (CRC) and Morris Williams, formerly of the Cincinnati Coalition of Neighborhoods, now running the Hamilton County Reinvestment Alliance. These three entities held protests and performed "street theater" in each of the three areas on the same day, coordinated media responses, and enlisted the help of their colleagues nationwide to call for the end to payday predatory lending.

Many of these colleagues proceeded to write about and advocate for the passage of municipal and state legislation to outlaw payday lending. This was extremely successful because the payday industry had concentrated its efforts on state legislators and had few weapons to fight the civic battles. After this episode, many antipredatory city ordinances also included anti–payday lending components. The use of the civic arena and its greater accessibility than the state legislature was the key. In the civic arena, the street theater was more effective and the playing field was not as skewed by money.

It is important to note here that often the goal of civic engagement is to stop some negative issue or policy or practice. Sometimes, the origin of the problem is a group of people or an industry that is persistent and well funded. When these circumstances occur, the community leaders and advocates have to be vigilant; even after a victory like the one described here, they must prepare for additional assaults because when great profits are at risk, capitalists will continue to try to do business, even if they must morph their products. The payday lending industry has done just that by promoting what they now call "deposit advance" or "short-term finance," which has the same draconian policies and can still lead to 300% interest over time and unpaid loan balances as well. These same advocates have had to organize again with a coordinated protest and press conference that occurred on June 4, 2013, literally as I was writing this section. The teaching point is that the tools of civic engagement may have to be used repeatedly to reach permanent solutions to a particularly resilient problem.

The Creation of the National Community Reinvestment Coalition

Son and heir to Robert Kennedy, the late senator and presidential candidate, Joe Kennedy was a very important congressman from Massachusetts in 1989. Like his father, he was a champion of the causes of the have-nots and a forceful, fiery advocate and speaker. He had used the tactics of civic engagement prior to his election to build an organization in Massachusetts that worked with the poor and working-class residents to bridge the gaps in their ability to provide heat and cooling in their homes. This nonprofit had as its mission the eradication of energy poverty in the state. Kennedy and the organization spoke out, organized residents, lobbied the legislature and the federal Congress, brought foundations and their dollars to the effort, and, eventually, established a program of relief that helped most of the families with a need in the state. They engaged municipal leaders, state leaders, and federal lawmakers to promote programs such as the Low-Income Energy Assistance Program, which provided federal dollars to the very poor. Kennedy got municipal leaders to match the federal dollars, and foundations helped the organization provide grants for water heater blankets, weatherization of doors and windows, fans and air conditioners in the summer, and funds to repair heating systems in the winter. They organized and brought "truth to power" with their studies and testimonials from the working class and poor, who became leaders in his movement. He formed coalitions among union members and the unemployed, teachers and firemen, politicians and businesspersons—all of whom participated in protests, meetings at city hall, and public rallies. He rode this and other successes to become the congressman from the first congressional district of Massachusetts, the seat of former speaker Tip O'Neill.

As a congressman, Kennedy became a booster for the use of the CRA to attack the problems of poverty and economic displacement in his district and throughout this country. He became the chief voice in Congress for the protection of the act, which had come under siege from Republicans and Democrats alike because of the extensive lobbying of the American Bankers Association and other banking trade groups. As congressional leaders, such as Representative Paul Kanjorski, Democrat from New Jersey, and Senator Phil Gramm from Texas advocated for the outright repeal of the law, or at least the gutting of its effectiveness, Kennedy felt the need to have additional support for the act from the grassroots entities that had begun to use it to level the playing field economically in their communities. These groups had won hard-fought success by engaging the banks and the cities within which they operated to use the act to hold the institutions accountable when they were pressed by CRA advocates to do more to assist the underserved communities that had been redlined. Kennedy called a meeting of all the Washington-based consumer advocates, ethnic groups, and community developers to address this issue. He acted as a community organizer on the national stage. He had to use the tactics that he had gleaned while doing local and statewide organizing in the energy assistance field to assemble, disturb, and motivate the Washington-based organizations to go back into the field and get the stories, anecdotes, and testimonies about how CRA was very valuable to underserved communities and neighborhoods and must not be repealed or changed; in fact, it should be expanded. Kennedy told the assembled group of leaders that if they did not organize and do it quickly, they would lose the CRA. He told them that this was no idle threat and that very powerful forces were embarking on a campaign to indeed kill CRA. The only thing that Kennedy thought would deter these forces were everyday folks from the congressional districts who could prove the effectiveness and impact of the CRA.

Kennedy suggested that they organize a national coalition whose sole purpose would be the saving and promotion of the CRA. He gave them examples of tactics that he thought would be effective in bringing others to the campaign. He suggested that they use the following strategies:

- Sign-on letters with Washington and in-district groups
- Studies of HMDA and other lending data
- Surveys of consumers and bankers
- Trips to Washington to meet with and educate key banking committee members in the House and Senate Finance Committee members—called fly-ins
- Briefings and consciousness-raising sessions throughout the country but especially in the districts of legislators who were anti-CRA

Representative Kennedy called for the inaugural meeting of the Washington insider groups to be held at the Center for Community Change (CCC), where Alan Fishbein and Debbie Goldberg had run a program that had largely been the best technical assistance unit on CRA in the country. Through the CCC, these two advocates and consultants had been presenting and developing education materials about CRA and how to use it for change in communities since the law was passed. The groups in attendance were as follows:

- CCC
- National Council of La Raza
- National Association for the Advancement of Colored People
- The National Congress for Community Economic Development
- Consumers Union
- First Nation
- Local Initiative Support Coalition
- Enterprise Foundation

The groups quickly coalesced, and the CCC provided pass-through capacity until the new coalition got its own tax-exempt status, known as a 501(c)(3). Bart Harvey, president and CEO, was elected the first chair of the coalition, which would be known as the National Community Reinvestment Coalition. The year was 1990.

The coalition held its inaugural meetings and hired new staff. The initial leader did not work, and within a few months, John Taylor, a community development corporation executive from Somerfield, Massachusetts, who had been a board member of the coalition, became its first real president and CEO. There were only two other staff members. The work began. John Taylor, being from outside of Washington, D.C., knew right away that the strength of the coalition would come from grassroots groups from around the country, which were actively using CRA to deliver resources and opportunities to underserved communities and neighborhoods. He went on to recruit from established CRA leaders, all of whom had been using civic engagement strategies to organize their communities around CRA. Many had used the linked-deposits strategy to get banks to be accountable. As described earlier, this strategy involved linking city, county, and corporate deposits to banks that had shown the ability to be responsive to all of the community's credit needs and were willing to reinvest in the community.

John Taylor recruited the following key board members:

- Ted Wysocki—Chicago Association of Neighborhood Development Organizations
- Alan Fisher—CRC
- Malcolm Bush—The Woodstock Institute
- Hubert Van Tol—The Memphis Organizing Project
- Irvin Henderson—The Community Reinvestment Association of North Carolina
- Morris Williams—The Collation of Neighborhoods
- Gail Burks—Nevada Fair Housing Center
- Lee Beaulac—Rural Opportunities
- Shelley Sheehy – River City Development

With this diverse board, the coalition began to recruit other members from around the country and began to weigh in on the legislative process. An early sign-on letter was promulgated to national and a few local groups and was sent to the committee chairs of the Senate and House banking and financial services committees, as well as the ranking minority members.

The coalition worked feverishly to get information out to the districts. Throughout America, a recruitment drive began that resulted in 130 members joining the coalition in that first year. This number included 90 grassroots members who met with their congresspersons in the district and in Washington. Street theater demonstrations were held throughout the country, and some of the organizers coordinated their activities such that the *New York Times*, the *Charlotte Observer*, and the *Los Angeles Times* covered similar events on the same day.

This activity took the civic engagement lessons of linked-deposit protests and municipal banking ordinances to the next level and was used to preserve the CRA. The legislators who were trying to repeal the act backed down, and the act was maintained.

From Assessment Factors to Real Change

As the regulators grappled with the fact that the act would not be repealed, the enemies of CRA started a campaign to convince the regulators that the safety and soundness aspects of banking trumped the CRA and should not be fully implemented. The regulators developed factors that helped them make more objective analyses of the compliance of financial institutions, such as the following:

- Deposit-to-loan ratios
- Complaints from community groups and individuals
- Number of meetings held with community groups
- Contributions to charitable organizations
- Track record in fair lending

These factors were used to give most banks an outstanding rating, even though they were not lending to all aspects of the community that were eligible, as the law stated. When Bill Clinton became president, he knew that there were improvements that could be made that would make a difference in communities that were underserved in all 50 states. So, as mentioned earlier, he decided to take a stand.

The Role of Gene Ludwig: The 41st Comptroller of the Currency in the Democratization of Capital

The most important step taken by President Clinton was to appoint Eugene Ludwig as the 41st comptroller of the currency. This constitutional post was the perfect bully pulpit and regulatory oversight post for a change agent, and that was what Ludwig was. He talked openly about the fact that banks were redlining poor and minority communities and violating fair lending and the CRA. He indicated that CRA loans could be good business and were safe and sound. He coined the phrase "the democratization of capital" as he ran the Office of the Comptroller of the Currency (OCC) as a regulator who cared about communities and realized that the banks and the consumers were both constituents of the OCC.

Under his direct supervision, the CRA regulations were updated. Hearings were held all over America to offer the opportunity to lenders, community groups, small businesses, and regulators to speak on how those changes should—and could—be made to both strengthen enforcement and maintain fairness to the institutions that would allow them to comply and prosper at the same time.

Impact: What Has CRA Accomplished?

To date, $8 trillion were returned to underserved communities as a result of this law and the civic engagement of its supporters. All banks now routinely have compliance systems that deliver resources and collaboration to communities. Although the most recent banking crisis did disturb this progress, institutions are returning to their earlier patterns of reinvestment now.

The Role of Civic Engagement in CRA

Only through the localization of the needs of low-to-moderate-income communities has CRA been able to become relevant. Agreements penned by national groups and large financial institutions mean little if they don't deliver capital, credit, and services to the low-to-moderate-income households, the small businesses, and the small farmers and nonprofits that generate the real economy of this country.

As we look at the current activities of groups such as Reinvestment Allies of North Carolina, the California Reinvestment Coalition, and the Woodstock Institute, the need for civic engagement has never been greater. The National Community Reinvestment Coalition (NCRC) has pioneered work on municipal ordinances around the country that hold the banks' feet to the fire, and this has resulted in far more receptive relations to community needs. This project has resulted in ordinances in New York, Chicago, Pittsburgh, and many other communities. The work that these groups are doing with the city councils and legislatures in their areas is driving predators out and building sustainable products to meet the real credit needs of the underserved. The future is bright but still contentious.

Test Case: Capital One: What's in Your …?

A recent example of the strength of this type of organizing and engagement is the Capital One® campaign that was led by NCRC. As Capital One tried to merge with ING, an Internet bank, NCRC challenged the merger and the changes that Capital One was attempting to make to the marketplace. Capital One's strategies are largely credit card based, as their well-known ad campaign has evidenced. Their small business credit cards would take most small business credit needs from a term loan at 6%–7% interest to a credit card line and balance at 20% interest. The disparate treatment violations are obvious but also the affordability aspects show that this type of credit could very often lead to the closing of a business as debt and interest overcome net operating income.

NCRC led a nationwide challenge that resulted in the Federal Reserve taking the unprecedented step of having national hearings on the merger. NCRC organized civic engagement groups in all 50 states to protest, write letters, send emails, demonstrate at bank sites, and disinvest from Capital One. These efforts eventually brought Capital One to the table to negotiate deals with many groups; the regulators did make some adjustments to the merger approval based on the input of community groups.

The Future of CRA Is Civic Engagement

The future of the democratization of credit and capital will come through the process of groups small and large engaging their elected officials, their appointed officials, and the regulatory bodies to speak truth to power and level the playing field for those who are underserved. This is the essence of civic engagement: to provide access to the corridors of power so that input can change policies to closely mirror what consumers and the public really want from their government and their business leaders. This engagement is the most effective tool for providing access and changes that help us generate a more egalitarian society.

Printed in the USA
CPSIA information can be obtained
at www.ICGtesting.com
LVHW081732141223
766435LV00005B/50